HALCYON DAYS

HALCYON

Halcyon Days

The nature of trout fishing
and fishermen

Bryn Hammond

SWAN·HILL
PRESS

For John, Bill, Nick.

First published in the UK in 1992
by Swan Hill Press.

British Library Cataloguing in Publication Data

A catalogue record for this book is available
from the British Library.

ISBN 1 85310 153 2

Printed in England by Livesey Ltd., Shrewsbury.

Swan Hill Press
An imprint of Airlife Publishing Ltd.
101 Longden Road, Shrewsbury SY3 9EB, England.

For a long time I believed, without thinking too much about it, that this vague but unmistakable happiness of fishing derived simply from the classic benison of water. Almost everyone knows that water — especially running water — will smooth out the wrinkles in tired souls. I don't think 'tonic' is quite the right word: 'balm' is nearer to the truth of the matter. I think that no one spends a few hours by a river without feeling a spiritual refreshment. But of recent years I have had to admit to myself that there is more to the peculiar happiness of fishing than the simple healing quality of water. There is something in fishing which acts like a reagent on the inherent property of water, and precipitates a solution ten times stronger than water taken, as it were, neat. It is the compound, water-plus-fishing, which for the passionate angler makes the complete and perfect experience.

. . . Of course, folk fish for different reasons. There are enough aspects of angling to satisfy the aspirations of people remarkably unalike.

Maurice Wiggin

Sleeping we image what awake we wish;
Dogs dream of bones, and fishermen of fish.

Theocritus

Contents

Introduction

Maurice Wiggin once said writers should learn and take to heart the first rule of the quoter: *never* to ascribe any quotation they may use to a source. Flatter your readers, according to Wiggin, and at the same time spread awe. Those who don't know the source will assume that they are alone in their ignorance and those who *do* know will feel set up for the day. Much as I have long enjoyed Maurice Wiggin's fishing and autobiographical writing, and only wish there had been more of it, I have deliberately disregarded his advice in this matter.

Instead, I have not merely acknowledged and identified the source material throughout this book, but fairly peppered the following chapters with quotations from other writers' books. This was done, not in any attempt to seem erudite, or to be honest, but because I believe the words I have quoted speak more aptly and succinctly than any I might otherwise have written to illuminate the points I have tried to raise. It can be left to the reader to best adjudge this treatment.

Many contemporary angling writers not only ignore the proprieties of quotations from other authors' works, but plagiarize like mad. Indeed, since the very first books on fishing, plagiarism has been much practised. Walton plagiarized William Samuel, as well as Thomas Barker, and used material from far more 'books of credence' than he cared to acknowledge. He had, however, by the time he had polished up *The Complete Angler* for the 5th edition in 1676, written a masterpiece that remains one of the world's great books — in spite of being about fishing rather than because of it.

Rather than similarly pepper the following text with complete source details (although this has been done in some cases) I have named the book or author in the text, and included a detailed list of source books as a select bibliography in an appendix. This has been done to avoid making what is meant to be an entertainment into a text book. It may also assist and encourage some readers to seek out and go back to the original books in their entirety. What I hope are my own are some, at least, of the ideas and notions and perceptions of the magic of fishing. But primarily this book is meant to be an entertainment and a vicarious form of fishing itself. In reading it no one will become a better fisherman, although it is hoped that some readers, at least, may even come to enjoy their fishing more, and perhaps feel more questing and experimental about it.

The careful reader may note that some quotations overlap or are in part repeated in different chapters. Where it was considered necessary to each chapter to leave this so, rather than cut out any repetition, this was done. The alternative would have been cumbersome footnotes, directing the reader's attention to a quotation in another chapter in the book. It may be said that much of this book is what a contemporary fishing 'personality' and writer has called the 'only here for the scenery' genre of angling writing. For this, again, no apology is made. There are more than enough how-to-do-it manuals for the most avid technicians.

Similarly there are overlaps of basic subject matter in various chapters, so that exact imitation in artificial flies may be discussed in the chapter, Prejudices in Fishing or, in passing in the specific chapter, Exact Imitation. I hope this will show the linking, continuous thread running through every aspect of fly fishing, weaving them into a single rich tapestry.

This book, conceived and begun in New Zealand in 1988, and completed in England at the close of the following year, is about the nature of fish, fishing and fishermen. Above all it is a paean in praise of trout; albeit that, at times, a somewhat jaundiced eye has been cast on this most noble of all fish. Equally so, if this book is a paean of praise about the gentle art of fly fishing, it does, in certain places, take a similarly acerbic and perhaps cynical view about the philosophies and practices surrounding it. Then, too, there is the third member of the trinity: the trout fisherman himself. Here, in similar fashion, he is seen warts and all, and not necessarily as a pretentious bucolic romancer in the tradition of the common perception of Izaak Walton, any more than he is depicted as a mindless moron engaged in a needless pursuit of cruelty; and certainly not as a member of an elite class pursuing an esoteric and ancient craft.

Some readers may wonder and even object to some of the subject matter pertaining to fly fishing in New Zealand in a book published in Britain; and a book that is neither a where-to-go guide, nor a how-to-do-it manual, nor even for that matter a book of fishing reminiscences. I hope the New Zealand content may do a little to persuade some readers away from the increasingly held belief that fly fishing for trout and the fish themselves are unique to individual countries; that, somehow, trout and trout fishing are so much different in Britain and the USA, or New Zealand or Australia, or Canada or Chile — as, indeed, some of the current swamis of the trade suggest. There is a magic sameness and universality in the nature of fly fishing for trout wherever these fish exist naturally or have been introduced with success. Fortunately, trout cannot exist anywhere and everywhere, otherwise their commonality would make them unappreciated. They are, in fact, splendid monitors of excellence in the environment, and in the last analysis it is water itself that is the measure of the quality of our habitat, as well as that of the trout. Beyond satisfying the trout's critical environmental needs and requirements the trout themselves know no national boundaries. There are, in all simplicity, just three species — everywhere: the brown trout (*Salmo trutta*), rainbow trout (*Salmo gairdneri*), and cutthroat trout (*Salmo clarkii*). Even the famed and splendid American brook trout (*Salvelinus fontinalis*) is not a true trout, but a char. All the rest is the human passion for speciation.

Above all this book is presented to the reader as an angling entertainment. There is a linkage, a common thread, running through the various chapters — indeed it is hoped this feature may be central to this book — yet, as books go, it is meant for browsing through as the fancy takes. And, in this manner, it has no real beginning and no real end.

Bryn Hammond
Taupo, New Zealand,
Hampshire, England.

Chapter 1
Why Men Fish

The title of this chapter must remain a question rather than consist of a plausible list of answers. Since time immemorial fishing writers have asked the question and philosophized about possible answers. Even those people who positively hate fishing are often led to wonder why other men persist in doing it, particularly with such singular and unswerving passion. No doubt, that first one of our primitive ancestors who forsook the net or trap or spear and took to the river bank or sea coast to fish with a rudimentary rod and line, and fished as much for pleasure as for food was looked upon by his fellows as being peculiar and out of step with the world of reality. And perhaps in those sentiments we reach as close as we are likely to get into the heart of the matter as to why men fish. Maybe that first and apochryphal sports fisherman was, albeit unconsciously, stepping outside the real world as perceived at that time. If that is so, as I suggest it may be, then we anglers who fish today are similarly, if fragmentarily, turning our backs on what most of our fellow humans call the real world.

But this does not really answer the question, *why* men fish; simply what happens to them when they do so. Angling has often been likened to an addiction, and those who know its thrall are unlikely to deny the suggestion. One difference between plain fishing and plain angling is that somewhere along the fisherman's path fishing becomes an event in itself, almost detached from and not necessarily concerned with the catching of fish. And then the fisherman becomes an angler.

The first known book on angling as sport fishing, the almost legendary, but very real, *The Treatise of Fishing with an Angle* or *The Treatyse of Fysshynge wyth an Angle* as it appears in the spelling of the day, advanced this view of angling as an event, as much as a practical means of catching fish. One frequently, but incorrectly, reads and hears that this purely sporting view of fishing only came about during the more effete later centuries. *The Treatise* was written in England sometime between 1406 and 1420. The earliest known version, transcribed from the now lost original, was made about 1450. The other version is the first printed text, which appeared in the second Book of

St. Albans in 1496. It is generally attributed to Dame Juliana Berners, Prioress of Sopwell near the Abbey of St. Albans, although modern scholarship by John McDonald and others has shown that, while the Dame herself was real, her authorship of *The Treatise* is almost certainly mythical.

The Treatise itself, however, is very real and fully authenticated to the early years of the 15th century in mediaeval England. For my present purposes I shall refer to Dame Juliana as the authoress, as is only right and proper. Anyone wishing to read the entire story of the text in a modern English version is enjoined to read John McDonald's *Quill Gordon* (1972) for a brilliantly researched and eloquently written study by angling's best and most knowledgeable historian.

Right from the start *The Treatise* differentiates between angling and mere fishing:

> Thus me semyth that huntynge & hawkynge & also fowlynge ben so laborous and greuous that none of theym maye perfourme nor bi very meane that enduce a man to a mery spyryte: whyche is the cause of his longe lyfe acordynge vnto the sayd parable of Salamon. Dowteles thenne folowyth it that it must nedes be the dysporte of fysshynge wyth an angle. For all other manere of fysshynge is also laborous & greuous: often makynge folkes ful wet & colde whyche many tymes hath be seen cause of grete Infirmytees. But the angler maye haue no colde nor angre, but yf he be causer hymself. For he maye not lose at the moost but a lyne or an hoke: of whyche he maye haue store plentee of his owne makynge, as this symple treatyse shall teche hym. Soo thenne his losse is not greuous, and other greyffes maye he not haue, sauynge but yf only fisshe breke away after that he is take on the hoke, or elles that he catche nought: whyche ben not greuous. For yf he faylle of one he maye not faylle of a nother, yf he dooth as this treatse techyth: but yf there be nought in the water. And yet atte the leest he hath his holsom walke and mery at his ease, a swete ayre of the swete sauoure of the meede floures: that makyth him hungry. He hereth the melodyous armony of fowles. He seeth the yonge swannes: heerons: duckes: cotes and many other foules wyth theyr brodes, whyche me semyth better than alle the noyse of houndys: the blastes of hornys and the scrye of foulis that hunters: fawkeners & foulers can make. And yf the angler take fysshe: surely thenne is there noo man merier than he is in his spyryte. Also who soo wol vse the game of anglynge he must ryse erly, whiche thyng is prouffytable to man in this wyse, That is to wyte: moost to the heele of his soule. For it shall cause hym to be holy, and to the heele of his body, For it shall cause hym to be hole. Also to the encrease of his goodys. For it shall make hym ryche. As the olde englysshe prouerbe sayth in this wyse. Who soo woll ryse erly shall be holy helthy & zely. Thus haue I prouyd in myn entent that the dysporte & game of anglynge is the very meane & cause that enducith a man in to a mery spyryte: Whyche after the sayde parable of Salomon & the sayd doctryne of phisyk makyth a flourynge aege & a longe. And therfore to al you that ben vertuous, gentyll and free borne I wryte & make this symple treatyse folowynge: by whyche ye may haue the full crafte of anglynge to dysport you at your luste: to the entent that your aege maye the more floure and the more lenger to endure.

I had intended to use a modern English version of the above and subsequent excerpts from Dame Juliana's *Treatyse*, but for reasons of copyright the original mediaeval text has been used. In this, it is hoped, the reader will find more poetry and charm, as well as a sense of continuity with the origins of fishing. It does one thing superbly well. It clearly and categorically sets the tone for sport fishing as it should be. Many of the earlier — and even present-day — fishing writers couldn't have been more wrong in their macho attitude to the origins of angling and to what it's all about: The very first known angling book reflects that, even then, the sport of fishing was all important — *Piscator non solum piscatur*, there is more to fishing than catching fish.

The sentiments of *The Treatise* are as apt today as they ever were:

> I charge you, that ye breke noo mannys heggys in goynge abowte your dysportes, ne opyn noo mannes gates but that ye shytte theym agayn. Also ye shall not vse this forsayd crafty dysporte for couetysenes to the encreasynge & sparynge of your money oonly, but pryncypally for your solace & to cause the helthe of your body and specyally of your soule. For whan ye purpoos to goo on your dysportes in fysshyng ye woll not desyre gretly many persones wyth you, whiche myghte lette you of your game. And thenne ye maye serue god deuowtly in sayenge affectuously your custumable prayer. And this doynge ye shall eschewe & voyde many vices, as ydylnes wyche is pryncypall cause to enduce man to many other vyces, as it is ryght well knowen. Also ye shall not be too rauneous in takyng of your sayd game as to moche at one tyme: whiche ye maye lyghtly doo yf ye doo in eury poynt as this present treatyse shewyth you in eury poynt, whyche sholde lyghtly be occasyon to dystroye your owne dysportes & other mennys also. As whan ye haue a suffycyent mess ye sholde coueyte nomore as at that tyme. Also ye shall helpe yourselfe to nouryssh the game in all that ye maye: & to dystroye all suche thynges as ben deuourers of it. And all those that done after this rule shall haue the blessynge of god & saynt Petyr, whyche he theym graunte that wyth his precyous blood vs boughte.

Despite its appeal, none of this in any way tells us anything about *why* men fish, but rather how someone (supposedly, but unlikely, to have been a woman) tells us how and with what attitudes we should go fishing. We shall need to pursue changing attitudes down the centuries, long after the time of Dame Juliana more than five hundred years ago, in order to arrive at some place closer in time to our own, to better understand just why men do fish — and with a far more singular and specific passion than seems to have been the model in the age of the Dame.

One hundred and fifty-seven years later appeared Izaak Walton's *The Compleat Angler*, described as 'that lovely, bucolic idyll, the most famous book in all the literature of sport.' It took Walton some twenty-three years between the 1st edition in 1653 and the famous 5th edition of 1676 to polish up that early fishing text book into some of the most eloquent, limpid prose ever penned. It wasn't that it took him twenty-three years to become bucolic or philosophical about his fishing, so much as his being a child of the times. In 1653 Walton produced a little fishing manual — now proven beyond doubt to have been plagiarized from *The Arte of Angling*, published in 1577 and now attributed, through the considerable scholarship of Carl Otto von Kienbusch and Gerald Eades Bentley, to one William Samuel. Plagiarism has ever been rife, and no less so than in angling books, although it would seem that Walton leaned on *The Arte of Angling* rather more directly than needs be if his intention was to use it merely as a source book. As interesting as anything is the discovery of how things in those days often went unchanged for a hundred years. The up-to-date fishing manual of 1577 was just as up-to-date in 1653 and merely required embellishment of its prose to present it again in 1676.

Between the time of Dame Juliana Berners and Walton's 1st edition there weren't that many source books available. These included Leonard Mascall's *A Booke of Fishing with Hook and Line* (1590), largely and clumsily pirated from the *Treatyse*, although some of Mascall's angling tips are being rediscovered, or reinvented today. Then there was John Dennys' *The Secrets of Angling* (1613), and another pirated text from Gervase Markham in 1614. Shortly before *The Compleat Angler* first appeared, there was printed a little book, *The Art of Angling* (1651) by Thomas Barker, a cook by profession, by avocation an excellent angler, who employed such skills to provide an endless supply of fish for 'his lord's table'.

The essence of these few source books, with the possible exception of John Dennys' poetry, was entirely practical: how to catch the greatest number of fish in the shortest possible time. In other words, it would seem that anglers had departed from the conservational philosphy of the Dame, and were mere pot-hunters.

By 1676 and the publication of Walton's 5th edition, coupled with Cotton's 1st edition as Part 2 of *The Complete Angler*, going fishing became more of an event once again, and the sentiment *Piscator non solum piscatur* (there is more to fishing than catching fish) became not only acceptable, but the prime reason for going fishing. In this respect Walton's influence was not only singular, but persists to this day and has permeated much of the vast literature on angling since that time.

But, insofar as this present enquiry is concerned, as to *why men fish*, there is much distance to go in angling attitudes before reaching that time when Negley Farson could write in presenting one of the finest fishing books of all time: 'This is just the story of some rods, and the places they take you to . . . This magic wand has revealed to me some of the loveliest places on earth.' In Walton's day the pace was slower and a single stretch of small river might well occupy a man's fishing for an unhurried lifetime. Yet anglers today increasingly move back to wanting to know and fish one stretch of one particular river well, rather than dissipate their passion by fleeting visits to a hundred different streams and lakes. For Walton:

> . . . as we have done this last hour, and sate as quietly and as free from cares under this Sycamore, as Virgils Tityrus and his Meliboeus did under their broad Beech-tree: No life my honest Scholar, no life so happy and so pleasant, as the life of a well governed Angler; for when the Lawyer is swallowed up with business, and the Statesman is preventing or contriving plots, then we sit on Cowslip-banks, hear the birds sing, and possess our selves in as much quietness as these silent silver streams, which we now see glide so quietly by us. Indeed my good Scholar, we may say of Angling, as Dr. Boteler said of Strawberries, Doubtless God could have made a better berry, but doubtless God never did: And so (if I might be Judge) God never did make a more calm, quiet, innocent recreation than Angling.

But Walton and his fellow anglers weren't just there to admire the scenery. For his old friend, Sir Henry Wotton, it was, he said,

an imployment for his idle time, which was then not idly spent: for
Angling was after tedious Study, a rest to his mind, a chearer of his
spirits, a diverter of sadness, a calmer of unquiet thoughts, a moderator
of passions, a procurer of contentedness; and that it begat habits of
peace and patience in those that profess'd and practis'd it. Indeed,
my friend, you will find angling to be like the vertue of Humility, which
has a calmness of spirit, and a world of other blessings attending upon
it.

To Walton and his contemporaries, it would seem what they liked best was
the leisure and the opportunity to go fishing:

Nay, let me tell you there be many that have forty times our Estates, that
would give the greatest part of it to be healthful and chearful like us; who
with the expence of a little mony, have eat, and drank, and laught, and
Angled, and sung, and slept securely: and rose next day, and cast away
care, and sung, and laught, and Angled again: which are blessings rich
men cannot purchase with all their money.

After Walton's day one is led to believe that successive generations of
anglers looked back with nostalgic longing, somehow seeing those idyllic and
bucolic fishing days as being something that contemporary living could no
longer provide. Right up to and including the time of the Industrial
Revolution, anglers looked wistfully backwards to halcyon days long since
gone — and to better fishing. It is my own suspicion that thus it ever was, and
is likely to be: rear vision has a romance about it hard to resist; a lotus land
where it was always yesterday. Maybe, after all, it hinges upon a dim race-
memory of the Garden of Eden.

We, too, are no different. However much we may long for our angling
tomorrows, we most often remember and relive our angling yesterdays.
Jonathan Swift was old when he recalled, 'I remember when I was a little boy,
I felt a great fish at the end of my line which I drew up almost on the ground,
but it dropt in, and the disappointment vexeth me to this very day.' To some
readers this is no more than the old, old story of the big one that got away. To
others it is quite different, and may be the key towards a better
understanding, not merely of why men fish, but of why they increasingly tend
to do it with such a singular and consuming passion.

Fishing has often been described as being a disease; a sort of terminal
affliction from which there is no respite or release. To anglers themselves this
sort of fishing state is pure bliss. Anything interrupting even the most
vicarious aspect of going fishing is held in contempt. But the appreciation of
the *enjoyment* of going fishing is, like the awareness of happiness,
retrospective. It needs to be looked back on. And almost always is. This is
perhaps the reason why all anglers remember the fish they lost, far more than
those they landed; and this despite old Izaak's warning to 'pray take notice no
man can lose what he never had'.

As for it being an addiction, few anglers would deny, albeit that most would
rather it be described as being a passion: 'Fishing is the one passion,' wrote
Logie Bruce Lockhart, 'that grows increasingly feverish, uncontrollable and
unreasonable with the passing years. As business preoccupations reduce
present opportunities, and advancing age reduces future prospects, every
moment spent rod in hand becomes more urgently precious.'

Another inkling as to the deeper-seated reasons why men fish may be found in what most displeases anglers in things proverbially said about them by non-anglers. Logie Bruce Lockhart again:

> It always was a mistake to believe that fishing, especially trout fishing, called for patience. It is, of course, a fever, an all-consuming lust that can brook neither opposition nor interruption. There comes a day, in late April or early May, when the breeze veers to the south-west, and the call of the river rises to an irresistible crescendo. For some of us it is the water itself that calls, the dancing of the ripples in the bright sun, which suddenly heats the anorak between our shoulder blades with all the tingling hope of a new season. For others it is the ardent worship of Spring's return to the river banks; or the deep urge for the hunt, the cunning pursuit, the delicacy of casting, the excitement of the rise, the fight and the capture, or the splendour of the trout's colours and texture fresh and gleaming in the water. Even in middle age, when in the distance I first see the river at the beginning of another year, I break into a run and am overcome with clumsiness in my impatience to get started.

But Lockhart, too, found there were many ages in fishing:

> For others especially in old age, this impatient lust is replaced by a steadier passion. Like true gourmets they derive their highest pleasures as much from anticipation as from action. The lucky ones among them have more time and money. The fever is not just focused on the fishing itself, but is spread for hours, days or weeks over the preparations for the final assault. The first crocus which opens to the February sun sends them scurrying to their fishing bags. They try their lines to hear the purring of the reel evoke the excitements of past seasons. They fuss around inspecting the joints of their rods, checking the hooks of their flies for rust; they re-grease the dry fly line and rearrange their old favourites: Greenwell, Wickham, Tup, Blue Dun, March Brown . . .

To Lockhart, as with his better-known uncle, it was the passion of angling that comes through again and again in his remembering: 'Trout fishing may start as a peaceful escape,' he warned, 'but it soon reveals itself to be a powerful drug which takes possession of us as an unalterable passion.'

However, fishing is not always seen as being either an addiction or a drug; and the act of going fishing not always regarded as being in the nature of a sorely needed fix. For Raymond Hill:

> The real charm, the real rest cure of fishing lies in its comparative solitariness. To be able to say I have not talked for six hours, nor fingered money, nor caught trains, nor bored any of my fellows, nor lied, nor sinned, nor breathed used-up air, forms at least a comfortable confession which, when repeated day after day for some weeks, cannot but restore health and nerves to a normal condition.

In Raymond Hill's list of the charms of fishing — for him it would seem ten good reasons why he went fishing — we have an early-twentieth century version of the reasons why Dame Juliana Berners so much recommended it almost five hundred years previously. Not all anglers, however, have seen the act of going fishing as being the great escape from the constraints of cities.

Lord Grey of Fallodon did record elsewhere that, whilst serving as Foreign Secretary, he longed for Friday evenings or Saturday mornings in order to escape from London and catch the train from Waterloo that would carry him to Hampshire for a few days' fishing. Yet, for Grey, it was more than just an escape from the great wen and the cares of state. He seems to have been aware that fishing somehow linked him with the natural world in a near mystical way: 'There are times,' he wrote, 'when I have stood still for joy of it all, on my way through the wild freedom of a Highland river, and felt the wind and looked upon the mountains and water and light and sky, till I felt conscious only of the strength of a mighty current of life which swept all consciousness of self and made me a part of all I beheld.'

Francis Francis also reveals something of this worship of the natural world, only found by escaping from the environment of cities:

> Far, far beyond all care: away from rates, taxes and telegrams, proofs, publishers' and printers' devils; where there are neither division lists, nor price lists, nor betting lists, nor any list whatever; where no newspaper can come to worry you or unsettle you, and where you don't care a straw how the world wags; where your clients are trouts, your patients worms, your congregation mountain black-faces, water-ousels and dab-chicks; your court, hospital or church the pre-Adamite hills with eternal sky above them; your inspiration the pure breeze of heaven, far, far above all earthly corruption.

In the same manner in which Jonathan Swift had that great vexation, even as an old man, about the great fish of his boyhood that 'dropt off' when he came to haul it out, so there is something of the perennial boy in the angler's pursuit of his sport. Patrick Chalmers saw it as providing a continuing link with his youth:

> And still the fair conceit I'd hold
>   That fishermen never grow old,
>   That with the daffodil's gold,
> That, with the cowslip's plenty,
> And with the loud and building rooks
> The man of rods and lines and hooks
>   Is always one-and-twenty.

To non-anglers the claim made by many anglers that there is more to fishing than simply catching fish rings as a patent untruth, an ever-ready excuse to explain away the fisherman's failure to do what he set out to do. This peer pressure to bring home the catch has sometimes been described as basic to the primitive origins of fishing. Personally, I doubt it. There seems more reason to believe that this measure of success or failure is of more recent origin, and ever increasing as time goes by. There may have been a time and place in our civilization when, if the fisherman returned home empty-handed, his family would go hungry. In the present age of frozen fish fingers and the like, this is unlikely. Yet, increasingly one notices many more anglers who are almost shamed by their wives and children to bring home the catch; to prove not only that they had been fishing, but — more importantly — that they were successful or (even more to the point) that they had not failed.

For generations the best of angling scribes have been telling their readers the very opposite. W. Earl Hodgson was generally considered to be a fairly practical sort of angler and angling writer; yet it was he who wrote, 'Paradoxical as the notion may seem, much of the fascination of the pursuit of trout, which never stales, springs from the knowledge that the pursuit will often be unsuccessful.' We shall come, in due course, to this view of fly fishing for trout as being the pursuit of the unattainable, nowhere ever described better than by those anglers who must live and work in cities, all too rarely escaping to the riverside. Perhaps there may be a clue here: that in order to appreciate the best of angling, one shouldn't have too much of it, that it is far better for a man to have too little.

Rarely have the delights and mysteries of trout fishing and of moving water been evoked more tellingly than by Nick Lyons, a citizen of New York City whose usual view of the sky is pierced and interrupted by the skyscrapers of Fifth Avenue:

> Nothing in this world so enlivens my spirit and emotions as the rivers I know. They are necessities. In their clear, swift or slow, generous or coy waters I regain my powers: I find again those parts of myself that have been lost in cities. Stillness. Patience. Green thoughts. Open eyes. Attachment. High drama. Earthiness. Wit. The Huck Finn I once was. Gentleness. 'The life of things.' They are my perne within the whirling gyre.

In *Bright Rivers* Nick Lyons longs for his all too brief forays out rod in hand, but must perforce spend most of his time in the very heart of New York City where, as he writes:

> In the evening on upper Broadway, two blocks from my apartment, lynx-eyed women stand near the bus stop as the buses go by, waiting. They wait patiently. Their impassive rouged faces show only the slightest touch of expectation; their gold high-heeled shoes glitter. Their dresses are exceedingly short. One of them hums, and the sound is like a low cacophonous motor, in perpetual motion.

No mean observer of the city streets, Nick Lyons is the epitome of the cultured New Yorker: Ed Zern described him as being 'that happy and compulsive combination of angler-poet-romantic', with rivers not only touching his heart and imagination but providing a vital link to the natural world. Does it help, then, not to get to go fishing too often?

There can be few anglers who have not often wished they lived alongside a favourite trout stream, or at least no more than a short walk away. It is perhaps the fly fisherman's most recurring and persistent dream. But would satiety creep into one's fishing if it was quite so easy? Would that tingling of the nerve-ends still be there in anticipation of every outing rod in hand? Would it be pointless to ask such a question as we ask now — why do men fish? — if the answer was simply because the river was there outside one's very door? For someone like Nick Lyons, 'Just knowing they are there, and that their hatches will come again and again according to the great natural laws, is some consolation to carry with me on the subways and into the gray offices and out onto upper Broadway at night.'

From this we can see that a vast amount of fishing is done vicariously, from the concrete canyons of New York, from the heart of downtown San Francisco, from office blocks in the City of London, from behind murky and dusty windows along a hundred city streets almost everywhere and anywhere.

'Must you actually *fish* to enjoy rivers?' asked Nick Lyons' friend the Scholar. To which he replied:

'It is difficult to explain but, yes, the fish make every bit of difference. They anchor and focus my eye, rivet my ear.'

'And could this not be done by a trained patient lover of nature who did not carry a rod?'

'Perhaps it could. But fishing is *my* hinge, the "oiled ward" that opens a few of the mysteries for me. It is so for all kinds of fishermen, I suspect, but especially so for fly-fishermen, who live closest to the seamless web of life in rivers. That shadow I am pursuing beneath the amber water is a hieroglyphic: I read its position, watch its relationship to a thousand other shadows, observe its steadiness and purpose. That shadow is a great glyph, connected to the darting swallow overhead; to that dancing cream caddis fly near the patch of alders; to the little cased caddis larva on the stream-bed; to the shell of the hatched stone fly on the rock; to the contours of the river, the velocity of the flow, the chemical composition and tempera-ture of the water; to certain vegetable life called plankton that I cannot see; to the mill nine miles upstream and the reservoir into which the river flows — and, oh, a thousand other factors, fleeting and solid and telling as that shadow. Fishing makes me a student of all this — and a hunter.'

'Which couldn't be appreciated unless you fish?'

'Which mean more to me because I do. Fishing makes rivers my corrective lens; I see differently. Not only does the bird taking the mayfly signify a hatch, not only does the flash of color at the break of the riffle signify a fish feeding, but my powers uncoil inside me and I must determine which insect is hatching and what feeding pattern the trout has established. Then I must properly equip myself and properly approach the fish and properly present my imitation. I am engaged in a hunt that is more than a hunt, for the objects of the hunt are mostly to be found within myself, in the nature of my response and action. I am on a Parsifalian quest. I must be scientist, technician, athlete, perhaps even a queer sort of poet.'

The Scholar smiles wanly and says, 'It all sounds like rank hedonism. And some cultism. With some mumbo jumbo thrown in.'

'Yes, I am out to pleasure myself, though sometimes after I've been chewed by no-see-ums until I'm pocked like a leper you wouldn't think that. There is a physical testing: the long hours at early morning, in bright sun, or at dusk; casting until your arm is like lead and your legs, from wading against the stiff current, are numb. That is part of the quest: to cleanse through exertion.'

'And the cultism and mumbo jumbo?'

'Some of trout fishing has become that, perhaps always was that. It is a separate little world, cunningly contrived, with certain codes and rules and icons. It is not a religion, though some believers make it such, and it is less than an art. But it has qualities of each. It touches heart and head; it demands and builds flexibility and imagination; it is not easy. I come to rivers like an initiate to holy springs. If I cannot draw from them an enduring catechism or from their impulses even very much about 'moral evil and of good', they still confer upon me the beneficence of the only deity I have been able to find. And when the little world becomes *too* cunningly contrived? Wit helps.'

Someone once remarked that the quality of fishing writing — that is its quality as literature — varied inversely to the quality of the fishing. That is not totally unlike suggesting that sackcloth and ashes and suffering provide a better path to the kingdom of heaven than the comfort of all the riches of this world. But I don't really believe it to be true. The United States has long provided some of the very best and most taxing fly fishing in the world, often with an intelligent sort of purity of purpose about it; not a blind adherence to outmoded cults. The United States has also produced much of the finest reflective fishing writing of all time, particularly on the question of why men fish.

Not all such writers have been so intellectually sensitive about it either; not because they lacked the intellectual equipment or approach, but rather because they often saw the event of going fishing in purely joyous terms, almost as if fishing was a form of pure hedonism they might indulge in without being considered beyond their establishment pale. Robert Traver, who in his non-fishing life was a Justice of the Michigan Supreme Court, possessed intellectual equipment of a high order. This, too, is reflected in his angling writing, but less in philosophical introspection than in the rumbustious joy of going fishing again and being where he most wanted to be, doing what he most wanted to be doing.

Traver, too, was perpetually pondering that question as to why men fish, but his findings were richly earthy and from the heart as much as the head. Robert Traver's angling philosophy was decidely functional: how else could it be for a passionate angler who said that fly fishing was such great fun it really ought to be done in bed. In a first attempt at defining why he fished, his reasons were profound, yet hesitantly negative. Unlike some commentators, Traver never suggested any superiority over other men in being an angler; in fact, quite the reverse. Even thinking of himself as 'a lawyer gone wrong', because he neglected so much to follow the siren call of trout, he saw all trout fishermen as a race apart. 'They are a dedicated crew,' he wrote, 'indolent, improvident, and quietly mad'. But, like so many others, he saw it as an addiction:

> The true trout fisherman is like a drug addict; he dwells in a tight little dream world of his own, and the men about him, whom he observes obliviously spending their days pursuing money and power, genuinely puzzle him, as he doubtless does them. He prides himself on being an unbribed soul. So he is by way of being a philosopher, too, and sometimes he fishes not because he regards fishing as being so terribly important but because he suspects that so many of the other concerns of men are equally unimportant. Under his smiling coat of tan there often lurks a layer of melancholy and disillusion, a quiet awareness — and acceptance — of the fugitive quality of man and all his enterprises. If he must chase a will-o'-the-wisp he prefers that it be a trout. And so the fisherman fishes. It is at once an act of humility and a small rebellion. And it is something more. To him his fishing is an island of reality in a world of dream and shadow.

Then later, he came to write what he himself called *Testament of a Fisherman*:

> I fish because I love to; because I love the environs where trout are found, which are invariably beautiful, and hate the environs where crowds of people are found, which are invariably ugly; because of all the

television commercials, cocktail parties, and assorted social posturing I thus escape; because, in a world where most men seem to spend their lives doing things they hate, my fishing is at once an endless source of delight and an act of small rebellion; because trout do not lie or cheat and cannot be bought or bribed or impressed by power, but respond only to quietude and humility and endless patience; because I suspect that men are going along this way for the last time, and I for one don't want to waste the trip; because mercifully there are no telephones on trout waters; because only in the woods can I find solitude without loneliness; because bourbon out of an old tin cup always tastes better out there; because maybe one day I will catch a mermaid; and, finally, not because I regard fishing as being so terribly important but because I suspect that so many of the other concerns of men are equally unimportant — and not nearly so much fun.

Thus Traver's testament becomes a more polished and poetical version of his earlier statement, but pronounced with greater certainty. Yet the similarity, or at least the hints of similarity, we begin to notice in various writers' attempts to describe just why they fish is not in the way they somehow echo each other's feelings. If there is any similarity in the words they write, then it can be little different from the seeming sameness, and the obscurity, of much writing on mystical experience. However, there is another common thread which comes to the surface from time to time.

This recurring and cautionary thread is one of chiding anglers not to take themselves too seriously, however serious fishing is to them in their deepest hearts. The point has been made in various angling tomes for hundreds of years without ever losing significance. We are warned to 'Remember that the wit and invention of man were given for greater purposes than to ensnare silly fish: and that, how delightful soever Angling may appear, it ceases to be innocent when used otherwise than as mere recreation.' Herein may lie the greatest paradox: how to reconcile this 'mere recreation' with what becomes 'an insatiable passion'.

British angling writing has often been redolent with the nostalgia of past fishing events. Rarely, however, during the past fifty or so years have many British fishing writers explored the introspective *why*?, as in why men fish. It is almost as if they take it for granted their readers know and understand full well, without being told. I suspect it is more to do with two prime, though dissimilar reasons. To begin with, the genre has tended to produce thoroughly practical anglers, averse to too much wonderment about it. Secondly, it is uncommonly difficult to do.

American angling writers, on the other hand, far from shunning any more than passing mention to such matters, have all but deemed it essential, however difficult. This mood gave rise to the happiest American invention of all, ever to influence the world of fly fishing. This was the fishing book in which few, if any, trout were reported slain, and where the decorations were generally in the form of drawings of living fish, rather than dreary photographs of very dead corpses of once proud trout. This is not to say, of course, that a trout fisherman should not be honest and, if such is the case, reply to the question 'Why do you go fishing?', say 'in order to try to catch and kill a limit'.

Fortunately, there are better reasons, and in learning more about why other men and women fly fish for trout with such extraordinary singlemindness and preoccupation, we may further develop our own progress along the angling path. American writers of note include two outstanding self-questioners in Odell Shepard and Ben Hur Lampman, to whom all fly fishermen everywhere should give eternal praise. Each of them wrote slim, sparse, highly literate angling books of extraordinary eloquence and grace. Their individual and separate pursuit of trout was unique in its constant questioning and wonderment. Prospective readers should not be dismayed by the titles of some of their books. Odell Shepard's *Thy Rod and Thy Creel* is one of them. But, if the title is off-putting, the contents are nothing short of sublime. Arnold Gingrich did much to rescue the book from the oblivion that followed its first publication in 1930. In *The Fishing in Print* he praised it lavishly: 'Today I can think of nobody who has written about angling more beautifully than Odell Shepard, at least since Walton, and I have almost the same feeling about Shepard's book that I have about Walton's, that it is almost a disservice to quote from it, because like *The Compleat Angler* itself, it should be swallowed whole, and then savored again at leisure.' Here is how Shepard saw the act and event of fly fishing:

> This mystery and challenging strangeness that the angler sets his will and wit to explore. Standing in one element, he invades another, striving to search it thoroughly. With a fifty-foot finger of bamboo and silk and gut he probes the deeps and the shallows, feels along the riffles, glides slowly out into bays of glitter, striving toward and almost attaining a sixth sense, trying to surprise the water's innermost secret law — but this, of course, he will never do. In other arts and crafts, and even in a few sports, we can distinguish the three stages of apprentice, journeyman, and master; but in angling few ever pass beyond apprenticeship, and masters there are none.'

This probing of the unknown is a constant and recurring feature of the mood and heart of angling; equally so is that vision of the fly rod, fly line, tapered leader, and fly being almost an extension of the fisherman's arm and hand and head — standing in one element, invading another. But even a writer as good as Odell Shepard failed for words when he asked himself *why* he fished.

> The charm of angling and the strong hold it takes upon many of us, have never been exactly explained. This is not because angling is mysterious in its nature, like poetry, but because its fascination is so inclusive, woven of so many strands. We attribute the pleasure it gives us to one cause after another, but after each attempt at an explanation we are obliged to say: 'Well no; it is not entirely that. There is something more.'
> I have heard men attempt to account for fishing by reference to our supposed 'ancestral memories', asserting that there is left in every modern man some relics or embers of those predatory instincts by which our primitive fathers kept themselves alive.

Shepard, somewhat reluctantly one suggests, accepts this atavistic view as being at least an interesting theory, but is at pains to disagree with the often heard contention by many experienced fly fishermen that it matters not one whit whether they catch trout or not. Despite his sensibilities, Shepard still believed that one of the prime purposes in going fishing was to catch fish. The denial, he felt, was a sort of convention by which anglers tried to explain to non-anglers why it did not bother or distress them when they didn't. It would seem that anglers have never bothered much to tell fellow anglers why they fish: there is no need to explain something to a man who already knows. Instead, anglers have tried to explain the great mystery to non-anglers or unsympathetic people who neither want to know, nor could possibly understand. Here is where angler-writers like Odell Shepard and Ben Hur Lampman come into their own. Instead of writing fishing guides or how-to-do-it manuals, they write of their fly fishing more philosophically, with their words aimed at equally addicted anglers, rather than beginners or those still hungering after hard fishing facts and hungering after fish.

Another recurring aspect of such writing is that much of the most reflective of it comes, not from people who were addicted fishermen in early youth, but from men who came to it as adults, often after a peak of sorts in lives that were active and more demanding than the norm. These men who become anglers in maturity often seem to have come to it with all the sudden impact and inevitability of religious conversion.

Edward Weeks was a distinguished essayist and editor of the *Atlantic Monthly*, one of the world's most liberal and enlightened periodicals. The nearest any of his several books came to being a fishing book was *Fresh Waters*, published in 1968. Of his conversion he wrote:

> You must understand that up to my fortieth birthday I looked on fishing as the most economical way of providing the table with that menu of clams — raw, steamed, or fried — lobster, and scrod which is native to Boston. That there was any grace or rapture in the business of catching fish I failed to perceive either in my study of Winslow Homer's paintings or on my repeated visits to a restaurant as savory as the Old Union Oyster House. Fish were for eating, and so they remained until the spring of 1938 when like St. Paul on the road to Ephesus I had an encounter and, rather against my better judgement, began to see things differently. I entered timidly into my new life but like all converts I became eager to tell others of what it feels like to be among the redeemed.

It came as a surprise to Weeks to discover that many of his Bostonian contemporaries were already similarly afflicted. Men he had known for years suddenly came to be seen in a different light. Of these acquaintances and friends before his conversion he wrote:

> I liked these elders and enjoyed playing backgammon and golf with them, and always the cocktail hour, but even as we were relaxing over the 19th hole, back would come that far look in their eyes and this cult-talk which sounded to me as mysterious as sex but not nearly so much fun. I did not realize until much later that what they were speaking was the private language of their double life, the symbol of those hours when, remote from their professional calling and domesticity, they were worshipping in the cathedral quiet of a clean-run trout stream.

I am especially sympathetic to this route along the angling path as it somehow mirrors my own. I was born in a valley between the Usk and the Wye with some of the best trout and salmon fishing in Britain virtually on my family doorstep. But my father was a golfer, as much a golfing addict as his son has now become a fishing addict. For some reason in those balmy and fishless days of my childhood and youth, although the rivers and streams nearby were teeming with fish, fishermen themselves were relatively few on the ground. For no particular reason I can remember, my family seemed to regard the fishermen we saw with something akin to pity — that these forlorn people did not occupy their time doing something useful or enjoyable. Some of these fishermen were townsmen engaged in the free fishing available to them. They stood in long, dreary-looking rows on the bridge over the Usk at nearby Crickhowell, fishing from the serrated, buttressed parapets, and they all seemed to wear overlong, fawn gabardine raincoats. Similar scenes were repeated on each and every bridge in Monmouthshire, Brecon, Herefordshire and Radnorshire.

Upstream and down from such free fishing, but mostly out of sight and mind, were the more exclusive fly fishermen. Far from marvelling at the swish and grace of the fly fishers' uncoiling casts I, if I observed them at all, only wondered why they weren't smart enough to fish from the bridge like the townsmen, dry-shod, able to dangle whatever was on the ends of their lines right in mid-stream if they were lucky enough to get the central serrated bridge bay, instead of trying to chuck the thing out standing in the river.

As to the fish themselves, salmon, sea trout and trout were foodstuffs we ate at home with relish, and as part of frequent family lunches and dinners at the Angel Hotel in Abergavenny and in similar hostelries abounding in that area. Somehow, I never seemed to associate the fish I ate with the boring activity of the fishermen we observed; nor did, to the best of my recollection, any of my family. It wasn't to be for another thirty years that I encountered the light. As it turned out, this was to be at the opposite ends of the earth, in Tasmania and in New Zealand.

Of his early days as a fishing addict Edward Weeks said, 'I seemed to be living in a wider horizon, aware of antennae I had not used before.' And of his later fishing days:

> I doubt if I shall ever outgrow the excitement bordering on panic which I feel the instant I know have a strong, unmanageable fish, be it brook trout, brown trout, cutthroat, steelhead, or salmon, on my line. I know that I have acquired patience and the love of casting lightly and accurately whether or not the fish respond. I know that the hot blood has cooled and that I no longer reckon in terms of how many and how big. The river we love, the fish we admire, have given us an inestimable treasure, for when sight fails and one can no longer thread a fly even when peering at it against the evening sky, when the hearing dulls, when the legs are too weak for wading, we still have the freedom to relive, not once, but again and again, the play of shadow and sunlight, the remembrance of fast water, and of that primitive strength which will move one's line almost beyond control.

Despite the literary eloquence and this obvious yearning to fish, we have learned little about why such a man as Edward Weeks did fish. He described his coming to it as being a conversion. So, is this as far as we may go in our enquiry without departure into the realms of fancy? Is to ask Why men Fish? as meaningless a question as that of the mediaeval theologians who endlessly debated how many angels could stand on the head of a pin?

Ben Hur Lampman's classic *A Leaf from French Eddy* is a beautiful book and a sustained paean of praise for fly fishing as a rite, but he, too, was aware that any attempt at answering the question could do little more than skirt about the heart of the matter, and raise even more impossible-to-answer questions.

One of Lampman's parleys into the reason why, nicely avoided the direct
question in turning it into 'What is this fishing?' In this he was confident:

> One has no difficulty in distinguishing mere anglers from your true
> fisherman. Though it is possible for the individual to be both angler and
> fisherman, or almost, it is a phenomenon of great infrequency for any
> fisherman to be an angler or to wish to become one. The fisherman is
> artlessly gratified by the simpler expressions of the urge to fish. He will
> fish, doggedly, happily, with the aptness of the perfect convert, in waters
> where a strike is extremely improbable, and at seasons when every
> natural sign is against him. He will fish when thunders are above, and
> lightnings streak the sky. He will fish with the sleet in his face and the
> wind chilling him to the marrow. He will fish with a knotted cord of
> cotton and the crudest of hooks. It is true that the finer gear of the craft,
> superlative, beautiful, masterly, is very dear to him — but the urge to fish
> is dearer. He fishes because he must fish.

Note here that Lampman uses the words *angler* and *fisherman* quite
differently from current convention. He writes of *mere anglers* and *true
fishermen*. Lampman himself was no latter-day convert to fishing. The first
fish he ever caught was a catfish from a lake in Wisconsin, just below Poskin's
dam, described with the typical Lampman detailed eye and remembrance of
childhood. This was long before his journeying westwards to Oregon into the
world of trout. But that first Wisconsin catfish had the same lasting effect on
him as any conversion in maturity. Of that day he wrote:

> It began for me with the capture of a catfish — the most personable and
> handsome catfish — in the black pool below Poskin's dam. I drew from
> the earliest water something more than a catfish — a charmed creature,
> weaving spells. If I required his life of him, he in his turn exacted a tribute
> that has not wavered. The sorcery of him has led me to my armpits in
> frigid mountain water, of which I derived twinges that linger; and to
> shores of summer where the sun flayed me, face and arm — and shall
> lead again. I, too, am well content.

Reflecting on a soon-to-come opening day, longed for throughout an
Oregon winter, Lampman muses:

> It is good to live in a land where there is plenty of trout fishing. You never
> tire of it, and never does the season open without the old tingling, the old
> response.
> People try to explain it, although this is unnecessary, but nobody ever
> has been quite able to do so, not even Walton. But most fishermen are
> agreed there is a quality in trout fishing that approaches the ideal. It is
> like the pursuit and realization of a pleasing dream. The trout is its
> symbol of abundant reward. It is something like this: We know, of
> necessity, that we can never have all to which we aspire, and we realize,
> too, that the dreams of aspiration have a way of fading, and yielding,
> until they are gone beyond recovery, and we have but memories of them.
> Is it sad? No. That isn't it. This is the common experience of mankind.
> We are reconciled to it, or nearly so. Yet men must dream of a time, if it
> be no more than a single day, when their dreams shall come true, even as
> they dreamed them. Now the virtue of trout fishing is that it, of all

pursuits, rewards the dreamer with realization of his dream. The trout are more beautiful than he remembered them as being, and the day, the scene and the occupation are at harmony. That is why men go trout fishing.

It has often been remarked by trout fishermen that when they are about the affairs of stream and rod, the events of yesterday and the necessities of tomorrow are singularly dwarfed in importance. They seem somehow to lack for real significance. The beauty of stream and forest, the beauty of the fish, the agreeable nature of the employment — these are real. All else appears to be of little moment, and to wear an aspect of trickery, as though men were both betrayed into and by it. It is for this reason that men go trout fishing, vowing that they prefer it to other recreations. Physically weary as they are before the sun is high, the truth is they are resting. They have rediscovered the escape. The stream they fish is running through their hearts to bear away the frets and worries of yesterday and tomorrow. All fishermen will know how it is, though it is uncommonly difficult to explain.

Why should it be that American writers have come closer to describing what virtually all addicted fishermen know and experience about those 'uncommonly difficult to explain' things than writers from other parts of the world? Is it because they have greater sensitivities about such matters? Is it because they are often better, not necessarily as anglers, but as complete anglers? Is it because Americans are less inhibited about what they really feel, and in no way embarrassed about describing and sharing those feelings?

Of one thing I am certain. Whether or not any reader now knows any more about why men fish I can have no gleaning. But should any reader not have felt that old tingling, that old response, in reading these words, and have not had similar awareness at times — even fleetingly — then he has not yet travelled far enough along the road towards his own angling Damascus.

Chapter 2
Heresies and Humours

The time has come for anglers everywhere to put back more fun into their fly fishing, and to regard it less as a mere means of slaughtering trout. With that point of departure in mind it had been my vague intention to write a lighthearted and frothy overview about fun in fly fishing; about sheer fun as well as humour and funniness, both from days gone by and the contemporary angling scene.

I have been doubly blessed in having good and wise angling friends, especially in New Zealand, with whom it is fun beyond compare to actually go fishing. But, in addition, they talk about fly fishing, and do so with much erudition, wit, humour and grace, but above all with an infectious sense of fun. They have passions for angling more total than I have known in other men, but hang on to that sense of the ridiculous, remembering Charles Bowlker's warning 'that the wit and invention of man were given for greater purposes than to ensnare silly fish: and that, how delightful soever Angling may appear, it ceases to be innocent when used otherwise than as a mere recreation'.

Many aspects of angling are held to be serious matters, but one departure that should be full of laughter, full of fun and tongue-in-cheek, must surely be in the matter of fly fishing heresies. Heresy is a large and emotive word that seems to leap towards violently expressed and unorthodox views. One dictionary definition is 'opinion contrary to the . . . accepted doctrine on any subject'. There is something of the heretic in us all, and as much in fly fishing attitudes and ideas as the more weighty matters of life. Without it we would still be living in caves and catching the odd and sickly fish with spears. In much the same way as we are led to believe that all the world loves a lover, so, too, the world has lingering sympathy with and affection for the heretic. Thomas Huxley once said it is the customary fate of new truths to begin as heresies. Every age needs its heretics to question current dogma and to be suspicious of dogmatic change, whereby a harmless, outdated and unimportant dogma may be replaced by a harmful, ultra-modern and important dogma that intolerably affects us all. Angling is no exception.

Sacred cows abound in the angler's world: one is that the dry fly must be employed either directly upstream, or only through that very limited arc of absolute dead-drift, before the dreaded drag skitters the floating fly across the stream in an unnatural and fish-scaring manner. This would be about as basic and gospel-truth fact as any to almost anyone dry fly fishing today, both expert and tyro. But is it true? Does it have any absolute substance beyond vague generalities? As yet there are no High Priests of the opposite school, but there are a few simple heretics. Amongst these is an American angling writer, Leonard M. Wright Jr., sadly little known and appreciated in Britain; a thinking man's angler if there ever was one, and perhaps at one time fly fishing's most celebrated iconoclast. He is best known for his 1972 book *Fishing the Dry Fly as a Living Insect*, subtitled 'A Thinking Man's Guide to Trout Angling: An Unorthodox Method', but deserves to be far better known for his 1975 volume *Fly-Fishing Heresies*. The surprise is that these two books didn't exactly rock dry fly fishing to its Halfordian foundations. There were ripples, to be sure; even a few palpitations; but in the end Halford's attitudes prevail.

In the first of these books Leonard Wright begins with a critical look at dry fly imitation of the caddis flies — those much neglected, but abundantly distributed aquatic insects that much frustrate fly fishermen. Adult caddis look nothing like ninety-nine per cent of all traditional dry flies because these have been patterned on mayflies. Caddis have no tails and fold their opaque wings in an inverted 'V', horizontally, covering their bodies. Mayflies, like most of our artificials, have long tails and upright translucent wings. Leonard Wright cannot have been the first angler to observe that caddis flies are extremely active both as they hatch out on the surface and when they return to the river for mating and egg laying. They twitch, flutter and zigzag on the water surface in a distinctive manner that the trout find irresistible.

Despite the fact that caddis flies are the most profusely abundant single insect on many waters to appear each year, virtually all the then available standard artificial patterns bore no relationship at all to the silhouette of the true caddis. Moreover, the newly hatched caddis does not float downstream with the immobile poise of the classic dry fly but, in Len Wright's words, 'seems to enjoy finding itself on the water as much as the average house cat does, and it protests nearly as vigorously'. Yet, as we shall see in a later heresy, it is now clear that several species of adult caddis freely and frequently return to the water and after climbing down a rock or aquatic plant stalk swim around at will.

Three hundred years ago, when rods were sixteen to eighteen feet long, the then popular method of dapping — bouncing the fly over the surface on a short line directly below the rod tip — duplicated this insect behaviour admirably. With modern rods of eight of nine feet and even less this is not possible other than at very short range and over very limited fishing areas. It is in addressing himself to this problem that Leonard Wright's heresy began. He advocated and perfected such dry fly fishing *downstream and across*: heresy of heresies. He threw his floating, fluttering caddis imitations three or four feet above the trout's lie, with a pronounced curve, bellying the line upstream; immediately the fly hit the water he gave the rod a short, sharp, upward twitch, sending the fly darting up current an inch or so. He then let out slack line to let the fly float, drag-free, for six or eight feet, enough and more to cover the lie of the fish. This 'sudden inch' so simulates the behaviour of a winged caddis that it will usually be taken if the presentation is made accurately and if the fly itself is a passing imitation of the caddis on the water.

There were still problems — how to tie passable artificials that would float in spite of having no tails, was not the least of them. But this is not intended to be a how-to-do-it account: for that the reader should go to Leonard Wright's books and those of the few other writers who have espoused his, and similar, ideas. The point here is to outline, very briefly, how angling heresy begins. In this case, two sacred tenets of the dry fly — upstream presentation and dead-drift — were attacked head-on by advocating the practice of the exact opposite.

On the rich chalk streams of England a century and more ago the mayfly hatches were undoubtedly prolific, consistent and predictable. Because mayfly artificial patterns were so successful as fish catchers it is hardly surprising there should have been such contemporary emphasis on the development of such dry flies. 'The Duffer's Fortnight' of the chalk streams merely emphasized the seasonal selectiveness of the trout: over a period of time the trout would feed exclusively, madly, irrationally and with abandon on one species of winged insect while disregarding all others. Humans are in no way different when at times they gorge themselves on a box of chocolates. Arnold Gingrich put it succinctly when he said there was no such thing as one peanut.

Mayflies are exquisitely beautiful insects which trout find to be delectably delicious: no small wonder then that both man and trout should be so preoccupied with them. What is incredible, however, is that a world-wide and entire rigid code of dry fly fishing was built up on such relatively brief seasonal appearances of a particular insect. Why and how did it come to be that for almost a hundred years the more basic food of trout among the other species of winged insects — the stoneflies, caddis flies, ants, cicadas, crane flies, midges, smuts — were all but ignored. It was perhaps less a result of Halfordian pronouncement from on high than of artistic development and artistic licence in fly tying. Who wouldn't prefer to create and copy, tie, look at, admire, and fish a gorgeous mayfly rather than a common housefly or drab sedge?

The majority of insects that end up floating on rivers, unlike the mayfly floating downstream serenely under full sail, were blown there, willy-nilly. They struggle and try to fly off, skittering across and upstream, anything but resigned to their fate. The across and downstream dry fly, the sudden inch, the rod-imparted lift and upstream twitch — even at times the first moments and last moments of drag — are often accurate, authentic, scientific, ethical, thoughtful, and devastatingly successful simulations of the struggles of water-borne, living insects trying to escape back into their proper environment. Dead-drift may be classical dry fly fishing, but is exactly what it says: dead drift. Trout much prefer the real thing and living insects.

Any angler-imparted movement to dry fly or nymph was such anathema to the angling establishment that shortly after the publication of his first book, *Fishing the Dry Fly as a Living Insect*, Leonard Wright happened to bump into Sparse Grey Hackle, the dean of American fly fishing. 'Congratulations, Len', he said, 'I see you've written an entire book devoted to the ancient art of trolling.'

It is increasingly prevalent to categorize, and fly fishing is no exception. Take, for example, the now rigidily compartmentalized dry fly, wet fly and nymph fishing, and the occasional bigotries attached to them all. The small, sparsely tied, soft hackled wet flies fished upstream in the way advocated by W. C. Stewart (1857), Theakston (1853), Jackson (1854), Cutcliffe (1863), Pritt

(1885), was without doubt nymph fishing in all but name, but was rigidly categorized as being wet fly fishing, with no slur given or intended. The proven successful patterns — black, red and dun spiders, olive bloa, coch-y-bondhu, yellow hackle, woodcock and brown, waterhen bloa, rough olive — were, perhaps unknowingly, all accurate nymphal patterns, with the soft hackles providing underwater flash and sparkle like entrapped air bubbles and trout-provoking movement of legs and other nymphal appendages. They were releaser patterns par excellence long before Niko Tinbergen. They represented nymphs for all seasons, not because anyone had just worked out that trout take ninety per cent of their food underwater, but because they had always known so. These were imitative patterns long before Skues, albeit developed for rapid, fast-flowing streams. Most of us change attitudes over the years and Halford was no exception. While almost obsessed with dry fly purism of dead-drift, total inert and passive presentation, he was still fond of quoting his friend George Selwyn Marryat's saying, 'You can imitate the nymph, but you cannot imitate the wriggle.' It was as if that alone was reason enough not to warrant giving nymph fishing any serious thought.

G. E. M. Skues, who seemed so emphatic that nymphing should be almost directly upstream, and fished either to seen or known to be present trout, could still write in his very first book, *Minor Tactics of the Chalk Stream* (1910):

> Of all trials of the . . . angler, perhaps drag is the worst. Yet even drag may be made use of on occasion, to add to the weight of the creel. Years back . . . I sat by a mill-head on a blazing and well-nigh hopeless September afternoon. The water was low, much of the head having been run off by the sawmill, and such little current as there was confined itself almost entirely to the centre. Brown and dirty-looking weeds topped the surface along my side of the head. Suddenly I detected a tiny dimple in a little spot where, among the weeds, an eighteen inch square of clean surface showed itself. I despatched my fly — a Landrail and Hare's Ear Sedge on a No.3 hook — and by good luck or good judgement it dropped neatly on the spot. I waited. Three minutes passed. Nothing happened. Then I thought to recover my fly and drop it again in the hole, but with rather less delicacy, so as to attract attention to its fall. But first I had to recover it. I moved it gently towards the side of the hole, but I could not prevent the effect of a drag on the surface. Yet ere the fly had moved three inches a good pound-and-a-half trout had it, and, after a game of pully-hauly in the weeds, was duly brought to net.

As if to propitiate his critics, of whom there were many, he added, almost coyly, 'This was a limestone stream, and not a chalk stream.'

Apart from the somewhat archaic 'Yet ere the fly had moved three inches . . .' those sentences might have been written by Leonard Wright himself. Or this:

> So I knotted on a good big sedge — I think a No.3 Silver Sedge — the water was glassy smooth, and the current would not have carried my fly the length of the open water (three yards long) in much under five minutes. I was afraid to cast above the fish, or to right or left of his head, for I knew it would send him scuttling to weed. I wanted to drop the fly just behind his eyes, but I misjudged, and it fell several inches short, almost upon his tail. I waited a moment; the trout lay still, but evidently

excited. Then I remembered my German experience and began to draw the fly along the surface. Immediately the trout turned and slashed it, and was soundly hooked.

Pure Leonard Wright again? Not quite; but Skues again in *Minor Tactics of the Chalk Stream*. Fishing the dry fly as a living insect was clearly being practiced by Skues as early as 1906. And my companions and I used the same minor tactic, with much success, on the wild brown and rainbow trout of good size but existing in relatively small populations, in remote mountain streams in New Zealand.

Similar heretical suggestions from Skues appeared in *The Way of a Trout with a Fly*:

> Kick. This is a quality which every hackled wet fly, for use in rough water, should invariably have. Without it, it is a dead thing; with it, it is alive and struggling; and the fly which is alive and struggling has a fascination for the trout which no dead thing has. How is this quality to be attained? It is a very simple matter. Finish (tying) behind the hackle.

Fly fishing has a longer continuous history than is often realized. Walton in the 1st edition of *The Complete Angler* in 1653 was saying, 'And when you fish with a flie, if it be possible, let no part of your line touch the water, but your flie only; and be stil moving your fly upon the water.'

By Oliver Kite's time there were but few lingering prejudices left in attitudes to nymph fishing, but it required a lucid master angler of Kite's temperament to overcome once and for all antipathy towards planned and intentional manipulation of the artificial nymph. It was Oliver Kite's masterly exposition and practice of 'the induced take' that gave a new and added dimension to nymph fishing; this from around 1957 until his untimely and early death in 1968. In *Nymph Fishing in Practice* he wrote:

> The take in nymph fishing may be either voluntary or induced. A voluntary take occurs when the fish seizes the nymph as it sinks after entering the water or at any time during the course of its free drift downstream. The significant point is that you remain absolutely passive, apart from methodically gathering in any slack line, until you detect the trout's voluntary acceptance of your artificial and strike on this signal.
>
> An induced take occurs when the fish disregards the artificial nymph until you deliberately attract its attention to it by animating the nymph with a short sideways movement to the rod tip. This causes the artificial to swim or lift slightly in the water in a manner so realistic that the fish is impelled to take it, perhaps involuntarily.

What is most surprising is that the induced take in nymph fishing, and Wright's fishing the dry fly as a living insect, should have been so radical when generations of sunk fly, wet and damp, as well as lure fishermen, had been quite deliberately trying to impart life and struggle to their offerings, without anyone ever suggesting it was anything but perfectly natural.

Oliver Kite probably sounded heretical when he said,

> Modern nymph fishing is sometimes referred to by the expression 'upstream nymph fishing'. This may be misleading. The term seems to emphasize the fact that the nymph is not fished downstream in the old

downstream wet-fly style, but in practice 23 of the trout I caught on nymph from the Avon in 1959 were taken on an artificial cast directly across the stream.

Directly across stream nymphing, the induced take, across and downstream dry fly fishing, the sudden inch, the upstream twitch, fishing the dry fly as a living insect, were and are not startling new discoveries, but clever and thoughtful restatements about things that many were beginning to forget.

James Leisenring is sometimes reckoned to be the 'Skues of America'. He corresponded with Skues for many years, developing the ideas of the wet fly and its use as a high art among angling techniques as opposed to the earlier intolerant purism of the dry fly.

Leisenring's innovations can hardly be called heresies but were nevertheless far from fully appreciated. His book, *The Art of Tying the Wet Fly and Fishing the Flymph*, written in conjunction with Vernon Hidy, was first published in 1941. 'Flymph' was Leisenring's coined word for an artificial intended to represent that most delicious stage in the transformation of nymph to mayfly — at the moment when the emerging nymph becomes irresistible to trout; a revelation perhaps similar to a man who has long been eating peanuts, shells and all, who suddenly has a nut shelled for him and has the added pleasure of eating two unadulterated peanuts. Leisenring subsequently developed the 'Leisenring Lift', induced take and upstream twitch.

By the time the dry fly tyranny was at its height, art and artistry had so overwhelmed the traditional wet flies of the past, with gaudy, decorative, attractor patterns, that when they were eventually discarded with the arrival of the new dogma the baby was thrown away with the bath water. Some of the old wet flies — Cinnamon Sedge, Grannom, Greenwell, Red Spinner, March Brown, Wickham, Invicta, Peter Ross, Teal & Claret, Teal & Silver, and the rest — were, in fact, some of the greatest and most accurate imitative patterns of all time. They represented and fished like winged drowned flies, winged flies emerging, or the host of winged insects that return to the water and crawl down weeds and stones to lay their eggs underwater.

What many writers describe as the 'sixth sense' of skilful nymph fishermen may be nothing more, or less, than a not-easy-to-perceive refinement of the induced take, sudden inch, or all but imperceptible lift. The nymph is cast, whether to a seen or unseen fish hardly matters in this case, the expectant angler is honed for quick reaction; the line carefully mended; the tip of the fly line and what may be visible of the leader watched like a hawk. What actually happens next in order of sequence is perhaps debatable. The leader hesitates, pauses, moves across or upstream — there may be clearly or even barely perceptibly Skues' 'little brown wink under the water.' Or does the really good nymph fisherman in that very split second in which it is happening, or even, miraculously, a split second *before* it all happens, instinctively and surely draw his rod tip sharply but slightly to one side in a pre-determined and seemingly pre-ordained induced take?

Some angling heresies arose as a result of someone thinking the unthinkable, saying the unsayable, and writing the unwriteable in a fishing book. P. B. M. Allan was such a man, and his book *Trout Heresy*, published in 1936, was just such a book. In his view the quarry we seek with such singular passion is far from being the noble trout, but is a lowly, primitive creature of base and basic urges, which is neither cunning nor wise. Strangely, it seems that in the ensuing half-century no other angling writer has commented on this remarkably perceptive but non-idolatrous book. In it Allan ranges freely among what he considers to be the mucky, anthropo-morphized misconceptions fly fishermen have about trout. It was heresy of the first order.

The history of fly fishing for trout in England was well established even in Dame Juliana Berners time. In her *Treatise* she lists the twelve essential artificial flies and affirms that these came from earlier 'books of credence', now sadly lost to us. It has constantly amazed subsequent generations of anglers, even to this day, that these twelve flies have survived to our time, and in not too modified a form have continued in general use. This is not as remarkable as some commentators have suggested, for they are all imitations of natural insects, and there is no reason to suppose that the insect fauna of this country has changed radically since the fifteenth century. P. B. M. Allan had the temerity to propound the theory that their survival is due not so much to their ability to catch trout as to the failure by succeeding generations of fishermen to work out the psychology of the trout and to tackle the problem from the right end. Allan was mindful of the can of worms he was opening:

> Woe betide him who lays hands on the revered monuments of antiquity, the teachings of our forefathers through generations, our very birthright! Would that I were not a fly fisherman myself; for then I should at least be spared the most hateful of epithets — renegade! I shudder even as I pen the word: shall I who have spent the happiest days of my life on Kennet, Itchen, Test, in company with friends dear to me as brothers, be no longer of that glorious brotherhood? Must I forego my birthright — the inexpugnable right to catch trout where water flows and line may lawfully be cast — because I have dared openly and unblushingly to advance a theory contrary to the established use of ages?

As is often the case when presenting heretical beliefs to an all too cosy establishment, Allan leavened his arguments with a certain amount of lightheartedness and humour; a common device in order to avoid seeming quite deranged and over the top. In such a manner heresy and humour are often found hand in hand. By anticipating hostile reaction, and by making light of it, it is sometimes possible to avoid anathema by presenting a caricature of heretical beliefs. With such levity Philip Allan, in fact, pounds home his basic idea:

> Throughout the centuries fishermen have regarded the trout as a sagacious animal possessed of great cunning. It is a comfortable doctrine. Your impulse therefore on reading the next sentence will be to consign this book to the flames. For I submit that the trout has no more brain than a lizard — less indeed, since he is lower in the scale of animal creation. But read on: do not condemn me on account of the dire corollary that if the trout has no more brain than a lizard and can yet outwit you, your own mentality must suffer by the comparison. I am (at least I pray that I may be) your brother fisherman and not so skilful as you, and I would not willingly rate my own mind with that of an amphisbaena.
>
> The legend of the trout's sagacity is as old as the art of fly fishing, and it arises from man's conceit. If the trout can outwit us, the lords of creation, he must be superior to us in cunning.

By the time of the dry fly ascendancy the trout had become endowed with most of the finer human attributes. Even Skues, in 1921, asserted that the trout is endowed with sport, high spirits, jealousy, curiosity, rapacity and tyranny. Allan was quick to point out that an animal as low in the scale of life as a fish performs its life-cycle in accordance with the dictates of instinct. It is unable to 'reason'. It has not the power to meditate over its actions. It can do no wrong, where its natural functions are concerned, simply because it does not possess the power of *choosing* between what is good for it and what is bad, other perhaps than in its choice of suitable foods. Instinct decides these things for it. 'It cannot,' in Allan's words, 'play pranks with its body like a dry-fly man. If it is hungry it cannot refuse to eat. Surround it with its accustomed food and, conditions being suitable, it will eat till it is gorged, then lie torpid as an alderman after his Christmas dinner, until digestion enables it to eat again.'

Philip Allan, it seems, was concerned lest his critics confound him, over this matter of whether or not the trout has the power of choosing between one thing and another. As he saw if, if you offer a trout six flies at once and it takes one of them, it may well exercise the power of choice within the instinctive urge to eat. That is to say it will take the fly which (a) it sees first, or (b) appears most like a living insect, or (c) most closely resembles the insect upon which it has just been feeding, or which its instinct or experience informs it is good to eat. But wary of the philosophy of logic he asserts:

> If you think to catch me by placing a hungry trout in a position like unto that of Professor Buridan's ass, that is to say precisely half-way between two succulent flies, suggesting that without a power of choice outside instinct the fish would starve to death, I will confound you even as the Professor confounded those students of his. But beware! it is nearly six hundred years since Buridan died, and we know more about animal psychology today. Yes, even such an arrant heretic as I must needs allow the fish *discernment* in the taking of *suitable* food. But lest you should think I am giving my case away I must add that such discernment is, at its best, instinctive; at its worst, extremely fallible.

It is not intended here to summarize P. B. M. Allan's book *Trout Heresy*. Indeed the reader of these pages is enjoined to read the book in its entirety. It is not important to agree with, or attack, Allan's heresy; only to record how and in what manner some near doctrinal truths have been attacked and how such heresies have become no more than long-forgotten tilting at windmills, or become, in turn, accepted truths held commonplace. Aspects of other heresies are dealt with in other chapters of this book where they are more appropriate and relevant to the subject matter.

Leonard Wright, whom we have already met, was obviously cast in much the same mould as P. B. M. Allan. His second book, *Fly Fishing Heresies* (1975), although irreverent, is witty, erudite and sprung from a far more genuine passion for trout fishing than the bulk of how-to-do-it manuals. Wright, very much a member of the prestigious American fly fishing establishment — more traditional and orthodox than its counterpart in Britain — became disenchanted with the classic style of American dry fly fishing because of its blind acceptance of tired dogma and traditions that had resulted in losing sight of the main aim — the catching of trout.

To him the sport had become as highly ritualized a performance as bullfighting. Both pursuits were straitjacketed by rigid rules, hobbled by out-of-date choreography, and had little relevance to the catching of their quarry. Yet, desperately serious about it all, like most fishing heretics, he proclaims a sense of fun and funniness about it all, recognizing that fishing in itself is not of much special importance, but knowing as Robert Traver did, that neither are most other pursuits,

> because, in a world where most men seem to spend their lives doing things they hate, my fishing is at once an endless source of delight and an act of small rebellion . . . and, finally, not because I regard fishing as being so terribly important but because I suspect that so many of the other concerns of men are equally unimportant — and not nearly so much fun.

Iconoclasm subsists on a healthy sense of fun. But there is a thriving trade in less-than-genuine heresy where secondhand ideas are served up as new and soon become the new dogma of the age. Trout fishermen, too, should beware of such teachings, however currently fashionable they seem to have become. The new and spurious dogma is immediately recognizable by its total lack of humour and humility. Better to acknowledge as Lord Home has done that 'fishing is unquestionably a form of madness, but happily, for the once bitten, there is no cure.'

The one-time popular novelist Rafael Sabatini was less well-known as a fly fisherman, but wrote of:

> . . . the tyrannical fascination which angling holds for all those who have been initiated into its mysteries.
>
> 'The riddles it presents are endless; as fast as one is resolved, or appears to be resolved, by the pertinacious and thoughtful, another confronts him challengingly and engages his efforts. Sometimes the solution of one riddle is in itself the creation of another. And so, this endless tyranny goes on. Only those become weary of angling who bring nothing to it but the idea of catching fish.'

Heresies are part of that magic. Humour needs to be too.

Chapter 3
The Evening Rise

For most New Zealand fly fishermen, and generally for fishermen everywhere, there is day fishing for trout and night fishing for trout, with the twain rarely, if ever meeting, let alone overlapping. Yet, to a man, they are likely to hold decided (and invariably different) opinions about the evening rise.

For the most part, other than on specific fishing holidays, the angler has to travel some distance in order to get to quality dry fly or nymph fishing. Most such fishing forays tend to start as early in the day as possible, and by late afternoon most of us begin to wilt and tire, so that our companion's suggestion to pack up and head for home in time for a drink or two before an evening meal at a civilized hour, usually falls on willing ears. Indeed, it has been my personal experience that New Zealand affords such an abundance of daytime fishing, it has been beyond both my physical capabilities and my inclinations, to continue into the twilight hours. The prospect of a Scotch or two, or a dry martini at home, seems to signal the end of another fishing day, and a contented willingness to put away one's fly rod and head homewards.

However, New Zealand has long had a dedicated band of night-time fly fishermen, who never venture out, or at least never begin fishing until total darkness envelops the chosen place, often at river mouths entering lakes. But theirs is essentially lure or streamer fishing.

Somewhere in between lies that little understood time of twilight, when it is neither day nor night. It comes long after the day-fishermen have gone home, and before the night-fishermen deem it wise to approach the riverside. It is also one of the most magical times for fly fishing. The Evening Rise! Even the words have a near-mystical ring about them! It is noteworthy, too, that — however incorrectly — the evening rise in literature is so often given the dignity of capital letters.

Yet twilight itself is simply an astronomical phenomenon; a time when it is neither day, nor night. The sun sets beneath the western horizon, yet the light of the sun, now no longer visible, illuminates the sky in much the same way as an electric torch shone from outside a room on to the ceiling in an adjoining room will throw a diffused and shadowy reflected light downwards about the room. Later, when the earth's rotation on its axis takes the sun still deeper beyond the western horizon towards a new dawn somewhere to the west, night itself will fall in varying shades of blackness, where not long before the last glow of twilight persisted. To the navigator this magic time is simply the period of astronomical twilight, for the duration of which many of the stars are visible, but the sea horizon still shows as a definite line.

There is little twilight at the equator, or seasonally between the Tropics of Cancer and Capricorn. In those latitudes the sun goes down more or less at right angles to the horizon. In the temperate and colder latitudes the sun's apparent path angles across the sky. Even after setting, its path angles downwards, so that nightfall takes that much longer to descend upon the place. Towards Arctic and Antarctic latitudes twilight may last all or most of the summer night. And it is in the temperate to cooler latitudes that trout generally flourish. They are at home with relatively long twilights.

In New Zealand twilights are generally of shorter duration than, say, in Britain or the trout habitat areas of Canada and the United States. Towards the far south of the South Island the twilights more closely approach these longer, while towards the north of the North Island the twilights are comparatively shorter.

What happens in the natural world of the trout during these times is both complex and imperfectly known. For the purposes of this brief enquiry it is better to examine how anglers themselves are affected. Much of our angling literature originated in Britain, or at least has been much influenced from that direction. Much of our present-day fly fishing philosophy and attitudes is an amalgam of British and American influences — and the evening rise, however vaguely understood, is held to be one of the basic pillars of that tradition. Yet not too much is ever written about it and, what there is, is often couched in language almost as obscure as the growing night that ends it. It describes exasperation, frustration and near despair, and rarely the magic the anticipated nightfall seemed to promise.

To Viscount Grey the look of the evening rise was the best part of it:

> Numbers of trout appear to be rising frequently and steadily and confidently, but when the angler puts them to the test, they disappoint him. On some evenings the trout cease to rise after an artificial fly has once been floated over them; on others they continue to rise freely, but will take nothing artificial, and the angler exhausts himself in efforts and changes of fly, working harder and more rapidly as he becomes conscious of the approaching end of the day.

An interesting point made by Grey was that, despite occasional success, either the trout seem to rise short, or the angler spends too much time unsuccessfully over a stubborn fish, always on the point of great success without attaining it.

Lord Grey was, of course, writing about the English chalk streams. In those hallowed waters the events of the evening rise were codified by men like Alfred Lunn:

> The first flies likely to come down are the spent spinners of the Olives, Iron Blues and Watery Duns, and these chiefly females, and a few freshly hatching Watery Duns, augmented on occasions by various dipterous insects that we know generally as 'smut'. These are followed by more

fresh and spent Wateries and still a little later, between the lights, Sherry Spinners, Blue Winged Olives and, finally, Sedges.

A dull or rough or wet evening would still give you Wateries, B.W.O.s and Sedges — often great quantities of the two former — but no spinners with the exception perhaps of a few Spent Iron Blues, Olives and Wateries coming down in a sheltered spot.

In Lunn's view there are fewer fish caught in the evening on a fly different from what they are feeding on than in the daytime. This he put down to the fact that evening brings very definite hatches of particular types of fly, with not so many miscellaneous oddments coming along. The type of food changes with such rapidity during an evening rise that it is essential for success to change at once to suit both the individual fish and change of fly. Lunn advocated an immediate change of artificial fly after landing a trout on a certain pattern, not waiting to give it 'just once' to the next fish which may be feeding on something different.

Lunn made a few interesting points worthy of most anglers' consideration: no fish is worth more than a few casts — he may be feeding on something small; your fly may not be fishing correctly; there may be slight drag; or the trout might be aware of you. Best change the fish, rather than the fly. Even at the risk of putting a fish down, get your fly over him quickly. There is more chance in the evening than at any other time of catching two or more about trout in consecutive casts, so get in a hurry but not in a flurry.

Some angling writers have described the evening rise as being the duffer's half-hour. Once in a long while it might be so, but the honest angler will frequently admit to its frustrations and fishlessness.

Sporadically, throughout daylight hours, there may be hatches of duns, nutritious and more than acceptable to the trout, but too sparse and irregular to induce purely selective feeding patterns. Some early-season flies may return to the river to mate and die as spent spinners soon after midday, but for the most part the mating dances only begin as the light fades from the sky. There is ample evidence that trout are inclined to ignore these early daytime spinners in favour of the more nutritious newly-hatching duns, but by mid-summer all available food goes through a phase of relatively short supply. Only then in the few succeeding months will there be a good evening rise of trout to spent spinners, and of sufficient intensity to ensure purely selective feeding.

Leonard M. Wright once pointed out that the usual indication of selective spinner-feeding comes from the trout's position in the pool and the type of rise it makes. When trout are rising gently and regularly in the lower half of a long quiet pool at dusk the angler may be confident of spinners. Wright suggested that although you may not see any flies in the air or on the water, you shouldn't doubt their presence. He points out that this, in fact, is strong supporting evidence; caddis or duns, the other two most likely causes of a rise, would be clearly visible in such smooth water.

In the early part of one recent fishing season, about mid-November, Bill Crawford, a fishing companion, and I decided to stay on beyond dusk on the Manganuioteao to observe and fish the evening rise. The Manganuioteao is a big, wild and scenic river, tributary to the Wanganui, in the central North Island of New Zealand. It is a noted trout stream for browns and rainbows. Throughout the day we saw precious few rises and now, even as the light faded as we sat on the bank just below the long, glidey pool, watching and waiting, it seemed that a moonless dark would descend on the river without disclosing the presence of a single trout.

Then, suddenly, about halfway across the river and perhaps fifteen yards upstream of the tail, there was a single, gentle rise. The same fish rose again — and again — and was soon followed by no more than a few well dispersed others.

We waded in below the tail and took up positions to be able to cast almost directly upstream to the rising fish. Time and again the trout would rise to our flies, but never to be hooked. Darkness sped on disturbingly fast, until it was too dark for me to see to change my fly, but by this time trout were rising almost everywhere throughout the bottom half of that long slow pool. They were even rising within a rod's length of where we stood, between us and the fish we were casting to; and continued to come at the fly at almost every cast, but never quite connecting.

For many hours earlier throughout that day we had fished just there, or lower down, without seeing a sign of a single trout. Now, as darkness fell on the river, it was alive with rising fish. There was no limit bag — not even a single fish landed — and we came away pleasantly tired after a long day; not frustrated by the evening rise, as one might suppose, but humbly aware of it. As Lord Grey had written almost hundred years earlier, the *look* of it was perhaps the best of it after all.

Any frustrations in this direction may be dispelled by reading how other anglers have fared. John Waller Hills recorded the evening rise from as early as a month into the fishing season and even on the coldest nights, but nowhere in full swing until the height of summer. He wrote:

> It is an unsatisfactory thing, this evening rise. You get fish, certainly, but you seldom get as many as you feel you ought. And the mind is weighted with an unpleasant apprehension of finality. Daylight has a definite end which nothing can prolong . . . The trout, too, during an evening rise are always difficult and often exasperating.

Hills, too, divided the evening rise into well-defined segments. The first begins about an hour before sunset. This he called the casual rise. The second phase starts after the sun disappears below the horizon and ends when it is too dark to see a small artificial on the water. This is the small fly rise. The third rise then opens and runs for something under half an hour, rarely longer. This is the sedge rise. Writing of the English summer he continues:

> The casual rise may begin any time after six. Trout move languidly, often taking indecipherable insects. They are difficult, because at no time in the twenty-four hours are they so readily put down. A cast which would pass muster in the stillest noon sends them off like a shot. I suppose this is due to the slanting light. And it is not easy to see what they are taking. Altogether they are a high test of skill.
> . . . The small fly rise has a very different appearance indeed. If it be a good one, trout rise not languidly but eagerly, sometimes madly . . . the movement had started as though on the stroke of a clock. And often this sudden beginning will come immediately after the last rim of the sun has disappeared.
> . . . During the casual rise fish are, I think, usually taking spinners. During the small fly rise, either duns or spinners, or occasionally nymphs. It is often very difficult to see whether they are rising or bulging; or, if they are rising, what they are rising at. During the casual rise, too, the fish, though picksome and hard to please, are not particular about

pattern: but during the small fly rise they settle down to one article and refuse everything else. Your fly must be exactly right, or you get nothing till dark. During the casual rise fish are often unapproachable; during the small fly rise they are easy to approach and hard to put down, but hard to catch. You no longer need crawl or kneel, you can stand up. As the dusk deepens, you can get nearer and nearer.

. . . As I look back over many evening rises, I get the impression of more failures than successes. Not absolute failures, perhaps, but relative; one brings away the sense of not having done as well as one ought. Fish rise so confidently and so often: there are so many: you do not put them down, for they go on rising: but though they are taking winged fly, you they will not take.

On the occasion of that early-season evening rise on the Manganuioteao, it was our first outing of the fishing year without chest or even thigh waders, just ankle-high wading boots and long cotton twill trousers. Throughout the day the sun had been moderately warm to dry trouser legs often wet to the crotch as we fished up the adjacent pools and runs, often coming out to lie on the bank and soak up the welcome and warming afternoon sun. But during that evening rise I, at least, was cowardly reluctant to wade to the goolies plimsoll in the chill water, facing the mile or so walk back to the car before the longish journey home. To have reached those tantalizing trout rising like mad halfway up the long pool would have meant wading around a massive rock, known to be more than goolie-deep. It was here that caution took the upper hand. Bill and I will never know for sure what piscatorial delights may have awaited us had we been brave enough to overcome the chest-deep water and stood upstream of the tail of the long pool above us.

W. H. Lawrie, that wise Scottish angler, writing under the pseudonym of Arnold B. Scott, had this to say:

This is one disturbing exception to the general rule or rules of good representation. It is something of a mystery, but it occurs during the late evening rise and frequently reduces even the most expert fly fisher to despair and profanity. Something happens towards sunset which upsets all normal rules of successful representation and no one seems to know what it is. At such a time, very often, the angler's most effective day-time patterns cease to be effective and are completely ignored by trout which go on feeding as though their lives depended on it. The humiliation generally persists only during this evening rise, for later, when darkness sets in, trout revert to normal rules once more, as is well-known to those cheerful fly-fishing heretics who suffer from insomnia or who abandon the couch of sloth to practise night fishing with fly and so irritate all the good members of the fly rod who cannot do without sleep and who deplore the disgustingly good baskets of over-size trout taken under the cloak of darkness.

As one might expect, Halford's view of the fabled evening rise was somewhat personal: 'As a rule,' he observed, 'although the fish are evidently well on the feed, such evenings are most disappointing, and more often than not the fisherman gets a blank, or at best returns two or three fingerlings, instead of scoring among the *sockdollagers*, as Francis Francis so aptly named them.'

But Halford, true to form, went on to suggest:

The most probable reason of his ill-success is that he is excited and flurried, keeps moving from one feeding fish to another, seldom placing his fly accurately, and continually moving upstream to cast to a fresh fish. He is in such a hurry that he does not even dry his fly, and after a few minutes has become so utterly demoralised that he cannot differentiate the rise of a yearling from that of a three-pounder. Another reason for the non-success of the dry-fly man on such an evening often is that the fish are taking the nymphs under water, and not feeding at all on floating insects. The advice to give a beginner is that he should spot a good fish rising well and stick to it until he has either pricked it or set it down.

Note how Halford's view differs from that of Grey and Lunn.

Reactions to the evening rise in New Zealand — at least in the pages of angling books — is really quite fragmentary and passing. As often as not the time of the evening rise has been regarded as a curtain-raiser before getting down to the real business of night fishing. The further one goes back in the New Zealand literature, the less it seems to have been even noticed. Spackman, author of New Zealand's first-ever fishing book, went little beyond noting that 'the last hour before dark and the hour immediately preceding the dawn are favourite times for the trout to feed'. It must be remembered, however, that Spackman mostly fished the lower tidal reaches of the North Canterbury snow rivers, where aquatic insect life would have been relatively insignificant in the diet of trout.

To Captain Hamilton, author of New Zealand's second angling book, and who fished rain- and spring-fed rivers in the North Island, it was not all that different:

At night, in warm weather, good sport may sometimes be had. When there are moths and suchlike about a very slight breeze is the best, as it allows of their lighting on the water and attracting the trout to the surface. Casting over the rises will be found satisfactory; but in pools — and at night particularly — trout cruise about more, so that casting a good many times in one place where trout are about may be remunerative. When nearly dark, and in the dark, good-sized flies, rather larger than those used in daylight, and fairly strong gut, are the best.

But before Spackman or Hamilton, as expert local anglers, were moved to write their books, that indefatigable angler-traveller, William Senior, had already written and had published *Travel and Trout in the Antipodes* (1880), partly, at least, about angling in New Zealand. Senior's observation, one suspects, contains in a nutshell why so few anglers fish the evening rise. Taking down his fly rod after a day on the Cust, he wrote, 'On the hillside there was a modest tavern, where we spent a pleasant evening and slept the sleep of the just in homely beds, while the winds roared and beat in strengthening tempest.'

In the intervening years between then and now the evening rise has been paid passing lip service and mention by anglers and writers alike. Maybe the fishing at the other times of day was far too satisfactory to warrant any deviation from heading home for that welcome evening meal at a civilized hour. Additionally, on most of the rivers I fish, wading can be fraught with enough problems even when the sun is high, but treacherous when the shadows lengthen and the water surface begins to look like old pewter. And even if one can wade out without too much difficulty, the way back out of the river to the path by which one came is often not without its hazards and discomfitures.

Somehow, to me at least, Captain Hamilton seems like a figure out of history, while Dr J. C. Mottram has an air of modernity about him. Yet Mottram's New Zealand trout fishing took place only six or seven years after Hamilton's book *Trout Fishing and Sport in Maoriland* was published in 1904. The difference between the two is nothing less than astonishing. Mottram's first angling book, *Fly Fishing: Some New Arts and Mysteries*, was undated in its 1st edition, but was probably published in 1914. His knowledge of fly fishing was obviously greater and in advance of Hamilton's, and fresh out from chalk-stream dry fly and nymph fishing in England Mottram would most certainly have been knowledgeable about, and familiar with, the evening rise.

Mottram's approach to his New Zealand fishing was different than most:

> There I unconsciously did a very wise thing, I toured over both islands with a rod under my arm, not seeking fishing, but taking it as it came. Had I taken the advice of others I should have missed all the best, the most sporting, and the most artistic of the fishing; instead I should have gone only to certain places — I call them slaughter grounds — where is quantity but no quality of fishing.

Mottram's first mention of evening fishing occurred on the Waikato River, just below Taupo, undoubtedly somewhere between what is now the boat harbour at the outlet and the approximate site of the then unbuilt Huka Lodge. There, on a very broad shallow, he had two evenings' very interesting fishing. He was warned that he would not get fish although it was well known that each evening the water boiled with them.

> At 4.30 p.m. I was by the water and all was still. At 5.00 a heavy fall of spinner began. A few fish rose and I killed one on a spinner. At 5.20 all was quiet again, at 5.45 duns began to hatch out, and by 6.00 the air was thick and the water covered with them and boiling with fish. I cast duns of all colours, sizes, and shapes, but I never had a single rise. At 6.30 it was over. I was nonplussed, but on the way home in the dark, I started, for suddenly I saw my mistake. They were all bulgers, and I remembered that I had never seen a dun taken. The next evening I went fully armed with nymphs and slew many fish. Never shall I forget the rush of a four-pounder down stream and across that wide shallow. The line fizzed across and through the waters, the pace was tremendous. I played him as hard as I dared, for I was anxious not to waste time, but it was ten minutes before I was done with him.

That second evening Mottram was likely to have been the first angler to have knowingly cast an artificial nymph to a rainbow trout in the Taupo region — possibly the first ever in New Zealand.

But Mottram was far from impressed with the quality of North Island fishing in those days before the First World War. Somewhat grudgingly, one senses, he said of the Lake Taupo rivermouths, 'These fish can be taken with a dry fly. Sometimes of an evening they will rise at sedges on the lake, rarely at duns in the rivers, but of true dry-fly fishing there is none. There anglers count their season's catches by the ton; this is no place for the dry-fly purist.' Sadly for Mottram he never got to the right rivers. He was not to discover the abundance of excellent dry fly fishing in so many of the streams in the Taupo region.

He does recount having been directed towards one river in the district by the driver of the coach in which he was travelling, although this happened to be the Waikato about ten miles below Taupo. The coach driver said, 'Yes, there are plenty of fish in the river. If you go down that road you will come to a wide shallow, where every evening for a little while the water boils with rising fish. Many have fished there, but they always return empty-handed.' Mottram goes on:

> The following day I was there before time. At close on 5 p.m. the air became filled with spinners; soon a brisk and very brief rise took place at spent gnat. Having no suitable spinners, I hastily tied one by the waterside, just in time to slay one fish. This phase now passed, and another, or I should say the other, the evening hatch of duns, began: there were fleets of them sailing down, and flights of them slanting up, and the water boiled with fish. For half an hour I cast hackle duns and winged duns, large duns and small duns, bright duns and dull duns, over scores of fish, but I never had a rise; on the way home puzzling over the matter, I called to mind that during that wild half-hour I never saw a fish actually taking a floating dun. Were they all bulging? Next evening I armed myself with emphemera nymphs; very soon the riddle was solved, for after a grand fight one of my nymphs was unhooked from the mouth of a fat rainbow trout. This happened on the Waikato River about ten miles below Lake Taupo, out of which it flows, a great clear river of constant volume. It was not dry-fly fishing; on other occasions I have observed this preference of rainbow trout for nymphs to duns.

The occasion obviously impressed Mottram, for it seems he described the same event in two separate chapters of his book. Philosophically, he adds, 'There may be dry-fly fishing in the North Island; I neither found it nor heard it spoken of.'

Long before Mottram fished in New Zealand around 1910-11, George Edward Mannering had begun a long fishing life that spanned from 1892 to 1942. Mannering had seen Spackman fishing the Selwyn River on one of his first outings. Although he became a convinced fly fisher after many long years of live-baiting and spinning, Mannering's conversion to the fly was more a matter of convenience than conviction. But he was typical of anglers in those days, and probably considered himself to have been a well-rounded and versatile exponent of the art. The delightful and fascinating section of Mannering's book, *Eighty Years in New Zealand — Embracing Fifty Years of New Zealand Fishing* (not published until 1943), is the most detailed record by any one angler. Mannering's text is heavily peppered with statistics and records of almost every catch he ever made. The text, too, is equally peppered with accounts of 'fishing the dry fly' and 'fishing the evening rise', but closer study shows that these phrases were used much like buzzwords are used today: they made it all sound so much better. To Mannering and his friends, fishing the evening rise meant fishing the usual downstream wet fly as dusk approached.

In what may be the first mention of our subject in New Zealand angling literature (but remembering that Mannering's book was not published until 1943, and presumably written not long before that time from diaries) he tells the following tale:

At Christmas, 1899, I was at Kumeroa with my family; a brother banker was also there with his family. We were all invited by Mr Fountaine to his house, to see the new century in. Quite a large party assembled to be entertained with dancing and billiards and meals at all hours. Towards daybreak we went out to find our horses to drive some miles back to Kumeroa, but they had been 'planted' and we were told that we were to stay to breakfast, which consisted largely of cherry pie, not to mention further liquid refreshment. We got back safely about 6 a.m., but I did not feel like bed in the bright sunshine, so took my rod and made for the river, coming back a few hours later with a heavy basket of trout.

On many occasions I fished the evening rise with the fly there, mostly with Jack Mackie. I recollect one catch we had of 23 fish averaging 3lb. In the evening we always used to get the larger fish. It was all wet fly fishing. We knew nothing about dry fly fishing. That came later. Our favourite flies were Governor, Peveril of the Peak, Coachman and Governor Alyord (a fly I do not see nowadays — it was simply a Governor with a teal wing). Black Quill Gnat, Hofland's Fancy, Red Spinner and Greenwell's Glory were also good taking flies, fished wet.

Later, at Taupo in 1904, we have an account of Mannering and his friend Ivan Logan fishing the evening rise from the Taupo wharf! During the same holiday, when they stayed at the Spa Hotel, he records, 'In the evening, after dinner, it was our practice to walk to the river at the Crow's Nest, or to the mouth of the hot creek to fish the evening rise. Fishing by the Crow's Nest one had to be careful not to get a dose of hot water when the geyser went off.' Even in those days dry fly fishing and fishing the evening rise were all things to all men.

Somewhat later, a peripatetic English fly fisherman, A. H. Batten Pooll, described his trout fishing in New Zealand in the season 1934-35 in the book *Some Globe-Trottings with a Rod* (1937):

(1) New Zealand trout are not quite like other trout. E.g., one day in April when I was fishing the Forks river in South Island there was a very heavy rise of brown dun (*Deleatidium lillii*), yet not a fish rose. In spite of this another angler fishing dry caught, on a red-bodied Peveril of the Peak, a three pounder which he kindly allowed me to dissect; the autopsy showed that the fish had not taken a single winged insect, and only contained a very few nymphs and caddis. A trout which prefers an artificial to the natural fly on the water can hardly be regarded as altogether normal.

(2) There is not as much fly as on most European streams.

(3) Most fish are caught when trout are not rising — more than one New Zealand fisherman with many years' experience assured me that seventy per cent of the fish they caught were taken on the dry fly when there was no sign of a rise; that was not my experience, but the season was abnormal.

(4) In place of the evening rise there comes on, just as it gets dark, the evening bulge (the whole river boils), which lasts from a quarter to three-quarters of an hour; this occurred on nearly every river I fished, and is made at the caddis of two sedges, *Olinga feredayi* and *Pycnoceutria erecta*; that of the first has a small curved olive-yellow case, while that of the latter is very small and of a grey colour. Some evenings there is a rise of duns and a fall of spinners;

occasionally these are taken, and the best chance with the dry fly is when the bulge first starts; once it has got going, usually everything but caddis is ignored; there are, of course, exceptions. When it has become dark it is often best to fish wet, striking the 'pluck'; many are caught this way, especially in the Manawatu.

(5) The bulge which occurs on the Waikato appears to be at the nymphs of three Ephemeridae, *Coloburiscus humeralis*, *Atalophlebia versicolor* and *Deleatidium cromwelli*; at any rate, I did not come across any caddis in the autopsies I made when I was there in March, though it is possible that there is a caddis bulge at other times of the year, as a small dark-winged sedge (*Hydropsyche colonica*) definitely forms one of the chief foods of the trout in the Waikato.

Few present-day anglers would dispute many of those points. Although there may be less fly life on New Zealand trout streams than in many of their overseas counterparts, there is no doubt that there is also generally less awareness among New Zealand anglers of what aquatic fly life there is in and about the streams they fish. The vast majority of New Zealand fly fishermen have not trained themselves to see the often rich aquatic insect fauna that does exist, and see neither the nymphs in the shallows through which they wade so carelessly in indecent haste to get chest-deep into the river, nor the presence of hatching duns, often in considerable numbers.

It needs to be said, however, that nowadays in England, fewer and fewer fly fishermen are aware of this rich tapestry of life, while in New Zealand an increasing interest is being shown and, along with it, entomological knowledge and fishing wisdom.

Familiarity with, and fondness for, certain modes of fly fishing are both understandable and laudable, but they have become so rigidly exclusive that New Zealand fly fishermen often regard them as law. For example, it became established truth that central North Island trout fishing meant Taupo and Taupo alone, and its fishermen — whether they were occasional anglers, indoctrinated fanatics, knowledgeable and often delightful angler-authors, or Government Tourist Bureau officials — stated quite categorically that in the rivers running into the lake itself the only fishing was late autumn and winter fishing, when the rainbows came in on their spawning runs. Another myth was that the browns and rainbows of these waters were only catchable on traditional lures fished deep and downstream.

There was night fishing as well as day fishing, to be sure, but the two were quite separate and in no way interconnected by twilight. Some odd anglers no doubt fished the dry fly on the Tongariro from the earliest days, but would have been looked at as being cranks or plain ignorant of local revealed truth.

Joe Frost came to New Zealand immediately after being discharged from the British Army after the end of the First World War. Before long he was living beside the Tongariro and soon set up the first specialist fishing tackle shop in the then tiny village of Tupangi. The proud sign over the door read: JOE FROST — TUITION IN DRY-FLY FISHING. What is odd is that no-one seems to have thought it was odd, yet possibly not one visiting or local angler in a thousand ever fished anything but the downstream deep-sunk lure.

Joe Frost undoubtedly learned the craft of dry fly fishing as a youth in his native Herefordshire, but he seems not have have attempted in any way to convert the Taupo traditionalists; he simply preferred to fish the big and sprawling Tongariro River upstream with a floating fly, mostly in the early and midsummer, and mostly during the evening rise. An evening rise on the

Tongariro would still be considered nonsensical by most aficionados, yet it exists and is a steady and regular phenomenon. In Joe Frost's day there were no doubt bigger and better browns and rainbows resident in the river, which he at least and perhaps those he taught, caught in the summer months on the dry fly during the evening rise.

Joe Frost said that the upper reaches of the Tongariro were particularly suitable for dry fly fishing, especially in the broken water and the ideal side eddies where only short casting was necessary. Such fishing is available from November through to May, although Frost recalled that the evening rise was best and most prolific in early season. He warned anglers not be put off by the fact that few or no fish could be seen rising throughout the day, saying that browns and rainbows could still be risen to take a dry fly during the day by searching and fishing likely water, although the evening rise would bring the cream of it.

Today, the evening rise itself is just as predictable, but the trout that may be caught are often likely to be mending kelts that have chosen to remain in the river, rather than dropping down into the lake, or juvenile fish. Pools such as Major Jones where, in winter, anglers are often crowded shoulder-to-shoulder, are often empty of anglers on fine summer evenings when splendid hatches come on, and the trout are rising in the shallows along the river's edge.

Due to Joe Frost's influence, and success, dry fly fishing on the Tongariro and other Taupo streams became increasingly popular by the 1930s, but more or less had died a natural death by the time of the end of that other War in 1945. Now, in the late 1980s, another resurgence of fishing the evening rise is apparent; no doubt influenced by more and more anglers fishing for sport and less because of a compelling need to catch a limit of big fish.

Frost, of course, knew Alan Pye of Huka Lodge well. Pye, at the other end of the lake, was achieving world-wide fame on account of the magnificent evening rise sedge fishing on the Waikato just below Taupo, although strictly speaking the dry sedge fishing bordered on night fishing and often extended into the night itself, long after twilight itself.

For several years shortly before and following the Second World War it became almost obligatory for notable and even non-notable anglers who stayed at Huka Lodge to write something afterwards of their experiences fishing with Alan Pye. F. W. Pickard, the American author of *Trout Fishing in New Zealand in Wartime* (1940), was typical of them:

> A species of sedge is the characteristic fly of the Waikato. The fly appears in small numbers at about sunset. Twilight is short in this valley and as darkness sets in the hatch of flies becomes on many nights a matter of millions. The water is covered with them and they swarm by the hundred and thousand about the fisherman, and even on the Lodge porch, attracted by the electric light, they whirl about like swarms of bees. With such myriads on the water it seems strange that the imitation on an angler's leader will be singled out by a trout, but results prove that exactly this happens, thanks largely to the excellent replica provided by Alan Pye's dry fly which is the universal lure when the hatch is on. Earlier in the day an imitation of the nymph takes many fish.

Meanwhile, it must be understood, both long before Joe Frost's time, and long afterwards, dry fly and evening rise fishing was extensively practised on other streams in the North Island and throughout the entire South Island, as being perfectly natural and not at all unusual. For some reason it never seemed to get such a good press or widespread publicity. During the 1950s-1960s it probably reached an all-time low, when the deep-sunk downstream lure was held to be the be-all and end-all of fly fishing everywhere and anywhere. Even knowledgeable angling visitors from overseas — fly fishermen who in their home waters were often considered to be bigoted in their dry fly purism — were seduced by local practice in New Zealand into believing that New Zealand trout, especially rainbows, would not rise to a dry fly, and that there was no evening rise anyway.

But the taunt and the enigma and the puzzle of the evening rise was more enduring than any man-made fashions in fly fishing. Among more recent observers, John McInnes comes straight out with it:

> The evening rise puzzles me; but for some anglers it is a most glorious time when they can put aside the day's anxieties to relax by effortlessly catching a couple of fish for breakfast.
>
> Rarely is it like that for me. One perfect summer's evening on the Mangatainoka fish rose steadily for an hour. Dry fly, spent fly, nymph deep, nymph in the surface film; not one took a fish.
>
> When I do catch evening rise fish, it is often more by accident than as a result of a deliberate ploy . . .
>
> Frustration in fact often reaches high pitch. One recent year for several nights in a row, all the trout in one pool motored around like submarines just below the surface, dorsal fins protruding like periscopes. Were they gourmandising something minute — collecting it with open mouth more or less by the bucketful? I don't know. In the half light nothing could be seen. I caught nothing; nor did any of my friends whether they were visitors or local experts.

John McInnes ends his chapter on the evening rise thus:

> The evening rise? It's an enigma. I wished I could make it work for me. I can't — not yet anyway — and I take just a little comfort from the fact that many others on the bank, around firesides, and in literature tell of their perplexity. But the minutes and hours after that? Success then is often sweet. Where would we be without sedges, moths, and beetles? They have a special power.

So, for John McInnes too, the evening rise remains an enigma and an illusion, just a curtain-raiser towards the real business of night fishing.

Similarly, George Ferris called the evening rise 'that mad gambol', but says the trout invariably rise well up the pool, usually in the fast water; only falling back to feed right down to the tail of the pool when the rise proper is on. But fishing the evening rise was, to Ferris, 'a mad, anxious and tense business'. Rarely ever fishing the evening rise itself, Ferris used that time to 'scout around the various reaches, noting the lay of the pools, and the presence and position of snags, the speed of flow and the location of shallows. When darkness falls I approach these pools quietly and begin to fish.' Once again, the time was but a prelude to the more serious business of night fishing — although, for Ferris, the best of this was fishing a dry fly upstream, not necessarily casting a wet fly across and down in the traditional style.

Keith Draper had obviously whetted John McInnes's appetite for the evening rise by that thoughtful chapter in *Angling in New Zealand*, 'The drowned spent spinner'. Describing his own apprenticeship to the evening rise on a central North Island stream, Keith Draper says, 'It was seldom as simple as it seemed. In spite of continuous feeding activity, I would only catch the occasional trout, except on special occasions when I might be lucky enough to catch two, or maybe three.'

But Keith Draper also records that he would sometimes cast to one fish for half an hour before it took his fly. Another of his personal discoveries was that, at times when the steadily rising and obviously feeding fish would ignore and go on ignoring his well-presented and well-tied and appropriate dry fly floating like a cork, a wet fly, say a coch-y-bondhu — cast upstream on a floating line with a well-greased leader, would take fish after fish. The trout may have been taking spent spinners but were not averse to a nymph. Moreover, he then discovered (as a result of being without a fly floatant) that a spent female Twilight Beauty of his own design took even more fish after it had sunk through the surface film. The trout were taking the spent flies just a centimetre or two beneath the surface.

Steve Raymond, that splendidly percipient and sensitive American angling writer from the Pacific Northwest, has fished throughout New Zealand and wrote of his experiences in his recent book *The Year of the Trout*. It was after fishing the Clutha in the stretch that runs out of Lake Wanaka that he wrote most perceptively:

> It was there that I found some of the most exciting fishing I experienced in New Zealand.
>
> I reached the river late in the afternoon of a fine sunny day and found a hatch of unbelievable proportions under way. Mayflies, countless thousands of them, were hatching in the lake and drifting down on an accelerating current that carried them into the river. There were whole fleets and flotillas of them, dark blue in color, some almost black, and yet their wings somehow caught the sunshine and reflected it so that the river seemed full of shining sparks. Waiting to receive them were hundreds of trout of all sizes, rolling and porpoising in the current as they captured fly after fly.
>
> Feeling the familiar surge of excitement that comes from such a sight, I waded out quickly within casting distance of the nearest rising fish. Among the flies I'd brought were some size 16 Blue Uprights that had served me well back home; they seemed too small to imitate the naturals that were hatching here, but they were the best I had, so I knotted one to the end of my leader and began casting. The little fly floated down on the current and quickly became lost among dozens of naturals, and I realized there was little chance a fish would find it among all the real ones on the water. But surprisingly one did: After several casts, my fly disappeared in a splashy rise and suddenly I was fast to a running fish.

It proved to be a 2½ pound rainbow, nickel-bright and in perfect condition. Raymond rose two other fish but missed them both,

> before the hatch began to fail at the onset of the early autumn twilight. For a while there was a lull, but then a hatch of sedges came. Like the mayflies, most of the sedges emerged in the quiet waters of the lake and were carried down by the current to the river, and soon the infant Clutha's surface was covered with fluttering, ungainly insects. I captured one and found it was about the size of a No. 10 fly pattern, with a green

body and dark wings, and this time my fly box yielded a perfect match in size and shape and color. But for some reason the trout seemed less interested in the sedges than they had been in the mayflies, and only now and then did fish rise within casting reach.

Far out in the center of the flow, well beyond the reach of any caster, it was a different story; there I could see fish rising steadily, and most of them were very large. Their rises were violent, the sounds of them audible above the sounds of the river, and they pushed water out in awesome rings. But soon it was too dark to see anything at all, and I reeled in and began the long climb up the hillside to the level spot where we had camped.

Steve Raymond fished the same place the following evening. It was cool and overcast, and the mayfly hatch did not repeat itself. Rises were occasional and sporadic, but after fishing patiently he eventually got a four-pound brown on the dry fly. 'Toward evening,' he wrote, 'the sedge came on again, as thickly as before, and in the brief frenzied moments before darkness I rose and hooked another good fish, but held it only briefly before the fly came away.' That evening's fishing he described thus:

My score . . . was not impressive — four fish risen, three hooked, two broken and one lost. But it had been wildly exciting fishing and I had thoroughly enjoyed every moment of it. I also took comfort from the thought that success, like beauty, is measured in the eye of the beholder, and one standard of success in fly fishing is the ability to fool large and difficult fish with a floating fly. By that measure it had been most successful.

Brian Turner's editing of *The Guide to Trout Fishing in Otago* (1983) made it perhaps the best fishing guide book ever published in New Zealand — perhaps anywhere. Wherever throughout the book there is mention of fishing the evening rise, or beyond that time into night, there is a touch of magic in it. Of the upper Mataura:

Midsummer evenings bring superb hatches of caddis. The insects erupt from their cocoons in the stony habitat of ripples. They burst through the surface and struggle into the air. Trout line up to take them, often extending in echelon far down into the slacker water below the origin of the hatch. It is important to identify what is going on at such times, because mayfly imitations will be totally ignored when a caddis hatch is happening. The accepted tactic is to fish across-stream, or even downstream, allowing the fly to drag on the surface. Any small caddis imitation will do: presentation, rather than pattern, is what matters.

And of the lower Mataura one learns of more frustrations associated with the evening rise:

Duns, spinners, or half-hatched nymphs — any of these may focus the trout's attention, and the angler must determine exactly which it is. As a further complication the trout may not be feeding on mayflies (or caddisflies) at all. Dense hatches of chironomids — small midges — often appear on summer evenings, and provoke an avid rise. This is a difficult situation. Chironomids are too small for realistic imitation, and the best approach probably is to pick out a fish and try him with a very small, dark-coloured nymph. Move on to another one if there is no immediate sign of interest.

Mataura trout, as a general rule, are not unduly fussy feeders. A blank evening can be very discouraging, especially when the trout are rising thickly. But take heart. Next day the sun will burn again; the stream will flow and the mayflies hatch. Next day your luck will alter.

Someone once said the chief feature of the evening rise was pleasurable anticipation; someone else that it was but the prelude to the generally much better sedge fishing that came on just afterwards. Certain words run through most written and spoken observations concerning the evening rise like a constant, if tenuous, thread. They are words like exasperation, frustration, maddening, inexplicable. Fly fishing has a habit of cutting its disciples down to size all too frequently, although, of course, it is the trout's doing, not the magical act of fly fishing itself.

The angler does not have to fish the rise for long before discovering that flies may be coming down in large quantities and trout may be rising all over the place, yet all his offerings are completely ignored. Of this state of affairs, C. F. Walker once said that on occasions — and this always seemed to him the crowning insult — you cannot even put them down: they simply continue to enjoy their evening meal as though such things as fishermen and their impedimenta did not exist, until you have the uncomfortable feeling that you have suddenly been turned into a ghost! When driven almost to the verge of frenzy, Walker's only advice was to keep an iron control over your nerves!

The myth of the evening rise is not that it doesn't or only rarely exists. It does happen, damnably on time, almost everywhere. The real myth lies in the often hushed and sanctimonious terms in which most anglers speak of it, almost with bated breath, while the truth is more likely to consist of fantastic hopes becoming disillusioned reality.

The evening rise! Who was it who said of it, 'The hymns written in its praise are poetic fancies'?

Chapter 4
Fisherman's Luck

For non-fishermen it is all a matter of luck. Even some fishermen will greet others already about their sport, and in passing enquire of them, 'Any luck?' But if it is all based on luck, then why is it that ten per cent of anglers catch ninety per cent of the fish? Or, put another way, why do ninety per cent of anglers only catch a meagre ten per cent of the fish? Is it that by some odd chance a favoured ten per cent of fishermen get ninety per cent of the luck? Why is it almost universally believed that luck remains the fundamental element in going fishing? One reason, of course, is that the myth is put about by that 'unlucky' ninety per cent of anglers who only catch ten per cent of the fish; many of whom remain genuinely puzzled by their continuing lack of success, while others find it a useful way of explaining away their almost always empty creels or fish bags.

First of all we need to examine if the 'lucky' ten per cent are simply better fishermen, and therefore deserve their extra success. After all, no one is surprised when better footballers score more goals than less expert team mates; few people are puzzled when a Botham knocks up a century; or when Boris Becker wins at Wimbledon. Although good fortune on the day in question must come into the equation, no one ever says that it was all to do with luck. The winners are acknowledged experts in their various games.

What then constitutes an expert fisherman? Is it someone who can cast prodigious distances? Or tie flies with some extra in-built magic? Or who understands the subtle and variable moods of fish, whether salmon, trout, bass, cod, or mackerel? Is it a combination of all these assets that assures success?

One needs only to have fished for a season or two before discovering that, while such prowess and technique are quite important to success in fishing, it is far from being of paramount importance. Something seems to sort out the men from the boys. Something does. And it certainly isn't luck.

Like any other pursuit there always is a small element of luck in fishing. To start with the fish must be there if the fisherman is to catch them. Knowing where to go, and when, is important in this respect. But luck alone, both good and bad, must be ruled out in the common instance of two anglers fishing alongside each other from, say, a boat, pier, river bank or trout lake, when one constantly outfishes the other. Nor can it be argued that technique alone is responsible for success. The technically proficient angler who can cast a trout fly to water unreachable by the man fishing alongside him is not necessarily the most consistently successful one of the two. However, it is probable that most of the 'lucky' ten per cent do enjoy basically sound techniques — but far from always, and this allows us to discount that element as the one we are looking for.

In any case, techniques in fishing, at least sufficient to reach a moderate proficiency, can be learned through some practice. Therefore, if adequacy in angling ability was something that could be acquired by anyone willing to bring to it that necessary diligence, then nine out of ten fishermen would be on average equally successful, with perhaps the remaining ten per cent split between those experts who always caught fish with consummate ease and those who hardly ever caught anything. But it's not like that.

The fact remains that ten per cent of all anglers catch ninety per cent of the fish. Always. Everywhere. Consistently. If skill and pure expertise can be ruled out as being the core reason for this phenomenon, and if the random nature of luck will not sufficiently explain it, then there is no alternative but to recognize that the real reason may lie in an area beyond basic human experience and the most profound human knowledge.

Most anglers come quickly to recognize that certain other fishermen they know or may see fishing appear to have an uncanny ability to catch fish consistently; what is more, they always know when to cease fishing, either for the day, or temporarily. Most observers put it all down to luck, or explain it with comments such as 'Well, so-and-so has the "hands" for fishing,' suggesting that the successful angler somehow 'feels' or wills the fish to take his fly or bait. Other observers have suggested that super-successful angling requires nothing more than having supreme confidence when fishing. Most anglers have experienced at some time a surge of confidence when fishing with a certain fly, for example, and caught fish. But, if they then lose that fly in a fish, or a snag, or in a tree, and have no other fly of the same pattern or even size, then that confidence is shattered and they fish on without success.

Fishing with a deliberately keyed-up sense of confidence has been described as positive fishing. It is more a state of mind than a fishing technique. Most anglers remain totally unaware of its possibilities; others only occasionally experience the fleeting sensation of it. I know two fly fishermen who can turn it on at will, and likewise turn it off, for it seems to require intense concentration and single-mindedness that cannot always be sustained at will, or not at all. One lucid observer has described it as climbing up to a plateau of awareness, at which point a state of flow is reached, as if the angler is connected to the fish by the means of his rhythmic fly rod, uncurling fly line, turning over leader, delivering the artificial fly all but irresistibly to the trout or salmon, so that the strike is almost anticipated. To Odell Shepard it was

> . . . this mystery and challenging strangeness that the angler sets his will and wit to explore. Standing in one element, he invades another, striving to search it throughly. With a fifty-foot finger of bamboo and silk and gut he probes the deeps and the shallows, feels along the riffles, glides slowly out into bays of glitter, striving towards and almost attaining a sixth sense, trying to surprise the water's innermost secret law. But this, of course, he will never do. In other arts and crafts, and even in a few sports,

we can distinguish three stages of apprentice, journeymen, and master; but in angling few ever pass beyond apprenticeship, and masters there are none.

Now, although Odell Shepard is hinting at the fisherman in one world attempting to invade another, and to connect with the inhabitant of that other world, the trout, by means of that gossamer fly rod, fly line, leader and fly; he is also aware that the performance of the act of fly fishing is almost ritualistic and other-worldly. And there, in the midst of all that poetry, he comes out with that old-fashioned and out-moded expression 'sixth sense'.

Whatever words are used to describe, however imperfectly, this not uncommon experience, there is one general and total agreement: the event is a departure from what we choose to call reality. It becomes an infiltration into another world. Even the 'escape' theory takes on an other-worldliness. For Odell Shepard,

> One can play the piano while thinking of the morning's mail, or one can watch a baseball game while planning a bank robbery, but in order to fish successfully, at any rate for the nobler species, one must give one's whole attention to the sport in hand. And this is the reason why a trout rod is the best magician's wand for exorcising the ghosts of care.

Our human trouble is that we regard other-worldliness as being 'up there' somewhere, in a universe outside that of our own small planet and still further beyond our understanding. And this is reasonable, because we stand under the arc of heaven and look upwards and outwards. Yet we are familiarly surrounded by the frontiers of inner space in our daily lives, here on earth, wherever we encounter the veil of water, whether it be the seas and oceans, or the shimmering reflective surfaces of lakes, or the deep pools of streams and rivers, or even the leaden, mirror-like curtain of the riffles of a shady brook, reflecting our world, with only vague and ghost-like innuendoes of what lies and lives therein.

This is man's everlasting fascination with water. Few men can pass over a bridge without gazing into the water beneath. No fisherman can ever do so. The trouble is that most of us see little but a reflection of our own world, up here. We see the reflections of the clouds and of sunlight; we see the broken, fluttering images of waving trees, of birds flying overhead, and narcissus-like, the reflection of our own selves. But the true angler is fortunate in that he strives to see beyond the shimmering veil of the water's surface into the world beneath, and therein lies the magic of it all. Of such an experience J. W. Hills once wrote, 'I felt receptive to every sight, every colour and every sound, as though I had walked through a world from which a veil had been withdrawn.'

More recently in their brilliant Introduction to *The Magic Wheel*, an anthology of fishing in literature, David Profumo and Graham Swift observed:

> There remains, however, perhaps one abiding and underlying reason for angling's literary dimension, which may be put in this way: the writer repeatedly attempts to transform the world, to see the world anew, to approach it, indeed, as if it were *another* world; the repeated experience of the angler is precisely of a confrontation with another world, or, of what may stand for it, another element. Water, in short, is all. More than anything, it is that glinting, tantalizing horizontal veil, the surface of

water, dividing so absolutely one realm from another, which gives angling its mystery, its magic, its endless speculation.

I have already referred to two fishing companions of mine who are both superb natural anglers, and who seem to be able to attain this state of flow and supra-awareness when fishing almost at will. They do not know each other and live half the world apart. In character and fishing attitudes and philosophy they are poles apart; only in this remarkable and singular ability to catch fish when other people can't are they similar. One of them, Bill Crawford, who lives and fishes in New Zealand, is not only a master of the art of fly fishing, but can turn on this total participation, total involvement, total awareness, total flow and supreme confidence at will. And I mean at will: exactly as and when he chooses to be in that higher state of consciousness.

But, as if the air is too rarefied there, as if it is too intense, he does not stay there long at a time, but comes back to where I am; to an angling world where at times casts may be sloppy, flies hang up in the plumes of toi-toi; great brown trout are spooked; legs get heavy with clambering river banks and fording swift and turbulent rivers, and even the end of the fishing day and the drive home becomes a welcome prospect.

It is difficult to be precise when talking about this 'paranormal' aspect of fishing, although most fly fishermen have experienced it at some time, however briefly, and recognize it when they do.

Two angling authors who have been most lucid about the philosophy of fly fishing and its occasional paranormal manifestations were both Professors of Philosophy at august universities. A. A. Luce was also a Doctor of Divinity and in his *Fishing and Thinking* (1959) he concentrates mostly on the ethics of fishing. Professor C. W. K. Mundle in *Game Fishing: Methods and Memories* (1978) examined both the ethics and, possibly for the first time ever, the possible paranormal happenings in fishing. Each wrote with the combined authority of being linguistic philosophers of note, as well as being informed and expert fly fishermen.

Professor Mundle, who was also President of the Society for Psychical Research, was the first angling writer to risk public ridicule by suggesting in print a connection between psychic phenomena and angling phenomena. Earlier angling authors had sometimes hinted at such a connection. Sir Edward Grey (afterwards Viscount Grey of Fallodon) wrote in 1899, 'It is as if there were some magnetic influence in the angler's confidence, which disposes the salmon to take the fly.' Ian Wood, in 1957, called it 'the angler's extra sense'. Hugh Falkus wrote, 'Often I know beforehand when I am going to catch a fish,' and adds with some reluctance that he is forced to believe this involves so-called extra-sensory perception.

My long-time fishing companion in Britain, Trevor Housby, most certainly often knows when he is about to catch a fish. Time and time again I have seen his apparent calm tense suddenly with an almost electrifying intensity as he anticipated the strike of a large bass off the Needles or the certain take of a Test trout he could not at that time see. Fishing for seen fish with some success may be attributed to Positive Fishing, but fishing blind, while still anticipating the strike anything from a few seconds to a minute or more in advance of it actually happening, simply has to be paranormal and beyond easy explanation. It is, however, so well documented and generally recognized among some anglers to be irrefutable.

Psychical research always was and still is fair game for scathing criticism and scorn, with its paraphernalia of ghosts and spirits, poltergeists and gypsy ladies with crystal balls. But today, there is a body of scientific evidence that gives credence to the real existence of psychokinesis, which can be approximately defined as the influencing of external objects purely by thought or volition. It was this hypothesis that Professor Mundle not only believed in, but recognized as having implications for fellow anglers.

He observed that in recent years many experiments had been designed to determine which psychological factors help, and which hinder, the exercise of these psychic powers. One discovery, confirmed by different investigators, was that confidence promoted and lack of confidence inhibited success. It was found, for example, that in card-guessing tests, if a group of people were divided according to whether or not they believed that they could get above chance scores, the 'sheep' (those who had expressed confidence that they could do it) got average scores *above* the chance level, while the 'goats' (those who lacked such confidence) got average scores *below* (not just at) the chance level. That being so, Mundle was convinced that the angler's confidence was relevant not, or not solely, because it affected his own physical actions, but because it enabled him to exert a psychic influence upon his quarry.

It was also apparent that in every known example of such psychic involvement there was a decline-effect, whereby the greatest success occurred at the beginning of involvement, gradually tailing off to nothing. This might suggest that some people may be able to intensify their concentration beyond normal parameters, but only briefly. It might also suggest that fatigue, or anything approaching fatigue, is anathema to the condition. There can be few fly fishermen who have not often become aware of a sudden, quite different sort of tiredness come over them, beyond which fishing is impossible.

Mundle realized that there was another implication to be drawn from this. Many psychical researchers had reported that if a successful subject continued to work for very long in the same experimental conditions, so that the monotony of his task induced boredom, his scoring level declined; but that *any* change in the conditions which revived the subject's interest invariably restored his high scoring — until the new method in turn became boring to him.

The moral Professor Mundle drew from this from the angler's point of view was that so long as he is not catching fish he should keep on making *some* changes to sustain and restore his confidence. This need not necessarily be a change of fly pattern, but perhaps a change of size, or by a change in presentation or retrieve. The often-quoted recommendation to fish the fly in which you have the most confidence suggests that one should rarely change flies. But reflect now on how often you have caught a fish immediately after changing your fly.

Of other implications of his hypothesis Mundle amusingly and astutely mentions that American investigations have reported that 'psychic' powers are stimulated by a small dose of alcohol, but diminished by a large dose. He wisely leaves it to anglers themselves who mix drinking and fishing to decide whether the theory fits the facts!

For those readers who consider it unwise to drink themselves into an effective state of flow and confidence prior to fishing he recorded a hitherto unpublished conclusion drawn from his own experiments and records of his own fishing. Analysis of his performance showed not only a decline from the start of a run, but also a recovery in scoring level in the last few trials, so that when a graph was made of the subject's performance score it formed a U-curve. Mundle then adopted a private ritual which is, in fact, very common among anglers and regarded almost as a superstition. It is always to have three *more* casts before stopping for a snack, or at the head or tail of a pool, or at the end of the day. The Professor was surprised and pleased by the frequency with which he hooked a fish with one of those three for-luck casts, especially the third. 'In three successive years it worked in the same Kincardine pool — just as I turned about to wade ashore and to start winding in, a salmon took hold of my fly. This ritual sounds like a simple superstition. Still, you can try it without telling others.'

Might this be explained by some slight aberration of time itself — a time-slip of sorts that momentarily puts the angler in touch with something that, according to his watch and his ordinary state of awareness, has not yet actually happened. Far fetched as that might seem it is extraordinarily difficult to suggest any other explanation.

Although, to the best of my knowledge, he never wrote about it in respect of fly fishing, J. W. Dunne, the author of *Sunshine and the Dry Fly*, an acknowledged angling classic, also wrote two of the most significant books ever on the time-slip mechanism and aberrations of time in dreams or waking thoughts. Dunne was a most distinguished mathematician and far from being a way-out crank. Coming from any less notable a man, the theories propounded in those two books, *An Experiment with Time* and *The Serial Universe*, may well have been subject to much scorn and ridicule. Dunne's basic proposition was that, leaving aside the charlatans and tricksters for whom it was grist to their particular mills, there was no doubt that some people at some times could and did have cognizance of events that had not yet occurred.

The French philosopher Henri Bergson, also, likened our lives to being afloat in a river of time, as if we were being swept along by the current, but at often varying speeds, and that which we call the real world was what we saw on the banks of this river. But there were back-eddies, too, and little floods and freshets, so that the sequence of events wasn't necessarily like a magic lantern show or even a movie being projected on a continuous time scale. Time slips forward were thought to be sudden spurts of speed ahead of the main flow such as might happen if the mass of water was being squeezed through a narrow channel with a consequent increase of speed of flow; while aberrations of time that led to time past were seen as being back-eddies away from and opposite to that main flow.

Dunne's one fishing book is purely scientific in its approach, although it does examine the instinctive origins of fishing and its hold over enormous numbers of people, men especially. Nowhere does it even suggest the existence of any subliminal element in the way or manner in which we fish, and wonder why. Perhaps he was working on a book that might, had it ever been completed and published, have thrown more light on this matter.

It is generally believed that solitude is the single necessary requirement for circumstances leading to a sort of communion with nature. There can be no doubt that solitude helps, but mountain climbers know solitude, so perhaps do prisoners, so do ocean-going single-handed sailors. But such 'lonely' men don't always or indeed ever enter this higher state of consciousness. If the sailor isn't necessarily aware of it, then water alone cannot be the fundamental ingredient. It must be something else. That something else is fishing itself: not any sort of fishing, but fishing with total concentration and pre-occupation and involvement, so that the shimmering veils of water between human fisher and the hunted fish are sometimes, briefly and fleetingly withdrawn.

The mystery, thank God, remains. Otherwise fishing would lose much of its delight and much of its essential uncertainty. It has to be a mystery. Total understanding and comprehension of the other world of water would do nothing but spoil us for fishing. The idea that water is all, and that the shimmering veil between air and water should forever remain so, separating us from the fish, is to be nurtured rather than regretted. Long may the mystery remain. André Gide is not generally known to have been a fisherman, but he once pondered and confided in his Journal that, 'Fish die belly-upward and rise to the surface; it is their way of falling.' This was perhaps Gide's way of acknowledging the everlasting mystery of fish.

Let not, however, the harsh fact of being one of the unfortunate ninety per cent of angling duffers put anyone off. Far from it. Take heart. Be even supercilious about the other favoured ten per cent, for theirs is not necessarily or always a happy state. Without the element of uncertainty always present in the sport of angling it would no longer remain a sport. Whether an angler catches fish with consummate and nonchalant ease because he is a member of that ten per cent elite, or whether because he is fortunate enough to be fishing, say during a spawning run up the Tongariro, in New Zealand, he may well catch a limit bag with similar ease, the burden such an angler bears is a sad one. For one thing, it is more like work than play. For another, there is nothing to envy in those fishermen who seem to have eliminated the element of chance from their fishing. It has been said that weather conditions, height of water, season of the year, popularity of streams or stillwaters, whims and caprices and conflicting engagements of the trout themselves, make no difference to these gentry: they lay their calculations, adjust themselves to circumstances and always catch fish. Odell Shepard said of such super-fishermen:

> My own attitude towards these anglers, if they can be called that, is respectful but quite unmixed with envy. It would be pleasant to have their knowledge and skill, of course, but one would not like to know that one had it. To my thinking there is something even vulgar in such self-confidence, and it seems to me almost as ugly in an angler as it would be in a lover. The man who is absolutely certain that he can catch trout under any and all conditions has not longer any good reason that I can see for doing so. He has ceased to be a sportsman and has decayed into a mere professional fish-catcher. Henceforth he might as well buy his trout from his butcher and leave the streams to those who can still enjoy them.

But those words, however wise and true, remain cold comfort to the angler who wants to catch more fish because he hardly ever catches more than the odd one, and tries hard to do so. But, as Izaak Walton observed, 'For Angling may be said to be so much like the Mathematicks, that it can ne'r be fully learnt; at least not so fully, but that there will still be more new experiments left for the tryal of other men that succeed us.' Take comfort from such success you might have, and be thankful for it, and — in Izaak's words again — go a'fishing.

Chapter 5
Evolution in Trout
and Salmon Flies

Most fly fishermen will be aware of the forces of evolution apparent in the history and development of artificial flies. This evolution is a process of natural development in the art of fly tying, as a result of innovative patterns, the use of new materials, or some new step forward in the light of man's increasing knowledge. Few anglers, however, would think there is any connection whatsoever between the development of fly tying and the Darwinian theory of natural selection. This is to suggest there may be.

This, it must be understood, is nothing to do with deliberate, cognizant, experimental development resulting in new and more successful fly patterns, but rather of an almost accidental, uncognizant, blind thrust; a purely random natural selection. The first inkling of it, specifically as far as fly fishing is concerned, occurs in an uncommented-upon chapter in Arthur Ransome's last angling book *Mainly about Fishing* (1959). Ransome's thoughts on the subject were specific to salmon flies, but although it was easier at that time to propound such a theory applicable to salmon alone, excluding trout flies, there are compelling reasons for the same processes to apply to artificial fly development as a whole.

'You must always have confidence in your fly.' This was Ransome's first piece of advice to the fisherman. 'Similarly', he went on, 'if you are given to theorising about your fishing, you must always have confidence in your theory. But this does not mean that you must always have confidence in the same fly, or, for that matter, in the same theory.'

Generations of fly fishermen have wondered why salmon can be caught on artificial fly after they have entered rivers on their spawning runs at a time when they no longer feed and, in fact, are no longer capable of ingesting and digesting food; living instead on the huge reserves of energy built up during their active and voracious feeding in the sea. Objections to the question of why salmon take the fly are centred around this one fact. A noticeable feature of *how* a salmon takes the fly is in how the fish mouths the fly and swims off with it lightly held in its maw; which, in fact, is exactly what it does having taken hold of a bunch of worms or a prawn bait.

There is no deliberate act of swallowing as a hungry, feeding fish might do. If, indeed, the angler strikes too soon after the salmon moves off with artificial fly or spoon, or bunch of worms or prawn, in its hold, the chances are the bait will be pulled out of the fish's mouth. There is a critical time, however, when a judicious strike will firmly hook the fish. Could this be because the salmon, having in a reflex action taken into its mouth something specifically reminiscent of the sort of food it used to enjoy suddenly finds to its annoyance that the object is being dragged away, so chomps upon it with extreme vigour, driving the hook home in its jaw.

Neither salmon, nor trout, nor indeed any fish possess arms and legs, hands and fingers, feet, even an extendable tongue, with which it can touch, hold, taste, frighten, strike, hit, or otherwise intimidate a real or imaginary enemy. If it wishes to drive off such a threat the only part of its body with any chance of doing so is its mouth; either to touch or push or nudge the intruding object with the ultimate threat of eating it.

In the same way the roar of the lion and the wide-mouthed gape of the crocodile may sometimes be a prelude to killing for food, but may also be a mere threat, perhaps in protecting territory. Sometimes it may be a purely reflex gesture, doing what it is programmed to do, or a defensive gesture and a prelude to flight.

In the case of the salmon in the river taking the angler's fly into its mouth, although it would be exactly the same if the hook was baited with a bunch of worms, the fish has no inclination whatever to swallow and eat the object. It may respond, as has been said, because it is reminiscent of the food the fish previously lived upon during its sojourn in the sea. That is one theory. It may, however, react to the presence of the angler's artificial fly in front of its path in the only way it knows how (the pre-attack grimace), and with the only physical means it has (its mouth). Given enough time, unless it hooks itself, it would have rejected the artificial fly (or bunch of worms) and spat it out.

In the case of the trout, the fish may be actively feeding and will take an exact imitation of some aquatic food, or even an impressionistic suggestion of it, with no more gusto than it might take a fly or lure that looks like nothing in nature and was never intended to. A temporarily non-feeding trout may well let the more exact or impressionistic artificial pass by disregarded, but may be more likely to attack, and eat, the outlandish and obvious fraud, as witnessed by the success of many of the more outrageous hardware trout lures. Once again its mouth is the trout's chief weapon. Biting at something, for both trout and salmon, has no more significance than the urge of a small boy to kick an empty can lying in his path.

It was always assumed that, in any use of its mouth, a fish was concerned solely with the process of eating. Yet it had been known for centuries that, while salmon cease feeding altogether on entering fresh water, they will freely take an angler's artificial fly.

Up to the 1960s nothing was known beyond the most general surmise as to where Atlantic and Pacific salmon went when they took to their respective oceans, or what they ate during their high seas sojourn. For this reason there was no basic imitative concept or intention in the creation and development of salmon flies.

Even in the very earliest days of fly fishing for trout it seems that the artificials had the intent of copying nature, even if often in a non-specific way. Most of Dame Juliana Berners' famous twelve trout flies are very much recognizable in nature. There can be little doubt that salmon were sometimes taken on these early prototype trout flies, but generally speaking the horsehair lines of the times, and the rods they used, were no match for a fresh-run salmon. In any case, as most monasteries, abbeys, nunneries, and similar religious houses straddled and owned most of the best salmon rivers in England, Wales, Scotland and Ireland — at least in the more peaceful regions — there had been a long history of the incoming salmon being trapped and netted to provide food for the religious on the countless holy days spread throughout the church year, when meat was prohibited to them.

It is likely that as sundry improvements in trout fishing tackle came about, in order to make the catching of fish easier, as well as more satisfying from the point of view of the sporting ethic that was already old in the age of the Dame in 1496, the odd salmon was taken on the artificial fly. Henceforth, there would not have been any deliberate attempt to make flies tied specifically for salmon any different than those used for trout. Certain points, in time, would have been noticed and remembered — the size of the successful fly, its colour — especially in those features that set it apart from the generally sombre-hued trout flies. The chances are that bigger flies came to be favoured — after all, the salmon was a much bigger fish — and it is highly likely that in some departure from the more generally used 'sad-coloured' wools and feathers the evolving salmon fly took on gaudier hues. By the nineteenth century salmon fly-tying and the encyclopaedic catalogue of 'essential' patterns had raised fly fishing for salmon into being an esoteric and expensive art.

Yet throughout this long and slow period of development there was no deliberate intention to copy the basic food of salmon. No one had any idea of where the salmon came from, except that it was from the sea, or what they ate. Even the advances of scientific enquiry during the eighteenth and nineteenth centuries hindered rather than helped man's understanding of the king of fish. Young salmon parr and immature fish before their seaward migration were actually observed to feed as voraciously as trout on the same sub-aqueous food items. It was assumed from this that the adult salmon must similarly feed in fresh water, no doubt on sandeels and elvers, and in this manner it came to be overlooked for centuries that adult returning salmon feed not at all in fresh water. As Arthur Ransome pointed out, talking about elver imitations:

> By dressing such flies, we can, at times, catch salmon, but we do not thus solve the problems of the salmon's natural food, but merely evade it. We can, if we choose, follow an entirely different line of reasoning, that seems to me to provide complete justification for all those other fly-dressers who, disregarding white moths, dragon-flies, caterpillars and even little eels, have unashamedly through many years (three hundred at least) been dressing flies for fun, flies for which they could not have pointed to a model. They tie their flies for fun and catch fish on them. This is the test and the only one that matters. The catching of their fish gives them every right to laugh at the would-be realists. The salmon is the final arbiter, and if there is one thing about the salmon of which we can be sure it is our own ignorance.

Since Ransome wrote those words great leaps have been made in man's knowledge of both Atlantic and Pacific salmon. In the Atlantic it stemmed from the redundancy of so many Danish trawlers during the early 1960s when Iceland was vigorously contending the depletion of its great cod fishery by the rapacity of trawlers from Britain, Norway, Germany, and other western European nations. The Danes took themselves off to friendly (to them) waters in Davis Strait which separates Greenland „and Baffinland in the Canadian Arctic. There, by means of practical investigation, spurred on by the compelling commercial need to catch fish, they found the true and centralised home and feeding grounds of salmon in the sea. It was in those cold, bleak, fog-bound waters that the salmon fed mightily on krill, a euphausid shrimp, found there in prodigious, near solid shoals. And it was there that the Danish gill-netters reeked such havoc and depredations on the salmon that they never recovered from the onslaught against them and, almost certainly, never will. '

Not long afterwards Russian and Japanese commercial fishermen discovered the equally rich deep-sea feeding grounds of the Pacific salmon and steelhead trout in the northwest Pacific Ocean between Kamchatka and the Aleutian Islands. There, too, in another ocean, they made war on the salmon. Within a few years they had all but wiped out the the stocks of several species.

It was now known on what and how and where salmon in the sea mostly fed. Only now can we see how Darwinian natural selection may have most subtly influenced the fly fisherman's less slaughtering pursuits of the salmon over past centuries.

For someone like Ransome, pondering on salmon fly development in the years prior to these discoveries, there were tantalizing benefits to be gained, if only it was known exactly what it was that salmon ate at sea:

It is difficult not to believe that if we could tie flies that would remind a salmon of the things that have fattened him so fast, things on which he has not merely fed but so over-fed as to be ready for a time to eat no more, he would be ready at least to break his fast and to taste those things again. Now, as to what those things are like who can tell us better than the salmon? It is to him that the dresser of flies for fun continuously appeals. He is the judge who decides on the future of the flies submitted to him. No fly-dresser goes on dressing a fly that does not catch fish. A fly may delight the human eye, but if it does not interest the salmon little more is heard of it. Flies are like books. Out of many thousands only a very few survive their publication. A ruthless form of Natural Selection has been at work for all these years, with the salmon as the Natural Selector. This has applied both to the making of flies that copy known objects and to the making of flies that in some way resemble and in other ways differ from artificial flies that have been approved by fish. This form of natural selection has led to the survival of certain characteristics and the disappearance of others. With the slow realisation that butterflies and other winged things can hardly be normal food for salmon has come a marked change in the general shape of salmon flies. Wings, for example, once wide and gaudy, have been shrinking and are now 'worn', as the fashion experts say, fitting closer to the body. An even more important change has been that they have grown more and more diaphanous. We have found ourselves trying to let the body be seen, ghostlike, through the wings. At the same time, by letting himself be caught on certain flies, the salmon has, as it were, expressed his preference, if not for particular feathers, at least for the flies dressed with them. Speckled mallard hackles and barred teal feathers hold their place in the fly-dresser's box all but unchallenged. Now why? May it not be that these feathers contribute in some way to the likeness of our salmon flies to creatures we have not been able to copy because we have not seen them, creatures on which we have had as yet no sure proof that salmon feed, convinced though we may be that very soon the scientists will be giving us just the proof we lack? They will tell us where he feeds, and on what. In the meantime, *if* the salmon feels inclined to take our flies because they remind him of something he has once upon a time tasted in that great secret restaurant of his, then, in the only way he can, he is helping us towards a solution. As the years go by, 'the survival of the fittest' must be bringing our flies to resemble more and more the things for which the salmon mistake them. Sooner or later the oceanographers will tell us where to find the salmon actually at his meal. They will be caught with food in them. Gigantic marrowspoons will then come into their own and there will be as little mystery about tying flies for salmon as there is about tying flies for chalk-stream trout. Whether we shall be better off for that, I do not know. It is inevitable, for 'each man kills the thing he loves' and none more surely than the scientist for whom a mystery is what a clockwork toy is for a child, something to take to pieces.

As it happened, the knowledge gained did not lead to any particularly deadly new salmon fly that copied the krill. In fact, just as Ransome had forecast, salmon fishing worsened over the subsequent years: man had gone irreversibly far in destroying the resource itself. But some points are worthy of our consideration.

Shrimp and prawn flies, both representational and impressionistic, have been developed and are much used for salmon fishing, as indeed has the use of preserved prawn baits in spinning for salmon in rivers often far from the sea. Perhaps more importantly, it might be considered that Arthur Ransome's preoccupation with these ideas, being confined to salmon and artificial salmon flies, failed to show that similar natural selection forces are at work in the evolution of trout flies. Ransome was the most liberal of anglers, scorning dogma and pomposity. He was, nevertheless, as we all are, children of our own time. In Ransome's case, his was the immediate post-Halfordian period when the main aim and thrust in tying newer and better dry flies and nymphs was towards exact imitation.

Yet even now, thirty years since Ransome, we are less certain that ever as to exactly what and how trout see — beyond that they often see far too much. Slavish adherence in fly dressing to the models of more exact imitation has now given way to a more impressionistic approach. And here, I suggest, is how natural selection of the Darwinian kind is still with us. Fitfully, one step at a time, occasionally sideways or even backwards, fly tyers are perhaps reaching forward to models of what the trout sees, and the way in which it sees it. The same would also apply to the evolution of artificial flies that plainly imitate small fish, minnows, bullies, smelt; even those that imitate any other food creatures. Slowly we are coming closer to portraying their underwater appearance to the trout as the trout perceives the living creature. In other words creating an image closer to what and how the trout sees.

Ransome once tied up a fun sort of salmon fly; a fly that was not consciously meant as a portrait of anything;

> With perhaps a traditional Peter Ross among its ancestry; a fly with a body of gold tinsel, and fluorescent red and green, with a scrap of teal for wing and a small black hackle at the head of it, or with a few turns of grey partridge to serve both as wing and hackle. The fly had this much of reason behind it, that I had thought that if in some lights the green did not show up, the red would. That little fly had caught salmon in the very

lowest of low summer water and in the river at a normal height and it had been most consistently taken by sea-trout. I had thought of that fly as an almost shameful example of hitty-missiness.

Then, soon afterwards, an acquaintance, a zoologist newly returned from a round-the-world voyage in the Research ship, *Discovery II*, encompassing Arctic and Antarctic waters, showed Ransome new colour transparencies of planktonic creatures from the North Atlantic. 'There came a day,' wrote Ransome, 'memorable for me, when, sitting in my room in London, I saw, projected on the wall, greatly enlarged pictures of living organisms which it may seem that the salmon, acting as Natural Selector, rejecting some of our flies and accepting others, has, all unknown to himself, been inducing our fly- dressers, all unknown to themselves, more and more accurately to portray.

The first thing Ransome noticed in the photographs was that if (and this was soon afterwards proved to be correct) the salmon and sea trout do indeed feed on these planktonic creatures, the salmon has been right (as Natural Selector) in teaching us to avoid opacity in our artificial flies. The creatures of the plankton were essentially transparent. He also saw that most members of the plankton possessed long, flexible antennae and that the planktonic squid had long, straight beaks, both looking much like the terminal nylon monofilament of a fly fisherman's leader. But what startled Ransome most of all was that the translucent creatures of the plankton bore a touch of scarlet and a touch of pale green, the green no doubt from the phytoplankton on which they grazed.

I could not claim that nature had been imitating art and I knew very well that art had not been consciously imitating nature, but I could, I think, quite fairly feel that my little Port and Starboard fly, tied for fun, but in the tradition of fortunate flies, was something on the right lines or not far from them. The salmon and sea-trout had shown me that already, but it was really staggering, here in London, to be given this wholly unexpected confirmation from the depths of the Atlantic. It was as if, instead of a portrait being painted from a model, a model had appeared from nowhere to match an already-painted portrait.

The *Discovery II*'s monumental world oceanic research was completed in 1951. Since then it has been shown that salmon of all species, and sea trout, feed extensively on their oceanic foraging, not merely on the once-vast populations of adult krill, but equally on the planktonic krill living in temporary infant community with planktonic squid and other creatures. The sheer density of such planktonic abundance often has the consistency of thick soup, so that the fishes and whales feeding upon it are literally swimming in protein rich food.

As for comparisons with portraiture and artistic creation, it was Skues who said of artificial flies:

The shape cannot be precise because of the hook. and because of the action of the water on feathers, and because, in the case of a floating fly, of the refractive operation of light passing from air into water.

The colour may be suggested by translucency (or transmission), by reflection, or by both.

Action may be suggested by motion in or on the water, or by position on the surface, and by such a use of hackle as to suggest a buzzing action,
The imitation may be
Impressionist,
Cubist,
Futurist,
Post-impressionist,
Pre-Raphaelite, or
Caricature.
The commonest is Caricature.
It therefore catches most fish.

Ransome was transformed by what seemed to him something of a revelation. The coloured photographs of the soup-thick animal plankton gave a new meaning to the salmon's long-known liking for some particular ingredients in the making of salmon flies. He began to see them in evolutionary terms through recorded angling literature:

Those speckled feathers of the mallard to take the most obvious example, those features that were used in the seventeenth century by Cromwell's trooper, in the eighteenth by the North Country poacher, in the nineteenth by the Liverpool banker and by the Tweedside shoemaker, need no further justification than Mr David's charming portrait of the little squid clutching a camel's hair paintbrush with tentacles that, spreading from the centre like the fibres of a wound hackle, are speckled, or look speckled, in just such a way. I should like to fish with just such a fly dressed with two or three turns of mallard, in fact a modified edition of a Derwent Whirlie. Another of Mr David's pictures showed a brace of shrimp-like crustaceans not in the drab livery of the ordinary seashore shrimp but flaming scarlet, perfectly explaining why the salmon should welcome ordinary shrimps and prawns that have been boiled scarlet and bottled and sold to fishermen over the counter of a tackle-shop. Those two little shrimps, blazing on my wall, made Dr Pryce Tannatt's well-known 'William Rufus' (that has scared many fishermen but caught many salmon) seem the production of a realist. Touches of fluorescent material seem justified by the many luminous creatures of the ocean though probably we could easily use too much of it. We do not need our flies probing for fish with bulls-eye lanterns.

In Arthur Ransome's view there is a simple explanation why in so many flies we have come (taught by the salmon and sea trout) to use the sharply barred feathers of the teal. That barring on the teal's hackles most vividly suggests the segmented carapaces of shrimps and related species. The zoologist's photographs reminded him of an experience when fishing a sandy Hebridean estuary for sea trout and found a Teal and Green (although known only as a lake fly) much the best pattern. While wading ashore through the shallows he observed that he described as 'countless little Teal and Greens, tiny crustaceans, whose segmented bodies looked exactly like the teal feathers with which I had winged those flies. So many of the plankton's inhabitants have segmented bodies that it is not surprising that (if he feeds on little shrimps) the salmon has been training us to use those feathers.'
Yet freshwater shrimps and other crustaceans undoubtedly provide a much bigger proportion of the food of trout, even in those habitats where it is not

generally believed or known that any crustaceans occur at all. In Britain at least, if not yet in New Zealand, many passably realistic as well as generally impressionistic patterns of artificial freshwater shrimps are much used and with considerable success. Would small sparsely tied Teal and Greens do even better?

The surprise is that Ransome's thoughts, expressed in his book *Mainly About Fishing* in 1959, made such little impact on the current or subsequent angling scene. They seem to have been remarkably overlooked and uncommented upon. It is possible that some observant readers recognized his book as being the first step towards something new, and were only waiting for his ideas to mature. But Ransome was already seventy-five years old; eight years later he was dead.

Yet Ransome's view of natural selection at work in the evolution of salmon flies was nothing less than visionary and far ahead of its time. Something that puzzled him was why the use of some of the most exotic and unlikely features and materials in flies and fly-tying should have continued so long. A case in point was that of Golden Pheasant toppings. If a form of natural selection was at work — and he had no doubt it was — and, if the usefulness of the traditional and almost obligatory Golden Pheasant toppings was nothing but frippery, then their use should have died out. His view, however, was characterized by some splendid imagery:

> But what, you may ask, explains the usefulness of Golden Pheasant toppings, those fine gold fibres, naturally curved, that are taken from the crest of that exotic bird? Is it fantastic to imagine that they may in our flies have the importance of the colours that appear in the skin of a soap-bubble, but for which the bubble itself would be invisible? Millions of the creatures of the plankton are indeed transparent, not to be seen unless somehow delicately caged in colour. May not those toppings, so frail, so sensitive, serve, as it were, to frame emptiness and, like the faint evanescent colours of the soap film, to outline the shape of nothingness and so make the invisible visible?

Ransome's views, as has been said, were specifically concerned with natural selection being at work in the development of salmon flies, but the process is just as applicable to trout flies. In the latter case anglers and fly-tyers have been blinkered in their views because the food of freshwater trout has been clearly observable, while in the case of salmon at sea it was not. The error lies in how man views a hatching mayfly dun on the water, or a spent spinner returning to die, or the brief and fleeting view he has of an underwater nymph, or the more frequent view he has of the same nymph removed from the water, dead or dying out of its proper home. Such man-views, however studied and studious, see these creatures as we see them, not necessarily as the trout sees them. Equally so, the river or lake communities of the young larval, nymphal forms of all aquatic insects, as well as the young fish of all species, are virtually transparent in their earliest days. Furthermore, they often lead a planktonic community-like existence, feeding upon other members of the plankton. One additional point is that the parr of salmon and trout, and the young of pike, perch, and most fish, including the forage fish such as bullies and minnows, have the same segmented parr or blotch markings reminiscent of the crustacean carapace. It is, in fact, a significant feature of the most preyed-upon lake and river communities and a means of protection and camouflage at a time when they are at their most vulnerable.

A critic may ask, why does is it happen so often that a particular pattern of a new artificial trout fly enjoys huge success with anglers and fish, then suddenly seems to lose all its fish-catching effectiveness?

Tentatively, I would suggest that over a period of time, as it is tied by many different fly-tyers, often guided by availability of materials, or commercial considerations of making an object to a price, perhaps straying from the original pattern through laziness, cussedness, or plain ignorance, some other feature creeps in. It may be that this aberrant feature, although trivial and almost imperceptible to our eyes, and certainly of no spectacular significance, is the very one that leads the artificial fly along the path to oblivion by means of natural selection.

Fly fishermen have been aware of this much-repeated phenomenon for a long time, and it has become a commonplace that most artificial flies are tied to capture fishermen rather than fish. Of whatever pattern or type, shop flies are generally too large and bushy, overdressed and bulky. Anglers who tie their own, sparser flies generally tend to be more successful, and not because they are necessarily better fishermen. Dr J. C. Mottram commented on it in this way:

> It is remarkable how flies gain a high reputation, are used by a great number of fishermen, then gradually lose favour and, finally, are seldom found in the angler's fly-box. I think the explanation lies in the fact that professional fly-tiers gradually and unconsciously alter the character of the fly until it comes to differ widely from the original and is of no particular interest to the trout. Take the case of Wickham's Fancy: forty years ago it was a general favourite; it was dressed on an 0 or 1 hook, the setae were short and of red hackle, the body of flat gold tinsel and a sparse short body hackle of dark red cock, the wings were small single, not double, of light starling and projected forward, the head hackle was a few turns of medium red cock. The tinsel body gave a semblance of transparency; the fly was a splendid floater and therefore very good in the evening and in bright sunlight during the day; under some conditions of lighting it was an excellent imitation of the olive dun.
>
> The shop-tied fly is now entirely different: it is on much too big a hook, the body hackle is thick and conceals the tinsel, the wings are large and clumsy, and it is much too heavily hackled at the head; no trout could possibly mistake it for an olive dun, nor any other fly commonly on the water — thus comes about its present-day bad reputation.

It would seem the end result is always the same, no matter whether the artificials in question are dry flies, wet flies, nymphs, attractor flies or lures. Too many fishermen explain it away by saying that the trout or salmon, as the case may be, are becoming 'too educated' — whatever that means. They say that the fish have seen that particular pattern so often they know it to be a fraud. And so on.

For my part I think Arthur Ransome was right: the fish are trying to tell us something.

Chapter 6
Secret Places

Few anglers are without their own secret place, or at least a place not known to be frequented and fished by their angling acquaintances, or by anyone else, for that matter. It may be that a fisherman needs to have, in some basic and primitive way, such a secret place.

It was not until the eighteenth century, at least in England, that fishing books were expected to be guides to fishing waters, as well as being manuals of instruction. Although Walton named a few rivers, he was in no danger of having to share his angling delights with hordes of excursion anglers, simply because there was far better fishing available almost everywhere else throughout the country. Only travel was difficult, and most men led lives that rarely even took them into the neighbouring county, ten or twenty miles away. But, in those balmy days, salmon, trout and sea trout abounded in almost every river in the country. It was never too difficult to find a convenient trout stream.

In later days, as fishing books became where-to-go as well as how-to-do-it manuals, the where-to-go sections were generally little more than gazetteers to help pad out the book to a more acceptable size. But the habit died out in the Romanticism of the early nineteenth century. People simply wanted to read about other people's angling adventures, rarely aspiring to visit and fish those same waters. If names were mentioned at all, it was to bring some colour to the scenes portrayed, to give shape and meaning to carefully contrived sentences and paragraphs. Even after the advent of railways there was no mad rush to set off for distant rivers and lochs: there were plenty enough at hand. And the fishing didn't even begin to worsen until the Industrial Revolution was at its peak, by which time abject poverty kept most of the population away from the rivers and hard at work.

The real where-to-go fishing manual is of much more recent origin. It is substantially geared to people's essential laziness, by saving them legwork in finding out for themselves. It is often claimed as an excuse that time is money, and the angler-tourist just doesn't have the time to explore. But that is probably less true than many suppose. It has been my experience that most where-to-go fishing manuals in New Zealand and in Britain are bought by people who live on the doorstep, and that the fewest are found in the hands of overseas fishermen, who often have only restricted and expensive time available to them. It is generally the American fly fisherman who sets out to explore New Zealand's trout streams without the guiding light of the manual, prepared to take his fishing where he finds it.

A successful where-to-go guide book to one of New Zealand's most famous trout rivers stated baldly at the outset that the joint authors wholeheartedly subscribed to the policy that there should be no secret about where to fish and what to use. To them it was an unfortunate aspect of trout fishing that many anglers endeavour to keep to themselves where they fish and the fly with which they have most success. Since the river in question must be the most public, as well as famed, in New Zealand, and with a high profile worldwide, as well as being far more readily accessible than most, it would indeed be difficult to keep any secret pools and runs private for very long. More curiously, the authors believed that with such an abundance of fishable water in this locality it was 'a tragedy that many who visit the area spend valuable hours of recreation time on what often amounts to a fruitless fishing exercise.' Yet most more questing anglers would surely say their most memorable fishing discoveries have come about as a result of pressing on over the next hill or around the next bend, stumbling on fresh and hitherto unknown fishing delights. Delicious memories are rarely full of recollections of driving one's car right to the water's edge of an overcrowded fishing pool — or, at least, such recollections may not always be the happiest of memories.

Of all the world's fly fishermen, Americans are generally the least secretive and the most unselfish. On the other hand they are realists. Their land is vast, and their trout fishing waters are spread out across the entire breadth of a large continent. They number many more millions of anglers than most countries have populations, and they don't necessarily expect or hope to find good trout fishing on their doorsteps, but very often do. Furthermore, in a land where a huge number of trout fishermen habitually lay in wait in their cars and chase the hatchery truck on its way to liberate trout along the rivers, it must be advantageous for other fishermen, less obsessed by the need to catch instant and easy trout, to ply their fly rods along streams not so stocked and less easily accessible. The fish-truck chasers have a high profile and are very visible, but are certainly outnumbered by others who mostly fish for the event of fishing, and aren't averse to tramping in to less gregarious fishing places.

These fly fishermen undoubtedly relish their secret places as much as any. Like their counterparts everywhere, it is something like a game, and often simple expectation makes the extra effort entirely worthwhile. At least they have the general satisfaction that even if they do have to share the stream with other anglers who got there before them, there's a better chance that the early-birds tramped in there for exactly the same reason: they will at least be fishing close to kindred spirits.

Robert Traver once confessed that, whilst he has no misanthropist, he nevertheless liked and frequently preferred to fish alone. In his view, in a sense, all dedicated fishermen must fish alone; the pursuit being essentially a solitary one. Describing a stretch of a favourite river he loved to fish by himself, he called the place as being made for wonder and solitude; an enchanted stretch of river. On his way in, he would take his car so far, then walk in along a heavily overgrown track, but craftily avoiding using the old trail at first, in order to leave no clues, charging instead into the thickest woods before veering right to pick up the trail. This was Traver's secret place;

the whereabouts of which he guarded most jealously. Yet the same man was not averse to buying drinks in order to better wheedle out of others their secret places. As I've said, it has all the elements of being a game and, like games, can be played for fun or in deadly earnest.

To another American fisherman, the late revered Ben Hur Lampman, all anglers should have their own secret river, although to Lampman this was best a river in the mind and in the angler's imagination. My guess is that he knew the reality of such places rarely if ever exists. It is just that the fisherman who believes he has such a place, only rarely goes to it, and happens never to have seen another angler fishing there, thus maintaining the illusion that it is his own discovery.

In Lampman's limpid prose all fishermen should not merely know a secret river but *own* one. However, those proprietorial rights were wholly in the mind:

> Everyone should possess a river, to have and to hold for his own; and there is this about a river, that a thousand may have such rights in its glancing brightness, the moody green secrecy of its eddies, as one possesses. Everyone should possess a river, for a river, well owned, will seem somehow to cleanse its proprietor, as his river washed the soot and the shame quite away from small Tom the sweep. And in this region a river is simply obtained . . .
>
> . . . When one owns a river by natural right, as may any, not least of the pleasures of this possession are those that arise out of memory, as a trout will rise, either slowly, bright turning, or flashingly into the morning, to strike at the drifting fly. Sorcerous memory, alchemic, eudemonic, that permits one to touch once more the elusive pattern of yesterday — and, this is strange, in some manner to obtain yesterday more closely, to hold it more dearly, than when yesterday was itself the present. Who owns a river by natural right travels it with memory.

Often the most realistically described rivers are really only works of fiction. There are many discursive, reflective fishing books that seem to have no secrets: rivers are named, fishing pools are named, so that no subterfuge is suspected. The truth is that in many cases the named stream is only approximately similar to the real river; or they may be hundreds of miles distant from each other. Sometimes the river is either a total fiction or, if it does exist, is so cleverly hidden among the words that an intrepid explorer would be unlikely to find it. Unlike straight-out guide books, where the reader not only expects, but subsequently verifies the information given, the readers of the more discursive books are often carried along by the candour of the author. Rarely, however, does the reader set off at dawn to seek those same waters; if he does he will find they don't exist, or that what seemed to be clear and simple directions actually lead one to the town dump. The enjoyment is in the reading, he will try to put it into practice on his own river, not seek out that literary stream.

I once met a man who submitted a well-written, factual, and interesting article to a leading sports magazine, accompanied by honest photographs of trout caught and accurately described in the text. He didn't actually name the river, except to mention it was a tributary of a well-known trout stream that was clearly and truthfully identified. In fact, it was the only tributary, and a visitor from outer space armed with a book of road maps would have had no difficulty in finding the river. The article was at least as good as most. However, the editor declined to accept it, and wrote to say that his magazine required truthful, no-nonsense tales of fishing and hunting, with rivers named, and at least a couple of photographs of the place, and one showing a captured trout. The author was furious, particularly at the suggestion that his story may not have been true. He was so angry he sat down and wrote another, longer article straight off the top of his head. It was pure fiction about a non-existent river which he named by calling it by a Maori name of his own invention. The article described the hard slog into the river valley, the fighting browns and rainbows, the roaring waterfalls, dangerous rapids, even more dangerous river crossings — all describing an epic fishing adventure of which not a single word was true. Even the photographs showed some long-forgotten river scene taken from a main highway bridge some years earlier, and those of the two dead trout were similarly unauthentic.

The article was published, and the editor wrote to say this was the stuff his readers wanted. Far from suggesting that this was anything but a rare occurrence, this story goes to show that truth and fiction are often intertwined in such a fashion that fiction sounds better than truth.

There are two basic genres of a certain type of fishing writing. One comes across as being hard facts. The writers are writing from specific experience about specific places, and one is given the impression of absolute expertise and consummate skill. But sometimes, usually when writing about some overseas, often exotic, fishing destination, the writer dwells upon a place or a river or some specific fishing quite familiar to the reader, and then the local knowledge seems less than expert, often sketchy, often curiously out of date or inaccurate, as if compiled from tourist bureau brochures and handouts. Here what is presented as truth is often little more than fiction.

On the other hand there is the style of the more reminiscent, discursive writer who nowhere actually states that the story he tells is true or that the angling experiences he relates actually happened, just as he describes. Yet in this style of writing places and rivers and lakes are named and sound real enough to the reader: often sounding so real that it is assumed they must be real events possibly enlivened by some literary licence.

Yet the first 'style' of writing is far more likely to consist of fictions than the second. The more reminiscent writing may indeed be a distillation of events over many seasons, but as they are more likely to include angling 'failures', rather than to suggest ever-continuing 'successes', they are often more likely to be more factual than the 'hard-facts' style of fishing writing.

A paradox for readers of the two genres of this type of fishing writing lies in that the aficionados of the first hard-facts style usually deplore the second style as being archaic, artificial, only-here-for-the-scenery stuff, with no value for serious fishermen. Yet the opposite is more likely to be true. This same paradoxical expectancy on the part of the reader expects it to be true.

Many trout anglers think that Ernest Hemingway's 'Big Two-Hearted River' is the best fishing story ever written. There is a Two-Hearted River in the Upper Peninsula of Michigan in the same area where Hemingway fished as a young man, but it was a poor trout stream even in those days. Almost ten years later, writing in a Paris apartment above a lumber yard, Hemingway struggled to write a key short story that would somehow knit and hold together (as well as pad out to book size) his first collection of short stories. He already had his alter ego character, Nick Adams, in several of his earlier stories. Now he took Nick trout fishing in the Upper Peninsula.

Hemingway looked back on summer days of boyhood fishing the Fox River with a gang of school friends. But now he had Nick Adams go back there alone, as a man, after a war, and because he liked the sound of the name better he called it the Big Two-Hearted. The scene was true enough, but it incorporated the most memorable features of every river Hemingway could remember. But the fishing was how Hemingway preferred to remember it for the purposes of his story, and in so doing he created yet another Hemingway myth. Even to this day tourists flock to the Big Two-Hearted on pilgrimages along the Hemingway trail. Just as they go to bars in Key West and Bimini where Hemingway never drank, so they go to the Big Two-Hearted River where Hemingway never fished.

Even Ernest Hemingway's son Jack was fooled by it and took himself and a party off on a fishing expedition in his father's footsteps to fish the Big Two-Hearted he found to be unfishable. Only afterwards did he discover that he had been to the wrong river. Ironically, on the long drive into Upper Michigan they crossed a road bridge over a fine-looking trout stream, the Fox, but pressed on towards the 'true gen' of the more romantically named river of his father's story. Everything about the Big Two-Hearted was full of abject disappointment: it was a small, featureless, disenchanting stream edging by sand dunes until it emptied out into Lake Superior. Ernest Hemingway had just liked the name, and who can blame him?

Robert Traver, that erudite Michigan Supreme Court justice who had fascinated the world with his *Anatomy of a Murder*, then fishermen with *Trout Madness*, *Trout Magic* and *Anatomy of a Fisherman*, knew far too much about the Upper Peninsula to have been fooled like Jack Hemingway and countless thousands of other Americans along the Hemingway trail. Long after the once remote and obscure Two Hearted River had become a sort of combined literary shrine and tourist mecca, Traver pointed out that both the word 'Big' and the hyphen had been added by Hemingway. Traver was a real fisherman who confessed that when one is trout fishing sometimes even two can be a crowd while anything over three is a milling throng. He was perfectly happy to see the myth become established in American literary and fishing lore, for while the hordes of visitors trampled to death what was left of the Two Hearted River, and phalanxes of fishermen waded out to where Nick supposedly stood, casting flies and spoons and spinners into the troutless stream, they left the Fox alone for fishermen like Traver himself.

As a secret place, the Big Two-Hearted River says much about such places in the minds of fishermen. They are rarely quite so secret or so desirable as fishing paradises as the myths about them suggest. But mistaken identity can likewise creep into the most seemingly factual accounts of such anglers' eldorados. Let the peripatetic, ever questing fisherman beware: the best fishing is usually around the next bend.

Robert Traver used to call anglers who readily divulged knowledge of their secret spots 'Kiss-and-Tell' fishermen.

> Most fishermen swiftly learn that it's a pretty good rule never to show a favourite spot to any fisherman you wouldn't trust with your wife — a rule that possesses the further utility of narrowing the field fast. Show your secret Shangri-La to the wrong fisherman . . . and the next time you visit the place you are more than apt to find *him* there ahead of you, quite often leading a guided tour.

Traver wasn't enamoured of the breed of kiss-and-tell fishermen and made noises against them in a way considered uncharacteristic of American anglers:

> Worse yet, if the place is really good and the character knows how to

spell, chances are you'll soon be reading all about *his* intrepid new fishing discovery (meaning, of course, the fabled place *you* so foolishly showed him) in your favorite newspaper or outdoor magazine. For these are the compulsive squealers on good fishing waters who keep writing those glowing confessional articles one keeps reading, typically called 'The Ten Best Trout Spots in Michigan' or 'Monster Browns at Your Back Door' — usually accompanied by photos and detailed maps. And I'm not now talking about those ill-disguised and often gaudily misinformed local-booster pitches, the main aim of which is to fill local coffers rather than visiting creels, but rather of hard, reliable dope about really hot fishing spots. These latter are the charming kiss-and-tell fishermen to whom I now give the back of my hand.

What it is that compels these strange characters to keep snitching on good fishing spots, especially in writing and to perfect strangers, has long baffled me. Fortunately for the preservation of my own few remaining favorite spots, I've never gotten to know one of these characters intimately. Accordingly, I can only speculate that their odd obsession must somehow accompany a particularly lardy ego, one so driven by a primitive desire to show off and be top at any price that its possessor is willing at one swoop to kill both his reputation for piscatorial discretion and the doomed spot he's just squealed on.

These kiss-and-tell fishermen must lead damn lonely lives, one would guess, or else have to keep moving around one hell of a lot in order to find a new batch of sucker fishermen they can con into showing them still newer spots to tell on. This is so because the normal ordinary close-mouthed fisherman need only get burned once in order to clam up and spread the alarm.

It was Traver again who pointed out that paradoxically these kiss-and-tellers probably help save more good fishing spots than they ever ruin. Their very presence makes other fishermen more wary and suspicious and close-mouthed than ever, reluctant to show their best spots even to tried and trusted fishing friends, which in turn sharply reduces the fishing pressure on those remaining spots that have so far escaped the 'broadcasting flannel mouths'. A feature of this, in Traver's view, is that many anglers are more likely to show their secret places to visiting fishermen than to other local anglers.

Harry McShane, a splendid fly fisherman and for many years a doyen of the Taupo scene, was often asked by less adventurous anglers the exact whereabouts on a particular high country river he had been fishing with such notable success. If by deduction they had approximately located the spot, he would say, 'No. Not there. Around the bend!' The authors of the New Zealand fishing guide book mentioned at the beginning of this chapter would have considered this attitude selfish and anti-social. To this particular fisherman's way of thinking, the very opposite is closer to the truth. The sort of angler who expects free top-quality fishing information is guilty of abject laziness and of wanting to muscle in on other men's hard-won discoveries. It really makes no difference whether they get the information directly or indirectly from a local expert, or from the pages of a book or magazine. What they want is something for nothing, or at least without personal effort. Nothing is more certain that the rewards of fly fishing can sometimes be beyond compare, but such rewards rarely come without personal effort and doing much of one's own legwork.

Chapter 7
Numeracy

Numeracy, according to some dictionaries, means an understanding of basic scientific concepts. It does not even warrant a mention in the 3rd edition of the Shorter Oxford Dictionary. However, for present purposes I take the word to mean exactly what was intended by David Profumo's and Graham Swift's use of it in their Introduction to *The Magic Wheel*, An Anthology of Fishing in Literature. They give the word the benefit of inverted commas, thus 'numeracy', meaning in angling terms, an abiding preoccupation with the numbers of fish caught and their weights and vital statistics. In such usage it is a marvellous word because it says something about certain fishing attitudes, objectives, and philosophies that no other word quite manages to convey.

So, staying with *The Magic Wheel* for the moment, we can best see in what context Profumo and Swift used it with such dazzling clarity:

> If one feature of nineteenth-century angling literature was a certain bravado, another, not unrelated feature was its increasing 'numeracy'. Accounts of fishing are peppered with figures, measurements, avoirdupois. The record books are out. Walton may have appreciated a good-sized fish, but he seems not to have produced the scales at every opportunity. The statistical obsession is a modern obsession.

Profumo and Swift observed that another phenomenon came with it of which statistics are only a symptom. If the seventeenth century transformed fishing from a trade into a pastime, and the eighteenth century transformed it into a sport or recreation, the nineteenth century and our own have transformed it, to its own cost many anglers would argue, into competition. Competition, that is, not between angler and fish but between angler and angler.

The Magic Wheel is not an anthology of fishing writing but an anthology of fishing in literature. True, most of the familiar authors are represented, but the criteria to include or not include differed from most such collections. In this selection we have Aristotle rubbing shoulders with Aflalo, John Bunyan with Thomas Barker, Chaucer with Cotton, John Donne with J. W. Dunne, Hugh Falkus with J. A. Froude, Oliver Goldsmith with Zane Grey, Halford with Rider Haggard, Longfellow with Andrew Lang, Howard Marshall with Guy de Maupassant, Ovid with George Orwell, Arthur Ransome with John Ruskin, Saint Anthony of Padua with Skues, Izaak Walton with Virginia Woolf, and Ed Zern — as might be expected — in a category of his own.

The book ends with an excerpt from David Duncan's *The River Why*, as magical and captivating a book about fishing as anything ever written, although perhaps a book about fishing only in the sense in which *Moby Dick* is about whales:

> Like gamblers, baseball fans and television networks, fishermen are enamored of statistics. The adoration of statistics is a trait so deeply embedded in their nature that even those rarefied anglers the disciples of Jesus couldn't resist backing their yarns with arithmetic: when the resurrected Christ appears on the morning shore of the Sea of Galilee and directs his forlorn and skunked disciples to the famous catch of *John 21*, we learn that the net contained not 'a boatload' of fish, nor 'about a hundred and a half', nor 'over a gross', but precisely 'an hundred and fifty and three'. This, it seems to me, is one of the most remarkable statistics ever computed. Consider the circumstances: this is *after* the Crucifixion and the Resurrection; Jesus is standing on the beach newly risen from the dead, and it is only the third time the disciples have seen him since the nightmare of Calvary. And yet we learn that in the net there were 'great fishes' numbering precisely 'an hundred and fifty and three'. How was this digit discovered? Mustn't it have happened thus: upon hauling the net to shore, the disciples squatted down by that immense, writhing fish pile and started tossing them into a second pile, painstakingly counting 'one, two, three, four, five, six, seven . . .' all the way up to an hundred and fifty and three, while the newly risen Lord of Creation, the Sustainer of their beings, He who died for them and for Whom they would gladly die, stood waiting, ignored, till the heap of fish was quantified. Such is the fisherman's compulsion toward rudimentary mathematics.
>
> Statistics are a tool upon which anglers rely so heavily that a fish story lacking numbers is just that: a Fish Story. A fish without an exact weight and length is a nonentity, whereas the sixteen-incher or the twelve-pounder leaps out of the imagination, splashing the brain with cold spray. The strange implication is that numbers are more tangible than flesh; fish without vital statistics are fish without being. And this digital fisherman-consciousness has seeped into most facets of life.

Despite any inclination towards a somewhat different point of view, it is extraordinarily difficult for anyone to argue otherwise than that the prime objective in going fishing is to catch fish. Indeed, many anglers would argue that the peripheral delights and charms of fishing — from streamside entomology and flytying, to the more subtle joys of anticipation and escape, the immersion of the angler's soul and heart and mind in the balm of being out there fishing, the natural beauty of stream or lake, the beauty of the fish themselves, companionship — that all these things, however deeply felt, are nothing and mean nothing unless there is the satisfaction of catching fish, preferably big ones, and great numbers of them.

Piscator non solum piscatur, there is more to fishing than catching fish, is both the splendid motto of the Flyfishers' Club and a splendid sentiment to be encouraged and advocated. Unfortunately, it seems, all of us fishermen pay little more than abstract lip-service to the proposition. We remain disconsolate and discontented if we end a fishing day without a limit bag of fish, and even if we do catch a few are dissatisfied with any but big fish.

There is nothing wrong in a fisherman setting out with the intention of catching fish. Why else go fishing, one might ask. What perhaps is wrong, and it is a fairly recent attitude, is the way in which we have become brainwashed into the belief that in being fishless at the end of the day the fisherman has failed miserably. One can accept that the fishless angler will be disappointed, but it is nonsense to write off his day as an abject failure of which he somehow should feel ashamed. The fishing always was better in days gone by — in some respects at least. In the Middle Ages in Britain there were fewer people, and far fewer fishermen, but far more fish. But even in those halcyon days there were fishless days among them, even for those clerics and religious orders who commanded many of the best fishing rivers. It was Dame Juliana Berners, as early as the fifteenth century, who advised anglers:

> Dowteles thenne folowyth it that it must nedes be the dysporte of fysshynge wyth an angle. For all other manere of fysshynge is alos laborous & greuous: often makynge folkes ful wete & cold, whyche many tymes hath be seen cause of grete Infirmytees. But the angler may haue no colde nor no dysease nor angre, but yf he be causer hymself. For he maye not lese at the moost but a lyne or an hoke: of whyche he maye haue store plentee of his owne makynge, as this symple treatyse shall teche hym. Soo thenne his losse is not greuous, and other greyffes maye he not haue, sauynge but yf ony fisshe breke away after that he is take on the hoke, or elles that he catche nought: whyche ben not greuous. For yf he faylle of one he maye not faylle of a nother, yf he dooth as this treatyse techyth: but yf there be nought in the water. And yet atte the leest he hath his holsom walke and mery at his ease, a swete ayre of the swete sauoure of the meede floures: that makyth hym hungry. He hereth the melodyous armony of fowles. He seeth the yonge swannes: heerons: duckes: cotes and many other foules wyth theyr brodes, whyche me semyth better than alle the noyse of houndys: the blastes of hornys and the scrye of foulis that hunters: fawkeners & foulers can make. And yf the angler take fysshe? surely thenne is there noo man merier than he is in his spyryte.

The mediaeval English of Dame Juliana Berners' *The Treatyse of Fysshynge wyth an Angle* has been quoted, rather than the modern English transcription, not for its quaint archaic language, but rather to show that, for all its antiquity, it expresses a view of fishing generally held to be modern. Though written at the beginning of the fifteenth century, the words ring true at the end of the twentieth, despite all the changes in the fishing itself. Far too many supposedly modern attitudes stem from the current surfeit of how-to-do-it fishing manuals that spell the gospel according to the latest angling guru, but always pressing the point that limit bags are always attainable; that the fish should be caught quickly to be sure of them; and suggesting by inference that the guru always catches a limit bag every time out. In this, I suggest, they do infinite harm, both by setting generally unattainable standards for the average angler, and by setting a minimum goal to be achieved. Far too many angling writers continue to equate limit bags with success, and anything less than a limit bag on each and every fishing outing with failure. Worse still, these gladiators of the angling scene set a deplorably bad standard in putting the maximum permissible limit bag of fish caught as a base minimum towards which the angler should aim and apply himself. It really is a nonsense, and makes a nonsense of going fishing for thousands of average fishermen who might otherwise have their sights on other goals and achievements, enjoyment being not the least of them.

But limit bags have in themselves nothing whatsoever to do with numeracy in fishing. Bag limits are a fishery management tool. For commercial reasons they are unavoidable, and no alternative seems possible. However, by setting an upper limit, many fishermen often stay on to catch one or two fish in order to achieve it, when otherwise they might have long since packed up and gone home, quite content with a fish or two and a happy day's fishing.

Numeracy is all to do with what the angler does after catching the fish. Does he weigh and measure and record all such details? Does he simply admire the beauty of the fish before stuffing it in his bag, out of sight and out of mind, except perhaps for a brief recollection of that spurt of adrenalin and heightening of the senses that came momentarily in its capture?

Some numeracy, of course, is nothing but habit. The British have a natural inclination towards scales: every fish caught must be weighed (and, of course, the added ounces sneaked in); while most Americans will simply measure their trout, recording that it was a sixteen-incher or whatsoever. In New Zealand the trout fisherman is more likely to weigh and measure the fish and look up its condition factor on a sliding scale as a measure of its excellence, although this habit has noticeably decreased in recent years.

In bygone years, for some fishermen, in some places, numeracy was superfluous to sheer quantity. Andrew Lang once lamented, 'Even then, thirty years ago, the old stagers used to tell us the water was overfished . . . 'Tis gone, 'tis gone, they cried: not in our time will any man . . . need a cart to carry the trout he has slain.' Numeracy, indeed, may result from the after-effects of such depreciation in the fishing. In the absence of cart-loads of trout it may perhaps be that these disillusioned Scottish fishermen actually started to count their catch and weigh it.

New Zealand was first settled by immigrants from Britain who took along with their household baggage salmon and trout rods, reels and lines and flies, to a land where the rivers and lakes were empty of these species. Trout and salmon were unknown. It was a troutless, salmonless land. But before long acclimitization burst upon them. The main thrust, as far as introduced fish was concerned, was to acclimatize the Atlantic salmon. Except for a few remaining fragile and stunted land-locked populations, this was not successful, but brown trout flourished. Ironically, the early settlers wanted and only requested fertilized Atlantic salmon ova. In that first successful shipment that left the London docks in 1864 on board the *Norfolk* bound for Tasmania, there were 118,000 Atlantic salmon ova. These were obtained by James Youl, who supervised the shipment on behalf of the Australian and New Zealand acclimatization societies, from fisheries on the Tyne, Tweed, Severn, Ribble and Ettrick. On the final day of loading, almost immediately before the ship sailed, Frank Buckland and Francis Francis arrived on the scene quite independently of each other (but, one suspects, with some rivalry between them) each bearing unsolicited gifts of fertilized brown trout (*Salmo trutta*) ova, which they persuaded Youl to take on board as an afterthought. By comparison with the 118,000 Atlantic salmon ova (*Salmo salar*) already stowed in the ship's ice-house on deck, the brown trout shipment was small: 1200 ova from Buckland and 1500 from Francis.

Frank Buckland was a great Victorian naturalist eccentric, while Francis Francis was editor of *The Field* and perhaps the most noted fly fisherman of that era. Buckland's contribution was taken from a single pair of fish, by Buckland himself, from a branch of the River Itchen at Bishopstoke, near Winchester. Francis Francis's contribution came from trout taken in the River Wey, at Alton in Hampshire, and from the River Wycombe, at High Wycombe in Buckinghamshire. It is highly likely that at least part of the shipment came from sea trout parent stock. Later, when the sea-going tendencies came to light in New Zealand streams, it was Buckland who blamed Francis for the error. But, if error it was, it was an exceedingly propitious one.

It is, indeed, fortunate that Youl was perusaded to take on board this small shipment of trout ova, each packed separately in two small wooden boxes. From these, in due course, sprang the parent stock of all the brown trout that were to populate the streams of Tasmania and Victoria, and to thrive in the virgin waters of streams throughout New Zealand.

In 1867, 800 ova from the second generation progeny at Hobart were shipped to New Zealand. Of these, only three trout hatched; all of which escaped. Two were recaptured and by good fortune proved to be a male and a female. They were reared to maturity, and although there were later introductions of both brown trout and sea trout ova, today's stock of brown trout in New Zealand come from these first two fish. The brown trout flourished magnificiently in New Zealand waters, soon growing to prodigious size. They were followed by the rainbow trout and quinnat salmon from America. And all flourished.

When the first New Zealand trout fishing season opened in 1874 the stage was set for numeracy in fishing to become established on a gigantic and mind-boggling scale. Size was always important among the criteria for establishing the relative merits of trout and salmon — at least for brown trout, then rainbows in their turn, if not for quinnat salmon. Exceptionally big fish were commonplace and angling reminiscences of bygone years abound with tales of trout less than ten pounds being thrown back almost contemptuously.

Despite this numeracy of weight and numbers there is little actual record of accredited trout and salmon captures along the lines of national records. It seems these early anglers were too busy fishing to bother about such details. In any case the trout themselves were all magnificent, and the browns, being all descended from a single pair of fish, were almost clones of each other. Until the season of 1926 anglers in the Taupo/Rotorua District were restricted to taking not more than 120 lb of trout per rod per day. Right up to the 1930s it seemed common to record only the total weight of a day's catch. This may have been because the average weights of all the trout actually kept were similar and it hardly required stating the obvious. It wasn't until 1927 that T. E. Donne stated that 'the record of takes of big fishes is not of particular interest to the experienced angler; to him the charm is in the *fishing*."

But the fishing diaries were out, even if the record books stayed closed. Donne recorded some figures from the Lake Rotorua Rod & Gun Club:

First year, 6952 trout weighing 13 tons 13 cwt 3 qrs 21½ lb. Second year, 15,043 trout weighing 25 tons 16 cwt 0 qrs 22 lb. Third year, 22,140 trout weighing 38 tons 10 cwt 3 qrs.

From the Waters of Taupo, Mr A. D. Shilson took over four tons of trout, about 50-50 each of rainbow and brown on fly and minnow, but fishing on his feet, not trolling from a boat. During the last four weeks, he took from the Tongariro River, 504 fish weighing 4287 lb; his best takes being:

May 5th,	25 fish, 205 lb.
May 9th,	30 fish, 273 lb.
May 27th,	29 fish, 232 lb.
May 28th,	27 fish, 205 lb.
May 31st,	28 fish, 228 lb.

He pleaded guilty to being tired after taking the 30 fish on the 9th May, and excused himself because the river was rapid and the big fish very strong. It is recorded that one angler took one ton of trout from Lake Taupo and the Tongariro River in one month.

Another early fishing writer, G. E. Mannering, tells of a 23-lb brown trout from the Rangitata, and of a 39-lb quinnat from the Rakaia. In 1911 Mannering and his friend, Dr Nairn, fishing off the Waitahanui rip, took nine trout weighing 96¾ lb. He goes on to say that previously, in 1904, he had observed numbers of enormous trout in the Waitahanui that would take nothing by day, and he knew not how to catch them at night. It was on this visit he first met the celebrated Ernest DeLautour and saw him catching exceedingly large rainbows, which no one but he knew were there. Immediately after being instructed by the eccentric DeLautour, Mannering caught a 14¾-lb rainbow which he landed a quarter of a mile away in the rough waters of the lake, and immediately cut up into pieces lest others discover its size. In 1912, in two day's fishing on the Tongariro, Mannering took 12 fish; the largest 15½ lb and the average just over 11lb. Meanwhile his companion, Ivan Logan, took trout up to 17½ lb.

But even going back to the first ever fishing book in New Zealand, W. H. Spackman (1892) records a brown trout of 16½ lb taken in the Shag River in 1878; two of 18 lb each from the Taieri in 1881; and another of 22 lb from the Puerua in 1883. Spackman also tells of two brown trout each weighing 34 lb shot in Lake Heron in 1884. In the euphemistic parlance of the time they were said to have been taken on a silver spinner. At the time of writing his book in 1892 Spackman records the then largest trout caught on rod and line as being one of 26½ lb caught by a Mr Lambie of Leeston, fishing in nearby Hall's Creek with live bait. Another fine brown trout was a 25-pounder taken from the same place by Mr Beetham, the Resident Magistrate for Christchurch. And so on and so on. The books are peppered with avoirdupois.

Even in more recent times (and in the more recent metric weights) there are well-authenticated accounts of brown trout approaching 20 kg. A brown trout found dead in the Southland Waiau in 1981 weighed 14 kg. Another brown of 12.8 kg was caught in Lake Whakamarino near Waikaremoana in the same year.

But these are more accounts of big fish rather than clear-cut examples of the prevailing numeracy. What is most noticeable is that the disciples of numeracy never, ever mention having had a good day out fishing, or to have in any way enjoyed the experience. So potent was the force of numeracy that blank days were simply omitted, rather than simply never mentioned. Even Mannering, who was rapt with weights and numbers, was coy over the shameful matter of blank days. 'It is natural,' he wrote, 'that in recalling incidents in angling, one should recall successes rather than failures. There have been many, many failures and blank days. You can't photograph a blank day. There is nothing to photograph.'

Blank days were anathema to numeracy. They were shameful blots on the pages of the records. They were banned.

But vague and less arithmetical numeracy can have its charm. Witness Frederic F. Van de Water in his delightful book *In Defense of Worms — And Other Angling Heresies*:

> We of Peter's Brotherhood talk a great deal of the dimensions of fish, usually fish that we have failed to land, yet to all of us the length and weight of such trophies are of slight material importance. We welcome the rise and the stiffened line and the quivering arc of the rod for what we shall find lodged in our brains, rather than our creels, when the conflict is over.
>
> For some reason, explicable perhaps by mystics or psychologists, the taking of a memorable fish stamps on our minds forever not only the place of his capture but the very smell of the air and the quality of the light. Something, perhaps the excitement of the struggle, embeds these matters permanently in our memories.
>
> I cannot now remember the weight of the largest pickerel I ever took, but I do recall as though it were yesterday, and not a quarter-century ago, the dark October water, the riddled lilypads, the maples ablaze on the pond's far shore, and a length of green water weed that, tangled in my line, followed it, rippling like a serpent.
>
> I have seen a man revisit a stream he had not viewed since childhood and, pointing to an eddy below a cliff, say in the pleased voice of one who greets an old friend: 'That's where I caught my first trout.' Compared to fishermen, elephants are unretentive.'

In the true style of numeracy, of course, the actual numbers of fish caught, or of their individual and aggregate weights, and the vital measurements of each and every one, are not simply accorded to the giants and monster fish. A real numerist is as diligent in recording the vital statistics of delicious but tiny brown trout from a Scottish burn, or a puny pounder of a stew-fed rainbow from one of the poorer commercial stillwaters, as he would be about a veritable giant of either species. Never mind the quality, feel the width.

But ask a number of anglers to explain why there should be this obsession with weights and numbers, and you will find a bewildering range of replies. The preoccupation with the avoirdupois of fish is described differently by almost every individual fisherman for whom it looms importantly. For one it will be justified as a basic reality: that the only purpose in going fishing is to catch fish. For others the reality will be economic: if one is to pay quite considerable sums of money for the rights and privileges to go fishing, then it becomes encumbent upon every angler with any gumption to work hard at catching the maximum number of fish, of the maximum possible individual size and weight, as soon as possible after starting fishing. Such argument is based on the grounds that the trout may be catchable now, at this particular hour, but may be uncatchable by this afternoon. And soon we come up against all manner of pseudo-philosophic arguments that the trout themselves should not be the be all and end all of a day's fishing, that, somehow, it is vulgar to fish primarily for the purpose of filling one's deep-freeze. Then we cannot ignore the undoubted fact that poor anglers who habitually go home fishless become adept at explaining away their lack of success. Such reasons are endless: the day was too hot and bright; too many fish were caught yesterday, and the fishery owner is known to be mean and penny-pinching in the matter of re-stocking; that the unlucky angler couldn't get at any of the choicest spots from which the fish were easy to catch; that he didn't have with him the fly line he really wanted, or the particular pattern of artificial fly the trout wanted that particular day to the exclusion of all others; and, perhaps worst of all, the often fatuous excuse that it doesn't matter — all but suggesting that the fishless, unsucessful angler actually best enjoys it that way.

In no other sport or leisure pursuit is abject falure quite so much lauded because we know in our hearts that the experience is good for our souls. The direct thrust about the prime purpose in going fishing often comes from surprising sources. J. W. Hills, not exactly a man thought to be a fishmonger, had this direct but cautionary message:

> Lastly, do not forget that numbers are an angler's measure of skill. They are the currency in which he is paid. An artist likes getting a thousand pounds for a picture, and not entirely because he likes the money. He likes that, of course, but he also likes a large sum because it is the measure of his worth. It may not be the true measure, for posterity may assess him differently, but it is the only certain one, and after all most painters whose works are now famous were well paid in their lifetime, according to the standard of the day. So with the fisherman. The man who comes home with twelve trout may be a better angler than he who under the same conditions catches six-and-thirty. He may be. He may not care to catch more. But if you are to grade the two according to skill, you have no other test except either numbers or weight, and in northern rivers, where trout run much of a size, it must be numbers.
>
> I walked down, picked up my first box, swung it on to the opposite shoulder, and staggered home with 15 lb on my back. I was well content.

In much the same manner several fishing writers have spoken of the fundamental pleasure of feeling the heavy weight of a fishing bag cutting into their shoulders on the long trudge home. It is a recurrent theme of pleasure being burdened at the end by something less than pleasure.

A point not made, I think, by the editors of *The Magic Wheel* regarding the sudden emphasis on this numeracy in fishing throughout the nineteenth century, was that it was compounded by the sharpening divisions and total segregation of game and coarse fishing. Before the Industrial Revolution the people of Britain fished for whatever species were readily available to them in streams and lakes close by their homes. A poor man might fish exclusively for salmon or trout, while a rich man a hundred miles away might have fished for roach and tench and perch and pike with equal obsession. The new wealth and the new polluting degradations of the industrial age changed all that; as much as the changing times changed the ownership of riparian rights. The worsening of available fishing, the new exclusiveness of changing ownership under the new industrial barons, together with the growth of industrial slums, all contributed to creating a new social caste of devoted coarse fishermen. The rivers and canals readily available to them suffered the brunt of industrial pollution. The fish deteriorated in quality, if not in numbers. If any sport was to be had in fishing alongside a stinking gasworks then it had to be based upon competition between the fishermen themselves, with keepnets, scales, prizes, money and trophies to be won, and some little glory for the champions after a hard day in the pits or in the factory furnace room. It begat a numeracy of gross total weight, the weigh scales becoming the only judge of excellence.

Not without reason such a single criterion assumed a priority more important than the fishing itself. It was all to do with winning, with success.

At about the same time the arithmeticians were astride the noble salmon rivers and the preserved trout streams. It was an obsession of the Victorian age to measure and weigh everything. Brought about by the enquiring lay minds of that time, Science had become king and was given a capital S to distinguish it from lesser pursuits. It was the age of the gifted, often eccentric, amateur. People collected things, from fossils to bird's eggs. Everything was measured, weighed, and recorded. Such attitudes spilled over well into this present century and I remember well my first school chemistry lesson (a mite more than one-third into the twentieth century), eagerly awaited from a master who had once worked with Rutherford. This barren, awful first lesson consisted of about twenty of us eager young boys having to write down and commit to memory the unexciting and simplistic statement that 'The old chemists made three mistakes. They relied too much on outward appearances. They made insufficient use of the balance. And they failed to measure everything. We must avoid these errors.'

There can be few anglers, whose schooling finished prior to the recent revolution in educational methods, who do not well remember those exercise books, on the covers of which were printed the multiplication tables from one to twelve, and the now archaic tables of Imperial and other measures with those only vaguely understood items of drams, grains, pennyweights, gills, pecks, bushels, nails, links, chains, furlongs, roods, and all the rest. Although few if any pupils ever learned them all in parrot, rote fashion, as was expected of them, it is hardly surprising that such an era bred entire generations of addicts of numeracy, whether they became fishermen or not. Is it to be wondered that even now, with the twenty-first century almost upon us, we live in an age when a goodly percentage of fishermen are obsessed by the vital statistics of the fish they catch, and always record them with such exactitude and, even, sometimes, slight exaggeration?

It is tempting to digress into other angling legacies of Victorianism — bag limits, size limits, seasonal limits — and to wonder whether they have any real validity as we approach yet another century. Without limitations there would be no point in numeracy. And many such limitations are sociological and aesthetic rather than based on sound scientific principles. Take the case of bag limits, for example. Most literate trout and salmon anglers not only observe whatever regulations exist in the water they are fishing, but suppose that all the grand, respected, learned names in the history of game fishing would have been fervent believers in the divine rationality and necessity of bag limit regulations. But not a bit of it. Take John Waller Hills, of blessed memory, for example. He said (in the wisdom of old-age): 'I do not believe in limits: I do not think you can overfish big rivers. Most clubs impose them, some going further and restricting not only the number of trout you may catch in one day, but the number you may catch in a season, or even the number of days on which you may fish, which is to treat the angler as a malefactor, allowed out only on ticket-of-leave.' But this is not the time or place to ponder these things. After all, we are discussing numeracy in angling, not the rules and regulations governing it.

Although it has been remarked that Izaak Walton seems not to have rushed for the scales every time he or his companions caught a fish, it must be said that he did sometimes reach for his tape measure. " 'Tis enough honest Scholar, come, lets to supper. Come my friend Coridon this Trout looks lovely, it was twentie two inches when it was taken, and the belly of it looked some part of it as yellow as a Marigold, and part of it as white as a lilly, and yet methinks it looks better in this good sawce.'

Perhaps, then, when all is said and done, we are all numerists at heart; otherwise we would not be fishermen.

Chapter 8
Prejudices in Fishing

We who fly fish for trout know full well that ours is the acme of the angler's art, the epitome of everything best in fishing, the pinnacle of human experience, a never-ending joy for all our days here on earth; that, about the affairs of stream or lake, with rod in hand and eager expectancy in our hearts, we are the happiest of mortals, almost in harmony with heaven itself. There can be no doubt whatsoever that we fly fishers are fully aware of this condition; just as there can be no doubt that it is all absolutely true. But, in knowing this truth, we fall into the trap of vanity, and in so doing we are the undoubted snobs and bigots of the angling world. We are rotten with prejudices and conceits. At least some of us are.

In some parts of the world of fishing the fly rod itself is just a tool of the trade for use in certain places and under particular circumstances. Such anglers will switch to fishing with spinning rods, or boat rods, or deep sea game fish rods, surfcasters, baitcasters, as the case may be to suit the circumstances, the conditions, the place, and the quarry. The complete angler may also be certain that fly fishing is the very summit of this total experience and beyond compare, but will be without the bigotry, the false snobbery and the hypocrisy that so badly characterizes many of us.

Contrary to some popular views, this hypocrisy and snobbery is not to do with exclusiveness and class as such, but is rather geographic. Many New Zealand anglers are certain that theirs is an egalitarian, snob-free society; that the bastion of snob-ridden fishing attitudes, based on the exclusivity of class and the power of money, lies in the chalkstreams of England and the great salmon rivers of Scotland. In this, it is humbly suggested, they may be wrong in all respects except that of money. Even in New Zealand ample money can certainly buy one better fishing nowadays than used to be the case. Helicopters, expensive fishing lodges, the better of the available guides, the ownership or leasing of land adjacent to some of the best waters, have all in recent years become available to those with money. The cost of the actual licence to fish is peanuts, anyway, as any honest fisherman knows. But it can still be awfully expensive, even prohibitive, to go fishing where one might like to go. In this manner it is no different from the Dee, Spey, Helmsdale, Test, Itchen, or even the great salmon and sea trout streams of Norway, Iceland, Ireland, Argentina, Chile or anywhere else. It all boils down to money, to whether one can pay for it, or is willing to pay for it. As for the egalitarian bit, New Zealand does score on one point. If a would-be angler wants to fish the choicest waters in the country, nothing will prevent him gaining access to the fishing other than the cost of getting to it; whereas if the same angler wished to fish, say, the Houghton Water, money alone would not get him a ticket in. This may be exclusiveness but *fishing* snobbery, definitely not, for you would be as likely to see the same people *spinning* for salmon, *feathering* for mackerel, *groundbaiting* for carp in a nearby lake; *livebaiting* for pike on a day ticket pond, or even *fly fishing* for stocked rainbow trout on a small stillwater fishery. The sort of snobbery some New Zealand anglers may suffer from is one concerned with methods, not social distinction or money.

Fly fishing is just a method and a means of angling. It may be the best of all the methods, and as superior to spinning for trout and salmon, as spinning is to netting the fish out, or using gelignite, but it is still just a method and a way of fishing. A fly rod does not automatically confer any superiority on an angler using one. Far too many people, unfortunately, think it does.

Every development in fishing methods and techniques has come about in order to make the catching of fish more certain, even easier, while still complying with local regulations, customs, and mores. There are fishermen around who still believe that dry fly fishing was 'invented' to make trout fishing yet more difficult by ritualizing it into a cult. This is really all stuff and nonsense. It developed out of experiments that made the catching of trout in certain rivers and at certain times easier and less a matter of chuck and chance it. But, however superior, more stimulating and satisfying it may be, it is still not holy writ. Its use in no way confers upon its practitioners any angling superiority, however much they think it does.

A dry fly bigot can be insufferable — and any other variety of angling bigot is just as unsufferable. Both types are fishing bores. The problem lies — if, indeed, it is a problem at all — in the nature of angling itself. In many ways it all boils down to geography and the whims of fortune and fate. Insofar as freshwater fishing is concerned, the only species available to New Zealand anglers (with the exception of eels, which are only rarely fished for as a deliberate quarry by means of rod and line) are brown and rainbow trout and quinnat salmon. Whatever other salmonid fishes are available to the angler are so localized and ungeneral as to be excluded from this sort of consideration. In most parts of the world it would be considered bliss indeed only to have such fish at one's doorstep. Coarse fishing has hardly dented the surface of the New Zealand angling scene, but will, despite the vociferous opposition that any proposed extension of its present boundaries and restrictions receives. In turn, it too will develop its share of zealots and bigots, for as fishing practices go, it is even more likely than game fishing for trout and salmon to throw up its cults and dogmas. Interestingly, salmon fishing in New Zealand, being almost universally spinning, has remained the most egalitarian form of all freshwater angling; whereas in Britain salmon (albeit Atlantic salmon, not quinnat) are variously fished for by fly fishing, spinning, worming, and even legalized netting. Exclusiveness has come about from the restricted use of and access to certain, in fact, most rivers. But as the cost of salmon fishing escalates, so does the acceptance of all likely methods widen. In this manner there are adequate market-related buffers to put too much emphasis on the superiority of one fishing method over another, based on people's desire to get their money's worth. Yet fly fishing for salmon is undoubtedly on the increase in Britain; not for reasons of snobbery or cultism, but because it is more satisfying and provides far better sport.

It needs to be remembered that cultism, bigotry, humbug and snobbery in fishing practices are entirely man-made. An interesting feature of present-day New Zealand trout fishing is an inheritance from contemporary anglers' great-grandfathers and how they regarded the nature of fishing itself, and their need to codify or control it immediately following the acclimitization of introduced species. Dr Donald Scott of Otago University has pointed out that, almost without exception, restrictions on angling methods decrease progressively as one proceeds from north to south. This, in fact, is the mirror image of what happened in Britain, where angling restrictions and restraints generally increase as one travels southward from John o'Groats to Land's End. In other words, the attitudes were in people's minds before the arrival of the trout, and still persist today more than a hundred years later.

The very mention of worming, and even spinning, in the North Island of New Zealand, particularly in the northern half of the island, is anathema to most trout fishermen. Yet many of those same anglers would be considered unethical fishmongers by many Southland and Otago fly fishermen who live and fish cheek by jowl with practitioners of the ancient art of worming, especially upstream worming. In truth, one would think it would be the other way around, but it isn't.

Some attitudes spring from deep personal conviction, but far too many are based on sheer prejudice, ignorance and parochialism. Sadly, things seem to be getting worse, rather than better, as far too many anglers climb on passing bandwagons, espousing causes that sadly tend to give fishing and fishermen a bad name.

A case in point lies in nymph fishing. Less than a decade ago nymph fishing in New Zealand was virtually confined to occasional visiting overseas anglers, a small band of local fly fishermen who had practised the method for years, and those who stumbled on it in the pages of British and American books. Contrary to a now popular belief, nymph fishing had been part of the New Zealand fishing scene, at least in the hands of those first pioneering souls, for sixty or more years before the nymph fishing explosion took place on the Tongariro. It wasn't until the late 1970s that a few brave fly fishermen turned defiantly to fish upstream into the faces of often arrogant and bigoted downstreamers, and caught limit after limit in runs and reaches that previously had been considered fishless.

Yet, within a few years, the nymph fishermen were joined by bunches of yahoos who fished like angry and anti-social predators. It was the era of the Globug and the bug-eyed so-called nymphs that soon deteriorated into nothing but float fishing with illegal methods. The wheel turned full circle. The 'nymph' fishermen were now the villains of the piece, while the old-guard wet fly downstreamers were suddenly reinstated to the top of the ethical, authentic, good-guy heap. Such is the speed of change. Such are the vicissitudes of fishing. Such are the frailties of dogma, humbug, and bigotry turned loose.

Angling dogma, if examined closely, often turns out to be based on disputes as to proper interpretation of existing regulations. If, however, the interpretation of any particular local rule or regulation is open to dispute, then the rule or regulation itself is at fault. Quite obviously certain waters have to be protected, and the best way to protect the fishing and the fish by good and sound management is to impose sound, sensible, workable and acceptable regulations — the purpose of some of which will be restrictive in terms of angling methods, bag limits, seasonal limits, and so on. With sound management and sound regulations there should be no conflict. Sadly, all too often, there is.

Much prejudice and humbug in fishing attitudes stem from localized misreading of the regulations. For example, anglers who live and fish in those areas where year-round, no close-season fishing is permitted in some places feel that such rules should be universal. They also tend to feel that there is much merit and sound management in the concept. New Zealand's Tongariro River is open for year-round fishing when many adjacent streams are closed. But because the winter months provide by far the best fishing, during the spawning runs of rainbow trout entering the river from Lake Taupo, many would argue that, without winter fishing, there would be no fishing at all worth bothering about. Yet, angling and fisheries management pressures are rapidly moving towards opening up all the surrounding rivers to winter fishing. Meanwhile, anglers in, say, the South Island who have long accepted and abided by the close season regulations, are not merely glad to put their rods away after closing day, but think it both ethically and angling-wise to do so.

If regulations impose strict limits on angling methods, they should be abided by willingly, not grudgingly. But just abiding by, say, the fly fishing only regulation, in no way elevates the complying angler into a higher plane, as some bigots would have us believe. There is little or no merit in fly fishing in itself *per se*. Fish-hogs and fishmongers are just as likely to wield a fly rod as a spinning rod. Any visit to the Tongariro in winter will provide adequate visual evidence that this is so; here it is common to see so-called anglers fishing in groups of six or more carting away obscene numbers of fish strung over a tree branch.

Fishermen who may have progressed from worm to spinner to fly fishing are rarely bigoted in their views. Generally speaking they do not regard their elevation to this pinnacle of the angler's art with anything but sheer thankfulness, but certainly not with any feelings of superiority.

Americans, for the most part, are less prejudiced about their fishing than their New Zealand counterparts. They, furthermore, tend to see fishing as an event in itself, to be enjoyed quite separately from glee in the numbers of fish caught. They are also more inclined to view their fishing with a sense of humour encompassing all permitted fishing methods and techniques. Lacking any sense of humour about it is probably what besets so very many New Zealand anglers today, and an increasing number of British anglers, too, in their common pursuit of numbers and weights by which to measure the success, or otherwise, of every fishing trip.

Two American books spring to mind that best illustrate this attitude of freedom from humbug and self-deceit in fishing attitudes. One is *In Defense of Worms*; the other *The Even-Tempered Angler* with the marvellous sub-title of *Being a Treatise in Praise of the Fine Art of Bottom Fishing Together With Remarks on the Other Varieties of Fishermen & Fishing*. But before pondering the angling philosophies of these two American books, with roots as deep and innovative as the very origins of the United States itself, it might be prudent at this stage to examine certain attitudes and the roots of possible prejudice among New Zealand and British fishermen.

New Zealanders are convinced that theirs is a just, decent and egalitarian society, especially within the portals of sport, with no doors closed on grounds of class, creed, or the lack of money. Like most generalizations, many of which are flawed, such observations have acquired the status of gospel truth on account of being so universally and constantly repeated. Insofar as fly fishing is concerned, most New Zealanders started with it, rather than with some other form of fishing, for purely geographic reasons. In much of the more densely populated areas of both islands trout fishing is restricted to fly fishing, and is synonymous with it. Trout fishing is fly fishing. In some districts where more liberal regulations have long been established it may be more general for youths especially, but also beginners of all ages, to catch their first trout on worms or other natural permissible baits, or spinners. Graduation to the fly rod is considered to be a natural progression; it not only opens up the legal availability of fishing everywhere, but, most importantly, is a more efficient way of catching trout — an advantage rather than a handicap.

Additionally, there is no specific kudos in catching trout, believing it to be superior to other species of freshwater fish, because, with few and very localized exceptions, there aren't any other species of freshwater fish, not counting eels. And even eels aren't that common, and are mostly considered as loathsome creatures to be avoided. Throughout New Zealand the superiority of the trout is a matter of being the only contender; there simply aren't other species of fish to attract the freshwater angler.

In Britain, however, things are different and do not necessarily remain the same through succeeding generations. During the past hundred years the once humble trout has become the centre of a cloud of bias, prejudice, and what Bernard Venables called an astonishingly fervid dogma. He wrote:

> Earlier generations took the trout more naturally. It was a fish, and a good one, one of many for the angler's delight, but towards the close of the nineteenth century it was completely totemized. Those that were dedicated to it no longer thought of fish in a general sense: they thought, reverently, of trout, and of vermin. Into the latter category went all the rest, the sleek and gleaming tench, the subtle carp, the perch, all of them, matter only for contemptuous extermination. Just the salmon, as another divinity, was excepted.

Bernard Venables called this period 'a great but turgid era' that, though past, the effect of it still lingers on in many honest angling hearts. To him, writing in 1953, an angling generation had arisen with a broader view. This very nearly mystical esteem in which Victorian and Edwardian devotees held the trout, and which gave rise to the rigid cult of the dry fly, led to, or was based on, a basic misconception of the trout as a fish:

> Tacitly or openly it was regarded as a creature on a higher plane than other fish, one without their grosser appetites. Therefore, *per se*, it did not grub indelicately for things on the bottom; it eschewed all worms, grubs, snails, and horrid things. It sipped only fastidiously at the surface, taking only the minutely fashioned, beautiful ephemeral flies. Anyway, if it did not, no decent angler and gentleman should notice the fact.

But such attitudes, far from being confined to fishing, were universal in Victorian society, which not only pretended that women didn't have legs, but insisted that even table legs should be draped and covered by long, overhanging cloths, as legs (whether female of flesh and blood, or table legs made of wood) were somehow suggestive of the sort of depravity needing to be curbed.

Insofar as fishing was concerned, the supposed delicacy and superiority of the trout was equally absurd:

> The trout like any other fish is a lusty beast. It likes its food, and for its main support appreciates substance. The eating of flies is but a small facet of its appetite, though to the angler an important one. To catch a trout with a little imitation of a natural fly is more meticulous and enjoyable than catching it by other means, but a large lobworm will often appeal to it more. The priests of the Dry Fly School thought it was more moral to use a fly.

Notwithstanding the ascendancy of the dry fly as a result of Halford's rigid orthodoxy, the origins of prejudice stem from much earlier times. Such prejudice lay in the nature of fly fishing itself, and how it was always considered to be modern and state of the art — yet wasn't, not by any means. From angling's first traceable beginnings it was recognized that the sweetest pleasure was to be had in the capture of trout if an artificial fly was the means of the deception, that there lay the most beguiling piquancy; but earlier anglers never hesitated to use less refined methods when they seemed likely to catch more fish. 'Inevitably,' wrote Bernard Venables, 'for such is the nature of angling, these methods became refined to a delicacy not less than that of fly fishing. Worm fishing for trout, for example, quite early in angling's history became distilled to the art of the upstream worm in low clear water, which demands a most fastidious skill.'

Even so, trout fishing means pre-eminently fly fishing. And of this there were two kinds, wet fly and dry fly. The origins of fly fishing in Britain are lost in the obscurity of the dark ages, but by the time the first book on fishing in the English language was printed in 1496, *A Treatyse of Fyshynge wyth an Angle* by Dame Juliana Berners, fly fishing was not only well established but had an abundant lore and tradition. The Treatyse gives a list of twelve essential artificial flies, still recognizable as imitations of the same natural flies seen by anglers today. It is often said that subsequent angling writers, including the near-sainted Izaak Walton himself, slavishly copied and plagiarized this same list of flies right down to the nineteenth century. What is generally overlooked, however, is that there was a compelling good reason: they were such good flies. Venables observed that the basic aspects of fly fishing remain extraordinarily constant through all the books down the centuries. Many of them, if their outmoded idiom is disregarded, have an astonishingly modern ring about them: there is a constant if variably-paced progress along one path.

Yet, in respect of angling methods other than fly fishing — bait and bottom fishing, for example — they often smack of witchcraft and sorcery. Witness the unguents, ointments and pastes and receipts commended as baits 'compelling fish to bite' recommended right up to the mid-1800s and still used in sundry versions today, judging by the advertisements often seen in the more vivid sporting and fishing magazines.

But as far as fly fishing is concerned, that earliest known list of twelve flies from the *Treatyse* became a prototype and basic theme in a steady advance towards the enormous list of flies today. It has been pointed out that the only significant changes have been in the means used to attain the constant object, the suggestion by artificial means of the tiny fragile perfection of the natural flies upon which the trout feed. With much perception and by cutting through the swathes of mere wrappings, Bernard Venables pointed out that the fly is the important thing. The rest — the rod, the reel, the line — are together a propulsive agent to bring the fly to the fish. Despite countless innovations, there has been only one major revolution, the invention of the reel. To deceive a fish a leader must always be used of a strength too slight to resist a dead pull of the fish's whole strength, requiring a buffer of some sort to absorb at least a part of the pull. This role is now shared between the elasticity of the rod and by the reel. The fish pulls and the rod bends, yielding to the fish but resisting it. The advance of the reel was to allow the fish to run off line when the bend of the rod neared the breaking strain of the leader.

So, despite the slow steady advances in other aspects of tackle, the famous list of twelve flies was deemed amply sufficient: what Izaak Walton was to call 'a Jury of flies likely to betray and condemn all the Trouts in the River'. Dame Juliana copied the necessary twelve artificial flies from earlier unnamed and unknown 'books of credence'. From then on each succeeding angling author even more slavishly copied out the list, and with less understanding, as the Dame's dozen of some time before 1492 makes more sense to present-day fly fishermen than do the copy-cat lists in later books by Mascall, Markham, and Barker. Even the *The Arte of Angling* (1577) by the Rev. William Samuel, afterwards plagiarized by Izaak Walton, continues to list the now famous twelve flies without comment or qualification.

In Bernard Venables' view the great spearhead of change began in 1651 after a long period of what he referred to as a time of uncreative quiet. Then, in the short space of twenty-five years, a small group of angling writers appeared with ideas that became near dogma in fly fishing, continuing unchanged for several centuries.

Contrary to most more recent observers' views, the man who perhaps started it all was the most unlikely man to have been an angler in the first place, let alone a stridently innovative one. Richard Franck was most unrepresentative, yet this was to be his role. Most angling historians have all but vilified Franck because of his nature, failing to recognize that he was the first to question this long period of uncreative quiet and blind acceptance of much handed-down and misunderstood lore, grown dim with the passage of time. Throughout the ages most views have agreed that, broadly speaking, anglers have been of the easier kinds of men, those, in Bernard Venables' phrase, 'of more genial mould'. Franck was the very opposite, 'a dark and rigid man, a man of a vast and prolix pomposity, a prater, a pedant, a coxcomb of drear absurdity.' He was a Cromwellian colonel and a narrowly religious man. Indeed the surprise is that he was an angler at all. It has been said of him, however, that 'it is plain he was a good fisherman though an intolerant one, and the greatest bore in the history of angling.' Franck is perhaps best known to those who have not read his book *Northern Memoirs* as the man who took contemporary issue with Izaak Walton, calling him a 'scribbling putationer' and *The Complete Angler* 'an undigested octavo.'

Harsh and ungenerous as those words may be to describe a book that has been through more editions than any other save the Bible, one can see the justice of Franck's reasoning. He was the first angling author to venture further than sylvan streams handily adjacent to towns and country inns. He sought and fished in the wilder waters he found in Scotland in the course of his soldiering. He was, moreover, a fly fisherman. His book, written in 1658 just five years after Walton's first edition, was intolerant that the first Walton regarded fly fishing as being no more than just another method, almost incidental to bottom fishing. And Walton, of course, was a bottom fisherman in heart and temperament. Franck's *Northern Memoirs* remains an almost unreadable fudge of circumlocution, but one feature does shine through its pages. Richard Franck was the first fishing writer to question and doubt and often scoff at those famous writers of books of credence from the past. He had no time for the teachings of Gesner, Dubravius, Aldrovandus, and thought that all the subsequent writers on these matters — including Walton — were equally unscientific, unpracticed, and lacking in personal knowledge of the subject. And he was probably right in that matter. He believed it was more important to get out there on a Highland river or loch and fish experimentally and intelligently, using one's eyes and wits for imitating nature in the deceits of fly fishing for trout and salmon.

Walton wrote most beautifully, but much of the fishing substance of his book was plainly lifted from earlier authors and shamelessly plagiarized from William Samuel's *The Arte of Angling*, written in 1577 but unknown until Otto von Kienbusch found and bought the only known copy in existence in London in 1956. It would be idle, however, to attach too much importance to Walton's obvious plagiarism. It was the common practice of the day, and considered scholarly to consult the earliest known authorities on every subject under the sun. Somehow it was assumed that in the history of mankind, things, including human knowledge, were getting worse, not better. For this reason great plausibility was given to the most outrageous utterances of the past. A reading of Walton shows his leaning back to the words of Gesner, Dubravius, Aldrovandus and the like on all matters from ichthyology to angling techniques. Then, of course, even more importantly, there was the divine approval given to fishing by Christ to his Disciples.

So Walton, in fact, was less a plagiarist than a born bottom fisherman, who happened to write most beautifully, who happened to hone up other men's ideas into some of the most lyrical prose in the language. In the twenty-three years between the first edition of *The Complete Angler* and the now more famous fifth edition in 1676, Walton himself polished and repolished his prose most eloquently. It was during this period, too, that he befriended Charles Cotton and fished with him in the Derbyshire Dove. Cotton's Part the Second in the fifth and subsequent editions of Walton's book raised *The Complete Angler* beyond being a classic, into the realms of containing a brilliant dissertation on fly fishing, written by a master fly fisherman. It at once took the book so far ahead of its time that its supremacy, even as a how-to-do-it manual, remained unchallenged for a hundred and fifty years.

The supremacy of the trout really begins after 1676. Previously, writers like Walton and his predecessors were more at home on the more sluggish, less rapid streams such as the Lea, close to London. Fishing for them meant fishing for a variety of species, of which the trout was but one. Henceforth the ascendancy of prejudice crept into angling, although it varied in progress from district to district, and even continues to this day — despite the present almost universal availability of stillwater trout fisheries throughout the length and breadth of the British Isles. Prejudice in such matters, with overtones of dogma and snobbery, has always been sociologically driven, especially in Britain where, until this century at least, it tended to decrease with travel north and westwards across the land.

But coincident with prejudice came a great leap forward in matters of innovativeness, technique and, above all, the development of fly dressing and the emergence of fly patterns more soundly based on nature and the nature of specific rivers and areas. Charles Cotton had escaped the manacles of the list of twelve flies: he named sixty-five patterns. The flies known in the south of England had been, and remained, bulky, large, heavily dressed. Cotton's were sparse, lightly dressed, slim, with the body no more than extending halfway down the hook shank. Cotton's artificial flies were the forerunners of the North Country and Scottish soft hackled flies that remain so even to this day; while southern flies still tend to be bulkier and more heavily dressed than their northern counterparts.

With the spurt of development following Cotton's contribution to the fifth and subsequent editions of Walton's *The Complete Angler*, a natural movement resulted in the upstream/downstream controversy still with us three hundred years later. Prejudice seems to have been accelerated by the most welcome and innovative new developments. Whether this was, and still is, a matter of regret is immaterial: this is how it happened.

As has been noted, this new innovative thrust was not confined to fly patterns. Hitherto most deliberate, intentional fishing was downstream, although the general tendency was to fish in the direction the wind dictated. As on most rivers, on average, the wind would have blown upstream on approximately as many occasions as it would have blown downstream, we may logically assume that once fly fishing assumed an ascendancy over bait and bottom fishing, numbers of anglers faced and fished upstream because the wind assisted their efforts at distance and covering the water. In the south of England at least, this variation never seems to have taken on any specific advantage other than of wind resistance or assistance. Meanwhile, however, in the north of England and in Scotland, definite advantages were being registered in upstream methods. To begin with, the sparsely dressed, soft hackled northern wet flies and spiders were — albeit unknowingly to the anglers themselves — imitating very well hatching sedges, hatching duns, drowned spinners, and that complex insect world which exists on or just under the stream surface. The northern anglers found that by upstream stalking and treading quietly they might approach so close to a fish that casting was possible whatever the direction of the prevailing wind. Generally the upstream anglers took bigger and better fish. Unnatural drag was reduced to a minimum, the angler remained unseen, and the downstream drift of float of the fly was far more realistic than the downstream wet fly being dragged down and across, which was guaranteed to alarm the older, wiser, and greater trout. Nevertheless, it was, and remains, easier to fish downstream. The current straightens out and forgives the badly cast line — hence the origin of the not necessarily true admonishment of chuck it and chance it. On the other hand, the upstream cast fly floats down or tumbles just beneath the surface in a most realistic manner. Providing the angler was in constant and total contact with his fly and was skilful, he generally caught more and better fish. It was from here on that better tackle resulted from the demands of anglers themselves. Tapered lines and horsehair or silk skilfully tapered down from the front of the fly line to the fly made such improvements possible.

It was all wet fly fishing. Upstream or downstream were the dividing and divisive choices. The downstreamer covered much more water per cast, but probably spooked far more trout that he ever caught. The upstreamer, on the other hand, covered far less water per cast and needed to be more skilful, and the fish he caught tended to be bigger and better. So much prejudice in fly fishing lies solidly in this antipathy between approaching anglers fishing towards each other, each conflicting with each other's water — and each convinced they have divine right on their sides. Thus it was in 1676. Thus it is today, and likely to remain so for many an angling tomorrow.

A view of this emerging split was expressed by Bernard Venables in an admirable passage which gives a key to the subsequent development of fly fishing:

> Till the nineteenth century, fly fishing, for all its developments, had been a simple art. It had been, like bottom fishing, in the main a bucolic pleasure of not very complicated men. In the earlier years of the new century it remained so; all classes of men pursued their trout and grayling as they did their pike and perch and chub, if all these were to be found in their own districts. But the future was gestating, if not obviously, from the first moment of encroachment by industrial development on the old rural simplicities. The path of fishing was set towards that time when fly fishing was to be isolated by an intense inquisitive scholarship. It is interesting that now, much later, the same trend is coming into bottom fishing, applied most particularly to carp.

Venables saw the erudite growth of fly fishing as stemming from the increasing preoccupation of anglers with the natural flies upon which the trout feed. In his view the *Ephemeridae*, in its various species, preoccupies both fish and fishermen during the greater part of the time that flies are being taken at all. It is surprising that Bernard Venables has not been recognized for being the acute angling commentator he undoubtedly was. Yet the increasingly rigid and dogmatic angling attitudes being adopted were not always rewarding anglers with the bigger and better bags of trout. Noting the near obsession with the mayfly, Venables said:

> About the end of May or the early part of June — the time varies from river to river, though it is constant on each river — the Mayfly Carnival opens. The Mayfly is a sensational insect; its affect on both fish and fishermen is profound. It is a very large fly, the female an inch in length without its whisks, the male three-quarters of an inch. At its first appearance trout treat it with reserve, seeming almost afraid of so great a fly, but this passes and a gargantuan feast is started which lasts for the three weeks that the Mayfly is on the water. Every trout in the river (and incidentally the chub and dace too if there are any), even those so large that they have ceased to pay attention to smaller flies, gorge themselves.
>
> It is firmly lodged in tradition that this is the time when opportunity is most golden for the fly fisher, the time when old hand and novice will come consummated away. It is called the Duffer's Fortnight (the last week of the Mayfly's season trout have become obese and torpidly indifferent). There is some truth in the old belief, but much less than the promise. In some seasons trout are more easily taken than at other times, some bigger ones are taken because they appear at no other time. But to a great extent the Mayfly Carnival is an annual disappointment. Success is seldom orgiastic. In a season of heavy hatches — and they can be so heavy that the air is clotted with the flies — the angler can hardly find a way to win the fish's attention to his fly among such a jostling crowd of natural ones. The hatch that is just a sprinkling serves the angler best: then he will find the fish greedy and expectant but not pampered.
>
> The Mayfly does not appear on all rivers; on those that know it not, its presence is not craved. It is a heady gift, almost a corruptive one. When it comes it induces in fishers and fish an intoxication: when it goes it leaves the latter somnolent and unresponsive, the former a little fallen from rare heights to a world where trout are dour.

Interestingly, among New Zealand fly fishermen, whilst the various species of mayfly are important in both their nymphal and dun and spinner form, far from there being a Duffer's Fortnight or anything approaching it, mayfly may be on the water and trout caught on a floating artificial on any day of the fishing season. I have seen many good trout, both brown and rainbow, caught on floating mayfly artificials on both Opening Day and Closing Day. If often seems that the colder, wetter, more blustery and inclement day it is, the bigger the hatch and the more selective the rise of trout to them.

But while New Zealand trout can be as exasperatingly and frustratingly selective as any chalkstream trout, it is certain they are less selective as to exact imitation in the dry fly patterns they are offered. They may be more difficult to hook and land, but for the most part they will take almost any small, well presented, preferably dark, well cocked floating fly put temptingly close to them. It is tempting from the angler's point of view to put this down to the relatively sparser natural fly life in the generally more turbulent New Zealand trout streams. Yet, given the hatches of mayfly can and do appear on any day throughout the season, one might suppose the trout would be even more cognizant of the species hatching at any particular time and be more selective in their decision whether to take it or let it float by.

Prejudice among New Zealand fly fishermen as a whole, tends to the belief that dry fly fishermen are effete and their art as contrived as that of their counterparts on the chalkstreams of southern England. Yet, paradoxically, for the most part, dry fly fishing in New Zealand is practised by the most hardily physical of anglers, pursued in the wildest places, with the trout inhabiting the most turbulent of rivers and best found in the fastest and whitest water. There are, of course, stretches of these rivers which are more limpid and glidey and where more browns than rainbows dwell. But, generally speaking, the approach to such sylvan streams is just as arduous as it is to the faster mountain torrents. Here we can debunk another myth. It is often said that once brown trout exceed a certain size they cease to rise to surface flies, subsisting instead on larger prey including their own kind. The same myth says that New Zealand rainbow trout never rise to surface flies at all. It has been my pleasure and delight to see that both propositions are sheer bunkum. Browns of all sizes, even the biggest of them, will not only rise but take surface flies steadily and with far less commotion than their younger smaller brethren. Similarly, rainbows of whatever size will rise almost joyously and far less suspiciously to a well presented and tempting dry fly. I have often seen them streak upwards from unseen depths in pools to intercept and take a large, succulent natural or artificial. Only prejudiced angling minds have it otherwise.

Prejudice has it that fishing the dry fly came about in order to make the catching of trout more difficult simply in order to exclude anyone less than expert, as well as to establish a rigid cultism based on exclusiveness. This idea is so much stuff and nonsense that it is hardly worth consideration. Dry fly fishing developed and came about in order to make the catching of trout in such streams easier and more certain. It was a minority of prejudiced people who took it up who turned it into a sterile cult. They were helped by Halford himself, who committed the cardinal sin of rigidly codifying fly fishing technique, and of establishing an orthodoxy based upon his own beliefs.

But if the dry fly brought along in its wake some of the least desirable prejudices in the history and development of trout fishing, so, too, did it bring some of its more sublime delights. On streams where trout may be stalked and seen rising to take natural insects on the surface the pleasures of dry fly fishing can be superlative. The fisherman's artificial fly cast upstream begins the downstream float, riding high on its hackles on silent unstirred water with no flaw in its smoothness save the rings of rising trout. Such water looks so much more likely to hold fish that may at any moment take the fly. Bernard Venables said of such moments that they provided the acme of all the fascination of dry fly fishing:

> Like all of the more profoundly delightful forms of fishing it has the heavenly paradox of peace — and how sublime and rare the chalk stream peace is — and intense excitement. The fish has been seen to rise, not once, a chance and aberrant rise, but consistently taking quietly from the surface each fly that comes fairly over it. Either from sight of it or from its position and the nature of its rise it is known that it is a big fish. Now the artificial fly has been cast and has fallen softly where it should go, a foot perhaps upstream of the fish. The suspense of that really only momentary but apparently interminable pause is so exquisite that the angler, most happily, never becomes inured to it. And, I think, only the most blandly polished performers ever get past that split second's unbelief when, the fish having risen, and the strike having been made, the first weight of the hooked fish is felt.

It is noteworthy that prejudices often arise immediately following some new technical development in tackle and of delivering the fly to the fish. The angler's ability to catch trout is thus enhanced, and the occurrence of such prejudice has little or nothing to do with whether that technical leap forward was the change from greenheart rods to exquisite split cane, or from fibreglass to boron composites. It may be a sudden development of fly lines, or of leaders, or of materials used in the tying of the artificial flies themselves. Halford and his rigid orthodoxy sprung out of the development of split cane fly rods that could punch out a dry fly into a wind if needs be, sink home the hook point with the merest turn of the wrist, and provide the power to hold a fish from running upstream disturbing every trout in the river.

Similarly, New Zealand orthodoxy — but this time the rigid orthodoxy of the downstream sunk wet fly or lure — arose out of the general and relatively inexpensive availability of big, heavy, powerful cane rods then used for salmon fishing in Britain. Even the down and across methods were transplanted some twelve thousand miles. Even the same traditional fully dressed salmon flies were used until more readily available native bird plumage gave rise to a growing list of successful, indigenous wet flies; it was found then that a Matuku or, later, a Mrs Simpson or a Parsons' Glory would catch as many or more big rainbow trout as a Silver Doctor or Durham Ranger. A New Zealand orthodoxy became established. By the 1930s it was as prejudiced and intolerant as any Halfordian doctrine and dogma. And so it remained for another forty or fifty years until its supremacy was challenged.

Visiting anglers were always less prepared to accept that any absolute supremacy existed. Overseas anglers like Mottram never succumbed to the directive to fish that way, and tended to seek their New Zealand fishing away from the more popular places where gregariousness and shoulder to shoulder angling practices only fostered and strengthened the current national fly fishing orthodoxy. There were, however, many visiting fly fishermen, who not only went along with their hosts' dogmatic beliefs, when it is plain they knew better, but went on to promulgate the practice and to write about it afterwards in words of fulsome praise. Dedicated and skilful dry fly and nymph fishermen from Britain and the United States came to New Zealand almost as a pilgrimage. Once there they would line themselves up in the Waitahanui Rip with the other devotees; fish equally gregariously on the Tongariro; then declare it to be the finest and most perfect fishing they had ever experienced, taking home vast quantities of Hamill's Killers, Craig's Nighttime, Fuzzy Wuzzies, Taupo Tigers, Mrs Simpsons, Spa Specials, Parsons' Glories, Scotch Poachers, Rabbits and Red Setters to relive past glories on their home streams.

Many New Zealand angling authors, exemplified in the immediate post-war generation by men such as Budge Hintz, were considered to be oracular in their pronouncements concerning all aspects of fly fishing for trout. Prior to earlier books by George Ferris, Keith Draper, and slimmer little angling commentaries by Adair McMaster, and a book from G. B. Hobbs who had already lived many years outside New Zealand, trout fishing was singularly identified with fishing a big lure downstream on a sinking line then twitching it back before repeating the process. In river or lake the technique remained the same. What is more, the method caught plenty of trout, especially rainbows, for few anglers deliberately went after browns, and there was a general but erroneous belief that their numbers in relation to those of rainbow trout were small and declining.

It seems that no one ever considered there might be better and more pleasing ways of fly fishing for trout. It is apparent that these dedicated New Zealand anglers were already aware of dry fly and nymph fishing, and possibly of fishing small wet flies upstream and down, but they were insistent that the only way to fish for the big rainbows was by their long-established method inherited directly from British salmon fishing earlier in the century. It was considered the height of piscatorial elegance, the very summit of angling experience which could never be bettered or improved upon. This was very much like the acceptance of the Halfordian dogma of the dry fly at the turn of the century, which stood firm for fifty years and traces of which linger on all around the world even today.

The New Zealanders were prepared to accept, up to a point, new flies, but by and large the list of patterns of Taupo/Rotorua and Canterbury lures was complete and unchanging by the time of the immediate post-war years. Like Halford and his disciples in 1910 when dry fly purism was at its height, anyone who fished otherwise was considered no fisher at all, and anyone who questioned the dogma was considered ignorant and unreasonable. To such men angling had reached the final pinnacle of perfection; the future was the blissful and endless repetition of a paradise.

Even when, as early as 1926, visiting overseas anglers such as Zane Grey came to New Zealand they headed straight for Taupo and were at once espoused to the deep-sunk across and downstream lure. No one after Mottram in 1911 seems ever to have questioned it or wondered about its universal and total acceptance. Some would argue that, provided the method caught trout, why change? Why tinker with a system so good? A few of these issues are taken up in other chapters of this book. Suffice it to say here that generations of fly fishermen who fished in this manner seem to have fished with blinkers on. Many of them were the most literate of men and probably familiar with the world of fly fishing literature; yet they remained totally untouched by the angling writing of men like Francis, Senior, Cutcliffe, Grey, Ronalds, Stewart, Halford, Dewar, Skues, Gordon, LaBranche, Hewitt, Dunne, Mottram and many others, right up to the time of Sawyer and Kite. They were convinced, of course, that all these writers were only concerned with and knowledgeable about small and insignificant trout in lesser waters in Britain or the United States, and that nothing they wrote had any significance whatsoever for New Zealand trout or New Zealand fly fishermen. If they considered any overseas parallels at all, it was confined to comparisons with fly fishing for Atlantic salmon on both sides of that ocean. It must be one of the strangest head-in-sand attitudes in the history of fly fishing anywhere.

Some would say thank God we have now entered a better informed age, a more enlightened era of fly fishing following on from the nymphing revolution of the late 1970s and early 1980s, and in many ways they would be right. Except. Except that yet even more outrageous edifices of prejudice are being built up around the new nymph fishing cult, which puts Globugs and Muppets, as well as the people who use them, on the latest pedestal of angling excellence.

I mentioned earlier two remarkably unnoticed American books; one, *In Defense of Worms* (1949) by Frederic Van de Water; the other, *The Even-Tempered Angler* (1983) by Louis Rubin. In quite different ways both books take pungent and witty looks at the art of angling through a series of contemplative essays. There can be little doubt that few fly fishermen anywhere have read either book. The superficial would have been put off by their titles alone; the self-considered purist of whatever prejudicial persuasion would have turned tail on reading the various chapter headings. Some examples: Men I Won't Fish With; In Defense of Worms; The Purist and the Dub; Heart or Belly; Worse and Less of It. These are all from the earlier book. As for Rubin's book, he didn't have the heart to give his chapters significant titles, choosing instead to launch off into witty, erudite and not always admiring examinations of the nature of fishing, and especially of fishermen.

Louis Rubin is an all-round fisherman himself, in no way in awe of fly fishing for trout, and generally prefers bottom fishing for other species from boats. Despite this purely personal preference, his acerbic and penetrating eye reveals a greater love of, and a far greater knowledge of trout fishing and trout fishermen than the vast majority of singularly dedicated trout fishermen.

Van de Water was a reformed trout fisherman but in eschewing worms for the artificial fly had sweet reason enough not to deny his past:

> I have worked my way up to the fringes of angling aristocracy by never using worms any more — or, hardly ever — though I still am a better fisherman with such bait than I ever shall be with a fly. I commonly employ the latter, just the same. Post-maturity has furnished me with too many troubles for me willingly to undergo the additional anguish a worm-user must suffer when a purist is around — embarrassment, sulky defiance, and a sense of treachery, all horridly emulsified and endured under the contemptuously pitying regard of his betters.
>
> Yet though I am practically a reformed character and have come up in the world, I can find in myself little of the climber's usual itch to defame his origin. Instead of detestation, I discover in my heart, when I look back at my former abject position in the fishing hierarchy, a reprehensible wistfulness and a sneaking regret. After all, fish prefer worms; why should not I?
>
> I profess to scorn worm-fishing because so many authorities have told me I must. Morality of all varieties is, after all, only the voice of the majority, or even a minority devoted to noise. A messiah frequently is he

who can yell loudest and longest. Decalogues and decibels have more in common than most people suppose.

Reformation has done its worst for me. I turned from worms to flies in a spirit of snobbery, in the hope of being considered by my fellow-anglers as something a little better than hopelessly plebeian. I normally fish with flies now, partly from habit, partly because I have grown to enjoy it, but that enjoyment has not blinded me to the unfair scorn visited upon the lowly. I wish a prophet might rise among them. There is much to be said for worm-fishing and worm-fishermen.

It never is. The practitioners of this discredited art are a humble, inarticulate folk. They are among the meek who, year by year, enjoy increasingly less prospect of ever inheriting the earth. They do not proselyte; they do not preach. They only want to have their fun in their own simple way, which, on some counts, gives them warrant to scorn the angling purists.

The scorn, however, always is upon patrician faces.

'What are you using? Oh, worms! Well!'

Thereupon the malefactor flinches and retires into himself like a box turtle. Fly-fishing is a needless complexity, an affectation, a vanity. The worm fisherman knows it, yet he shudders and tries to hide the tomato can.

Strong words, perhaps, and sufficient to arouse the ire of most complete fly fishers. Yet need it to be so? While I have met some fly fishermen who were haughtily patrician, as well as being fishing snobs, for the most part fly fishermen are quite ordinary folk, although usually prejudiced to excess in *some* of their attitudes.

It is commonplace that to some insensitive Europeans all Chinese people look the same; in the same way, to insensitive Chinese all Europeans look the same. In much the same manner, to non-anglers all anglers are the same. And the picture they have of them is not good: amusedly tolerant of the most urbane and informed, and downright scathing of the most bigoted. Only anglers themselves, it would seem, are ignorant of this prevalent view. Instead, anglers generally wallow in a Waltonian picture of themselves as good natured, harmless sportsmen somewhat obsessed with fish and fishing. The popular view, however, is more likely to be of a rather indolent and melancholic creature, somewhat furtive of habit and mean of nature. Or even as congenital liars, obsessed by folly, 'the epitome of a sedentary simpleton, a deranged yokel, hypnotized by the tiny tip of his float, hunched Rodin-still on the bank of a river, probably in the rain, possibly inebriated, and invariably fishless.' A fly fisherman might complain that one does not sit indolently on a river bank, mindlessly watching a float, inebriated, and fishless, but such is the stereotype of an angler in the collective unconscious of non-anglers.

Such a view differs markedly from how anglers see themselves, particularly how fly fishermen see themselves. Despite our addiction to fly fishing, those of us so addicted deep down long for the universal approval we heap upon ourselves as God given. Angling literature is full of such divine posturing. None so better or succinct, to my mind, than a melodious passage from Norman Maclean's *A River Runs Through It*:

In our family there was no clear line between religion and fly fishing. We lived at the junction of great trout rivers in western Montana, and our father was a Presbyterian minister and a fly fisherman who tied his own flies and taught others. He told us about Christ's disciples being fishermen, and we were left to assume, as my brother and I did, that all first-class fishermen on the Sea of Galilee were fly fishermen and that John, the favorite, was a dry-fly fisherman.

Being equally addicted I delight in that passage, but am cynical enough to wonder whether, perhaps after all, it does not speak volumes about anglers' more basic prejudices. We began this chapter by stating, quite categorically, that fly fishing for trout was the most perfect enjoyment and fascination anyone might have. The trouble is that you may know this sheer nugget of truth, and I know it, but most other people don't and never will. Paradoxically, it is a self-evident, self-fulfilling, self-perpetuating prejudice. But we who fly fish for trout know it to be true.

Even a New Zealand angling writer as urbane, gentle, and gentlemanly as Greg Kelly, whom it was my great privilege to know as a friend, was not without a particular attitude to fly fishing its critics would call snobbish and prejudiced. In his delightful book, *The Flies in my Hat*, Greg Kelly refers to his favourite dry flies stuck in his fishing hat — Greenwell's Glory, Dad's Favourite, Coch-y-bondhu, Tup's Indispensable, Kakahi Queen, Red-Tipped Governor — as his 'bunch of little snobs', and went on to write one of the best-ever New Zealand trout fishing books, based largely on his experiences with these flies. Yet dear old Greg Kelly, too, must have been seen to be overly concerned with angling prejudices by many of his contemporaries. Yet all who knew him knew he wasn't.

Perhaps it is not any particular prejudice in fishing each and every one of us should seek to conquer, but prejudice itself.

Chapter 9
Don't be Afraid of Being an Angling Duffer

It was said that Queen Isabella of Spain, then about seventy years old, was asked by one of her favourite Court ladies, who was at least forty years younger than the Queen, when it was that people lost their sexual desires. 'Oh! I've no idea,' replied Her Majesty, 'You would have to ask someone much older than me.' Not being strong on historical anecdote, it may have been Catherine the Great, and not the Queen of Spain at all, but the story serves to introduce my present subject well.

In approximately the same way I've always believed that no one actually ever *gives up* fishing once addicted to it — particularly fly fishing. Longevity or physical infirmity might often prevent an ageing angler from actually going fishing, but in no sense is fishing itself abandoned: the physical activity of going fishing now has to be enjoyed vicariously in remembrance, or in the pages of books, or in conversation with those not so handicapped.

Yet the American author George LaBranche actually gave up fly fishing because it was too easy for him. No challenge remained. No uncertainty. The outcome was known before the beginning: if there were any salmon or trout present he would catch them with consummate ease. No reason remained why he should even bother to try.

Poor sod!

Far from having reached the pinnacle of angling excellence, he seems to me to have reached rock bottom. While George LaBranche was without doubt a remarkably fine and innovative fly fisherman whose name is assured to be long remembered and revered, I can't help but feel that, somewhere along his angling path, he lost the way and took the wrong direction towards the sterile way of mere technical legerdemain.

Andrew Lang was one of those famous, prolific Victorian authors who churned out volumes of literary criticism, essays, verse, children's stories, novels and so on; he could write books on any subject, and did. He is remembered among fly fishermen mostly for that delightful book *Angling Sketches*, published in 1891. A very good fishing companion of mine can't stand it because of the famous chapter 'The Confessions of a Duffer', which opens the book and sets the tone for what is to come. To Lang there was no false modesty in the confidence with which he proclaimed himself a duffer at fishing:

> Some men are born duffers; others, unlike persons of genius, become so by an infinite capacity for not taking pains. Others, again, among whom I would rank myself, combine both these elements of incompetence. Nature, that made me enthusiastically fond of fishing, gave me thumbs for fingers, short-sighted eyes, indolence, carelessness, and a temper which (usually sweet and angelic) is goaded to madness by the laws of matter and of gravitation. For example: when another man is caught up in a branch he disengages his fly; I jerk at it till something breaks. As for carelessness, in boyhood I fished, by preference with doubtful gut and knots ill-tied; it made the risk greater, and increased the excitement if one did hook a trout. I can't keep a fly-book. I stuff the flies into my pockets at random, or stick them into the leaves of a novel, or bestow them in the lining of my hat or the case of my rods. Never, till 1890, in all my days did I possess a landing-net. If I can drag a fish up a bank, or over the gravel, well; if not, he goes on his way rejoicing. On the Test I thought it seemly to carry a landing net. It had a hinge, and doubled up. I put the handle through a buttonhole of my coat: I saw a big fish rising, I put a dry fly over him; the idiot took it. Up stream, he ran, then down stream, then he yielded to the rod and came near me. I tried to unship my landing-net from my buttonhole. Vain labour! I twisted and turned the handle, it would not budge. Finally, I stooped, and attempted to ladle the trout out with a short net; but he broke the gut, and went off. A landing-net is a tedious thing to carry, so is a creel, and a creel is, to me, a superfluity. There is never anything to put in it. If I do catch a trout, I lay him under a big stone, cover him with leaves, and never find him again.

A little later, as if anticipating the question, Lang continues, 'Then why, a persevering reader may ask, do I fish? Well, it is stronger than myself, the love of fishing; perhaps it is an inherited instinct, without the inherited power. I may have had a fishing ancestor who bequeathed me the passion without the art'.

Andrew Lang wasn't proud of being an angling duffer, but had simply grown accustomed to it and loved angling all the more in spite of it. I also suspect that he wasn't perhaps quite as much of a duffer, or at least a hopeless, unmitigated duffer, as he made out. To Lang, 'fishing is like life; and in the art of living, too, there are duffers, though they seldom give us their confessions. Yet even they are kept alive, like the incompetent angler, by this undying hope: they will be more careful, more skilful, more lucky next time.'

The desire to attain technical excellence and skilful ability in any chosen field of human activity is admirable. This applies as much to fly fishing for trout as it does to running a four-minute mile or to earning a living. Anything really worth doing is worth doing well, or at least as well as possible. But fishing, by its very nature, by its intrusion on the angler's part into another world, is really to do with uncertainties. Therein lies its charm, its appeal, and its magic. Otherwise it is nothing itself. One might as well buy fish at the fishmonger's, a cheaper and far more reliable source. In fly fishing some technical excellence is basic to success, but it is far from everything. The superb caster who achieves unbelievable distance with shooting heads or double hauls or some other trick of the trade almost always casts over and beyond the best fish. The grass in the next field isn't always greener; it merely looks that way from a distance.

Andrew Lang was in many ways more fortunate than the fly fisherman of today. Scottish streams in 1891 did have their fair share of 'professional' fishermen. These were men who made their living by supplying trout to local hotels and fish merchants. They were very local in their activities and somewhat secretive about them, so little leaned on the purely-for-pleasure angler. Their present-day counterparts live on in many remote parts of Scotland in the guise of boatmen/ghillies at some lochside hotels where their employment by guests is either obligatory or nearly so. Elsewhere there are fishing guides and tackle dealers, but most anglers are amateurs. When an angler is urged to be 'professional', what is usually meant is a subtle pressure on the novice angler (mostly from the more basically instructional magazines and books) to become more competent, more technically proficient, more successful in terms of trout in the freezer than in the pleasures he gets from the event of going fishing.

To the more traditional fly fisherman's way of thinking 'professionalism' is often a sterile philosophy that must, sooner or later, pall, and lead anglers down to the sorry stage that George LaBranche reached when he gave up fishing because it was too easy. Duffers, on the other hand, never give up fishing. They enjoy if far too much to do anything so silly.

Far from advocating that today's fly fisherman should turn his back on technical ability in his craft, or do without the best assistance possible, or first-class tackle, it is best that an angler should be taught to cast competently by an expert, or by the close study of a first-class book. Similarly with quality in tackle. Buy and use the very best; not only is it cheaper in the long run, but is far more pleasurable and reliable to use. If it so happens that, by dint of hard practice, you end up being able to drop a dry fly on to a saucer from sixty feet away, then fine, marvellous; such ability will often be rewarded and always greatly admired. But, if you can't do it, then don't worry too much about it.

In many respects the proliferation since the late 1970s in the numbers of smaller stillwater trout fisheries throughout Britain has spawned a less than admirable trend in fly fishing techniques as perceived by the accepted experts. Our modern gurus fish many of these smaller, private trout fisheries regularly. Rarely at Damerham, Leominstead, Two Lakes, Avington, does one not see one or two personages of the trout fishing world.

And, almost without exception, they stood — or sat! — on one bank of a very small lake, casting their flies right across to the far bank before twitching them back. You do just that, and so do I; it is human nature to do so. But apart from covering more water per cast there is really very little advantage in it. The sort of gurus I'm talking about almost always chose a thirty-yard distant target so that they might faultlessly and effortlessly put their fly at the far extremity of the fly line — prodigious feats of casting ability and much admired by the populace at large. The gurus almost always caught their limit of four fish — but, then, so did almost every other angler — and mostly at the very end of the retrieve, with barely a yard or two of fly line outside the rod tip.

Fishing in New Zealand is, fortunately, a very much different activity, yet many anglers somehow think that prodigious distance casting is essential to success — and thereby miss the crux of the matter. The chances are that there are as many trout close under *your* bank as there are across that wide river. The ability to cast a long, accurate line will often be the key to success, but not always, and rarely essential to it. Some of the most consistently successful stillwater and stream fly fishers rarely have more than twenty or thirty feet of fly line extended beyond their rod tips. They have no need to cast prodigious distances. In fact, most long distance casters actually cast their flies over and beyond most of the fish, often putting down those close inshore in the process. Better to think of it as Oliver Kite did, not as a 'cast', but as a 'chuck'.

Comment is made elsewhere in these pages of the harm done by some current angling gurus in suggesting to less expert fly fishermen that anything less than quick limit bag achieved in an hour or two is tantamount to failure on the angler's part. Many such gurus are far less purist in their methods than their magazine articles and books suggest. And their wham-bang bag limits aren't quite as regular or quick as they would have the reader believe. This present chapter aims to counter the claim made by some current masters of the fly fishing scene that technique, and technique almost alone, is essential for success.

Far from giving an essay on *how* to fish, my present intention is rather to dispel gloom in those anglers who feel they can't, who feel (or feel they may have been made to feel) they are duffers.

If fly fishing for trout is not pure pleasure, then it is nothing. Despite guru pronouncements to the contrary, angling duffers enjoy their fishing far more than do the gurus. To start with they know that fishing is, or should be, a recreation, pure and simple. Think of that lovely word 'recreation' — 're-creation'. If *going* fishing isn't 're-creation' for you, then perhaps you may have missed the point of it all. As for the gurus' lack of enjoyment, I once in my early years in New Zealand asked an astute fishing friend just what sort of man so-and-so was — this being a leading guru in that country where, blessedly, there are but few fishing gurus. 'Well,' replied my friend, eyeing me thoughtfully, 'He's a man who seems to have declared war on trout.'

I just happen to be a totally addicted and passionate fly fisherman. But I, too, am a bungler. My casting is often terrible, inaccurate, sloppy. My flies find toi toi fronds and manuka and hawthorn snares with unfailing accuracy. Fishing in Britain my flies find equivalent snags in every overhanging tree, in every bush behind, with equal precision. I fall in, which might just as well because my waders leak anyway. I carry on my fishing person a thousand nymphs, dry flies, wet flies, but can never find a single one I'm sure I need. While trout fishing I get sunburned, bitten, wet, day-dreamy, while my companions fish with unfailing excellence and consummate ease. My fishing vest is full of spools of the best nylon monofilament, but never the breaking strain I sorely need. I get mad at my handicap of having to change from polaroids to reading glasses to tie on a fly, and often even then find it difficult. If it rains — when the heavens open — I discover that my neatly folded parka is back in the car four miles away, not in the capacious back pocket of my fishing vest, where it's supposed to be. These are not exaggerations, either, as any of my fishing companions would vouch.

But, neither would any of those same companions deny that I fish with a passionate and consuming joy, as much so as they do themselves.

Sometimes I even catch fish.

The beauty of being something of a known bungler is that it doesn't really matter whether one does or not. The important thing — the only important thing — is going fishing itself.

It isn't even that fishing itself is so important. As Robert Traver so wisely commented, 'I fish not because I regard fishing as being so terribly important but because I suspect that so many of the other concerns of men are equally unimportant — and not nearly so much fun'. Traver, a High Court Judge, believed of the trout fisherman that 'under his smiling coat of tan there often lurks a layer of melancholy and disillusion, a quiet awareness — and acceptance — of the fugitive quality of man and all his enterprises. If he must chase a will-o'-the-wisp he prefers that it be a trout. And so the fisherman fishes. It is at once an act of humility and small rebellion. And it is something more. To him his fishing is an island of reality in a world of dream and shadow.'

So, if you happen to be something of an occasional bungler, too, neither despair nor deplore it. Everything is relative. Join the club. It has some honourable members quite apart from Andrew Lang: Sir Humphry Davy, Robert Traver, Nick Lyons, Arnold Gingrich, Robert Bruce Lockhart, Ben Hur Lampman, Viscount Grey, Odell Shepard — to name but a few. And I've never ever heard of a passionate bungler who ever gave up fly fishing for trout.

While most of the fraternity positively idolize George LaBranche, and I accept that he wrote a penetrating and classic book, I still think what I most irreverently said of him at the beginning of this chapter — poor sod!

Chapter 10
Night Fishing

Few fly fishermen remain indifferent to night fishing or develop a take-it-or-leave-it attitude about it. Without exception, it seems, they either love night fishing or hate it. The reasons why this should be are not as straightforward as they first appear. Some such reasons have been examined in the chapter 'The Evening Rise', where it was seen that, for many anglers, what they called fishing the evening rise was no more than a trivial prelude to, and getting into position for the real business of night fishing.

Despite the fact that fishing for at least some hours of the night is perfectly legal, if not throughout it to the following dawn, night fishing has had a long and bad history almost everywhere of being associated with poaching and other malpractices. Such an idea no doubt horrifies many avid night-fishermen, many of whom are purists in their preference for fishing in total darkness.

Night fishing has been called many names, not all of them flattering: the black art, for one, suggesting an activity that should best be practised in the clear light of day, not when honest men should be in their beds. To better understand why such notions have come about we have to go back to seventeenth century England, to a time when so many other legends still affecting our lives today were born.

James Chetham, whose book *The Angler's Vade Mecum* was first published in London in 1681, had this to say of night angling:

> In the Night usually the best Trouts bite, and will rise ordinarily in the still Deeps; but no so well in the Streams. And although the best and largest Trouts bite in the Night, (being afraid to stir, or range about in the Daytime;) yet I account this way of Angling both unwhomson, unpleasant and very ungentiel, and to be used by none but Idle pouching Fellows. Therefore I shall say nothing of it, only describe how to lay Night Hooks; which, if you live close by a Riverside, or have a large Moat, or Pond at your own House, will not be unpleasant, sometimes to practice. But as for Damming, Groping, Spearing, Hanging, Twitcheling,

Netting, or Firing by Night, I purposely omit them, and them esteem to be used only by disorderly and rascally Fellows, for whom this little Treatise is not in the least intended.

That Chetham then goes on to describe in some detail sharp practices that would make the most arrant poacher blush for shame, seems neither here nor there: he had set the record straight by condemning night fishing out of hand. He wasn't alone in such beliefs. But as often as not the earlier angling writers' distaste for night fishing was as much based in their ignorance of the habits of trout, as on ethical considerations. The ethical disapprobation only crept in along with the dogma of the dry fly in the very late 1800s.

Another celebrated angler's vade mecum, this one *The Complete Angler's Vade-Mecum* by Captain T. Williamson was published in London in 1808. As the book was subtitled as *Being a Perfect Code of Instruction on the Above Pleasing Science*, there can be little doubt the good Captain felt sure of his factual knowledge. He had this to say:

Fishes in general do not seek food during the night, though in the very hot season of the year, when the sky happens to have been remarkably clear during the whole day, and especially towards sun-set, they will come on the feed during very late hours. Such must be considered as adventitious; for we may set it down as a rule, from which few exceptions will be found, that animals of every kind retire to rest as the day closes in; becoming more disposed to sleep than to eat.

It is likely, in the light of gentlemenly activities and way of life in 1808, that Williamson preferred a pre-prandial and post-prandial drink either side of a lavish dinner, and had little first-hand knowledge of what went on in the natural world outside his house during the hours of darkness. As to disinclination to fish at night, I must confess to having somewhat similar views. But Williamson chose not to fish at night because he believed the trout had retired to their rest. Strangely, however, he goes on to commend night lines baited with chicken guts or worms set out for eels *and* trout. Captain Williamson was a great believer in setting night lines and recommends they should be secured by means of attached bricks, rather than with stakes visible above the river surface, for although stakes are preferable to bricks in that they cannot be dragged about by eels and other large fish, 'they cannot be so well concealed; and, as all who lay night-lines are, to a certainty, watched by various classes of idlers, and especially by the professional fishermen, who cannot bear to see a fish but in their own nets, it is an object of some moment, to adopt such measures as may counteract the wiles of the vulgar.'

Recounting personal experience, Williamson continues:

I have often found my cord one or two hundred yards down the stream, with several eels and other fishes fast on my hooks; and sometimes I have had the mortification to find my whole apparatus laying on the shore; no doubt robbed by the fishermen, who watched my motions, and got up time enough to be before me.

Once indeed, I was eased altogether of my cord and lines, but had the satisfaction to learn, that the thief, who often gave cautious hints of his trick, was sent to display his dexterity to better purpose at Botany Bay.

Here we have a contemporary account of the sort of offence then punished by transportation to Australia.

Captain Williamson's sentiments suggest he was the sort of angler unwilling to expend too much energy in the pursuit of trout or any other fish. Not only did he draw the line on staying out late, but was equally averse to getting up in the mornings to see to his night-lines. The tradition, of course, was long established, and the unnecessary wasting of vital energies by overmuch physical activity, was not only frowned upon, but considered foolish.

Even Walton, the father of sport fishing, preferred to retire to a quiet inn before the end of day, to be entertained by a sweet serving wench throughout a sumptuous dinner, before sleeping in sweet lavender-scented sheets, rather than stay out fishing. Walton, too, shared that view of conserving one's vital energy for more important things. He may not have been as essentially practical about it as Captain Williamson, but still thought of it in this way:

> And now, Scholar, I think it will be time to repair to our Angle-rods, which we left in the water, to fish for themselves, and you shall chuse which shall be yours; and it is an even lay, one of them catches.
>
> And let me tell you, this kind of fishing with a dead rod, and laying night-hooks, are like putting money to Use, for they both work for the Owners, when they do nothing but sleep, or eat, or rejoyce; as you know we have done this last hour, and sate as quietly and as free from cares under this Sycamore, as Virgils Tityrus and his Meliboeus did under their broad Beech-tree: No life, my honest Scholar, no life so happy and so pleasant, as the life of a well governed Angler; for when the Lawyer is swallowed up with business, and the Statesman is preventing or contriving plots, then we sit on Cowslip-banks, hear the birds sing, and possess our selves in as much quietness as these silent silver streams, which we now see glide so quietly by us. Indeed my good Scholar, we may say of Angling, as Dr Boteler said of Strawberries, Doubtless God could have made a better berry, but doubtless God never did: And so (if I might be Judge) God never did make a more calm, quiet, innocent recreation than Angling.

Walton, of course, was an angler of the day, not the night. He nevertheless knew more about the trout's habits than Captain Williamson, even though *The Complete Angler* preceded Williamson's book by 150 years. Despite current views to the contrary, men don't necessarily or always grow wiser or more knowledgeable in succeeding generations. Plagiarized or not, Walton had a better knowledge of trout behaviour:

> You are to know, there is night as well as day-fishing for a Trout, and that, in the night, the best Trouts come out of their holes: And the manner of taking them, is on the top of the water with a great Lob or Garden-worm, or rather two, which you are to fish with it in a place where the waters run somewhat quietly (for in a stream the bait will not be so well discerned.) I say in a quiet or dead place near to some swift, there draw your bait over the top of the water to and fro, and if there be a good Trout in the hole, he will take it, especially if the night be dark: for then he is bold and lies near the top of the water, watching the motion of any Frog or Water-rat or Mouse that swims betwixt him and the skie; these he hunts after, if he sees the water but wrinkle, or move in one of these dead holes, where these great old Trouts usually lie near to their

holds: for you are to note, that the great old Trout is both subtil and fearful, and lies close all day, and does not usually stir out of his hold, but lies in it as close in the day, as the timorous Hare does in her form: for the chief feeding of either is seldom in the day, but usually in the night, and then the great Trout feeds very boldly.

Having said that, old Izaak continues with more detailed instructions, but admits to a personal distaste for night fishing:

And you must fish for him with a strong Line, and not a little hook; and let him have time to gorge your hook, for he does not usually forsake it, as he oft will in the day fishing: and if the night be not dark, then Fish so with an Artificial flie of a light-colour, and at the snap: nay, he will sometimes rise at a dead Mouse, or a piece of cloth, or any thing, that seems to swim cross the water, or to be in motion: this is a choice way, but I have not oft used it, because it is void of the pleasures, that such days as these, that we two now enjoy, afford an Angler.

Walton, then, got all the kind of fishing he wanted, during the day, but was well aware of those big Trouts that bite best on the blackest of nights. His sentiments tend to be repeated in this day and age, not by those anglers who have a lust to catch more and bigger fish, but by those who value most the quality of their fishing, and of the peripheral delights arising from it.

By the mid-19th century, many of the earlier attitudes to angling were undergoing change due to personal persuasion and a growing belief that fish were not simply provided by a bountiful God to be slaughtered by men in obscene numbers. An early glimmer of this came in Francis Francis' *A Book of Angling* (1867), 'I will now give a few simple and useful directions as to night-fishing,' wrote Francis, as if to spare the reader from what was to come, or at least lead him into it somewhat gently:

But I may premise that I wish night-fishing were generally abandoned, for I believe it materially injures the day fishing, by rendering the fish much more shy than they would naturally be if only fished for in the day-time. There ought to be some period during the twenty-four hours when the trout can feed safely without disturbance or the fear of a hook before them; but as fly-fishing is now conducted there is not; and this naturally makes the fish suspicious of every lure, while big trout get so shy that they seldom, in small streams, get into really good condition at all.

Williamson's Vade Mecum and Francis' Book were separated by a mere fifty-odd years, yet they seem to have been written a thousand years apart and on different planets.

The ascendancy of the dry fly and the formalized rules that with it, soon brought about a change in most places to prohibit night fishing as being unethical, but the prohibition was really an attempt to curb poaching on increasingly stringently preserved waters. Do not forget that, despite the subsequent dogma, dry fly fishing came about to make the catching of trout, at least on some waters, easier. As a result many lucrative fisheries were being overfished. The rules and regulations had to be tightened: even the syndicate members had to be made to catch fewer fish: The *cult* of the dry fly was, in part, at least, to do just that in a gentlemanly fashion. Night fishing was one of the first prohibitions. It was deemed right and proper, and quite ethical, to fish the evening rise; but to fish only for rising trout, and to use the exact floating imitation of the natural on which the fish happened to be feeding at the time. Even more importantly, it was considered imperative — either by prohibition, if not by ethical conviction — for the angler to cease fishing at once when he could no longer see his artificial fly on the water.

It is interesting to note that when trout and trout fishing were established in New Zealand the prohibitions regarding night fishing (where they did exist, or as they crept into legislation) were formulated in order to help curb excessive poaching — not because of ethical considerations. Jumping ahead some hundred years in New Zealand fishing, the same criterion exists to this day.

There, as the demand for angling grew, the *ad hoc* imposition of restrictive regulations imposed by the multitude of regulatory bodies became layered one on top of the other — often imposed as a purely local measure for no better reason than it seemed to be a good idea at the time. There was little or no consistency in the regulations themselves, or about what they were supposed to achieve. Generally speaking, throughout New Zealand, there has always been a tendency for restrictions to increase progressively from the south to the north. In the extreme south there have been few restrictrions on method, but in the North Island a large proportion of waters have been reserved for fly fishing, although this, too, is presently undergoing change.

Throughout the hundred or so years of trout fisheries management in New Zealand there has been considerable emphasis on restrictive regulations — size limits, bag limits, seasonal limits, methods of fishing, permissible artificial flies and lures, even baits — but little concerning the duration of the permitted fishing day, or whether there was any need for a restriction of the hours when fishing was legal. It would seem that such restrictions as do exist — say, those of the Taupo fishery, where fishing is permitted only between 5 a.m. and 11 p.m. — were imposed as a deterrent to the nefarious practice of poaching, in that rangers would be more active during the day and early evening. Presumably the regulation was based on the supposition that *anyone* abroad on the rivers and lakes between 11 p.m. and 5 a.m. was up to no good. In actual fact, of course, it took away from the scene, at precisely 11 p.m., all good and honest anglers, and left the field clear and safe for the most blatant poachers. As a deterrent to poachers and poaching, it was a poor one — poorly thought out and poorly executed.

How did this state of affairs come about? After all, trout and trout fishing were well established in the more liberal South Island long before the North. Was it as a result of Government intervention in controlling at least some of the subsequently established trout fisheries? Was it as a result of bureaucratic method and attitudes — a sort of early 20th century glide time? Many recent commentators, particularly fisheries research scientists (themselves no strangers to bureaucratic processes) have suggested it was more to do with anglers themselves, and selfish attitudes that sought to preserve and promote strict fly fishing only, as being more sporting than the open slather of the deep South. Yet, even the most cursory acquaintance with South Island fishing attitudes and ethics throughout the period in question shows it to have been far more generally purist than was common in the North Island — and as for permissible methods of angling, merely more tolerant and less bigoted. One hardly needs to look far in the central North Island to discover that much of the supposedly pure fly fishing ethic is little more than lip-service to the regulations, and nothing to do with anglers' personal fishing ethics.

It isn't as if central North Island trout fishermen were averse to night fishing on ethical grounds, because they flocked to the stream mouths to fish until

11 p.m., and only reluctantly packed up even then. It certainly wasn't, and isn't now, a conservation measure. If it is a measure of anything at all, it is an arbitrary hour picked upon as being appropriate for honest men to be home in bed. It only goes to show the folly of over-regulation and the absurdity of trying to explain it away on purely ethical or management grounds.

If someone owns both the waterway and the fish, as is the case, say, on the Broadlands trout fishery on a carrier stream of the River Test I used to fish, the fishery owner can impose any restrictions he likes, mostly for security reasons and to conserve the fish stocks. Fishing there was permitted from 10 a.m. to an hour after sunset but, because the fishermen were paying well for the privilege, it tended to be loosely interpreted. In any case, it included inside its limits a long enough angling day, enough for any reasonable and well-adjusted man.

Of course, it's only a matter of personal preference. In New Zealand, fishing as I do some of the high country streams of the central North Island and rarely nowadays much further afield, I get all the fishing I have the stamina for between the time of getting to the riverside after a 7 a.m. breakfast at home in Taupo, and a general (if not fixed) desire to get home in time for a dry martini or a Scotch or two before dinner at a civilized hour. Critics will say that's all well and good for someone who lives in Taupo and doesn't have to restrict his fishing to holiday times, or snatched days on occasional weekends, and these are valid points. Nevertheless, the vast majority of Taupo-style aficionados of the dusk to 11 p.m. brigade of fly fishermen in the rips of streams entering the lake live here, too. And, often, that's why they live here.

This night fishing must be even more of a disease than day fishing. It seems to spoil a man for day fishing, what's more; but there must be more in it than the frequent big bags of trout often taken after dark.

To the real night fisherman, the chief attraction lies in the dark mystery of it. The dean of night fishermen, L. James Bashline, devoted an entire and very good book to the black art. To Bashline, and to countless hundreds of thousands of dedicated night fishermen spread around the earth, it is the acme and the peak of fly fishing experience.

They must be more tactile than most of us, doing things more by feel and intuition and other senses. We lesser mortals get hung-up on the backcast even on fine, bright, clear days; have difficulties enough wading rivers when every boulder on the bottom is clearly visible; have problems enough tying on a fly or changing a leader tippet in bright daylight, let alone Stygian darkness. There must be something, too, about the companionships of night fishing, for night fishermen rarely fish alone, whereas day fishermen mostly long to be alone and have the preferred stretch of river or the pool to themselves. Bashline called the fraternity 'The Night Watch':

> The sun was down. The light which illuminated the huge clock in the court house steeple was turned on. From several directions came figures carrying fly rods, already strung up, with jiggling wet-fly droppers dancing in cadence with each step. For this group the evening meal was over, any important worries had been laid aside for tomorrow, the important business was coming up.

Such was Bashline's conversion to night fishing, he calls the chosen river place 'the shrine' and his fellow fly fishermen of the night 'the disciples'. Certain artificial flies are referred to as having 'mystical significance':

Fishing after dark has an aura of mystic charm. Nighttime adventures always seem to offer an extra bit of excitement and flavor — and so it is for the after-dark angler . . . Not all fishermen have that extra unexplainable compulsion to seek their prey at night. It's a tough game that will never draw a horde of followers. The dedicated night man is a trophy fisherman. He fishes for the love of the game, and he seeks only to sink his hook into a fish capable of putting a bend of consequence into his rod.

An interesting point about night fishing I came across recently in re-reading a noted American angling book was that the practice of night fishing arose in the United States during the earlier decades of this century because the acclimatized brown trout in the streams of the eastern states had driven out the native American brook trout, and the browns proved so hard to catch, the only means of getting them was under the cover of a dark night. As always, most new or changed directions in fly fishing are designed to make it easier to catch trout, not to make it more difficult.

W. H. Spackman, author of New Zealand's first angling book (1892) records that 'Trout fishing is allowed during the whole twenty-four hours, as during the greater part of the summer the large trout are seldom caught in the day time except in rapid water.' But Spackman, too, was aware of the frustrations and disappointments of night fishing:

One can never say at what particular hour the trout will feed by night, the last hour of day and the first before the dawn being generally found the best, but at any moment the feeding-time may begin, often without any apparent reason. Frequently on a summer night as many as twenty or thirty rods will be engaged on this particular stretch of river (the Selwyn) for hours without one of them getting a run; yet hundreds of fish must have seen the bullhead or inanga, and refused it. Three of four hours of this will choke off most of the fishermen; but an enthusiast or two, with true Sassenach consistency, will fish on in hopes of something which will gladden their hearts. Sometimes it comes, and then two or three great trout will be taken in an hour, weighing, more, perhaps, than he can conveniently carry; or that something wanted may not come at all — hungry, and weary, and sleepless, and fishless, he sees the dawn breaking over the everlasting hills, and, anathematizing the wretch who invented all-night fishing, vows that he has been made a fool of over it for the last time.

But, in the end, once hooked on it, the fishers of the night always go back to it, succumbing once again to its subtle charms. Among present-day New Zealand angling writers, Keith Draper, a master, all-round angler, with an all-round point of view, puts it thus:

Of all angling times, night is the most productive. Large trout which have been uncooperative all day long move into the shallows or the slow glides at the tail of the pool where they begin steadily to feed. During the hours of darkness many a large trout, proven almost impossible to take during the hours of daylight, has been caught. Angling statistics the whole world over show this is to be an indisputable fact.

Large sea-trout which have been nervous and timid all through the day will readily fall victim to a carefully presented fly during the hours of deep darkness. The large cannibal trout in his deep river hole will remain indifferent to all manner of baits and lures during daylight but will take a properly presented lure or bait after dark, often smashing the angler's tackle in the process. Schools of lake-dwelling trout will move into a bay or stream mouth after dark, feeding excitedly as they go, falling easy prey to the angler's fly.

. . . I like night-fishing, though I realise there are many who just can't stand it. There are many who claim they can make quite enough tangles during the hours of daylight without compounding their troubles through lack of light. Besides anglers who have this very legitimate reason, there are those for whom the night holds no charm whatever and they see little profit in fishing in a sea of inky darkness where any spells of inactivity are unrelieved by the prospect of at least scenery of passing interest. To yet others, the night is a time of deep-seated and unconscious fear to be avoided at all times.

I feel myself that night-fishing has a charm all of its own and that the cool all-enveloping darkness is a luxury to be delighted in, especially after a long hot summer's day. I am not referring here to the deepening twilight with colour-shot sunsets which is in itself a thing of absolute beauty and wonder — this is the time of the evening rise — a moment of sometimes brief and hectic activity. The real angling rewards come later when complete darkness has enveloped the countryside and the mad frenzy of the last minutes of light is replaced by the steady solid feeding of the trout.

Later on Keith Draper turns to an essential component of success:

Much of a night fisherman's skill lies in his fingers. The sense of touch is tuned to a considerable degree by years of practice, with the result that every movement of the line is felt. Any change in pressure or drag tells when the line is being swept through the current or when the fly is loitering in the edge eddies of a stream.

On many occasions no tug will tell you your fly has been taken. An indefinable something tells you that the swim of your fly has altered and that an immediate strike is called for. What has happened is that a patrolling trout has taken your fly and continued swimming towards you. No tug could possibly be felt as the line draws in a bow behind the fish and this causes an alteration in the tension between the line and your fingertips. In these circumstances you must pull in line until you come firm and then strike, because the fly has only been lightly pulled into the corner of the trout's mouth by the bow in the line. When struck, these fish immediately surge into action and, since the pull of the line is from behind, they take off in the opposite direction, towards you. Such situations are very tricky as many of these fish are only pricked. At the first firm pull of the line they panic, and unless you can tighten immediately and drive the hook in, there is every chance of them jumping and ridding themselves of the cause of their fright. Many anglers of no great experience in night angling (or indeed day angling for that matter) seldom realise this fact.

W. H. Lawrie, that wise and knowledgeable Scot, when writing *The Truth about Trout Fishing* under the pseudonym of Arnold B. Scott in order, one suspects, to be slightly shocking, commented that the tradition that night fishing is in the nature of an abomination has persisted to the present day, and that today's main objectors are:

1. Those who are so fond of the comforts of the couch of repose — and this includes all anglers who have themselves been caught in the matrimonial snare — that they cannot or will not abandon them.
2. Those who are afraid of 'things that go bump in the night.'
3. Those who fumble in the dark, have no 'hands', and whose other senses have more or less degenerated.
4. Those who have never fished at night and on that score feel qualified to condemn night fishing severely as an unsporting method.
5. Those who would not condemn night fishing if the method did not produce such disgustingly big baskets of over-size trout.
6. Those charitable souls who imagine that all deeds done in the dark are necessarily shady deeds.
7. Angling authors who desire to maintain a reputation for respectability.
8. Publishers of fishing books who dislike dangerous originality from those who are idiotic enough to write fishing books.
9. Dyed-in-the-wool Poachers who dislike the presence of dyed-in-the-wool anglers.
10. River-keepers who imagine that every night fisher is a salmon poacher in disguise.
11. Village Constables who imagine that all nocturnal sportsmen are burglars in disguise.

But Lawrie was quite serious about his beliefs as well being humorous about them:

Notwithstanding such universal condemnation, let it be stated truthfully, fearlessly and frankly that night fishing, particularly night fishing with fly, is a clean and skilful and exciting pursuit, a highly profitable one, possessed of its own strange charm and appeal and demanding abilities and senses such as are never dreamed of by the fearful, the feckless, the feeble, the fiddlers, the fuddlers and the fogies. Night fishing has been cruelly misrepresented, libelled and slandered and very widely misunderstood . . . There are many to whom night fishing will never appeal, but that is no reason for condemning a method of fishing available for those who enjoy it, and still less is there justification for ignorant derision. In fishing there is much of faith, still more of hope and all too often precious little of charity, which is surprising as we are told that it is the greatest virtue of the three.

That famed American angler-author, Sparse Grey Hackle, alias Alfred W. Miller, dean of American fly fishing authors and Boswell of the purist fraternity, had this to say, almost hidden away in the delightful pages of his own book, *Fishless Days, Angling Nights*, revealing a different view. Describing an occasion of night fishing, we find him casting a big black wet fly, albeit upstream. But he was doing so because of the magic of night fishing:

I unhooked and returned him — gently, because I was grateful to him for providing a little action; stowed away my flashlight and felt for my pipe.

Only then did I realize that my heart was pounding slowly and heavily, like a burned-out main bearing.

That is night fishing, the essence of angling, the emperor of sports. It is a gorgeous gambling game in which one stakes the certainty of long hours of faceless fumbling, nerve-racking starts, frights, falls, and fishless baskets against the off-chance of hooking into — not landing necessarily or even probably, but hooking into — a fish as long and heavy as a railroad tie and as unmanageable as a runaway submarine. It combines the wary stalking and immobile patience of an Indian hunter with sudden, violent action, the mystery and thrill of the unknown, a stimulating sense of isolation and self-reliance, and an unparalleled opportunity to be close to nature since most creatures are really nocturnal in habit.

As I sit here writing these last words of this chapter, the sun is setting over the hill to my right beyond my study window. To my left, through another long, tall window, I can see the still sunlit waters of Lake Taupo, within a few minutes' walk of where I sit writing. There is bright sunlight over the waters of the lake, but beyond them, several miles eastward of the far shore, there are massive rainclouds building up over the Kaimanawa peaks as dusk approaches.

I haven't fished at night proper for a very long time but, having written what I've written this afternoon, shall I succumb to the call of the approaching night and take my fly rod and go to a little stream mouth that slides, rather than tumbles, into the lake not ten minutes drive away, or shall I be slothful and fearful and feeble and fiddling and fuddling and fogie-like, and simply join my wife who is waiting for me in the living room, to mix a couple of dry martinis for us to sip while we talk about the events of our day before eating dinner?

Tomorrow night perhaps? The view across Lake Taupo is even more dramatic now, with ruddy reddish glows of the departed sun reflected on the massing rainclouds across the lake. But the view from the living room is even better, so I think I shall end this now and sit there, sipping my martini, watching the storm clouds gathering as darkness comes on, telling myself there's always tomorrow night to go fishing.

Chapter 11
Catch and Release

Catch and release in trout fishing is an emotive issue in the United States. In recent years it has become that way in New Zealand. Now certain voices in Britain are speaking up for and against its practice in fly fishing. In many other angling practices — upstream or down, wet or dry fly, nymph or streamer, floating or sinking lines, gently twitched retrieves or savage stroke-hauling hard enough to pull off a fish's head — remain very much a matter of personal choice and preference, although some are regulations imposed by the controllers of the water being fished. While often strongly held as matters of conviction as well as preference they do not as a rule inflame passions. For various reasons the matter of catch and release does, and few fly fishermen seem able to remain indifferent about it.

So far, in Britain, it has hardly raised more than a ripple from certain quarters. Many trout fisheries specifically own the trout for which their clients fish, and they transfer that right of ownership to the angler who fairly and squarely catches and lands that fish according to the rules of the particular water. The trout, then, is a commodity to be caught but once, then killed and subsequently eaten. That is the object of the exercise and the reward for success. Nevertheless, the issue of catch and release is growing and will not go away.

In the United States, where catch and release did not necessarily begin, the practice has become codified in recent years in a manner ranging from dogma to just plain common sense. In many waters, it came to be recognized that a trout was too valuable a commodity to be caught only once. But this mostly stemmed from the changing mores and fly fishing philosophies of certain groups of American fly fishermen, rather than as a result of practical deliberations by fishery managers, who tend to regard trout in much the same way as other renewable resources such as crops.

Even before commencing this examination of catch and release in trout fishing it is necessary to remind ourselves of a few salient points. It was not invented in the United States by Trout Unlimited only a few years ago, although that admirable body of fishermen have done much to publicize and spread their gospel far and wide. Catch and release has been practised in one form or another, not always effectively, for as long as men have fished with rod and line. Food gatherers and sportsmen have long practised the release of fish too small for, or in excess of their needs. They were put back to grow bigger, and to be there for another day. This would have entailed safe release, so that the fish would not die. And this depended largely on the size of hook and bait, and how deeply the fish had engorged it. It also depended on the care and skill of the fisherman.

Long before angling degenerated into the rigid divisions of game and coarse fishing, men would catch and release 'unwanted' species without any specific thoughts of the superiority of one species of fish over another. As the varieties of coarse fish actually used as food lessened over the years (largely one feels because of changing eating habits) more and more unwanted fish were being returned to the water. Any reading of Izaak Walton shows that he and his friends (and remember he came from the more affluent and cultured end of society) enjoyed a dish of chub as much as any fish. According to Walton the art lay in the dressing and the cooking:

> Look you Sir, there is a tryal of my skill, there he is, that very Chub that I shewed you with the white spot on his tail: and I'le be as certain to make him a good dish of meat, as I was to catch him: I'le now lead you to an honest Ale-house where we shall find a cleanly room, Lavender in the Windows, and twenty Ballads stuck about the wall; there my Hostess (which I may tell you, is both cleanly and handsome and civil) hath drest many a one for me, and shall now dress it after my fashion, and I warrant it good meat.

When Walton issues any doubts about eating certain species at all, it is only to do with size. On the subject of pike he has this to say:

> But if this direction to catch a Pike thus, do you no good, yet I am certain this direction how to roast him when he is caught, is choicely good, for I have tryed it, and it is somewhat the better for not being common, but with my direction you must take this Caution, that your Pike must not be a small one, that is, it must be more than half a Yard, and should be bigger.

Then follows a detailed recipe for the baking of the pike, using sweet-marjoram, winter-savoury, pickled oysters, anchovies, sweet butter, mace, claret, oranges, garlic. Roasted according to Izaak Walton's instructions, 'This dish of meat is too good for any but Anglers or very honest men; and I trust, you will prove both, and therefore I have trusted you with this secret.'

The Complete Angler, while not a 17th-century cookery book, does at least give some clues as to why 'coarse' fish were to become neglected for the table. Instant food may have taken a further three hundred years to catch popular usage but people, it seems, even in Walton's day, were starting to be always in a hurry: 'But first I will tell you how to make this Carp that is so curious to be caught, so curious a dish of meat, as shall make him worth all your labour and patience; and though it is not without some trouble and charges, yet it will recompence both.' Here, too, follows a detailed account of how to cook him.

In similar vein Walton goes on to extol the culinary delights of tench, perch, eels, lampreys, grayling, minnows, as well as trout. Fishing was fishing in those days. But they fished with unfailing zeal and, even if they didn't practise catch and release as such, they did at least at times return unwanted, immature, or out of condition fish back to the water. No doubt many such fish died. Nature, we know, was bountiful in those days.

It was the development and charm and refinements and sheer artistic pleasure of fly fishing that brought about change. Trout, together with only a few other species, were the fish that avidly took the anglers' artificial flies. Trout caught on small artificial flies were lip hooked; easily, quickly, and safely released without any apparent injury and none at all if done with efficiency and dexterity. Increasingly, there was more point in releasing trout rather than gullet hooked fish of other species that would probably die anyway. In the same way that trout were the perfect fish for fly fishing, so too were they the perfect fish for releasing unharmed. Nowhere was this practised more than in those places where anglers fished as much for sport as for food. The trout, however, was in an awkward situation because its flesh was generally held to be the best of all fish for food, requiring simple cooking, not needing Walton's additional thirty oysters, anchovies, garlic, bottle of claret, and handfuls of various herbs and spices in its preparation. The trout, instead, provided the nearest thing to an instant breakfast or supper: not many minutes in the ubiquitous frying pan and it was a dish fit for a king.

What perhaps finally made the absolute division between eating game fish and not eating coarse fish arrived as a result of the Industrial Revolution. Pollution spread wherever the factories and mines and iron works belched forth their toxic smoke and poisonous gases, and spewed their foul wastes into the rivers of Britain. Before such massive pollution and rapid degradation of the rivers trout and salmon ranged everywhere, because there was clean, clear fast water and suitable spawning grounds almost everywhere throughout Britain. But trout and salmon are sensitive monitors of water purity and could no longer live in waterways where some other species, if not flourished, then survived after a blighted and tenuous fashion. Such fish were eagerly fished for, but were no longer eaten as food. Hatters may have gone mad from their ingestion of mercury compounds, but had trout and salmon been able to survive in waters polluted by such effluents, and had people other than hatters gone on eating them, then half the population of these islands would have gone mad.

The result was that, as a direct result of the Industrial Revolution, catch and release became universally practised insofar as coarse fish were concerned, but totally abandoned in the case of game fish. Trout and salmon suddenly became too valuable — despite that old story about apprentices going on strike because they were forced to eat salmon five days a week. Thus catch and release, which came into its own as a viable alternative directly as a result of fly fishing for trout and salmon, soon came to be no longer practised except for those species people couldn't eat anyway.

No one, to the best of my knowledge, ever actually used the words catch and release until the American organization Trout Unlimited began to preach that gospel. Something doesn't necessarily only begin to exist after someone else gives a name to it, but nowadays, especially in matters to do with angling, one might think this to be the case. We seem to live in an age of namers, of people who go around putting tags and labels on everything, often claiming that they invented it. In America, where catch and release in trout fishing actually started as a named activity or policy, it is clearly meant to be a desirable and suitable fly fishing practice to be used on some designated waters — usually fragile ones as far as the continuance of trout fishing is concerned, where the trout population is not merely under threat but doomed to extinction unless something radical is done to change the process. Such a situation may occur whether stocking is carried out or not, and is invariably caused by gross overfishing. Its opponents argued that, particularly in state Fish and Game areas, the present populations of trout — whether browns, rainbows, or even brook trout — were placed in those streams and lakes in order to provide sport for bona fide anglers, and that (whether one entirely agrees with it or not) the destiny of such fish is to be caught and killed and subsequently eaten by anglers. Certainly, many parts of the United States still have viable and established self-sustaining trout populations not requiring man's intervention in order to maintain adequate fishing, but would be wrong to think of it as being a vast wilderness of wild and unspoiled rivers and lake systems, teeming with wild and lovely trout avid to take the first fisherman's fly. But the view of America, particularly from certain quarters in Britain, tends to be a stereotyped one — in much the same way as the reverse is true *via-à-vis* a certain type of American's view of Britain.

Today, in some of the British angling press, there is much nonsense talked about the threat of catch and release being exported lock, stock and barrel for imposition in Britain whether it is logical or not, whether it is fair or not, and whether it is necessary or not. It is true that some converts to the cause of catch and release in America do come across with all the fervour of religious bigots. One thing is probably certain: there is far too much uninformed and overstated opinion about it on both sides, particularly from those who fear their often easy and killing fishing is threatened by a bunch of dooleys.

Like most misunderstood ideas this one is a real minefield for the unwary. It is not a simple universal issue. There is no particular right or wrong. It is far from being a simple fisheries management tool to extend the working, useful lives of trout, enabling them to be caught and caught again until, eventually, they die in contented old age. The issue is meaningful in so many different ways to so many people; it involves questions of ethics, vegetarianism, the charge of cruelty in angling, economic management and necessity, religious ordinances, greed, selfishness, value for money, people's rights, fair play. You name it, somewhere the discussion will lead in all manner of unexpected directions. Some people, on the other hand, are convinced the whole thing is a non-issue; not just dead, but non-existent. One thing seems fairly certain. Whatever happens, it won't simply go away.

Before we consider how and in what fashion this 'new' dogma has reached Britain it might be as well to examine its earlier impact in other countries where trout fishing is taken very seriously, as well as to look at what its advocates are really trying to say and do. Having only recently returned to live in Britain after ten years of life and thirty years of fishing in New Zealand, in addition to a wide variety of fishing in North America, from steelhead and rainbow, as well as salmon fishing from Alaska down through British Columbia to the Pacific Northwest states of the USA, and other places, I feel a sense of *déjà vu* in arriving back in Britain at this time.

In an earlier book, *The New Zealand Encyclopaedia of Fly Fishing* published in Auckland in 1988, I wrote this in the section Catch and Release, although much else was said about it under other entries. I take the liberty of quoting it here because the book is not generally available in Britain:

Catch and Release
A contentious issue in New Zealand at present, and one that causes hackles to rise. There are many who defend the angler's almost God-

given right to go out and catch and kill fish up to the allowable limit. Other anglers view the present situation as impossible to continue; that unless restraints are imposed by edict or personal conviction — and soon at that — trout fishing, as we know it, is doomed.

Slogans abound: A trout is much too valuable to be caught only once; trout are a self-renewing exploitable resource; to release trout after capture is cruelty in itself: either they should be killed and eaten, or the angler should not be fishing in the first place — that, quite apart from needlessly tormenting poor fish, he plays God in releasing them after their ordeal, instead of dispatching them cleanly with a sharp blow on the top of the head. All good gutsy emotive stuff, but unlikely to assist any but the extreme believers on both sides.

Looked at as factually as is possible, there seems no doubt that there is far too much mindless slaughter and unnecessary killing of trout in New Zealand today. That it has gone on since trout fishing began here, is no justification in itself that it should continue, as seems to be a much heard argument, despite the capacious maw of the family deep-freeze. But in that respect it is difficult to believe that any more than a small fraction of the trout one sees being carted away from our rivers ever even get as far as the deep-freeze, often hundreds of miles away.

Many people liken fishing itself to man's primitive urge to hunt: to hunt, not only for food as such, but even more importantly to satisfy a basic urge that should not be too much repressed, as our modern way of life tends to do. This argument is really saying that the true hunter is more interested in the kill than he is in the act of hunting itself; that the kill itself is of more significance and should not be trifled with, or denied.

If that sounds too ridiculous to be true then consider the committed Christian attitude — fundamentalist to be sure, but still advanced as being provable by biblical authority — that man is lord of creation and that the fishes were created for his purposes. By this argument it can be said that an angler is not only justified in killing his entire catch, but furthermore should do so in order to avoid inflicting cruelty and playing with one of God's creatures.

But what of the advocates of Catch and Release? To start with, much of the debunking one hears these days, is that what it says is that *all* fish caught anywhere by whatever method should be released back into the water unharmed. That this is not so should be obvious. Trout caught by legal trolling methods in such a place as Lake Taupo obviously ought not to be released in order to comply with Catch & Release philosophies. To begin with they are more or less dead anyway having been hooked at 5 knots and towed around at the end of 100 yards of wire or lead line, then unceremoniously dragged into the boat. Secondly there seems little point in fishing for trout by such means in the first place unless the object is to kill and eat them. Most importantly, a vast lake and self-sustaining fishery like Taupo can withstand the sort of trolling fishing pressure it gets, provided that the regulations are not broken — and even does good by culling what might become over-population.

The Catch and Release principle is an entirely different matter when applied to year-round permissible fishing — including spinning — on small and comparatively frail streams like the Rangitaiki which tend to support small populations of average to rather better than average fish, all competing for dwindling food supplies due to forestry, run-offs, pesticides, pollution and the like. In once remote wilderness rivers such as the Rangitikei, upper Mohaka, Ngaruroro, etc — once truly wilderness experiences but now only twenty minutes by aircraft or helicopter from that same Lake Taupo — the rivers support small populations of larger than average fish that are far from being a seasonably renewable resource to be exploited like a crop. Herein lies the difference, and herein lies the heart of the matter of Catch and Release.

We live in an age of buzzwords, so shouldn't be too surprised that they have crept into fly fishing, although I can't help but feel that such jargon puts more people off than their use attracts. 'Limit your kill — Not kill your limit' is one such much bandied around expression, although it is direct and honest as well as being both sensible and essential advice.

In any case it is a good thing and good for a fly fisherman's soul (especially if he presses down the barbs of his dry flies and nymphs) to release *all* of the trout he catches in such places, and *most* of the trout he catches elsewhere.

Fisheries scientists often advance ideas less to do with straightforward scientific truth than with complying with the wishes of their political or bureaucratic masters in telling them what they want to hear. In any case, science never was especially noted for its monopoly of wisdom.

Dr McDowall subscribes to the idea that much of catch and release is sheer snobbery, encouraged by anglers who have so much time to fish and catch so many that they are sick of eating trout, never liked it anyway, or wouldn't know what to do with the fish if they kept them.

Somewhat tempering such a view he admits — uncomfortably, one feels — that catch and release can be a useful management tool, or where there are small populations of very large, very old fish. He stretches the egalitarian bit by saying that only overseas tourists or wealthy New Zealanders can afford to fly in to these headwaters for the fishing experience of a lifetime, and — unless these small populations of large trophy fish are preserved by catch and release — disaster lies ahead in the collapse of a little industry. He states that, in such cases, it is the fishing guides who take anglers into such wilderness rivers who insist on releasing all the trout their clients catch, or allow them to kill one for the taxidermist, and others only sufficient to eat at the camp — presumably as being an essential part of the total wilderness experience. This, he argues with some truth, is not for altruistic or conservational reasons, but simply to foster the continuance and preservation of their business by providing money over and over again in catching the same trout over and over again.

Dare I suggest it's not really like that at all: the sort of (mostly American) anglers who do helicopter in to such places with professional New Zealand fishing guides have long been catch and release fly fishermen by total conviction; not by imposition. More than one American angler has told me of their horror on discovering that guides themselves want to bring out dead fish — at least that some do; and enough to give their numbers a blemished name. Another point is that catch and release — as a matter of conviction — is much practised by many New Zealand anglers who are neither snobs, nor wealthy, as Dr McDowall has suggested.

Catch and release should be a state of mind. It should be a matter of getting an angler's priorities right; of sorting out the real reasons for going fishing in the first place. Of course it can be regulated by imposition but, like bag and size limits imposed by regulations, they only affect honest fishermen who willingly abide by such decrees. Catch and release should be practised by total conviction, in the places where it usually is, when the fly fisherman is quite alone.

That was written a few years ago from an informed but passionately held view of how things stood in New Zealand at that particular time. Not a great deal has changed since then, except that I'd guess more and more New Zealand trout fishermen would subscribe to that view. At about the time I wrote those words the American organization Trout Unlimited Inc. was fairly active in New Zealand. Whether it was necessary or not — and my personal view was that it wasn't — their activities bore all the hallmarks of international junkets. Apart from the choice fishing, there were dinners and speeches and presentations of plaques and scrolls honouring the efforts of the recipients, most of whom had probably never even heard of catch and release a few months earlier and weren't known exponents of the rite to those who knew their style and philosophy of fishing. This is not to say that all the professional fishing guides, fishing lodge operators, and private quite unprofessional fly fishermen, who either joined the association or subscribed to it by lip service, were all bandwagoning — but many of them, I suspect, were. The trouble about such eminently and seemingly respectable and purer than pure, whiter than white organizations with worldwide aspirations, is that they make enormous appeal to people whose main aim is to find a bandwagon on which to climb and hitch a lift somewhere in the direction of bureaucratic authority and, eventually, power. In some fishing circles in New Zealand at that time the prospect was both fashionable and desirable. It seemed to hold the promise of membership in at least half a dozen quangos that would, in due course, be appointed by Government and Government agencies. Blanket support of the principles involved came from some scientific and fisheries research bodies, as well as from some acclimatisation societies, tourist boards, fishing lodge owners, the professional guides association, to say nothing of the fishing tackle industry, and parliamentarians looking for votes as well as committees on which to sit. But there was no guts to it, and no clear sincerity or conviction. Yet, for eight years past, I had fished extensively throughout New Zealand, and particularly in the marvellous fishing waters of the volcanic plateau of the central North Island where I lived at Taupo, with a number of fellow anglers who were members of none of those causes yet had long practised catch and release as a matter of total conviction because it seemed the best and only basically honourable way of going fishing in the more fragile and lonely places where we loved to fish. If anyone wanted to catch a few trout to eat there were many places around the shores of Lake Taupo itself where generally, at the right time, a fish or two was to be got. And, during the winter run of rainbows up the Tongariro River — provided one could stand the crowds of fellow anglers — there was always the possibility of a limit bag of eight fish for the fly fisherman so inclined. In this manner, catch and release in the mountain and forest streams was not in any way doctrinal, any more than it showed any form of purism or dogma, nor were we jumping on a perceived popular bandwagon, for we fished alone and privately and never spoke of it except among ourselves.

Who really wants all those trout anyway? The small group of friends with whom I fished in such remote places never ever killed a trout. I remember one incident when the young son of one our party caught and killed a four pound rainbow unbeknown to his father. He said he wanted to cook and eat it that night at our camp nearby, and later we all somewhat mechanically, I thought afterwards, assisted in the cooking and eating. No one, I seem to recall, actually said anything about it, but I suspect that none of us really enjoyed it. We much preferred our basic but unstated policy to take in with us all the food we needed; half of which anyway we never seemed to eat.

If then a fly fisherman decides not to go on mindlessly killing trout he is faced with a dilemma. Is he to stop fishing when he was caught and killed the few trout he wanted, or — if he choses to kill none at all — is he to deny himself any fishing at all? Should he, in fact, give up fishing? By squeezing down the barbs, or using barbless hooks for very small dry flies and nymphs; by using a decent net instead of beaching fish; by using tippet material light enough to deceive the trout, but strong enough to avoid half-killing the fish by extending the so-called 'play'; by never lifting the netted fish out of the water except perhaps to photograph quickly; by carefully releasing the trout with wetted hands, holding it upright and steady until it is ready to swim off; by doing these things with consideration and skill, no harm is done to the trout. It may not exactly enjoy the experience, but that's life. Like yours and mine at times.

Like many other 'movements' and 'causes', catch and release, and the entire conservationist lobby in angling, is in danger of being taken over by zealots spreading yet another gospel. As has been said, in New Zealand, quite suddenly, without any slow build-up and certainly without much prior evidence of such attitudes, the national association of professional fly fishing guides espoused the cause with such fervour one might be forgiven for thinking they had invented it. Britain, not having such a body of professional guides (their nearest equivalents are mostly employed by fishing hotels, or as ghillies, or casting and fishing instructors), has a totally different angling scene.

Salmon fishing is so depreciated and so rigidly and expensively controlled that its problems have nothing to do with such abstruse and philosophic matters as catch and release. No one is likely to pay hundreds of pounds for the uncertain likelihood of catching a salmon, knowing that he will be obliged to return it to the water. Coarse fishermen release their fish anyway. Only their keep-nets might be questionable. Competition fishing for trout, despite the claims made for it and the increasing razzmatzz, is of less significance and importance than its sponsors and team members make out. And that leaves fishing for trout. Except locally in some places that really means fly fishing for trout. And that it turn really means trout fishing in the larger urban reservoirs or the smaller privately owned and operated stillwaters. Fewer and fewer fly fishermen have access to less and less stream and river trouting, and self-sustaining stocks of wild trout are increasingly rare. Like the reservoirs and private stillwaters, streams and rivers are wholly reliant on stew-bred and raised stock-fish, now commodities for purchase by any customer who wants them.

Now in a situation where a fishery owner buys mature stock trout he can do what he likes with them: he can kill and sell them at so much a pound from a roadside farm-gate type shop; or he can put them into a pond, with or without adequate natural food to sustain and grow-on the fish, and charge a fee for the privilege of clients being allowed to catch those trout, according to rules and conditions set by the proprietor. In fact most such fisheries insist on all trout caught being killed at once; thereby preventing anglers from practising a private sort of catch and release by not actually killing a limit which would mean having to cease fishing, or buying another ticket. This means that catch and release, as an angling philosophy, when introduced into the British Isles has no relevance in the case of stocked, introduced trout. The only thing it might do, in the case of the smaller stillwaters, is to diminish the financial burden of the proprietor in restocking — and result in a lake full of uncatchable, psychotic trout. For populations of wild, indigenous fish in running waters and certain more fragile lake or loch systems it might make more sense.

In recent months there has been some hoo-ha in the UK angling press concerning its importation here — with predictable reactions. What is not generally recognized is that catch and release, far from being universally obligatory in the United States, isn't even practised except by a small minority of anglers, and in certain, specific areas. In fact many American state-operated fisheries have rules that would surprise British anglers. These might include what seem to be novel management strategies. Typical would be waters where it is decreed that all fish *below* a certain size may be kept (the logic being that many anglers wouldn't want to keep them anyway and in addition most of them would die). This length is, say 6 inches. Between 6 inches and 10 inches the fish have to be returned to the water alive. (Here the management logic is that mortality rates are rapidly dropping in the larger fish and anglers want bigger fish. A trout 6 to 10 inches long, returned alive to the water, obviously has a chance to grow larger.) Fish above 10 inches may be kept. It must be said, however, that these rules would apply to areas where trout production was far from high, but angling pressure intense.

So far we have only looked fleetingly at a very few of the reasons why the proponents of catch and release lobby for its universal acceptance. Much of the North American argument is based on the contention that by catching and releasing trout the fly fisherman will not only feel good about it, but moreso enjoy the experience. It was in this respect that my New Zealand fishing came about, and in that country, and in the nature of the fishing I did, it was not merely valid but spectacularly true.

At that time and long before its recent fashionableness there was hardly ever a mention of it in New Zealand trout fishing circles. Despite the fact that c & r, as an angling method, had long been practised by many fly fishermen, I don't recall a single magazine article or fishing book chapter that even mentioned it in passing. It was a non-issue in the public domain. The first article to do so in a New Zealand angling magazine (*Flyfisher*, October 1985) — 'To Kill or not to Kill'), to the best of my knowledge, was written by my friend and fishing companion Dr Nick Bradford. Spread through two consecutive issues it was a good article, but hardly made a ripple. It was pointedly New Zealand in context and written about fishing the small forest streams east of Taupo, not of the big brawling rivers like the Tongariro that run into the lake itself. I can vouch for the sincerity in these words from it:

> This is not being written to try and pretend that I'm particularly virtuous, my friends would no doubt point out the error of that statement anyway. I am no more than a fly fisherman who loves fishing and who wants to preserve the good fishing we have, and even enhance if it possible. There are some lovely streams and rivers nearby, and they hold fish of good size but there are precious few in some streams. Even in those streams of crystal-clear water by stalking carefully and using polaroids, one may see only two or three fish in a mile or more of water. On good days when the fish can be caught, it would take only one skilful but thoughtless fisherman to deplete quite a length of good fishable water. These pools thereafter may remain empty of good fish for the rest of the fishing

season, so diminishing that, and every other angler's pleasure in the stream. When fish were plenty and anglers few they just moved on to another well-stocked river, but with fishing increasing in popularity and anglers becoming more mobile this is becoming less and less possible, and it is here that catch and release has its main advantage.

. . . Another argument against releasing fish goes like this: 'why should I release fish so someone else can kill it.' The counter to this is almost too obvious to state; the ball has to start rolling somewhere and as more people begin releasing fish it will have a snowballing effect, and soon you will find that you are not releasing fish for someone else to kill but fish that could well be there the next time you fish that spot.

. . . At this stage I would like to disgress and deal with attitudes to catch and release that surfaced in two recent New Zealand fishing books. The first book is *Tread Quietly* by John McInnes. Succinctly, his arguments are that we have divine dominion over the beasts and fishes, that one should not practice catch and release as this is irresponsible trifling with nature, and if a fishery is in danger of depletion then we should not go there or it should be closed until regeneration occurs. I do not think that many now believe we have divine dominion over other species; the irrefutable evidence from evolution is that we are just one species, though an exceptional and rapacious one, that lives alongside many thousands of other species who have just as much right to live here as we. With the sanction of 'dominion over the beasts and fishes' we have a pretty poor record of caring for them when one considers the countless species we have hunted to extinction. Neither do I agree that catch and release is trifling with nature. All angling is trifling with nature. Hook and play any fish and you are putting it through a stressful time. If the author wanted to avoid this stressful time for the fish and still kill fish, then the only way would be to kill fish instantly — shooting or dynamite would do it, and I'm certainly not advocating either. The author obviously enjoys his fishing but I feel he trifles more with nature by hooking, playing and then killing the fish that we do who release them carefully to the water.

Here is what John McInnes says. There can be no doubting his absolute sincerity although I, for one, cannot agree with him:

A common answer given in recent years to the fisherman's greed syndrome, has been to appeal for wide practice of 'catch and return'. 'Stalk the fish or find them from experience, catch them, admire them and return them to their element.' That's advocated by many a writer, many a magazine.

For me that won't do. Catch fish and return them? That is playing with nature — abusing it. Undersized fish? Yes, I put them back as is legally required, but by fishing selectively I leave them largely undisturbed, even in small-trout fisheries.

Even if we put aside the question of whether or not a fish feels pain, he is clearly panicked when fought to the point of being easily landed, de-hooked and released. Then he is in a rather parlous condition to face the rigours of stream life over the following few hours. He is also made more wary, less likely to be a daytime feeder. 'Catch and return' probably makes fishing harder for others — a very significant point.

But most importantly there is an irresponsibility about 'catch and return'; a violent trifling which says to the fish, 'we're too selfish to stop fishing but at least we'll put you back after we've exploited you'. The practice reminds me of chasing sheep around a field until exhausted before leaving them half dead. When that happens sometimes on the outskirts of cities it's vociferously condemned by society at large.

I grant at once that killing a fish is violent too. But if it's done quickly and properly and the fish is used for food, then it comes within responsible exercise of the divine mandate 'have dominion over the fish of the sea' — provided we extend the sea inland a bit! Killing a fish gives me no pleasure. I accept it as a necessary consequence of fishing; a prelude to eating the catch.

I guess I'm really appealing here to the concept of being a steward — a longstanding Christian image for care and responsibility. As well as having 'dominion' or power over animals and plants, men and women are asked by this notion to preserve, care and even heal.

To me it seems a pity that John McInnes — whom I know slightly — could not have been more influenced by Sven Berlin, whose imagery alone was influenced by the Old Testament:

> A good fisherman has just that amount of natural contact with the other world to be able to enter it without reason; for reason in fishing belongs only to those other men whose fishing is to compete with one another to catch so many fish that their egos, like their slime-destroying keep-nets, are bulging with their pathetic achievement. Whereas the just man has exactly that amount of cruelty and truth which sharpen the edge of the ecstatic moment when the float runs, and a being from another world withholds its own life and the fight begins; the hunter and hunted, both using all the cunning and the skill that nature has evolved to preserve and destroy life.
>
> . . . A fully evolved fisherman is interested in everything but the fish's death, and this is because in the heart of that ruthlessness which makes the true hunter there is love, a deep love for the quarry, therefore an understanding of the tragedy of its death and of the miracle of its life, shown so profoundly in the Salmon Shelter carving at Val d'Enfer in the Dordogne, done twenty thousand years ago. The heart of man and the heart of fish beat little differently then as now.

The paradox lies at the heart of catch and release, not in that it is wrong to kill a fish, at the right time and in the right place; but that it is wise at other times not to take that life simply because we have become conditioned to regard the *coup de grâce* as being the essential end to the catching of a fish.

As to a spiritual view of releasing fish back to the water unharmed, Sven Berlin, I believe, was perhaps closer to God when he wrote — albeit long before the catch-phrase 'catch and release' was coined:

> A young fisherman has the making of a man of vision who might learn to tie his own fly, fight his fish and then release it into the great stream of life for another migration. Until the time comes when the catching of fish is not the purpose of fishing. When asked why he used no bait the Chinese sage said: 'The idea is *not* to catch fish!' He became so in harmony with natural laws that he could hold the greatest fish on the slenderest silken thread. So also will the hunter put away his gun and the soldier his flame-

thrower, for in the end the spectacle of life is more beautiful and more deeply rewarding to the spirit of man than the carnival of death.

If I may be forgiven yet another reference to New Zealand it may assist in recognizing and differentiating between the disciples of the cause and the bandwagonners. Once again I will quote something I wrote in the New Zealand *Flyfisher* magazine several years ago:

For what it's worth it seems a pity to me that much advocacy of catch and release so far heard in New Zealand consists either of over-used catch-phrases like 'Trout are too valuable a commodity to be caught only once', to the almost obsequious deference many of our daily press journalists, spokesmen for the Government Tourist Bureau, and other people who often should know better, pay to the most minor and insignificant visitors from overseas. Recently *The Dominion* carried a 'news' item on page three stating that a certain gentleman had said that New Zealand anglers should practise and preach catch and release before it was too late. It was given the prominence of an authoritative statement from on high; it was totally unqualified as to where and when it should be practised; it was made by a visiting American, brought here with New Zealand taxpayers' money, and his authority seemed to stem from the fact that he was the Camping Editor of an American sporting magazine, not particularly noteworthy for its fly fishing content and always embarrassingly full of advertisements guaranteeing fishermen huge catches if only they buy and use secret oils and bait additives and use lures on which hang three sets of murderous treble hooks that would kill a shark, let alone a trout.

While it has been my experience that the majority of American anglers I've met fishing in New Zealand do return all or most of the trout they catch to the water, they are generally representative of a certain type of fly fisherman who do so anyway, whether American or New Zealanders. If New Zealand trout fishermen need preaching to, or re-education, then there are ample expert and passionate voices here, without our Government using tax money to invite overseas experts here, about whom I'd lay a bet the vast majority of dedicated fly fishermen in the United States have never even heard of; and who very probably aren't fly fishermen at all, but trot out some of the well-worn and old platitudes.

Many New Zealand anglers are more caring of the fish themselves, and more considerate of values, and concerned about the environment than their often pragmatic practices suggest. No one group or creed of anglers possess all the virtues, and many who practise catch and release as a matter of principle are sometimes seen going through the motions of releasing trout without considerate care, as if the action is an end in itself.

After this article was published in *Flyfisher* magazine I received a letter from a regular correspondent whose love of fly fishing is total, whose knowledge of the sport is enormous, and whose thoughts about it are models of sweet reasonableness and humanity. Far from chiding me for my views he most tolerantly and wisely pointed out things I had not said or had left unsaid, as well as the bigotry of my argument. He wrote:

I have fished for sea run brown trout on the West Coast; regularly at Moeraki and occasionally in rivers further south as far as the Hollyford and Kaipo.

My best sea run fish was taken in the Hollyford River above the McKerrow Island. That was in 1964. I marked his length, 28½ inches, on my wading stick; he was in very good condition and probably weighed about 12½ lb. His true measure was taken in the frying pan, he fed a large party of trampers who were camped on the island.

I am not a Kodaker and I can supply you with no photographic evidence of this capture or any other.

On the Coast capricious weather and difficult access to the best estuarine and upstream water protect the fish from all but stalwart anglers and poaching 'Coasters'.

The best fishing on the Coast is nocturnal; it is not your picnic angler's idea of fun. On a dark night you must be brave to stand firm on a boggy footing amid chest high flax and raupo while an eel nudges your waders or a stoat kills a screaming victim somewhere in the bush behind you.

I enjoyed your remarks about catch and release fishing in *Flyfisher* No.26. You chummed the water thoroughly and should get some good bites. Unfortunately my copy of *Flyfisher* is not at hand and I should read it again before writing any further. For now I will only nose about in the turbid water without taking the bait.

The fellow who kills a limit bag for the freezer and the fellow who releases twenty fish in a day and brags about his catch have a lot in common. What makes them different is their effect on fish stocks. Fish stocks are the business of fisheries management. Ideal management would control both the catch and the number of anglers with access to the fishing. Such management could also preserve elusive qualities of the angling experience, like the occasional enjoyment of solitude.

We hear and read a lot of precious nonsense from the practitioners of catch and release. The nasty aspects of c & r are often glossed over.

Here in Wanaka we have professional guides who take visitors trolling on the lake. The fish are taken on treble hooks and lead lines and then returned to the water. This practice apparently satisfies the professionals' code of conduct and the sensitivity of some clients. Other clients have complained to me about this obscenity and have regretted taking their outings.

There is also a perversion of c & r fishing. The angler may be happy to deceive the fish but not necessarily to land it. This is best done on a light tippet. Early in the season the Dingle Burn carries a stock of good trout. By February the fish are few and timid. Some fish show signs of injury, others carry a Light Cahill, Letort Hopper or Royal Wulff on a broken 6X tippet.

There is danger in the belief that c & r fishing is a carefree game where you drag 'em out and pop 'em back. A life is endangered; it is a serious business. Recently I had eight days fishing the Mararoa River. It was a great trip; but I find it difficult to forget an unhappy release. After careful attempts to revive a good fish it floated away belly up and out of reach. I was mortified.

As I think you pointed out in *Flyfisher* c & r fishing is not the sport of all American anglers. That is the conclusion we make from the visitors we meet in New Zealand.

I have sat in airport terminals in Kodiak, Dillingham, and Anchorage and watched hundreds of fishermen pass by clutching a rod in one hand and a chilly bin in the other. Some travellers carried only a rod. Had they been 'skunked' or were they the c & r men?

In New Zealand, where everyone believes they have a right to do as they please wherever they choose, the idea of controlled access to fishing waters suggests elitism and will be resisted until the resource is destroyed. I would be happy for Bob Jones to enjoy exclusive fishing rights to the Tongariro provided he cared for the fishing. I think I would take the lakes Mavora and Mararoa River; they also need someone to care for them.

I write from a fortunate situation. I live close to the Clutha and fish whenever I please. The fish are abundant and fishermen few. I can sit on the riverbank and even nod off for an hour without fear; I don't have to be out in the water casting to reserve my place. I have nothing left to prove and no one to listen to my bragging.

So if I take a fish and he is easily released, I release him. If he is not easily released, I kill him. If he is good condition I eat him, if he is not in good condition my cat eats him.

I should be happy. The trouble is I worry about cruelty. Do fish feel pain? How acute is their obvious terror?

Whoosh! there goes another bucket of chum!

Such sweet reasonableness, compassion, tolerance, and much angling wisdom — as well as clear thinking — typifies much of the most informed fly fishing thinking in New Zealand, even after several years of targetting and attention by Trout Unlimited Inc. (note the Inc.) and its converts.

It is indeed ironic that England, where fly fishing for trout was raised to a fine art, where more than in any other country the motto of the Fly Fishers' Club: *Piscator non solum piscatur* — 'There is more to fishing than catching fish', was meaningful, should have now become perhaps the only country in the trout fishing world where the pleasures of fly fishing seem only related to getting value for money and in sometimes sneaking into one's fish bag a trout or two over the allowable fishery limit.

It is even more ironic that it may even save British trout fishing from the possible onslaught of catch and release as envisaged in recent articles and letters to the editorial pages in the two most prestigious fishing monthlies. Such fears are probably exaggerated anyway and, such has been the enormous change in fly fishing for trout in recent years, that catch and release has little or no relevance here.

Hugh Sheringham once said that angling was a branch of human activity with its roots in culture as well as hunger. In that seemingly commonplace statement we have, in a nutshell, the essence of every possible angling dilemma.

We have considered in another chapter the vexing matter of cruelty in fishing, and from that standpoint the question of inflicting unnecessary pain on fish by what we anglers do in our often self-admitted passion in pursuit of them. When such accusations are made against anglers — and here we enter the matter of yet another chapter in this book — it will be as well to know where we all stand in the face of serious and far from friendly charges.

Catch and release is not the perfect and absolute solution to all of angling's ills. In some places and at some times it will not only help, but should be obligatory. The trouble is that it is a matter of the heart, not of the head. It is one thing to catch and release a desirable trout in front of an audience — whether a potentially critical one, or one that promises adulation and admiration. It is another matter to do so on a remote mountain stream when one is quite alone. As it happens nowadays fewer and fewer trout fishermen in Britain are in that situation. For the most part our fly fishing is done in commercially operated fisheries, at no small cost to the angler, where profit and loss is the bottom line.

One of the most lucid and sensible reactions from observers of the scene in Britain came in an article by Peter Lapsley in that excellent journal *Salmon, Trout & Sea-Trout*. Perhaps for the first time catch and release is looked upon, not as an alternative fly fishing philosophy or dogma, but as a managed means of fly fishing for trout, while the author wonders whether it has any relevance whatsoever in trout fishing the way it is — whether we like it or not — in Britain today. The reason for this is not hard to find. In those parts of the world outside the United States still blessed with wild fish and fishing, from self-sustaining stocks, and requiring the attention and intervention of man only in matters of administration of the resource, it is clear the only way in for catch and release is through the head. It is either a philosophy that appeals to the minds and hearts of fly fishermen, or it is nothing, quite without any relevance. But in countries where the number of anglers is greater, and more urbanized, yet less regulated, where the dwindling number of available trout streams become ever more exclusive, elitist, and expensive, the bulk of available fly fishing for trout is to be found only in the larger reservoirs (now being privatised) and the entirely commercial stillwater trout fisheries offering fly fishing in return for money and, hence, subject only to profit and loss. And where anglers gather to fish in such places they are generally looking for value for money, and this usually relates to the numbers of good trout caught and killed. While in New Zealand the message was aimed at the head and heart, where c & r belongs, in today's Britain the same message will have little effect where the fisherman's pocket is concerned — although certain protagonists will argue that supposedly higher ideals are at stake.

Peter Lapsley points to just such sources, remarking that while its new-found advocates in Britain see their new philosophy as being one of good sense, it may perhaps spring from attitudes more akin to greed, and contain the thrust of a new and ill-advised purism. These days a steady trickle of eminent and respected British flyfishers make the pilgrimage across 'the pond', fish some of America's finest rivers, and return home singing the praises of catch and release.

Here Peter Lapsley has hit the nail squarely on the head. Until recently it was generally Americans who made the pilgrimage across the Atlantic to fish in Britain, partly to escape the frenzied car-chasing of hatchery trucks on some of the more popular streams, partly as real pilgrims to fish in such fabled waters as the Test or Itchen or Dove — or even in stillwaters such as Blagdon. American flyfishermen, by and large, are generally more piscatorially literate and well-read than their British counterparts, and seek out and absorb the timeless redolence of well-remembered fishing books along with their fishing. It is part of fishing as far as they are concerned, and an important part at that — perhaps also they regard this pilgrimage to the historical cradle of fly fishing as being good for their souls.

Now, it seems, in order to get back to the heartlands of fly fishing to make a reverse pilgrimage to the United States. Meanwhile the current gurus of the English trout fishing scene are proclaiming a gospel of commercial stillwater fly fishing, barely fly fishing in anything but name.

If someone travels a hundred miles or more, as many do, to fish a favoured stillwater, paying £25 or more for a day ticket, and fishes competitively alongside other anglers intent on catching a quick limit, it is not altogether surprising that cost considerations seem never take into account the pleasures of a day out fishing, but simply the quick achievement of four trout on the bank, or the maximum possible aggregate weight, in order to justify the expense incurred. It is an attitude increasingly difficult to argue against. The joys — or otherwise — of a day's fishing are of no consequence to the vast majority of today's armies of British trout fishermen. Therein lies the rub. Therein lies the heart of the matter.

When earlier I spoke of restrictions and regulations governing trout fishing in New Zealand, I didn't suggest that by comparison with Britain they were egalitarian and generous. These are regional variations throughout New Zealand, but by and large a daily bag limit is likely to be eight brown or rainbow trout, although the regulations permit the release of fish up to that time when a full limit has been killed and retained. At about this time of writing, in the Taupo district — wisely if a little belatedly — the permissible daily bag limit is being reduced from eight fish to three.

An undesirable effect of such a relatively large number of eight fish in the daily bag is that it sets a goal to be aimed for, when otherwise the average angler would have stopped fishing and gone home after catching one or two fish. Additionally, simply by setting even a rarely attainable goal of, say, eight fish creates in far too many anglers' minds a sense of failure in not having achieved that limit. It is necessary to say, however, that in New Zealand trout and salmon are the property of the Crown until legally caught by fair means by a licenced angler when the fish becomes the property of the angler, but only after it has been killed, and only for his personal use. Trout cannot be sold or bought, although an angler may give his catch to another person.

Such considerations plainly have no bearing on the ways in which British anglers now do their fly fishing. Peter Lapsley observed that the British fly fishermen he knew of who had made the reverse-order pilgrimage to the United States, and returned singing the praises of catch and release, had been converted by a perceived need to conserve trout stocks and, perhaps, by personal distaste for killing trout unnecessarily.

Pointing out that there has been a noticeable tendency for some of these people to see catch and release as an end in itself, even as a virtue, almost as a new form of piscatorial purism, rather than simply as a means to a conservation end, as they extol its virtues blindly rather than seeking its selective use, Peter Lapsley mirrors almost exactly how the movement came to New Zealand and how it took root there. In yet another parallel development he notes that the fervent cry is often taken up by lesser men with lesser motives who simply wish to be permitted to go on fishing after they have already caught and killed a limit bag. In New Zealand, however, anglers are permitted to release any fish they may catch but have to stop fishing immediately they have killed a limit. Except here there is a difference. Quite apart from the fact that the New Zealand daily bag limit is generally twice that of most British commercially-operated trout fisheries, it is nowadays only very rarely obtainable; whereas, in Britain, the averagely competent angler *expects* to catch his limit, and usually does, and would be bitterly disappointed if he goes home with anything less.

Lapsley further points out that the United States is a huge and relatively sparsely populated country with an abundance of relatively lightly fished rivers. It is a country where many of its citizens have a strong outdoor, camping, hunting and fishing urge, as Peter Lapsley says, 'engendered into them almost from birth'. Even more importantly, the Christian ethic of man's dominion over the beasts and the birds and the fishes is almost central to much of middle American life, and middle America is where fishermen acquire their attitudes to the sport. Also fundamental to the American ideal is that the good Lord provided this dominion for the benefit of mankind as a whole, rather than for a privileged minority. One needs but look at American gun laws and the right to bear arms, and of the enormous and powerful opposition to any thoughts of change, to see how deeply this is ingrained in the psyche of most Americans. Little wonder, then, that not all movements can be transplanted lock, stock and barrel to another country with a totally different background. Little wonder still, that when such transplant occurs, there is a tendency for many of the newly converted to see their cause as a crusade. Meanwhile other lesser men with lesser motives (in Peter Lapsley's words) hijack the idea and use it for selfish ends, using the argument as a right to be allowed to go on fishing when they have already caught and killed a limit bag, regardless of the effect it may have on the water, on the fish, or on the fishery.

Fishing may be the most popular participant sport in the United States, but it generates relatively little revenue outside that of an enormous tackle trade. Different, to say the least, size and bag limits imposed by State authorites — of which previous mention has been made — have contributed to the use of other encouragements, such as the catchily-phrased slogan 'Limit your kill — not kill your limit'. As a basic slogan it can't be faulted. It is sensible, moderate, fair-minded, high-principled, modest, and most appealing. As a fly fishing philosophy in many of the open spaces and mountain rivers of the United States it is admirable. On many of the once remote mountain streams of New Zealand, with susceptibly fragile populations of big trout, it may be essential. On some similar streams in inland Victoria and New South Wales in Australia it may be the only way left. But in Britain in the 1990s it makes little sense on the vast majority of waters where anglers fish for trout.

Far from saying that British trout fishing is better in any way and therefore must not be spoiled by such limitations, there is much to suggest the very opposite. For better or for worse Britain has got what it has got, and must make do with it. Hopefully, our streams and rivers will be cleaned up and be re-generated but it would be wishful thinking to hope that any will return to the pristine, unspoiled condition they were two hundred years ago.

It would seem and is highly likely that the demand for trout fishing will further increase, placing yet greater strains on the finite resources (that is the streams) and creating an even greater need for more man-made stillwaters and for more carriers, or more fishable carriers, on rivers able to cope with them and on which carrier streams are a natural part. This, then, dictates that the commercial thrust will become even more commercial, until virtually all trout fishing will be at cost to the fisherman and based on the profits of the fishery owner.

Even now, noted English trout streams like the Test and Itchen have become almost totally reliant upon stocked farm-reared trout. As Peter Lapsley, himself a one-time fishery owner, has ruefully pointed out, the decision to stock a hitherto wild fishery almost invariably seems to draw the fishery proprietor further and further down the road towards complete artificiality.

This road towards artificiality is, however (and sadly in my belief), trodden more by fishermen themselves than by the fishery proprietors. Greed on the anglers' part then induces the manager to stock with more and more, bigger and bigger fish, as Peter Lapsley says, out of all proportion to the size and nature of the water, and which the water obviously cannot sustain. What continuance of numbers and size that can be obtained is entirely due to put-and-take, exemplifying the very worst aspects of the small stillwater fishery.

Simply in order to maintain a viable put-and-take trout fishery costs are going to rise. No doubt certain voices in trout fishing circles (and all wearing the purer than pure badge of catch and release) will be heard advocating its introduction to our stillwater fisheries under the guise of conservation. Sadly, these will include loud and often influential voices who really only want to go on catching record numbers and weights of trout where the object of the exercise will be to catch and release record numbers and avoirdupois of fish in the shortest space of time: in other words, coarse match fishing gone over to trout. At worst, many of the unhooked fish will die anyway after their ordeal or, at best, the fish will become so increasingly wary each time they are caught until, in Lapsley's words:

> Probably after their fourth, fifth or sixth mistake — they became effectively uncatchable. At this point they would have to be replaced with fresh, catchable fish if the quality of the fishing was to be maintained.
>
> Under such circumstances, on any intensively-fished water it is possible to envisage a bizarre situation in which so many often caught but un-removed trout have to be replaced that the lake or stretch of river eventually contains more fish than water. Less absurd but of more immediate concern would be the question of the water's ability to sustain the biomass of fish artificially introduced into it.

Many would dispute Peter Lapsley's scenario of these numbers of uncatchable trout, claiming that they could catch any trout under any conditions. It will be noted that most of the gentlemen who make such claims mostly fish (under the more public gaze at least) on certain, highly selected, smaller stillwaters, by specific invitation only, where the water has been even more liberally seeded than usual with large numbers of big trout, newly introduced immediately prior to the guru's arrival, and known by him to be comatosely available. It may still require skill of sorts to get them on the bank, but less than one is led to believe, and certainly less than for a trout that had been caught and released five times in the previous week.

It is one thing to catch and release a trout in a wild and brawling New Zealand river, or in the heartland of the best American fly fishing, but another thing altogether to do the same on a Hampshire pond of an acre or two. I have fished New Zealand streams and seen the same trout caught and released on two or more occasions separated by several weeks; but these have been in remote, hard of access, and lightly fished waters. I have also seen, in that same country, in more readily accessible and heavily fished waters, pools holding several trout terrified out of their wits, that did nothing but dart mindlessly from bank to bank, as if escaping from nothing in particular except perhaps fear itself, at the merest flash of an aerialized fly line or the glint of a fly rod whooshing through the air.

Catch and release is not merely an art of fly fishing, not necessarily learned or suitable for some fishermen, but it is one that should be used only in waters where it makes real sense and not simply imagined sense. Where and when it is practised, it should always be for the sake of the trout, not for the sake of the angler. If any benefits accrue from its employment then they are due to the fish alone. If not then it becomes an act of selfishness.

All this, of course, cannot be part of a blanket approach of attitude to Britain in its entirety. Thanks be it that there are some waters left, usually because they are far distant from intense angling pressure, where catch and release, properly done and for the right reasons, would make sound sense. On some Scottish burns one is aware of the frequent mindless slaughter of numbers of tiny trout that hardly warrant inclusion in anyone's frying pan. Where there are wild, self-sustaining populations of brown trout in Scotland, Wales and even parts of the North and West Country, there is place for well-intentioned catch and release in the interests of conservation. But unless it is done with skill and care and attention it is probably better to kill the fish.

Far too few anglers in Britain today seem to have any awareness of stress imposed on a hooked fish. Leaving the question of pain and possible cruelty aside for the moment, pause to consider what happens in the moments immediately following the hooking of a trout.

Until recent years stress was rarely heard of among human beings, let alone in fish — especially trout, that by their physiology are especially sensitive of it. Leaving aside the question of pain, we can still be sure that when a trout is hooked it doesn't enjoy the experience, and does its best to make the nasty experience go away. Whether the angler intends to kill or release a hooked fish it behoves all sensitive fishermen not to prolong unnecessarily that part of the business archly known as the 'fight', or 'playing the fish'. This can be aided by using the heaviest nylon tippet that will fool the fish yet enable the angler to land it speedily. There is no doubt that a hooked trout 'fights' within the proper meaning of the word. During this time the fish suffers considerable stress, causing a continual build-up and accumulation of lactic acid in the trout's muscle. If the fight is too protracted, the fish may not survive an extreme accumulation of lactic acid in its tissues, even if initially it swims away after release with all the outward signs of being unharmed.

In the ordinary course of events in the life of a salmon or trout, lactic acid builds up in the muscles while the fish is active, then naturally dissipates during rest or inactive periods when the blood rinses the muscles. In both salmon and trout, lactic acid begins to accumulate in the bloodstream immediately after heavy exercise or similar activity, building up to a peak in a few hours. From the time it starts to subside, twelve hours will elapse before the fish has regained a lactic-free state. A fish can be killed outright by a high amount of lactic acid in the blood. Death probably occurs either because lactic acid stops the heart, or because it blocks the oxygenation of the blood by the gills.

In respect of the expenditure of energy by trout and salmon, anglers should consider that the larger the fish, the faster it can swim. As a rough calculation the top cruising speed of most fish works out at 11 km/h for each 30 cm of length (say 7 mph for each 12 inches of length). Thus a 15 cm (6 inch) fish would be able to swim about 5.5 km/h (4 mph); a 45 cm (18 inch) fish at 17 km/h (11 mph). Additionally, fish can attain short burst speeds about 50 per cent higher than the maximum sustainable speeds. Thus, as salmon with a top sustained speed of 16 km/h (10 mph) might reach a burst speed of 24 km/h (15 mph) before leaving the water to leap over a waterfall or on that first dash after feeling the barb of the fly. Or a 38 cm (15 inch) rainbow, weighing 1.4 kg (3 lb) with a condition factor of 88 — that is a fish in its peak condition — has a sustainable speed of about 14 km/h (9 mph) and a burst speed of about 21 km/h (13 mph).

At the sustained rate, a fish can energize its muscles and remove the wastes from them via the bloodstream continuously at a balanced rate. At high burst speeds, the poisonous lactic acid builds up rapidly in the muscles. The energy for high-speed swimming comes from the glycogen stored in the muscles, although the supply available is extremely limited. The muscle glycogen supply of a rainbow trout is half used up in the first two minutes of heavy exertion. Once this store of energy is burned up, it takes more than twenty-four hours to build back to normal again. Consequently, a rainbow that has just ended a sustained burst of feeding activity (such as might be the case on several occasions throughout the day), or has broken your leader after being hooked, may have to spend a whole day or longer recuperating. Add even more stress in prolonging the 'play', in using angling 'skill' in not breaking your leader, and the chances are the fish will certainly die.

Despite that more physiological interlude concerned with the chemistry of fish, it remains at heart a matter more concerned with the psychological and philosophical processes of the angler himself. Bearing in mind what has been already said about the proper time and place and circumstances for catch and release, it has rarely been said better than Howard T. Walden in *Upstream and Down*:

> Returning a good fish to the water will fill you with a sweet and secret pride and leave no residuum of regret. There is an awareness of material loss, perhaps, as there may be in the donation of a handsome gift to charity, but the spiritual gain outweighs it.
>
> It is only when you lose a big one midway in the battle that the shock of loss seems insupportable. The ensuing emotion is comparable to nothing else in the whole psychological experience of humans. There is a more profound and most lasting sense of loss, but there is none more momentarily acute than that which seizes you when a big one gets away.

With good reason we should all perhaps take more to heart old Izaak Walton's words when he said to his pupil who had so suffered:

'Nay, the Trout is not lost, for pray take notice no man can lose what he never had.

Chapter 12
Exact Imitation
in Artificial Flies

Exact imitation in artificial flies is an offshoot of the formalism of dry fly dogma rather than part of the artistic heritage of fly tying. If there are two basic schools of fly tying then they would have to be those of Exact Imitation and Impressionism. Yet, paradoxically, some of the most slavishly exact imitation and representation has been in lures meant to simulate small fish fry, freshwater shrimps, corixadae, and other creatures often fished as deep as practicable on sinking lines, and so far from the Halfordian concept of dry flies and dry fly fishing that the dogmatists insist that the sunk fly is not fly fishing at all in anything but spurious name. Thus, at the outset, the two separate schools of exact imitation are strange bedfellows, to say the least, yet neither group seems aware of the similarities in their fly-tying philosophies.

Exact imitation, then, did not begin and end with Frederic Halford, albeit that he was the High Priest of the dry fly school. Some innovative developments designed to make things easier or more efficient tend to become central to new cults. They are apt to become so overlaid with false doctrine and reasoning that the original reason and cause of their coming into being gets lost and forgotten among the myths. There can be no doubt that dry fly fishing began to make it easier and more certain to catch trout on certain waters and at certain times.

It is likely that more paeans of praise have been sung about dry fly fishing, as well as more attempts at ridicule, than any other branch of fishing, anywhere, at any time. Such was its hold over people, and such was the purity of its proclamation throughout the trout fishing world that many good men were all but broken because of their non-compliance or contrary views.

As a mode of fly fishing it became so highly systematized that it became, in the words of John Waller Hills, the tyranny of the dry fly. Stripped of its dogma it remains what it was. As a fly fishing method and technique, on certain trout waters, at certain times, it can be a sublimely beautiful and satisfying way to catch fish. It is relatively easy to learn. It does not require quite as many of the canny skills required for consistent success in nymph fishing or, indeed, in fishing the traditional wet fly. It has an almost balletic choreography of sorts that exalts it above all other fly fishing methods, and it can have a passionate hold on its practitioners. Yet it was hijacked away from its true path even in Halford's lifetime although he was probably not responsible for this happening. Yet it is often practised by the most bigoted and inexpert of fly fishermen, for no other reason that they were brought up that way, and introduced to it — without any thought on their part, either then or subsequently — as to the truth of its doctrines.

Nevertheless, dry fly fishing is still practised all over the world — possibly, nowadays, more in other parts of the world than in England where it all began. America, New Zealand, Tasmania, Chile, Argentina, Canada — wherever trout are fished for, you will find dry fly fishermen and fishing. And for the most part in those countries, this mode of fishing has none of the overtones of elitism and snobbery often associated with its practise in England.

And it all began because of the doctrine of exact imitation in dry flies, not because of any inherent superiority as a method of fly fishing. It is interesting in reading Halford's books on the development and rise to ascendancy cf dry fly fishing to find that he began as a convert and pupil-disciple of other fishermen, and that he did not begin it all himself, as is commonly supposed. Chief amongst his mentors was, of course, George Selwyn Marryat and, hard at his heels after Marryat's early and untimely death, came Edgar Williamson. In Halford's view — and it is a view shared by many others, including Francis Francis and William Senior — Marryat was the greatest fly fisherman of all time. What Halford did was to codify and formalize dry fly fishing and to turn it from being a delicate, satisfying and unique method of fishing, enabling the angler to catch more trout more certainly, into a creed.

It was Halford's less intelligent and innovative acolytes who turned that creed into a dogmatic near-religion. And Halford's sin, if indeed he really did sin, was to believe the praise and honour heaped upon him and to act as if he was the sole fountainhead of truth. In other words he was guilty of vanity and self-deceit; a common enough and very human fault we all share, and of which no one is wholly innocent.

In fact, Halford began as a coarse fisherman. If ever a style of fishing had long been governed by ritual and popular belief then it was that manner of fishing for roach, perch, tench, carp and pike. By comparison trout fishing at that time, other than in Scotland and the north of England, where W. C. Stewart's dictum of upstream fishing with spiders and soft hackled wet flies held sway, was a no-holds barred affair of hauling out trout by whatever means seemed easiest at the time.

So, Frederic Halford, High Priest of the cult of the dry fly, began fishing at the age of six in a small pond in a meadow adjoining his parents' home in the Midlands. From this murky pond he and an older brother and sister learned to catch small perch and roach. Soon afterwards the family moved to London and young Halford was soon fishing the Serpentine, and from there, by the age of ten, he was fishing the Thames from bankside or punt. From now on he caught larger roach and bream. It was not long before the young man was sea fishing at Eastbourne, but it palled after catching a few whiting, pout, sea bream, congers and dogfish. Then he turned to trolling for bass, towing a handline behind a sailing or rowing boat. In this he soon discovered new and innovative methods, substituting a stiff pike rod for the handline and using a Nottingham reel and running line with a gut trace — to the disgust of the local boatmen. Halford's first trouting is best described in his own words taken from *An Angler's Autobiography* (1903):

From fear of being prolix, I must once more hark back to the river, and tear myself away from the fascination of the ozone-laden sea and its finny inhabitants. Barbel, bream, roach, dace, chub, perch and pike are only in season during the late summer, autumn and winter; the spring and early summer were therefore the slackest times of the fishing year. From April 1st to June 1st, according to the law of that epoch, no fish could be killed in the Thames except trout. We had all seen specimens of these magnificent Salmonidae set up in glass-fronted cases and displayed on the walls of the various riverside hostelries — deep, thick, short, brilliantly spotted, and generally very handsome trout of from say 5 to 16 lbs.

All had heard of the breathless excitement of hooking one of these monsters, of its headlong rush for fifty or more yards down the broken water of the weir, culminating in a leap into the air; and of the game fight following the first check, during which contest a considerable proportion escaped and a few were safely steered into the capacious landing net, to the intense gratification of the angler and his attendant. All the larger fish were killed by spinning, generally with natural baits — bleak, dace or gudgeon — and an occasional smaller trout was taken on a fly. It never was my good fortune to kill one with fly, and anything I could write on the subject would be mere hearsay. I knew nothing of fly fishing beyond an occasional try for dace or chub, and was not in those days much drawn to that form of fishing.

Any fly fisherman now reading those words for the first time (for the *Autobiography* is a scarce and rarely quoted book) will no doubt be surprised that the writer is none other than the august, austere, and near-sainted Frederic M. Halford. He continues:

Spinning, from my previous experience with pike, was comparatively easy, and later on, when live baiting for Thames trout became popular, this too presented no great difficulty. During the months of April, May and June most of my weekend holidays were devoted to trying to emulate the records of the famous Thames trout fishermen of the day; but although I had a most intelligent professional who spent much of his time in marking down the feeding places of the large fish and the hours at which they were most given to feed, my success was nothing to boast of. Occasionally the fisherman would hook a fish and hand me the rod to play it; sometimes I hooked one myself; some, as usual, got away and others were duly consigned to the well of the punt. Although I killed many, and a few of fairly good weight, I never secured a monster, and for many years had not succeeded in hooking and landing one over 6 or 7 lbs.

In the year 1870 I did fairly well, but having no written record, fear to give even approximately either the number or the weights. At that time, as will be shown in a subsequent chapter, my imagination had been excited by the dry fly, and on the few days when I could get permission on the Wandle had no desire to try any other form of sport. The last two Thames trout I killed, and the circumstances under which they were taken, are so indelibly fixed in my memory that I am tempted to give a brief history of their capture.

At that time my headquarters for the Thames were at Halliford, and one of the best of the local fishermen, George Rosewell, had a standing engagement to attend me with his punt. During the early part of the season we had killed a few fish varying from 8 to 3½ lbs, but it was a cold spring with high water, and until the latter part of May the flow over the weirs was too strong for *Salmo fario* to be much *en evidence*.

The first week in June Rosewell hooked a splendid fish, handed me the rod as usual, and after a very hard struggle we killed a fine trout weighing nearly 9 lbs. During the next week he wrote me that he had spotted two fish in Shepperton Weir, one a large one and the other about 5 to 6 lbs. On the 10th I journeyed down, and the early morning of the 11th found me in his punt, above the weir, he spinning a dace while I was live baiting with a moderate-sized bleak. It was a lovely morning, with the sun just breaking through the light mist, scarcely a breath of wind, and we were located at the part of the weir where the larger of the two fish generally fed.

Simultaneously we both turned round and caught sight of a fish feeding in the far corner below the weir. Of course Shepperton old weir has long since been removed, and the present ugly but probably more serviceable structures have been erected in its place.

. . . The fish we had seen feeding was under the bay close to the side of the ballast box. Cautiously the punt was pushed across so that my live bait could be slowly let down to the spot. Another moment and the fish showed again, this time some four or five yards nearer the centre of the weir. Another gentle push and the punt was in position, and as my bleak came into its view the fish dashed at it, was hooked, and rushed across and down the weir, throwing itself into the air two or three times. Rosewell, at my suggestion, put the punt ashore, while I steadied the fish, landed, and after a few gallant runs was on terms with it. It was a silvery handsome fish of about 5½ lbs, and was duly appreciated by a good friend whose dinner table it adorned the next evening.

Few readers, I suspect, are anything but surprised at this picture of Halford employing a professional to fish and hook trout, for him to play, and at the later account of the great Halford fishing for trout with live bait. The account continues with more of the same, culminating with the capture of a trout of 9¾ lbs, 'a more perfect specimen of a Thames trout I never saw.' Halford had the trout mounted and set up in a glass case.

This was my last Thames trout, and as the time went on the attraction of fly fishing, and especially dry-fly fishing, gradually impelled me to drop all other forms of sport to follow that which may fairly be described as more scientific and more engrossing than any other.

It was in May 1868 that Halford had his first day fly fishing for trout on the Wandle. Halford and his mentor that day began fishing downstream with a team of wet flies, but his friend (a visitor from the north, who was making his first acquaintance with the stream) soon realized that on the slow-running, gin-clear Wandle its only effect was to scare every feeding trout. It was other local anglers who impressed upon them the necessity of 'fishing dry'. In Halford's words describing this revelation on the road to his particular Damascus, it needed no second telling:

. . . and very little explanation sufficed to teach us the crude meaning of this expression. We gradually worked out approximately the number of false casts required to free the fly from moisture, and were soon converted to the doctrine of waiting for rising trout, spotting them and fishing them; and before the early part of the season was passed had both killed some fair fish, and were exceedingly keen for this form of fly fishing.

The conversion had taken place.

Before the end of that first season on the Wandle Halford discarded the use of all 'the so-called standard patterns, such as the Red Palmer, Governor, Coachman, Hofland's Fancy, and March Brown [because] the tendency of the younger school of dry-fly men even in those days was to pin their faith entirely on the upright-winged floating duns.' It was already clear that Halford was not only entranced by the method, but also felt that its purer form was modern and younger and in the vanguard of change. So, too, in that first fly fishing season the popularly used fancy patterns of dry flies were declared anathema and never henceforth used. Purism had begun.

Before migrating to the Test and other Hampshire chalkstreams Halford, in this most interesting of all his books, includes a chapter on fishing the sunk fly, which he, of course, other than very briefly on his very first day out, never did:

> Ninety-nine out of every hundred dry-fly men have gained their early experience in the use of a fly rod by fishing the sunk or wet fly. My case was an exception to this general rule, and perhaps my observations on the difference between the two methods may not commend themselves to all of my readers, and be deemed heterodox by some of them. I must confess that the sunk fly has never appealed to me with the same satisfaction as the floating fly, and yet I am fully convinced that to be a first-rate performer with the wet fly requires considerable natural aptitude and prolonged study of the subject.
>
> . . . He who for preference would find a feeding fish, stalk it, cast to it, and if successful rise, hook, and kill it, is evidently intended by Nature to be a votary of the floating fly. On the other hand, he who for preference will wander, rod in hand, along the banks of a mountain stream and cast his fly or flies upon it; in short, doing what is commonly called 'fishing the stream', on the chance of tempting the lively little trout to their destruction, is as evidently a born adherent to the sunk fly. Some of my friends whose experience of fly fishing, wet and dry, is far greater than my own, condemn my opinions. They urge, no doubt with good foundation, the argument that in many parts of the world, notably in the United States and New Zealand, the largest fish are therefore without exception killed on sunk flies.

He was, of course, not altogether right in that assertion. Writing the *Autobiography* in 1903 Halford had long been in earnest correspondence with the ardent Theodore Gordon in the United States, and should have been aware of the fact that, while it was true that the sunk fly and a distinct form of lure fishing was generally practised in New Zealand, even then it was the monsters of twenty pounds and more, both browns and rainbows, that were mostly caught by such means, while it was already long established that, *particularly* on fast mountain streams, browns and rainbows would rise spectacularly to a dry fly.

Indeed it has long been (albeit in recent years) my own most favoured mode of fishing in New Zealand, for there big rainbows can be induced to rise straight up in a mountain pool through ten or fifteen feet of water to take a dry fly with sheer abandon.

But, to get back to Halford in those earlier days, note how near-religious terminology has crept into his angling philosophy. Dry fly fishermen are 'votaries' of the art, while we are led to assume that wet fly fishermen are lesser, mere mortals. Shades of this almost symbolic relationship between matters of God and dry fly fishermen linger on in the minds of fishermen, even in specific ways. The reader may recall those lines from Norman Maclean's *A River Runs Throught It* quoted elsewhere in this book. For the young Maclean, a Presbyterian minister's son, Christ's disciples were fishermen and John, as the favourite among them, was assumed to be a dry fly fisherman. In that household 'at the junction of great trout rivers in western Montana' there was no clear line between religion and fly fishing.

As Frederic Halford moved on to codify and formalize his perception of dry fly fishing into a rigid, intolerant doctrine, it is little wonder that a holier-than-thou attitude should have crept into it.

Far from being in any way a humbug, Halford's knowledge and understanding of streamside life, of the ways of trout, and of 'the other side' in wet fly fishing, was enormous and in advance of his time:

> We believe that we know why Salmonidae take the floating fly, and are in consequence concerned to try and imitate the natural insect in size, in shape, in colour, and in its behaviour on the surface of the stream. There is, however, some room for difference of opinion as to what the wet fly represents. It may be taken for the active nymph of one of the Ephemeridae, or for the more supine pupa of one of the Trichoptera; it may be for one of the Corixae or other water-bugs darting through the water; or it may be for one of the Crustaceae, such as the water shrimp (*Gammarus pulex*), or the water wood-louse (*Asellus aquaticus*). It may fairly be urged that in rivers where natural insects and their larvae are few in number, the ever hungry trout will try every moving object carried down by the stream which suggests to them the idea of living creatures fit for food.
>
> Some readers may express surprise at the statement that the brilliant-coloured flies often used by the wet fly fisherman could be mistaken by the fish for these comparatively sombre-hued denizens of the river. Let the doubting one place a few of these larvae or Crustaceae in an ordinary aquarium and he will be startled by the rays of many coloured lights due to interference and refraction produced by their movements through the water. Some authorities are of the opinion that the motion of the fibres of hackle and fur convey a notion of life, and that the fish are attracted to and take the artificial fly mainly because it appears to be embued with life.
>
> In dressing imitations of the duns, spinners, sedges and other insects, some votaries of the wet fly imagine that in the rough broken water of rapid streams the natural insects are drowned, and the feeding fish often comes across them well below the surface. This probably is a fallacy, for certainly I have never yet succeeded in getting one of the Ephemeridae or Trichoptera so sodden as to sink it below the surface, although I have tried to do so and treated the specimens with considerable violence in attempting to effect this object.

One might think that Halford then would have had no objection to an artificial that specifically sought to imitate, as exactly as possible, a nymph fished beneath the surface. Yet, in what follows, he seems to be saying *chacun son goût*:

One of the great charms, however, of angling in all its branches is that it gives endless opportunity for difference of opinion and discussion among the followers of the various schools. Every good fisherman and every sportsman will urge his own particular view with all his might, but at the same time will be prepared to listen to the arguments of those holding opinions quite opposed to his own, and will ever be ready to respect these opinions and credit his opponent in argument with being convinced that his (the opponent's) view of the question is the right one.

All seems sweet reasonableness, so that one wonders at this stage what all the dry fly — wet fly antagonisms were about. Although it has been said that it was not Halford himself, but his disciples of the generation after him, who were guilty of the bigotries outlined elsewhere, one wonders whether in the eleven years after writing the *Autobiography* until his death in 1914, having seen the ascendancy of his dry fly code established around the world, he did not lose whatever tolerance he once had. If so, then it is sad. The dry fly practice and ethic was a good one, quite epochal in the long history of fly fishing. It deserved better than to descend, as it did, into a piscatorial Star Chamber that later tried, and damned, Skues and his new doctrine of nymph fishing.

It might seem that the doctrine of dry fly fishing has, in itself, little to do with the practice of aiming for exact imitation in fly-tying. But insofar as dry flies are concerned the one is entirely to do with the other; the doctrine is as much concerned with exactly what the angler's dry fly is meant to represent as it is with the technique of how to present it to the trout, and under what circumstances. But, as already mentioned, exact imitation is not only confined to the art of tying dry flies. Many of the nymphs, wet flies and lures, as well as hundreds of imitative patterns, strive towards exactitude by ignoring the general, overall effect of impressionism. Yet, in truth, so many of the dry fly patterns that claim a measure of exact imitation are, both to the human eye as seen in the angler's fly box, and to the trout as the fly appears from nowhere and floats downstream towards its lie, in all likelihood registered as impressionistic images. Paradoxically, it has generally been the case that when a fly-tyer comes up with a dry fly that looks remarkably like a specific mayfly dun or spinner, it is considered to be an estimable characteristic; but when another fly-tyer comes up with a remarkably lifelike simulation of a small fish, or damsel or dragon fly, or waterboatman or other aquatic bug, he is as often as not accused of departing from the true heritage and traditions of fly-tying. In other words, exact imitation in dry flies tied to represent a mayfly is good, while the same principle incorporated in the tying of a wet fly or lure is bad.

Equally paradoxical is that the doctrine of exact representation of the fly on the water that a specific trout was feeding on at that time — in itself the very heart of dry fly purism — infers that before the Halfordian codifying of dry fly practice, it had not been known, whereas plainly it had. Some of the earliest books proclaim it as a basic principle. Thus Walton, not a fly fishing purist, even by the standards of his time, declares:

You are to note, that there are twelve kinds of Artificial made Flies to Angle with upon the top of the water (note by the way, that the fittest season of using these is in a blustering windy day, when the waters are so troubled that the natural fly cannot be seen, or rest upon them).

And later:

> I confess, no direction can be given to make a man of a dull capacity able
> to make a flie well: and yet I know, this with a little practice will help an
> ingenuous Angler in a good degree: but to see a Flie made by an Artist in
> that kind, is the best teaching to make it, and then an ingenuous Angler
> may walk by the River, and mark what flies fall on the water that day,
> and catch one of them, if he see the *Trouts* leap at a fly of that kind: and
> then having alwaies hooks ready hung with him, and having a bag also
> always with him, with Bears hair, or the hair of a brown or sad-coloured
> Heifer, hackles of a Cock or Capon, several coloured Silk and Crewel to
> make the body of the flie, and feathers of a Drakes head, black or brown
> Sheeps wool, or Hogs wool, or hair, thred of Gold and of Silver: Silk of
> several colours (especially sad coloured to make the flies head:) and there
> be also other coloured feathers both of little birds and of peckled foul. I
> say, having those with him in a bag, and trying to make a flie, though he
> miss at first, yet shall he at last hit it better, even to such a perfection, as
> none can well teach him, and if he hit to make his flie right, and have the
> luck to hit also where there is a store of *Trouts*, a dark day, and a right
> wind, he will catch such store of them, as will encourage him to grow
> more and more in love with the art of *Fly-making*.

And intimations of the dry fly:

> . . . and when you fish with a flie, if it be possible, let no part of your line
> touch the water, but your flie only; and be still moving your fly upon the
> water, or casting it into the water, you your self being also always moving
> down the stream.

Downstream, albeit, but fishing on top of the water with a fly tied with art
to best closest imitate the actual fly on the water.

As in so much of fishing wisdom, nothing is as new as the advocates of each
succeeding generation often proclaim. Walton, no great shakes as a fly
fisherman, unlike his friend Charles Cotton, and despite having borrowed
ideas from earlier writers ranging from Dame Juliana Berners to Thomas
Barker, still advocated using an artificial fly tied to best simulate exact
imitation and to fish it on the surface.

By Halford's day great advances had been made in making fly lines that
could be greased to float better than anything known by Walton and his
contemporaries. Thus it was technique, just as much as the philosophy of a
new dry fly fishing creed and code, that gave rise to the establishment and
acceptance of the late nineteenth century dry fly dogma.

J. W. Hills in his *A History of Fly Fishing for Trout*, first published in 1921,
comments that even by 1908 the records of the Houghton Fishing Club on the
Test had never made any reference to the dry fly. In that prestigious club and
the River Test in general a much more liberal attitude prevailed until Halford
and his disciples made it their river and the very heartland of the dry fly ethic.
Francis Francis, was one of Halford's closest friends, was an all-round fly fisherman. He wrote, 'The judicious and perfect application of dry, wet and mid
water fly fishing stamps the finished fly fisher with the hall mark of efficiency.'

Hills comments on that:

> Halford is the historian of the dry fly. He did for it what Stewart did for

upstream fishing. Neither were pioneers, for both described what they did not invent; but both, by practice and writing, made an unanswerable case for the system they advocated. With Halford was associated a band of enthusiasts who devoted themselves to perfecting the art and spreading the creed. Among them they systematized the practice; they dealt with and solved technical difficulties; they developed rod, line, hooks and flies to their present excellence; and all that they acquired or invented was told to the world in sober and convincing English. Never was a reform worked out with greater ability or presented with greater lucidity.

. . . Halford's place in the history of fishing is well marked. He is the historian of a far-reaching change, and as such it is possible that he will always be read. He was well-fitted for the task. He possessed a balanced temperament and a reasonable mind. He took nothing for granted, and proceeded by observation and experiment.

. . . If he is to be criticised it is because like most reformers he overstated his case. He considered that the dry fly had superseded for all time and in all places all other methods of fly fishing, and that those who thought otherwise were either ignorant or incompetent. He did not realise, and perhaps it is impossible that he should have realised, that the coming of the floating fly did not mean that previous experience and previous knowledge were as worthless as though they had never been; but that it meant that from then onwards fly fishing was divided into two streams. These streams are separate, but they run parallel, and there are many cross channels between them.

It seems clear that fishing — especially fly fishing — needs its own historians, not just to record those events that most interest them, but like historians of politics and nations, and of the lives of eminent people, to examine it all in the light of hindsight, warts and all, and not simply words of praise.

But what, the reader might well ask, has all this got to do with exact imitation in artificial flies? As we have seen, there is sufficient tradition of exact imitation in the design and tying of wet flies, nymphs and lures to dispel the notion of any fixation on the development of dry flies in particular. But by lumping together exact imitation in every mode of fly tying, we would fail to see how central it was to the dogma of the dry fly.

Hills, once again, as the post-Halford historian of fly fishing saw it this way:

As I have said, fishermen when they cast their eye on flies and began to imitate them, proceeded on what we can now recognise as three distinct principles. Some imitated fly life generally, and produced an article which was a fair copy of an insect but could not be connected with any particular species or genus or group. Such flies are called fancy flies. They have many redoubtable advocates, drawn in modern times chiefly from Scotland. Stewart pinned his faith to his three famous hackles, his black, his red, and dun spider. No doubt each of those could with a little laxity, be identified with a specific insect; but he did not set out to imitate such, and chose his flies with an eye rather to weather and water. This, in fact, is the feature which distinguishes this school: more attention is paid to light, to the clearness of the water, and to the sky, than to the insect. Stewart has many followers to this day.

The next school use what are called general flies, that is, flies which imitate a genus or a group, but not an individual. They differ from the last in that they regard imitation as more important than light or water: but they consider that precise copying is impossible, and, if it were possible, unnecessary.

The third and last is content with nothing short of an actual copy of the individual species which trout are taking. Of these was Halford, who when he first wrote included fancy and general flies in his list, but at the end of his long life says that his full experience convinced him that specific imitation is best in all weathers and all waters. Of course these three schools merge into each other. A fly can be more or less general, or it can be on the borderland of fancy and general, or of general and individual. Take the Partridge and Orange as an example. It is fished in the north all year round, and may be called a fancy fly. But it is possibly the best imitation of the February Red, and when so used it is specific. And besides the February Red it also kills as an imitation of the nymph of the Blue Winged Olive, and as such is general. Or again the Wickham is regarded as a fancy fly, yet a trout must be keen sighted to distinguish it from a Red Quill, specific imitation of a Red Spinner. So there is no hard and fast line with fishermen, for most of us use all three sorts. Few are entirely fancyists or generalists or individualists. Yet the distinction remains and has been an important one throughout history.

Hills, on that score, chose not to enter into this particular controversy, as it had been waged (and was, indeed, continuing) with considerable acrimony. What he sought to do was record the struggle in fly tying towards exact imitation, culminating in the exquisite copies in use by the 1920s.

One feature of the ascent of the dry fly in English trout fishing, and of its rapid spread throughout the entire fly fishing world, was the way in which it captivated the minds and hearts of those anglers newly introduced to it. It seemed to bear the hallmark of modernity and excellence, and was in no way associated as it is in some places today, with angling elitism, snobbery, hallowed waters, and blinkered logic. In its appeal to youth there was no hint of old-fogeyism, and if it was at all elitist, then it was based on sheer and deserved excellence. J. W. Hills, not in *A History of Fly Fishing for Trout*, but in his much scarcer and little-read, *My Sporting Life*, not published until 1936, writes almost breathlessly, looking back to his initial conversion many years earlier:

It was in 1890, the year after I killed my first salmon, that I caught my first trout on the dry fly. Seven or eight years earlier, when I was struggling with the inadequate rod and ridiculously light line then thought essential for fly-fishing, and poring earnestly over Stewart's *Practical Angler*, surely still the best book of its kind ever written, a rumour arose, I know not how, it was in the air, that a great event had happened, that something called the dry fly had arisen. A novelty, doing for trout fishing what the breech-loader had done for partridge shooting. Something modern, forward-looking, reforming and sweeping away the errors of past practice, a new age and a glorious one. I listened eagerly, as did Amyas Leigh to Salvation Yeo. Here was something for the young, something imbued with the spirit of youth. I gathered every rumour I could, sat, a wondering disciple, at the feet of the only practitioner I discovered, until finally in 1886 I bought Halford's *Floating Flies and How to Dress Them*.

I do not know how often I read it. I believe I knew it by heart. So clear was the writing, so unimpassioned, so convincing that I, like most others, took it as gospel. I felt, as I have done since when listening to speakers who possess the matchless art of imaginative simplicity such as the late Lord Grey of Fallodon, that the contrary could not be true. I longed for a chance of trying out that entrancing theory. No fisherman of this age can realise the effect Halford's books had upon our generation. Before they appeared we had heard rumours, but they were vague, indefinite and contradictory. Then suddenly the whole of the new art burst upon us full-grown. We drank deep and we were intoxicated. I did not give up my north-country practice, far from it. But I regarded fly-fishing as divided into two unrelated worlds, a higher and a lower. Much water has flowed under bridges during the fifty years which have elapsed since Halford's first book. Two angling generations have gone by. The great ones who worked out his reforms have nearly all passed over. And I now see that the floating fly is part only of the whole, and when I say that it is not the highest I do not in the least belittle it. I express a belief which I hold deeply: that all sorts of fishing are at their summit co-equal; none is before or after the other. The dry fly has fallen into its place in the great hierarchy and a high place it is, but a different one in the minds of most modern anglers from that which it occupied in 1886. Then it stood alone, unapproachable. Now the sunk fly, even in Hampshire, has its honoured usefulness.

But Halford's book was a revolution and a revelation. I set to work to readjust myself. And I was fortunate. Andrew Lang was a member of the Whitchurch Club on the Test, and many times I went there with him to fish.

In *A History of Fly Fishing for Trout*, Hills writes with an admirable detached fairness of judgement. But fifteen years later, in the auto-biographical *My Sporting Life*, he is writing about himself, free of constraints, and with fifteen years of hindsight. Yet note that this was still prior to the Halford–Skues debate conducted by the Flyfishers' Club in 1938.

But if John Waller Hills looked back and saw the rise of the dry fly as having been a revolution and a revelation, then before long he saw and recorded the rise of what he called the counter reformation:

It was during the time that I fished the Ramsbury water that the revolt against the purist took place. In 1902 he reigned a despot: nothing was admitted but the dry fly. At least openly, for we did get fish, though rarely big ones, on a sunk alder or march brown or hare's ear in stiller waters when ruffled by wind, and an occasional heavy one in mayfly time on a sunk hackle; but we did not talk about it, and always left off when there was a chance with the floater. Red and ginger quills, wickhams, olives dark and light, whitchurch duns, detached badgers and some sedges, these were our stand-by. Spent spinners were unknown, and nymphs were not dreamed of. Nearly all our few patterns were winged. In 1899 Lord Grey of Fallodon thought four patterns sufficient. It was a time when Halford's very real invention and advance had reached its limit and had run itself out. We went to sleep over our oars. We became set and inflexible. And it was not until we read Mr Skues's *Minor Tactics* in 1910 that we woke up.

If Hills was in the vanguard of modernity and youthful thinking when he became a convert to the dry fly and a disciple of Halford, then he was way ahead of it in 1910. Reactions to the appearance of Skues' first book surprised him:

> It is strange to think that such a book, closely reasoned and modestly worded, not challenging the dry fly but supplementing it, was received by the great ones not with interest but with fury. That anyone should dare to attack Test or Itchen trout with anything that sank was regarded as indecent. It was hardly the pursuit of a gentleman. On many waters the rule Dry Fly Only was enforced: and, what is odd, this rule survives until today. Halford and his disciples were sure that they had finally settled the controversy. Their method was right, at all times and in all places. If you argued with them they copied Whistler, who was accustomed to say, when his opinion was disputed, 'I'm not arguing: I'm telling you.'

In the following years Hills often fished the St. Cross water on the Itchen with Skues, whom he came to admire greatly. In that same autobiographical chapter he wrote:

> If Halford is the father of the dry fly, Mr Skues is the begetter of that emancipated young woman, the nymph. Dry flies were known long before Halford, assuredly, and nymphs had donned their scanty skirts at an earlier age than this twentieth century: but Mr Skues, with a truly modern mind, taught them how to make up their faces, and showed them that the less clothes they put on, the more attractive they would be.

Only here — at long last — do we return to the present central issue: that of exact imitation. Hills again:

> Halford, as he got older, relied more and more on the exact copy. He was a great man, but opinionated: he did not believe that his theory of precise imitation would ever be shaken. I do not imagine that he read many books on fishing, probably regarding them much as the Caliph Omar did the library of Alexandria. When told by the Arab conqueror that there was a library of two hundred thousand volumes, and being asked what should be done with them, he replied: 'If they contradict the Koran they are impious: if they confirm it they are superfluous: therefore burn them.' This story, long ago disproved, is too good to be forgotten, and not unfairly represents the attitude of some discoverers. And Halford was widely followed, and exact imitation was generally practised. But much knowledge has been gained since then, and a change has come over thoughtful anglers. Then again there was Lord Grey with his four patterns and no more, and he, too, had many disciples. Here also opinion has swung in the opposite direction, and modern anglers are using a wider range of fly and are not sticking to the precise copy.

In that respect, even on the Houghton water on the Test, under the direction of William Lunn, the riverkeeper, Hills observed that the imitation had passed through a profound change, and that change is a continuous progress:

> We cannot tell where it will end, we can only note its present direction. Halford believed that it would result in a photographic copy, and that the

nearer you could endow every part of your fly with a meticulous likeness to the natural insect, the more the trout would want it. But they do not. Their eye resembles that of the educated European who prefers a sketch by Whistler to the most accurate example of poster art. Progress contradicted Halford's forecast. The movement seems to be accelerating and certainly it has not reached its peak.

We have come across Mottram only passingly here. Much younger than Halford, Skues, or Hills, he too was an early convert to the dry fly, but by the time he visited New Zealand in 1911-12 he was an ardent nymph fisherman. In all probability Mottram was the first angler to fish the nymph in that country where today its use is almost universal. What is surprising about Mottram is that his book, *Fly Fishing: Some New Arts and Mysteries*, 1914, shows him to have been a highly innovative experimental fly designer, years ahead of his contemporaries: so much so that he was generally treated with indifference or contempt by all of them, except Skues. His concepts of fly-tying broke away from conventional styles, pioneering the art of creating illusions and suggestions — silhouette flies and flies without bodies. Clearly, in his first book, he anticipated the work of fly designers fifty years later — even including a bead-eye streamer fly. Before 1912 he was using cork-bodied midge pupae to allow them to float just below the surface.

Yet Dr Mottram was the man who, later during the infamous Flyfishers' Club debate, did so much to destroy Skues' credibility and good name because Skues had departed from the strict Halfordian purism of exact imitation and dry fly only. Even so, Mottram, unlike Halford who had believed the opposite, still thought that the art of tying dry flies in exact imitation of the natural insect was even then only in its infancy. He was nothing but a forward-looking fly designer. In his view, colour, transparency, form, weight and buoyancy were all important qualities to strive for. Yet he remained a true believer in exact imitation.

What then is the situation now? Mottram realized that Halford had blundered in the colour and form of his artificials by looking at them from above and with human eyes, instead of from below and with the simulated eyes of a trout. In this respect, at least in the tying of dry flies, exact imitation has attempted to copy what the natural fly looks like from beneath, but still strives (within those limitations) towards accuracy rather than representation. Insofar as the design and tying of sub-surface nymphs are concerned, it is here that the fly-tyer's art has most closely achieved the near perfection of exact imitation. So lifelike are some of the best contemporary nymph and pupa patterns that, with the points and bends of the hooks removed, it would be difficult to distinguish the artificial from the natural.

Streamer patterns and lures, once assiduously copied from the natural creatures they sought to imitate, are now largely suggestive and impressionistic, usually singling out and exaggerating some dominant feature or characteristic, so that the tendency is to move away from any attempt at exact imitation or, indeed, of imitating any one creature in particular. If one looks into one of the overlarge flat wooden fly boxes so essential to the current stillwater fly fisherman's armoury, the beholder is mostly overwhelmed by a bright jangle of shocking and often fluorescent, day-glow colours that scream their presence in vivid orange, lime, yellow, and fiery reds. These are often displayed on one side of the open box, while opposite are arranged the so-called battery of 'nymphs' — often not noticeably smaller than the lures, and still arrayed with the same shocking fluorescent dressings of chenille and marabou, which do, except when the fishing gets hard, lure many uneducated stock brown trout as well as rainbows to their doom. They catch trout and that, for the majority of today's fishermen, is all that matters.

The outcome seems to be a movement away from any attempt at exact imitation in trout flies except from those specialist tyers supplying the dwindling numbers of stream fishermen, and from the vises of those growing numbers who tie their own flies and seek out the traditional arts. Fly-tying has little consideration for ethics these days, and neither does the practice of fishing itself, but this need not necessarily be bemoaned. As in all things, fashions and ways and means in fly fishing go in cycles, not least in the matter of flies. John Waller Hills was firmly of the opinion that the changing fashions in artificial trout flies were fish-driven, rather than fisherman-driven. When the trout have seen enough of them they will stop trying to eat them, forcing the fishermen to rummage deeper into their long discarded and disused fly boxes until, inadvertently, they tie on a forgotten fly the fish will take with heady abandon. If not, if one waits long enough (and that won't be too long either), exact imitation will be discovered again with all the fervour of a new doctrine. And when the new flies start catching trout, as they will, the discoverers will say, 'I told you so', as the new dogma swings into gear.

Chapter 13
Patience and Flyfishing

An almost universal myth about angling is that it requires an almost imbecilic patience. There can't be a single fisherman who has not had a non-fishing friend say to him, "Oh! I couldn't be bothered with fishing! I just wouldn't have the patience for it!"

There is in the collective unconscious a view of the angler as a forlorn and solitary figure sitting huddled on some riverbank waiting, with the patience of Job, for some poor fish to come and commit stupid suicide by impaling itself on the angler's baited hook or lure. My dictionary defines patience as being the ability to bear pain, misfortune, etc., bravely; ability to wait calmly; perseverance; forbearance when provoked.

I, for one, have never experienced anything remotely like that in many years of fishing all over the world. On the other hand, I must admit that I have never sat on a riverbank for hours on end watching a tiny float bob up and down in front of me. Once or twice I've float-fished for bass off deeply indented rocky shores, but it was no time or place for daydreaming or the long exercise of patience. I found worming for sea trout among the lanes of bladderwrack in Orkney and Mull not altogether to my liking, but far from boring or requiring patience.

Arthur Ransome once said that nothing was more trying to the patience of fishermen than the remark so often made to them by the profane: 'I have not patience enough for fishing':

> It is not so much the remark itself (showing a complete and forgivable ignorance of angling as it does) that is annoying as the manner in which it is said, the kindly condescending manner in which Ulysses might tell Penelope that he had no patience for needlework. Are they D'Artagnans all, rough-riders, playboys of a western world, wild desperate fellows who look for a spice of danger in their pleasure? Not a bit of it. They hit a ball backwards and forwards over a net or submit to the patient trudgery of golf, a laborious form of open-air patience in which you hit a ball, walk earnestly after it and hit it again. These devotees of monotonous artificial

pleasures who say that fishing is too slow a game for them seem to imagine that fishing is a sedentary occupation. Let them put on waders and fish up a full river and then walk down it on a hot summer day. Let them combine for an afternoon the arts of the Red Indian and the mountaineer and, in the intervals of crawling through brambles and clambering over boulders, keep cool enough to fill a basket with the up-stream worm. Let them discover that they have to take their coats off when salmon fishing on a day when the line freezes in the rings. Let them spin for pike in February, or trout in August. They will find that they get exercise enough. Some forms of fishing are sedentary, in the purely physical sense, in that after a man has baited a spot for carp or roach, or anchored a boat for perch, he keeps still. But he has not attained a sort of Nirvana, like a crystal gazer, isolating himself from nature by concentration on a miserable ball. His mind is not dulled but lively with expectation and, of all the virtues, patience is the one he least requires.

. . . What other people mistake for patience in anglers is really nothing of the sort but a capacity for prolonged eagerness, an unquenchable gusto in relishing an infinite series of exciting and promising moments, any one of which may yield a sudden crisis with its climax of triumph or disaster.

Perhaps there is less difference between the back-country, very physical fly fisherman in New Zealand or in British Columbia, and his sedentary counterpart on European canals, ponds, and gently flowing streams of easy access, intent on watching his float for the merest twitch, than even anglers themselves imagine. Whilst fishing, both are keyed up and hyperactive with expectation and anticipation. And the magic lies in the anticipation.

One of the less than admiring early-nineteenth century commentators on anglers and angling, James Henry Leigh Hunt, remarked on the astonishing lack of success fishermen suffered; so that he dubbed each one a 'prince of punters'. What non-fishermen see as being mindless patience is, in essence, the illogical likelihood of any of them ever catching a fish. To such men angling seems such a deplorable waste of time, a frittering away of life that might be better spent. Leigh Hunt recounts an often-told story, but fails to see that the lack of success he ridicules is really part of the very heart of angling and full of the supercharged expectancy of the fisherman about his business.

The tale is about a man and his family out walking along a riverbank. They passed a lone fisherman and on enquiring from him if he had caught any fish, he replied that he had caught nothing. That evening, on their return walk, they saw the same man still huddled over his rod, and asked again whether he had had any success. 'No,' he answered, 'but just an hour ago I had a glorious nibble.'

None but an addicted angler could possibly understand that much of fishing is really about Glorious Nibbles. Most certainly it has nothing to do with patience.

It may be, of course, that the magic is chemistry in motion, and nothing more. Might it be that this concentrated expectation and anticipation releases little shots of adrenalin into the angler's system; while a glorious nibble induces a yet more potent injection; and the take of a good fish and the subsequent 'battle' of capture or loss is nothing short of a longed-for fix of heady adrenalin? Are we anglers addicted to our own adrenalin? Are we hooked on what we know it will do *for* us, rather than what it is? I really don't think so, but it is a sobering thought should we become too lyrical and enthusiastic about it.

It will be known by passionate anglers, and should be becoming clear to any non-anglers who may have made the mistake of reading this book, that it is extraordinarily difficult to describe the 'feel' and essence of fly fishing without seeming to be either crass or bemused or most definitely odd. No sooner does one begin to penetrate layers of its meaning, than other layers appear out of nowhere. It is virtually impossible to write much about this 'feel' of fly fishing without sounding like a real Charlie. We have seen how extraordinarily difficult it is to write meaningfully about why men fish or why they praise it. Yet some do find occasional words that say all that is necessary — at least to fellow fishermen.

Arthur Ransome was such a man. Writing about that half-world in which fishermen can seem suspended when other men, non-anglers, see them as near imbecilic morons, Ransome told of that 'benign moment', adding immediately that it was difficult to define or explain, though every fisherman knows it:

> It is like one of those sudden silences in a general conversation when, in England, we say, 'An angel passes' and in Russia, in the old days, they used to say, 'A policeman is being born'. The day is not that day but another. Everything feels and looks different.

In a delightful little book, *The Pleasures of Fishing*, Logie Bruce Lockhart saw fishing as lust, rather than addiction: It always was a mistake, he wrote, to believe that fishing, especially trout fishing, called for patience. It is, of course, a fever, an all-consuming lust that can brook neither opposition nor interruption.

Even the writers of fishing manuals are tender about the scoffing jibes that mindless patience is a prerequisite of angling. In 1904, in *Trout Fishing*, W. Earl Hodgson saw it as a kinship with the arts:

> Patience, which so many persons suppose to be the necessary qualification, is certainly required; but it is not a thoughtless or inactive patience. It is not merely willingness to wait for an hour, or two hours, or a whole day, watching for an indication that the lure has proved attractive. Patience of that kind has but a small part in the sport. The befitting patience is more than a lazy or stoical endurance. It is continually alert. It embraces much more knowledge and a much greater resourcefulness of thought than are commonly imagined. It is a state of mind more complex than that which is necessary to success in any other pursuit on flood or field.

Salmon fishing, at least as practised in Scotland in those days, was free it seems of any odium on account of this supposed near-imbecilic patience. That most rollicking and rumbustious of all fishing writers, William Scrope, had this to say about it in his book *Days and Nights of Salmon Fishing*:

> I say then, and will maintain it, that a salmon fisher should be strong in the arms, or he will never be able to keep on thrashing for ten or twelve hours together with a rod eighteen or twenty feet long, with ever and anon a lusty salmon at the end of his line, pulling like a wild horse with the lasso about him. Now he is obliged to keep his arms aloft, that the line may clear the rocks; now he must rush into the river, then back out with nimble pastern, always keeping a steady and proper strain of line; and he must preserve his self-possession, 'even in the very tempest and

whirlwind of the sport,' when the salmon rushes like a rocket. This is not moody work; it keeps a man alive and stirring. Patience, indeed!

The bucolic, idyllic and romantic view of nature and of outdoor pursuits was not, as is often suggested, invented by the lyrical poets of the early nineteenth century. In England, at least as far as fishing was concerned, it had a long history going back before the age of Dame Juliana Berners into the mists of time. The Christian church had long sequestered most of the finest fishing waters throughout the kingdom. Just look at the sites of most abbeys, cathedrals, priories, nunneries, and other religious houses built astride and commanding the finest stretches of Kentish Stour, Ouse, Arun, Itchen, Avon, Dorset Stour, Axe, Exe, Dart, Bristol Avon, Teme, Severn, Wye, Usk, Taff, Kennet, Dee, Trent, Witham, Ribble, Yorkshire Ouse, Lune, Esk, Eden, Tyne, to name but a few that spring to mind, and not counting the hundreds of delectable fishing tributaries. It was suggested that the religious orders were needful of ready access to and availability of fish in order that they might faithfully observe the many holy and other fast days prohibiting the eating of meat. Whether for this reason or not, the great religious houses were mostly built on the flatter, more lush water meadows of rivers, affording the monks quick and easy access to the creation of fishponds, stews, carrier streams, weirs, and the epitome of the pastoral riverbanks that still persist in the public imagination as 'fishing waters'.

Added to this there was the deep-seated and mystical symbolism of fish, fishing, and fishermen underlying the Christian ethic. By Walton's day the associations were complete, except that the monasteries had long been sequestered by the Crown. Country landowners were no longer necessarily warring knights. They had time and leisure to enjoy the bucolic pursuits of the abundant countryside under a less demanding God who smiled upon them.

Even in the age of the Dame fishing was seen, by some at least, to be a sport and a wholesome sport at that, commended in their view by Christ himself. It seems little wonder than that patience, being an admirable Christian virtue of the times, should have become intrinsically associated with the practice of angling.

Long afterwards, when an emerging middle-class of British society took to the outdoors, rather than avoiding it whenever possible, they generally tended to walk beside well-trodden river banks close to towns and villages, through lazy and lush water meadows. Their view of fishermen was naturally sedentary. It was the fisherman who was sedentary, while they, out walking, were commendably active. In such a manner did the less than flattering populist view of the angler as a shiftless character take shape.

Soon after Wordsworth and his fellow romantics took to the hills and dales rather than remain in sight of the cathedral spire, the wildness of Scotland and Wales began to capture the popular imagination. Heroics were again to be admired. Men sometimes died salmon fishing. Fishing was to become work, albeit a splendid work that could capture a man's imagination as well as his mind. The more literary fishing became — and it most certainly did — the more it became adventure. Not many non-fishers, however, would have observed the likes of William Scrope doing battle with huge and powerful salmon. But thousands still saw the solitary fishermen huddled along sluggish river banks and the growing networks of canals. The picture of the typical fisherman was firmly established in the public mind, and, for that matter, still is.

Seen from a little distance a fisherman, even a salmon fly fisherman, rarely seems to be actually *doing* anything. To a non-fisher, if he doesn't have a fish on, it must be a boring occupation, hence one requiring this imbecilic patience. This attitude is far from being confined to places where coarse fishing, match fishing, and sea fishing of the end-of-the-pier variety may be seen at first hand. In New Zealand, for example, where coarse fishing virtually does not exist, and there are no seaside pleasure piers, there is still a generally held public view that trout and salmon fishermen are a strange bunch of people who have departed from the norms of reality by engaging in a sport requiring this same mindless patience. Yet the fishing I knew there was often exceedingly wild and rugged and remote. Whatever other qualities it may have called for, patience certainly wasn't one of them.

Previous mention has been made of Arthur Ransome's 'benign moment'. Another author, C. W. K. Mundle, a Professor of Philosophy, passionate angler and keen observer of paranormal aspects of fishing, wrote in his *Game Fishing — Methods & Memories* of the need to 'rest when tired' while fishing. For him there was a definite link between success in fishing and 'psychic powers'. Mundle's theory suggested that this height of concentration — what non-anglers confuse with patience — could be kept up only for brief periods, beyond which the angler became 'tired' and was advised to rest. What Professor Mundle called the exercise of 'psychic powers' may be the very same thing as Arthur Ransome's 'benign moment', and similar to what an American fishing writer, Robert G. Deindorfer, in *Positive Fishing* called achieving 'a state of flow'. These phenomena have been described in other chapters of this book, but in the present context they are associated with that undoubted form of super-concentration and involvement seen by non-anglers as being the exercise of patience. Patience, however, is a mere passive waiting for something that might happen, while the 'benign moment' is more an awareness that the hoped-for happening is imminent, and the 'state of flow' is the exercise of powers willing it to occur.

A. H. Chaytor, who was a barrister and not subject to flights of fancy, put it this way in a chapter of his classic *Letters to a Salmon Fisher's Sons*:

> That, my dear boys, is spring fishing all over. Pool after pool, looking perfect, and certain, as you feel, to hold fish, you fish over without a sign. Your high hopes are growing faint or have gone altogether, when, often at the most unlikely place, jump in your arm goes an electric thrill, and the one rise of the day has come and the fish is gone: or else, hardly knowing how it has happened, your nerves are found watching, and the half-raised rod is twitching and quivering with the line tight upon a plunging, splashing, rolling salmon, beginning a battle of anxious, growing hope, ending with a noble, glittering prize.
>
> As far as catching fish goes, you may now go home. Unless your lines are, indeed, cast in pleasant places you have had your only fish of the day, and you will catch no more. The memories of many days of spring fishing tell us so, and in our hearts we know it as we admire this shapely, shining fish. But, go home! do you say? Hang it, man, the day is only just begun. Go home! Don't you know that every cast that I make after this I shall feel certain that I am going to take another fish. I shall be fishing better than I have ever fished today. I've got one; nothing can make it a blank day now, and, with a little luck, I shall certainly get another.
>
> Well, this is called patience by those who don't know. But it is nothing at all like patience. It is hope, undying, unquenchable, the heart and soul of salmon fishing.

And elsewhere in the same book:

> And then there is the joy of fishing itself; of throwing a line whether fish take or no. It seems impossible to convey the reality of this as a separate pleasure, to any but honest anglers. 'You fish?' they say. 'What patience you must have.' Not at all: hardly anything is less true. Some of the most impatient souls alive are untiring salmon fishers; men to whom blank days or lost fish are but as whetstones to keener fishing on the morrow.

In Robert Deindorfer's view this singlemindedness in fishing he termed 'state of flow' was a sort of emotional high obtained through confidence and concentration. The flow did not come directly as a result of confidence or concentration, or both; but could not materialize unless those factors were present. Such a positive fisherman once told him, 'I get myself in sort of a groove. I'm happy and enjoying myself and I can feel the groove growing. Sometimes I get so wound up that I almost forget it's me catching the fish. I see the fish, see it jumping and thrashing and being pretty well handled. It's funny, but I'm always sure it's me on the other end of the line.' Deindorfer comments:

> During those times when a fisherman, an athlete, an artist, or almost anyone truly enjoying whatever it is he's doing experiences the soothing sense of flow, his skill, perception, and performance improve. The more consumed a participant becomes in spinning out beyond the limits of self-consciousness, the better he is likely to perform. Ballplayers sometimes speak of special moments when they are playing out of their minds, beyond the rim of their talents, in a zone they have trouble explaining later. Almost invariably those special moments unfold when they are feeling a happiness close to exaltation.

Anxieties and a sense of daunting challenge tend to inhibit natural flow. This is the common experience of beginning anglers, whose nerve ends tighten because the sport seems so bewildering as they progress into it. If fishing becomes too easy, the fish themselves too plentiful, too simple to hook, too defeated while they are being played, boredom may also take over. And boredom stifles flow just as much as anxiety does. Deindorfer quotes Daniel Coleman who said:

> The domain of flow is the band between anxiety and boredom. An alert mind resists boredom by keeping us involved in events around us. A relaxed body is the physiological opposite of tension. The two together — alert mind, relaxed body — combine to make us ripe for flow.

What makes fishing especially susceptible to flow is its basic simplicity. Keep it simple.

That English ecclesiastic among nineteenth century fishing writers, the Reverend J. J. Manley, put it this way:

> That patience is one of the virtues of an angler, is a trite theme. 'Ye have heard of the patience of Job.' Who has heard of the patience of the fisherman? An old angler and writer in 1692, says, with a slight touch of sarcasm, and perhaps after a blank day —

> 'If patience be a virtue, then
> How happy are we fishermen!
> For all who know that those who fish
> Have patience more than heart can wish.

But whether anglers have patience or not, certain it is that this virtue is a *sine qua non* for success. I hold they have it, and that the constant pursuit of their pastime is constantly developing it. Bad sport, like bad sermons, calls forth this virtue. That some anglers are impatient I admit; and doubtless they were so in Walton's time, as he advises them 'to be patient, and forbear swearing, lest they be heard and catch no fish.'

But as for this disclaimer, sometimes heard from anglers themselves, that patience *is* necessary in fishing, they have failed to understand the heart of the matter. We have read at the beginning of this chapter some of the views expressed by Arthur Ransome in *Rod & Line*. Developing the same line of argument he wrote:

> Something rather like patience may be required by the kind of fisherman who casts a fly mechanically and uniformly and is jerked into consciousness only by some extraordinarily altruistic little trout who in a passion of benevolence hangs himself on the end of an undeserving line. But such fishermen seldom persist and, if they do persist, learn to fish in a different manner. Fishing, properly so called, is conducted under continuous tension. The mere putting of fly or bait on or in the water is an action needing skill, an action that can be done well or ill and consequently a source of pleasure. Many an angler returns with an empty basket after a day made delightful by the knowledge that he was putting his float exactly where he wanted it, casting his fly a little better than usual, or dropping his spinner with less splash at greater distances . . . He knows that a mistake is all but irrevocable, that a first cast has a better chance than a third. His day is a long series of crises and demands on his presence of mind. Even in float-fishing so much depends on observation, on watercraft, on the reading of barely perceptible signs, that those who imagine that a good fisherman can watch his float and think of something else beside his fishing are very much mistaken. So completely does fishing occupy a man that if a good angler had murdered one of those people who prate about patience and were allowed to spend his last day at the river instead of in the condemned cell, he would forget the rope.

The ultimate test, in Ransome's view, is one of time; patience being a virtue required when time goes slowly. In fishing time goes too fast. Note, too, how often this element of time enters all such attempts at explaining what happens when an appropriately passionate angler is about his business. It is commonly said — though extraordinarily difficult to say it well — that it seems, both during the event and in subsequent recollection, as it time itself had slipped or warped. Odell Shepard, in *Thy Rod and Thy Creel*, observed that:

> One can play the piano while thinking of the morning's mail, or one can watch a baseball game while planning a bank-robbery, but in order to fish successfully, at any rate for the nobler species, one must give one's whole attention to the sport in hand. And this is the reason why a trout-rod is the best magician's wand for exorcising the ghosts of care.

Whatever else it may be, this elusive but certain quality of angling is far from being plain patience, or anything remotely to do with that singular virtue. Fishermen dream in their beds at night, the proper place for dreaming to be done. And fully evolved fishermen are those who, in Sven Berlin's words, are interested in everything but the fish's death. There can, perhaps, be no last word on this matter, except to quote Theocritus, who wrote three centuries before Christ:

Sleeping we image what awake we wish;
Dogs dream of bones, and fishermen of fish.

Chapter 14
Hands off!

Anglers often go to extraordinary lengths in order to remain unseen and unheard by the fish they seek to catch. Such measures frequently employ the camouflage and stealth of a commando; and rightly so, too, for they are necessary if the fish are to be deceived — and all fishing is based on deceit, deception and sleight of hand, making a feathered or baited hook seem like a free and easy meal. This is especially so in the case of fly fishing for trout, where the angler has to approach his quarry more closely than in almost any other kind of fishing.

Many fishermen have some knowledge of the optics of a trout's cone of vision, and of the refraction of a ray of light leaving the air and entering the water often permitting the trout to be able to see us before we can see them. Similarly the trout's upward field of vision outside its central overhead window consists of an opaque mirror surface enabling the trout to see what lies behind stones, boulders and tree trunks by means of its ceiling reflection, in what seems to us to be a remarkable refinement and extension of the business of seeing. Few anglers will not have seen trout shoot off for cover at their approach, however quiet and careful they think their bankside stealth has been.

Most knowledgeable anglers are fastidious about a quiet and unseen approach to their fishing, but few even stop to consider that of all the trout's remarkably acute senses perhaps the most dominant of all is its sense of smell. In comparison with its sense of smell, the senses of sight and hearing in a fish are relatively crude and limited. Yet the sense of smell in fish, and the use or misuse of it by the angler, has been well documented from the earliest times. Izaak Walton wrote of it as a slyly revealed secret:

> And now I shall tell you, that which may be called a secret: I have been a-fishing with old Oliver Henly (now with God) a noted fisher for both Trout and Salmon, and have observed, that he would usually take three or four worms out of his bag, and put them into a little box in his pocket, where he would usually let them continue half an hour or more, before he

would bait his hook with them; I have asked him his reason, and he has replyed, He did but pick the best out to be in readiness against he baited his hook the next time: But he has been observed both by others, and my self, to catch more fish than I, or any other body, that has ever gone a-fishing with him, could do; and especially Salmons; And I have been told lately by one of his most intimate and secret friends, that the box in which he put those worms, was anointed with a drop, or two or three, of the Oyl of Ivy-berries, made by expression or infusion; and told that by the worms remaining in that box an hour, or a like time, they had incorporated a kind of smell that was irresistibly attractive, enough to force any Fish within the smell of them, to bite. This I heard not long since from a friend, but have not tryed it; yet I grant it probable, and refer my Reader to Sir Francis Bacons Natural History, where he proves fishes may hear and doubtless can more probably smell: and I am certain Gesner says, the Otter can smell in the water, and I know not but that Fish may do so too: 'tis left for a lover of Angling, or any that desires to improve that Art, to try this conclusion.

As if that was not sufficient a secret Walton goes straight on with more:

I shall also impart two other Experiments (but not tryed by myself) which I will deliver in the same words that they were given me by an excellent Angler and a very friend, in writing; he told me the latter was too good to be told, but in a learned language, lest it should be made common.
'Take the stinking oil drawn out of Polypody of the Oak by a retort, mixt with Turpentine, and Hive-honey, and anoint your bait therewith, and it will doubtless draw the fish to it.'
The other is this: *vulnera bederae grandissimae inflicta sudant balsumum oleo gelato, albicantique persimile, ordoris vero longi suavissimi.*
'Tis supremely sweet to any fish, and yet *asafoetida* may do the like.

Bait additives — gunks and lotions to smear on more conventional baits — are with us still and even occasionally appear in advertisements in popular fishing magazines. Almost invariably they promise a bottle of a secret and irresistible recipe into which any fish or meat bait, or even spoon, spinner, lure or artificial fly may be dipped to ensure instant and bigger catches. Pilchard oil, sperm oil, menhaden oil, all have their recurrent vogues, while other less fishy concoctions based on aniseed or some essential oils are often resurrected to entice gullible fisherman, if not the fish. Some are no more than placebos by which the angler may have increased confidence, and so, in many cases, have more success.

In earlier years these bait additives were even more bizarre, and were part of the apothecary's art. Izaak Walton wrote, 'And some affirm, that any bait anointed with the marrow of the Thigh-bone of an Hern is a great temptation to any Fish.'

There were occasional tendencies to lure with tastes and smells such as we ourselves are often atracted to, as Walton says, 'There are almost as many sorts as there are Medicines for the Toothache; but doubtless sweet pastes are best; I mean, pastes made with honey or with sugar: which, that you may the better beguile this crafty Fish.' In Walton's day it would seem that anglers, even then, dreamed of a magic potion of bait additive. Here we find him back to his old tentativeness:

Not that but I think Fishes both smell and hear but there is a mysterious Knack, which (though it be much easier than the Philosophers Stone, yet) is not attainable by common capacities, or else lies locked up in the brain or breast of some chymical man, that, like the Rosi-crucians, will not yet reveal it.

The awareness of the senses of fish is there, but the search for the right bait additive is so shrouded in magic potions, alchemy and the search for the Philosopher's Stone by 'chymical men', that it fails to connect with how we see it from our present-day point view. But as in Walton's day we do too much anthropomorphizing over the matter. With fish this is especially dangerous as they live in a vastly different medium from our own. We cannot turn ourselves into fish, or can we ever fully appreciate what it must be like to smell under and in water.

Yet our human aquatic origins are still evident in the way in which our sense of smell is activated. We inhale minute particles of smell substances through our nostrils, but these first have to be dissolved in the mucous fluids lining our nasal passages before our brains can detect, register and recognize smell sensations. In fish the smell substances are dissolved in the water in which it lives.

The senses of sight, hearing, awareness of heat and of cold, awareness of changes in pressure, and that of touch or contact, may all be called physical senses in that in each one of them physical phenomena are received, which signals are then transformed into nervous energy. The senses of smell and taste, by contrast, are chemical senses, in that they transform chemical phenomena or messages into nervous energy.

In fish the smell receptors are located, like ours, in nostrils, but the nostrils themselves are quite unlike our own, and are not connected with the throat by means of nasal passages. Instead, the nostrils of the fish consist of two side openings leading into blind sacs where the organs of smell are situated. Here there are either delicate muscles or little moving hairs called *cilia* which keep a water current flowing in through the sacs and out via a rear opening.

The taste buds are located on the tongues of fish and are probably acutely aware of sour, salt and bitter senses, but perhaps not so much, if at all, of sweetness. However closely related taste and smell may be there is one essential difference. Smell is possible at a distance — sometimes a very great distance — whereas taste presupposes actual physical contact with the substance tasted. The sense of smell is rather like a sense of taste operating at a distance, helping the animal to find what is good for it to take into its mouth for final confirmation by taste that it will be good to eat.

Some fish that feed in turbid waters or forage along the bottom are provided with external taste organs in the form of barbels, so that they may taste things before taking them in their mouths. But, as virtually all fish sometimes have to cope with turbid waters and survive in such conditions, they too are provided with at least some external taste buds, usually clustered on their heads, but sometimes spread along their bodies.

Sharks have relatively poor eyesight and rely on their sense of smell in locating food. Experiments with sharks in tanks have shown how they will become animated and excited when broken up food such as pieces of fish flesh is thrown into the tank. They then start a regular figure-of-eight reconnoitre of the tank, and appear not to see the bait until they are right on top of it, when it will be taken with a lunge. If their nostrils are plugged with cotton wool soaked in vaseline the sharks show no consciousness or awareness of the food at all. This explains why sharks generally only attack wounded prey. It is also a well-established fact that sharks have been known to pinpoint a potential victim perhaps swimming or wading in a shallow part of a beach, well inside a line of swimmers, and home in on the hapless and unsuspecting victim in a searing speed attack while ignoring other closer at hand bathers.

Ships occasionally need to stop at sea while on ocean passages, either to repair some engine defect, or to do some planned engine maintenance, or sometimes even to waste time as economically as possible before arriving at their next port. For obvious reasons it is always best to do this in times of calm weather and away from busy shipping lanes. During my time in command of a wide variety of ships I always tried to choose the time and place of such stoppages to best coincide where fish and fishing might be expected. One of my very favourite places, after clearing the Panama Canal and bound across the South Pacific, was well offshore in the vicinity of the Galapagos Islands. But often there was little or no choice and stoppages might have to be made in even lonelier reaches of the oceans, or sometimes closer to continental coastlines.

Wherever we stopped, in deep ocean waters in the tropics or in shallower waters in more temperate latitudes, it would not be long, with some chopped up meat or fish thrown over the side, before pelagic fish and sharks would appear as if from nowhere. Most common of all in tropical waters were dorado (the dolphin fish, *Coryphaena hippurus*, not the mammalian dolphin, for they prefer a ship under way at speed); eager, inquisitive, incredibly fast and voracious. But always the ubiquitous shark, mostly of a single species at any one time, but almost always in packs of anything from five or six to more considerable numbers far too difficult to estimate. They would appear, as if from nowhere, however far from land, homing in on the scent of food from out of a seemingly empty ocean.

In the case of trout and salmon the sense of smell is acute, yet the development of the olfactory lobes of their brains is generally poor compared with, say, their respective optic lobes. This, it is suggested, is due to discrimination. Optical messages are received over an enormously wide range of light and dark, and the stimuli are well processed by the fish into pertinent information. Olfactory messages may be very basic. The chemical receptors alone are acute in their awareness, but the brain processing of the information is probably limited to interest followed by a searching pattern towards the source of the smell as being likely food, or else sudden interest based on fear and necessitating flight. The latter is the more likely prime use of the trout's sense of smell. Their habitat is such, and their other senses so acute and well developed, that only rarely will they need to hunt food by smell alone, although it will always be an additional attractor to the principal sensory information provided by sight, sound, and lateral line vibrations.

With salmon and trout one outstanding attractor compulsion of scent is that of the olfactory cues they receive in their homeward migration to their parent streams. This well documented, although still improperly understood, phenomena does not explain how migratory trout and salmon find their way across thousands of miles of apparently trackless ocean, but that is another matter. The olfactory cues of the parent stream must be diffuse and weak even close to the stream mouth with the effect of tides and ocean currents, yet the migratory fish not only find the estuary, but the main stream mouth, with unfailing and uncanny accuracy. They will ascend hundreds of miles, if needs be, before branching off into the proper tributary — and then several even smaller and lesser upstream tributaries — until they reach the gravels of their natal headwaters.

As for the way in which outward migrating salmon and trout, particularly all species of Pacific salmon, none of which fish had made the journey before, return to their oceanic feeding grounds, it is now thought that a residual race-odour of past generations in the gyral waters of the sea allows the young fish to know they have 'arrived' at their outward destination.

However marvellous and awe-inspiring this may seem to us, and whatever incredible dilutions of water composition and smell substances its achievement presupposes, it is still, I believe, a compulsive action by the homing fish. They have no choice in the matter. They cannot disregard the call. They cannot allow any other considerations to deter them. Especially in upstream migration they are not their own masters, or even in control of their own actions.

Research into the upstream runs of migratory salmon and trout have shown that the fish lose all sense of direction and purposefulness if their nostrils are temporarily blocked, but immediately set off upstream again when the cotton wool pellets are removed. It has also been demonstrated that certain smells put into the water above dam fish passes have totally inhibited the fish ascending. In one experiment fifty-four separate odours were used, including bear scent, sealskin, sea-lion scent, human scent, various other animal scents, fish oils, shark repellants — a very wide range of smell substances. Most had no effect on the ascending fish, but they reacted strongly to human smells, and to the scents of seals, bears, dogs and sea-lions — all of which caused them to retreat back down the fish-pass, although the introduced scents were more than a hundred yards above the fish at the time. A man's hand dipped into the water a hundred yards above stream ascending fish has been known to divert and stop them.

In experiments designed to show the repellent effect of smell substances always present on the skin of humans, as well as bears and sea-lions, it was discovered that this active substance, L-serine, elicited reactions at dilutions up to 1.30×10^{-10}.

It seems then not unreasonable that the fish will be aware of man's scent or odour on flies and lures he has handled. This may have particular significance for those anglers who may be more troubled and perplexed than others, by the frequency with which fish will mouth or pull at their flies without actually taking them. It happens to us all from time to time, but could it be that it happens to some anglers more often than not?

This human chemical substance of smell is something we all have, but perhaps in varying degrees. Maybe it is generated at certain times, or even in certain states of mind such as anger, frustration, or even fear. One thing we can be certain of: it is repellent to fish.

We handle our flies and keep them about our persons while fishing. If anglers even think of it at all, they probably suppose that the water itself will wash off any smell from their fingers. This is indeed a naive assumption when we have seen it is water itself that is the medium that carries the chemical messages of scent to the fish. The smell is there, impregnated in the object. It might wear off to our poor atrophying senses, but will not do so as far as the fish are concerned.

There are certain other amalgams of smells. Anglers often keep flies in empty tobacco tins that must forever afterwards imprint those flies with its odour. It doesn't matter whether trout find the smell of tobacco pleasant or repulsive. But they might either associate it with man, who is feared, or simply be repelled by its strangeness.

It is interesting to note that hatchery keepers handle trout pellets and throw them into their trout rearing ponds, and it is possible that some hatchery trout are conditioned from hatching onwards to this human scent and may even associate it with food. If so, it would not seem impossible or even improbable, that human scent might be an attraction to newly stocked hatchery trout in a small fishery, and that they might associate this human smell with food. This may provide yet another reason why newly stocked fish are relatively easy to catch. Nevertheless, hatchery stocked fish become more or less fully accustomed to the wild in a few days. It is axiomatic that if they don't, they are caught. Once forced to seek natural, available food their fear of man is instinctive — as every fly fisherman knows.

I used to fish a Hampshire chalkstream carrier stocked with brown trout and rainbows from the estate's own hatcheries. These, and the rearing stews and growing-on ponds were large and spacious, and incorporated in the maintream of a feeder to the stream itself. In this manner, although the trout were pellet fed, they had available to them an abundance of natural food from this rich alkaline chalkstream water. It was significant that these fish were harder to catch, and showed all the characteristics of wild fish, than others I sometimes angled for in another stillwater fishery that came direct from hatchery stocks where their feeding was totally artificial. They were raised in concrete stews virtually empty of any natural fly, nymph, or shrimp life. Even where it might have existed, the crowded life conditions for the trout would have precluded it, by sheer congestion as well as competition.

But, hatchery stock or wild fish notwithstanding, the survivors not only have, but use, all their senses and instincts to avoid man's intrusion in their lives. The thoughtful angler may do well to consider the sense of smell of fish as well as their remarkable avoidance response to him by way of sight and sound.

Even in this age of headlong scientific advancement we humans are still guilty of anthropomorphizing our view of the natural world. Our view of most other creatures and especially of the senses by which they become aware of and respond to their environment, seems increasingly governed by our appreciation of our own senses and sensory mechanisms. We are even guilty, at times at least, of thinking that animals *think* like us. And anglers are not less guilty of this anthropomorphism than the cartoon creators of Bambi and Yogi Bear. Fly fishermen observe a trout seemingly following their lure and assume the fishing is 'thinking' about whether or not to grab hold of it; whereas the trout, in truth, is responding to an unfolding chain of stimuli directing its actions, in which choice may not even figure. The trout is programmed to react to certain stimuli in a certain way. However much it may seem to be 'thinking' about its ultimate decision, it isn't.

In the evolution of all animal life the sense of smell was always the first to develop. Far from being primitive in the scheme of things, this sense of olfaction has in most insects, virtually all fish, and some animals such as dogs and bears and deer, been refined to such a degree of sophistication that it is only as a result of recent discoveries in molecular chemistry that man has begun to divine its secrets. Yet man once shared a closer affinity of odour perception with the rest of the animal kingdom than he does today.

Some species have found ways of codifying scent information as a means of communication. The means of transmission are analogous to our use of language, which in our case is based upon our most highly developed sense of sight. We give names to impressions we receive via our senses, assign descriptive words to thoughts, activities, positions in time or space, and then break up these words into sound elements, each of which we represent by a letter or group of letters. Such symbols, marked on a convenient surface, then provide us with a visible code that we can read and process again in our brain in order to conceptualize the thought or image encoded in the written words.

By such means fish such as salmon have 'invented' the equivalents of 'words' and 'names' for the experiences they have become aware of via their sense of smell. These 'words', reduced to a code of odorous particles, can be smelled again when required and these smells reprocessed in their brains to convey the original concept.

Writing in *Other Senses, Other Worlds*, Doris and David Jonas said:

> Smell signals have a quality we human beings do not immediately recognize: the large number of elements available for the synthesis of any particular odour. It has been found that the smell of a human being consists of twenty-four separate elements. Dogs could identify many more, but even in all their possible combinations and permutations, just twenty-four separate elements would be enough to identify every single human being in the world with as individual a mark of recognition as his or her fingerprints.

It is such by means that salmon are imprinted with the odour of their parent stream, and are able — often years later, after life at sea on the far side of the ocean — to home in to the main river then single out the same tributary where they were hatched.

Despite the vast sums of money spent on research and development of smell substances in the perfume and toilet industry, and despite the current near-obsession of some parts of the popular press to familiarize readers with the properties of pheromones, the real nature of smell substances themselves is little understood. Pheromones are sometimes in the news in the marketing and advertising of perfumes and other scented products. In this context pheromones are used as attractants — fundamentally sex attractants, however much we mask the image as being one of pleasant smells. Pheromones are basically hormones with an outside effect on other members of the same species. They are, in fact, essential in many functions of human and other animal life, and especially so for fishes and for insects. They are the building blocks of language or, at the very least, communication between members of the same species.

There is an apparently copious dictionary of odorous substances. Even now it is clear that the animals' scent language is not just a primitive substitute, conditioned by the medium, for the language of sounds and gestures, but an amazingly versatile, ingenious, and highly differentiated means of communication.

Even dead fish, as well as injured fish, produce an important pheromone. This too is an integral part of the communication strategy of their community, though little understood. We are so conditioned to seeing the sun, moon, stars — while many creatures either cannot see or only dimly see them — that we utilize certain visual information from these bodies, then use our brains to supplement this information by logical extensions of it and use these for navigation, for gaining knowledge of the universe, and eventually for technology based on this knowledge.

Other creatures only feel the warmth of the hidden or unseen sun, or sense cosmic electromagnetic emanations. It may be they further translate these received signals into olfactory terms, just as the instruments of astronomers can receive electromagnetic and other energy pulses, light waves, and the like, and register these in visual terms.

This idea is by no means as fanciful as it might first seem. Even among human begins who, by comparison with many other animals, are rather dumb to odour signals, we can demonstrate the remnants of the inherent acuity of the olfactory sense.

One of the substances that can be perceived independently by three of our senses is alcohol. We can smell it, taste it, or feel it if it is rubbed on our skin. But it takes 60,000 times the amount of alcohol for us to feel it on the skin, and 20,000 times as much to taste it, as it does to smell it. Our taste organs are equipped to perceive relatively large amounts of a substance, but smell brings us news of the presence of the most minute quantities.

Remember that this faculty of smell, vestigial and yet still so sensitive in human beings, is magnified a 100- and 1,000-fold in other creatures, we can begin to realize how potent, how malleable, and how refined an instrument for communication it could be if it were at the disposal of highly intelligent beings.

By way of comparison with an animal with whom all men are familiar, a dog's sense of smell is one million times more acute that a human's.

Another recent discovery is that many odorous solutions strongly absorb waves from both the infrared and ultraviolet portions of the spectrum, and perhaps it is significant that there is a connection between odours and the part of the spectrum that is invisible to us. Do fish, then, *smell* colours? Are feathers irradiated by waves either end of our visible spectrum somehow recognizable by olfactory means?

An interesting consideration is that odour signals are perceptible around corners or in other blind spots, and also in complete darkness, where sight alone would be useless. Because of these considerations, an intelligence based on the olfactory sense must be of a different nature from our own. Where at least the immediate past, and sometimes the more distant past, blends with the present in its immediacy, concepts and basic ways of thinking must be moulded by this kind of awareness. As Doris and David Jonas commented on this state of affairs: 'In *our* thoughts and terms of expression, the past is sharply distinguished from the present. A person out of sight is no longer with us. He *was* there, but he *is* so no longer, and out of sight, as the maxim has it, he is probably out of mind.'

How then can we imagine a 'vocabulary' of smell? Basically all our visual symbols are elaborations of the straight line and the curve. From these extremely simple elements, which are all that are registered by our retinas, our brain recognizes combinations that its associative apparatus converts into visual patterns and words to describe them. Colour is added by a similar process. When a light ray with a wavelength of 635 to 640 millionths of a millimetre bombards the retina, the brain interprets this and we 'see' red. The same light ray bombarding another portion of our anatomy is perceived according to the sense capacity of that organ. Our skin may perceive it as heat.

We tend to perceive odours in our minds as associated remembered images — a visual memory. It we smell a rose we remember what it looks like. We have no words to describe the smell of a rose and we cannot define it in terms of language. A primary olfactory intelligence could do this.

Any degenerative process, whether evolutionary or in the ageing of a single individual, begins with the loss of the most recently acquired function, while the oldest and once most vital remains to the end. In this manner old people may begin to lose their senses of sight and hearing, but not of smell. The potential for gathering information via the nose was an essential part of our past and remains with us even though it has been overlaid by the dominance of the sight brain and the neocortical layer that endows us with reason.

We have seen how those chemical messengers called hormones carry out vital integrating functions *within* any animal organism, while pheromones perform similar coordinating functions externally. The possibilities of scent are at least as subtle as words, although they convey their meaning on a different channel and to a different destination. Travelling directly to the emotional centre of the brain, they activate immediate responses, while words travel to the reasoning centres of the brain, which must re-interpret them and relay instructions to the appropriate executive centres. Scent language provides a direct line, whereas verbal language must pass through relay stations.

It is likely that so complex are olfactory creatures in odour perceptiveness and interpretation that this sense conveys a spatial patterning analogous to the three-dimensional quality of vision. In this manner it may be that if a dog smells, say, a deer, its olfactory brain receives graded messages from different parts of the deer's body, forming a three-dimensional pattern in the dog's brain. The dog will be able to perceive and recognize even in darkness what kind of animal it is, its size, shape, and anatomical features. But the dog would know more than we do, even via sight. It could also discern from the deer's various glandular secretions whether the deer is hostile or afraid, male or female, in heat or other states of health or mood.

Most animals probably interpret these kinds of odours only in their own species or in species with which they are closely involved, as in the predator-prey relationship. But cross-species scent recognition is common. This may explain why many species of fish are as terrified of the presence of men as they are of seals, sea-lions and bears.

The Jonas's postulate yet another possibility:

> An understanding of this 'in-depth' quality of the olfactory brain offers a tantalizing glimpse of the unexplored land of our emotions, which are closely linked to the sense of smell.
>
> We describe our emotions with words that have spatial connotations: '*wave* of pity', '*flow* of feeling', '*height* of ecstasy', '*depths of* despair', '*surge* of love', 'a *welling up* of envy'. Moreover we think of emotions as waxing and waning, persisting or lingering, which implies a diffusion over time, again not unlike the similar lingering qualities of the sense of smell. Beyond the spatial quality and its extension into time, there are other words — *overwhelming*, *overpowering*, *intolerable*, *unbearable* — that we use to describe both emotions and smells.

We cannot explain these things for the same reason we cannot define an odour — because it arises in a part of the mind over which reason has no jurisdiction.

It should be clear by now than man's sense of smell has diminished along the evolutionary path we seem to have taken, yet memories of its one time preponderance in our lives comes back at times, however fleetingly and hauntingly, from sources we little comprehend, so compelling that these occasional flashes leave us with a sense of *déjà vu*.

There are few of us who, at times, quite suddenly, and always quite unexpectedly, become aware of a long forgotten smell that carries us back to another place, another time, often childhood, by some aroma that seems to engulf our beings. This could be the scent of flowers or of a flowering bush, or of a country smell of new-mown hay, or of a farmyard; or it might be a smell, not of nature, but of industry or manufacture; or a domestic smell inside a particular house or building; or the aroma of cooking or baking; but perceived in such a way perhaps more direct into our past than anything else we ever experience.

As we have seen, olfactory messages are used in much the same way as language is used in communication. Other observers prefer to liken the nose to a camera. There seems no doubt that odour memories — pictures of a sort — are more persistent and longer lasting than visual images relayed to the brain. Even though man's sense of smell may be feeble when compared with that of a dog or a salmon, it is still a truly remarkable receptor.

So indelible is this picture that were you to smell an odour tomorrow that you had not smelled for thirty years, the chances are that it would not only be instantly recognized, but that it would trigger a whole flood of memories and emotional associations. This link of odour to emotion and memory has been a fruitful source of inspiration for writers since the earliest times.

In *The Senses of Man*, Joan Steen Wilentz wrote:

> The strength of these aromatic memories ultimately stems from their visceral connections in the nervous system. We tend to ignore these aspects today because our travels are undertaken for pleasure and at our leisure. Originally, however, travel for all species capable of locomotion — for early man, as well as for nomadic cultures still extant — was an urgent necessity motivated for life-preserving purposes. One travelled in search of food. Smell was the first 'distance' sense developed to aid that search. The primeval fish with a 'nose' no longer had to swim aimlessly or wait passively for a food particle to brush against him. He could travel to his dinner, guided by chemical clues — certain molecules detached from their source and dissolved in sea water. These were not food particles that came into contact with the body and excited a generalized chemical sense. They were simply specks, traces of substances that excited new mechanisms altogether. This marked the divorce of smell from taste. From now on taste would become associated with what was put in the mouth. Smell was the preliminary investigator. We sniff before taking the plunge.
>
> But a fish doesn't stop at sniffing for food. He sniffs to find out if there may be a shark around, or possibly a mate.
>
> Thus the sense of smell came to serve species-preserving as well as life-preserving functions. So successful was it in coping with these vital needs that in time the small lump of olfactory tissue atop the fish's nerve cord grew into a brain. The cerebral hemispheres were originally buds from the olfactory stalks. En route, other senses developed, and in man, they came to pre-empt brain space. Man's frontal lobes, his highly developed sensory-motor areas, his capacity for reason, imagination, and memory, in combination with the greatly enlarged auditory and visual centers, far exceed olfaction in importance. Man has become a microsmatic (small smelling) animal.

The American author, Henry Van Dyke, who wrote so well of fishing said: 'Of all the faculties of the human mind, memory is the one that is most easily led by the nose. There is a secret power in the sense of smell which draws the mind backward into the pleasant land of old times.' For Van Dyke, on that particular fishing trip, it was a leaf of spearmint.

Man himself is not aware of the range of those human smells — his own or those of other people — of which fish are aware and, moreover, in incredibly minute dilutions. Similarly it is naive to think that the human smells we talk of are derived entirely from secretions of our sweat glands. The human scent would be as distinctive and recognizable immediately after the most antiseptic-like scrubbing and washing. It is as much an essential and unique part of us as our fingerprints.

It has already been suggested that it may not be similar in quality or even quantity in all men. After all smell is the sensory perception of chemical molecules transferred from one object to another in a fluid medium such as air or water, and the body chemistry itself is in constant flux and change. But such changes need not be triggered by physical happenings: the food we eat, the air around us, our state of health, by way of example. Our scent is altered by emotional changes within us: anxiety, anger, fear, being but a few such causes.

We have seen that the olfactory lobes of a fish's brain may be large and complex yet lacking in discrimination such as is evidenced by similar development in the human brain. In this manner the sensory perception of the scent of possible food — while important to the fish — is not paramount to its success or survival. Yet the complexity of the awareness of fish to odours is such that they can smell fear or dangers and other anxiety-influenced states of mind in much the same way as they would smell a wriggling worm or some other odorous food substance. It is strange how age-old metaphoric human sayings turn up in nature as a result of scientific discovery. 'The smell of fear' is just such one of those far-fetched ideas that turn out to be scientific fact, rather than some old-wives' tale.

Some scientific observers have noted the existence of shock and warning smell substances playing an essential survival purpose in the lives of fish. Carl von Frisch observed a school of minnow fry swimming around, when a large minnow suddenly turned up. The young minnows did not flee, for they are not afraid of other minnows. The grown minnow was overcome by hunger, however, and snapped up a little fish. Now something remarkable happened: all the small fry, having only just escaped, stayed calmly where they were; but the cannibal at once showed panic fear and made off hastily. Was the criminal, von Frisch asked himself, seized with remorse for his crime? Such an anthropomorphic idea is quite untenable, of course. What had happened was this. The moment the big minnow tore up the little one, a shock substance was released from the victim's skin and mixed with the water. As soon as a fish of the same species smells this shock substance, it feels an irresistible urge to flee. Only the young minnows remained unaffected, because sensitivity to the shock substance does not ripen in them until the age of between four and eight weeks.

The curiosity that a predator should put himself to flight is only a fringe effect of a phenomenon widespread among fish, and one that was really 'invented' for a rather different purpose. Research showed that the shock substance is produced in special club cells within the skin by many species of fish that spend at least part of their lives in schools. The purpose of the scare substance is to warn all members of the school or shoal to flee from the danger area when one of them has been eaten by a predator.

Rainbow trout are gregarious when compared with brown trout and tend to move around stillwater fisheries at times in loose shoals. Since rainbows generally predominate in most such fisheries nowadays, this might explain why, when a trout has been caught in one area, and others might be expected to follow soon afterwards, it often seems to happen that the fishing goes off for some considerable time. The common explanation is that the commotion caused in landing the first hooked and caught fish causes the other members of the loose shoal to disperse. But could it be that the hooked fish in its fight releases this shock and fear substance into the water from the punctured skin penetrated by the hook? It seems that this shock substance is released only if the skin is injured. A frightened creature cannot actively release it in the way a bird sounds a warning call. In other words, it seems, the fish that raises the alarm must die first, or at least be injured, to draw the attention of the other members of the school to a danger.

This may help show the astonishing sophistication — if not actual discrimination — in the olfactory senses of fish. Like so many animals and other creatures closer to the total world of the senses than we are, they are able to register and react to anxiety, panic and fear substances that come to them as perceived smells whether from polar bears, sea-lions, or a predatory fisherman on the bank. Take note, again, how most anglers agree that confidence is an essential element in fishing success. And a confident fisherman will have dispelled all anxiety, as well as fear that he isn't going to catch anything.

But fear and anxiety smell substances are far from being all the story. It doesn't have to be an anxious man or polar bear whose hand or paw put into a river upstream of ascending fish can immediately inhibit and stop the upstream movement of the fish. It can be any man, or any polar bear. We humans can be sure of one thing. Whatever this mysterious smell substance, L-serine, is, we all have it and fish for the most part don't like it and flee from it.

Many anglers are sceptical that such human smell substances could possibly affect their fishing. One of the problems is that they rely too much on their own noses. Another problem is that they are convinced that the water itself inhibits and prevents the spread of a smell. As to the first of those objections, consider the familiar dog. When a man walks barefoot on the ground, he loses about four-billionth parts of a gram of odorous sweat substances per step. This does not sound much. Yet it is an enormous amount if we count the odorous molecules clinging to every footprint: many millions of millions. Leather shoes prevent some of it getting through. But even here with every step some billions of butyric acid molecules are being pressed through — an amount which any tracking dog can still easily discover. Rubber boots hold in even more, but by no means everything. The scent of the foot penetrates a brand-new rubber boot 0.2 millimetres thick within eight minutes. Rubber that is 2 millimetres thick absorbs odorous substances like a sponge within about 36 hours. Although the human nose notices nothing of it, a dog still smells it easily, and could follow such a track with ease, many hours later.

It is not difficult to see how fishermen can so easily transfer such smell substances to their tackle — especially fly fishermen to their artificial flies. Some scientific workers have suggested that, while both Atlantic and Pacific salmon are acutely aware of this substance and recognize it without fail, even in the most incredible dilutions, trout are less so. This, however, is unlikely.

The sensitivity of fish to odorous signals is quite remarkable. Sockeye salmon, for example, can sense an extract of shrimp in the water when it is present in dilutions of only one part to 100 million parts of water — equivalent to a third of a teaspoon (12 drops) in a large swimming pool

(23,000 gallons). Salmon have been shown able to detect extracts of seal or sea-lion skin at dilutions of one part per eighty billion — less than two-hundredths of a drop in that same 23,000 gallon swimming pool.

Anglers would perhaps do well to consider that, when we handle and touch our artificial flies, all of us to some extent impregnate the fur and floss and feathers with our particular man-smell. Some may leave this chemical message so strongly impregnated on their flies that trout or salmon will reject them as they would similarly avoid the same men if they placed their hands in the water upstream of the fish. When angling you are sending your fly — complete with its warning message — right to the fish's noses. It couldn't be more or better advertised.

Perhaps we should handle our flies less, or more circumspectly, when we tie them on, and never ever just to admire or look at them. Bruno Kemball was a famed angler in New Zealand. An expatriate Englishman who spent most of his working life in China, Bruno retired to New Zealand and in order to satisfy his consuming passion for dry fly and nymph fishing set up a small tackle shop and fly emporium on the banks of the Hinemaiaia River that runs into the lake a few miles south of Taupo. It would be incorrect to say that Bruno ran a shop, because he would not sell his flies (all of which he and his wife tied) to just anyone. The flies were taken from their trays by tweezers, and transferred into boxes by the same means if a sale was made. If anyone actually handled a fly Bruno would fume and rile and refuse to serve them. It was considered to be an amiable eccentricity, no more, and may have been prompted more by aesthetics than olfaction — but was it?

Some anglers swear that all such skin odours are undetectable to fish after wetting the fly in one's mouth with saliva, but this must surely be debatable. Some anglers anoint their flies after tying on with cod liver oil or other fish oil; not as an attractor in itself, but to mask and cover up the smell from their own fingers. I once fished briefly with a man whose legerdemain of tricks seemed infinite. That he was eminently successful as an angler was undeniable yet, at the time, I thought his rigmaroles bordered on the ridiculously bizarre and eccentric. He invariably brought sardine sandwiches on fishing trips and kept a small screw top jar of a paste made from a little sardine mashed up in its oil. With a pinch of this on his fly he was ready to fish — but not before. Some anglers use the slime of previously caught fish for the same purpose. At least one near-sainted fly fishing authority was well-known for carrying a rag soaked in fish oil, with which he wiped newly tied on nymphs and dry flies before offering them to the trout. No doubt he would have claimed he was merely covering up human and tobacco smells — and not being devious or cheating!

In New Zealand the Taupo fishing regulations clearly prohibit the use of any attractants or additives. Whether or not in countries such as Britain this use of fish and fish oils contravenes fly fishing regulations would be a moot point.

These considerations may go some way to explaining an additional or even imperative reason why fish sometimes come short to our flies, nudging and nipping at them, pulling at them, then suddenly turning away, the deceit discovered. This is generally attributed to insufficient interest or stimuli to feed or attack, or even to playfulness. Life is too much in deadly earnest for trout and salmon to play; they have no sense of humour — whatever other senses they may possess in great abundance. Insufficient stimuli may have a bearing on coming short, but equally likely is the olfactory message impregnated in that particular artificial fly — one that says to the fish 'don't touch it with a bargepole'.

The use of chum and groundbaits have been known among sea anglers and coarse fishermen for centuries. Yet, in the past, a study of the sense of smell seems to have had little practical application for the angler who seeks his fish with an artificial fly. Nor does it seem likely that the sense of smell in fish enters into the likelihood or rapidity with which it seizes a bait in fast clear water. Knowledge that the sense of taste is highly developed in most fishes emphasizes the need for a rapid strike with artificial lures, before the deception is detected and the counterfeit fly ejected.

The olfactory lobes of the brains of fish are relatively large and seem to suggest incredible lower limits of threshold smell detection, but little ability to discriminate. The significance of olfactory messages may be fundamental rather than discriminatory. The chemical induced stimuli may generally signify one of two possible responses: advance, investigate, attack and eat; or retreat, avoid, flee and hide. Fly fishing simulates the first response by visual means. In the latter case it would at least be wise to minimize such chemical messages in every way possible.

However delightful in themselves our artificial flies may be, and however much we may want to handle them for the sheer pleasure and contentment of it, we may be wiser not to do so. If you happen to be an angler who consistently fails to catch fish, or catch very few, despite all else being right in your tackle, technique and knowledge, then think on these things and even develop a taste for sardine sandwiches when you go a-fishing.

Chapter 15
Cruelty in Angling

From time to time charges against anglers of being cruel to fish are voiced with anything between mild disapproval and angry condemnation. Such charges are likely to become more vocal and difficult to refute. But, in any case, it behoves all anglers to better understand and articulate their own personal attitudes and beliefs if they wish to refute these increasing allegations of cruelty. Angling is said to be a cruel sport. It does little to help matters if fishermen try to brush aside such charges by saying that the urge to fish is age-old and cannot be denied; or that it is in the blood; or that there are worse ways of spending a day's leisure.

Far from suggesting that anglers owe it to the various anti-angling lobbies to answer their charges of cruelty — although it would only help matters if they were more articulate in voicing their views — they need to think out their own personal views on the matter, if only for the sake of demonstrating that they have at least given thought to the matter and consideration to the charges often made against them. The charge of cruelty should be taken seriously, for it is a serious charge. If it is to be refuted it must be done by clear and reasoned thinking, as well as by conviction.

It is no longer sufficient to quote biblical approval, or to quote chapter and verse that Christ's disciples were fishermen, although many anglers have done and still do argue that this is fundamental approval. The symbolism of fish and fishing in Christianity does in all fairness seem to place the act of going fishing as being admirably beyond reproach. Such, indeed, was the legitimacy of this point of view that angling, especially sport fishing in Britain and elsewhere, was seen to be 'the blameless sport', 'the gentle art', and an admirable leisure activity and even mild passion suitable for country parsons and rectors, for contemplative gentlemen, and for country folk who walked in the path of godliness. Such due accorded to the act of going fishing was far more than tacit approval.

But the biblical associations with fishing — especially with the New Testament — are essentially concerned with the approval of angling as an activity worthy of good men. There is never mention of cruelty in its practise.

It is assumed, quite fundamentally, that the beasts of the field and the fishes of the sea were included as part of God's creation solely for the benefit of man. Thus, to Izaak Walton, it was abundantly clear: 'And it is observable, that it was our Saviours will, that these our four Fishermen should have a priority of nomination in the Catalogue of his twelve Apostles, as namely first St Peter, St Andrew, St James and St John, and then the rest in their order.'

We cannot, however, pull over-simplistic quotations out of medieval and other hats just when it suits us to defend ourselves as anglers against the charge of cruelty. Not only have ethical values changed, but there is a danger of linguistic misinterpretation.

Take Walton again. In one chapter of *The Complete Angler* he is advising would-be fishermen how to catch pike, recommending a live frog as bait:

> Put your hook into his mouth, which you may easily do from the middle of April till August, and then the frogs mouth grows up, and he continues so for at least six months without eating, but is sustained, none but he whose name is Wonderful, knows how: I say, put your hook, I mean the arming wire, through his mouth, and out at his gills, and then with a fine needle and silk sew the upper part of his leg with only one stitch to the arming wire of your hook, or tie the frogs leg above the upper joynt, to the armed wire; and in so doing, use him as though you loved him, that is, harm him as little as you may possibly, that he may live the longer.

This single paragraph has brought more vilification of Walton over the ensuing centuries than the rest of the *Angler* put together. Foremost among such critics was Lord Byron (hardly regarded nowadays as much more than a dilettante champion, even of frogs):

> And angling, too, that solitary vice,
> Whatever Izaak Walton sings or says:
> The quaint, old, cruel coxcomb, in his gullet
> Should have a hook, and a small trout to pull it.

As if his doggerel had insufficient venom, Byron continued:

> It would have taught him humanity at least. This sentimental savage, whom it is a mode to quote (among novelists) to show their sympathy for innocent sports and old songs, teaches how to sew up frogs, and break their legs by way of experiment, in addition to the art of angling, the cruelest, the coldest, and the stupidest of pretended sports. They may talk about the beauties of Nature, but the angler merely thinks about his dish of fish; he has no leisure to take his eyes from off the streams, and a single *bite* is worth to him more than all the scenery around. Besides, some fish bite best on a rainy day. The whale, the shark, and the tunny fishery have somewhat of noble and perilous in them; even net fishing, trawling, etc, are more humane and useful. But angling! No angler can be a good man.

For my part, Byron was talking rubbish, but his sentiments fall on more sympathetic ears today than they did when Don Juan was first published.

Despite the archaic language, any angler today well understands that Walton was simply writing prettily in the way of his times. 'Use him as though you loved him' is, in effect, a direction to inflict as little pain as possible on the luckless frog in question.

But here we stumble on a crucial element of cruelty. It is often said that cruelty is the voluntary infliction of unnecessary or avoidable pain. Inanimate things cannot be cruel: they have no volition; they cannot act voluntarily. They may be unpleasant, but they cannot be cruel. There can be no cruelty in angling unless it is in the angler. If the critics say that anglers take part in a cruel sport, what they are really saying is that angling has an unpleasant side to it, which of course is the fact, and we should not fudge this issue.

Angling involves pain and death. The angler then inflicts pain and causes death. Some people, so constituted by nature that they cannot do those things without revulsion, ought not then, go fishing. But such people should not make the charge of cruelty against those who do. The pain inflicted by the considerate, humane angler is very slight, for the most part, and very brief. Pain and death come to all living things; and death at the angler's hand, if he lives up to the sportsman's traditional code, is in almost all cases more merciful, quicker and less painful than death in other forms, including death from 'natural causes' — if there is such a thing in the fish-world.

A key point in the definition of cruelty is the word *unnecessary* or *avoidable*. The infliction of pain *per se* does not constitute cruelty. Surgeon, dentist, judge, all inflict pain during the course of their duties. No one would dream of calling these vocations cruel, or the men who perform them cruel, provided no unnecessary pain is inflicted. Angling implies the infliction of a small amount of pain, and death; but so does almost every meal we hungry mortals take. If the critic is to establish his charge of cruelty against angling, as such, he must be able to show that all forms of angling involve the infliction of wanton or unnecessary pain; and that cannot be shown of traditional angling for trout and salmon, by fair means, in the right spirit and for the right object. It is undeniable that angling, done in the right spirit, makes men sensitive and thoughtful. And herein lies a paradox.

It can be argued that it is cruel to hook and release trout, but not cruel to hook and kill them. Cruelty is largely in the mind and motive, but the primary object of justifiable angling may be to catch fish for food. Although there are many pleasures incidental to angling, these cannot justify the infliction of pain or death. This argument at once prohibits anglers who are not interested in trout as food. Should an angler fish for fish or fish for pleasure? The fundamental truth is, of course, that there is nothing terribly wrong in the pursuit of pleasure, although the pleasure itself is not the proper object of angling.

If this, then, is so, then the best defence and justification for fishing is that the angler is killing fish for food. In Britain, where there is much coarse fishing, only most sea anglers and trout and salmon fishermen come into this category. In New Zealand, where I have lived and fished a great deal, there is only very limited and regional coarse fishing, so that the vast majority of freshwater anglers do so in order to catch and kill and eat salmon and trout.

This, in itself, creates a dilemma. There can be little doubt that charges of unnecessary cruelty can be brought against some trout fishermen — these are often boat fishermen who habitually throw down still-living fish to die slow and lingering deaths amongst the beer cans and other debris at the bottom of the boat. Yet the fly fisherman using barbless, tiny dry flies or nymphs, who most carefully and lovingly unhooks every trout caught for undamaged return to the water, would be considered reprehensible for tormenting and playing with the fish he has no intention of killing for food.

The enormous growth of stillwater fly fishing for trout throughout Britain has brought to the sport many hitherto exclusively coarse fishermen, particularly those who fished in matches where the use of keep-nets was obligatory until the total catch could be weighed and recorded at the end of the competition. Keep-nets themselves, even in coarse fishing, attract and deserve much criticism on the grounds of cruelty. A new phenomena, and not a pleasant one, has emerged in the increasing use of keep-nets on still water trout fisheries. Even if the fishery rules state categorically that all trout caught must be killed immediately, there is ample evidence of this being flaunted, with live trout being put into keep-nets and even bank-tethered landing nets. The trout, under terrible stress, terrified and sometimes frightened to death, are not (as the perpetrators claim) 'being kept fresh'; on the contrary they seem destined for inedible doom. And with this current practice it is not possible to deny avoidable and unnecessary cruelty.

It is ironic that, almost simultaneously throughout the trout fishing world, the expert catch and release fly fisherman who never kills a trout is being attacked for tormenting the fish in playing God while seeking intense pleasure, while the often less than careful fisherman, who treats trout as a food commodity and something in direct exchange for the money it has cost him, and who sometimes is guilty of inflicting avoidable pain and suffering on the fish he catches, is being lauded as being direct and honest and straight to the point.

Before we come to look at current anti-angling lobbies and the arguments of Animal Rights groups, it might be prudent to see how more recent fishing writers have responded to the charge of cruelty. However sonorous and mellifluous may be the words of Izaak Walton, it would be disastrous to counter contemporary lobby groups with anything but equally contemporary logic and commonsense.

By and large there have been three responses from fishermen regarding the charge of cruelty in their sport. Some have admitted it to be true — at least partly true — but essentially part of the natural world in which we live, where we ignore certain truths and imperatives at our peril. Others propound subtle but compelling arguments based on more philosophic examinations of the nature of man and his intellectual place on earth, rather than as a hunting animal. The third group, who considerably outnumber the others, seem either unaware of the charge or do not let it bother them one jot.

Now let us consider those people who are opposed to angling in any shape or form, and who seek to have it banned, either by general concensus or by legislation. Until recent years there was virtually no anti-angling lobby. Some undoubtedly well-meaning people on the fringe of organizations like the RSPCA were perhaps basically opposed to angling, but mostly theirs was an anthropomorphically centred idea that cruelty was largely in the killing. However, the well-intentioned people who once behoved the rest of us to be kind to dumb animals — which most of us fishermen are, anyway, to a remarkable and wholly laudable degree — have become a pushover for the new zealots on the radical left of everything. Not the chic radical left of the salons, but the new radical left of the towns and cities, who claim they are the true protectors of the countryside, who claim to know what is best for farm animals, and dogs, and birds, and fish, and the whole animal creation. Not all, perhaps, but at least an ambitious core of such people have burgeoned into organizations like the League of Animal Rights and similar campaigning bodies. Quite apart from claiming to be the inheritors of the countryside at large, they also claim to be the true inheritors of the spirit of Richard

Jefferies, that prophetic 19th-century poet-naturalist — which they patently aren't.

In earlier years, when good and kind people campaigned for a better deal for pit ponies, and sought action against those who were cruel to dogs or cats, they saw their efforts in terms of human fairness and decency. The move towards active radicalism came in with anti-stag hunting, fox hunting, and such; but the protesters found that their adversaries were often rich, powerful, confident, and not easily cowed — quite apart from the fact that their sport took place on the move in often remote, damp and cold places. In recent years the anti-bloodsports lobby has sought softer, more easily accessible targets, found closer to urban areas; often their own kith and kin coarse fishing or trout fishing in the ever-increasing number of stillwaters throughout the country. Their activities have included vandalising fish breeding ponds and stews, causing the trout and other fish far more cruel deaths than they could ever have at the hands of the fly fisherman. Their declared intention is to have all angling banned. One suspects that it is really terrorism that these people enjoy. Their aim will not succeed, but the zealots' enthusiasm meanwhile knows no bounds and with some support from certain church groups is likely to continue and become even more belligerent, and to be exported to other parts of the world.

Much angling writing is marvellously mellifluous stuff, redolent of the streams and lochs and tarns of the deepest, loveliest countryside. And so it should be in this loveliest of all sports. The members of the Leagues of this and that, however, are quick to point out that fishing is not only essentially cruel, but selfish. In this charge the real and true fisherman is again maligned. Hear how Sir Robert Bruce Lockhart phrased it in *My Rod My Comfort*:

> The desire for solitude is the most pleasant disorder of our times. It is man's natural reaction to the speed of modern life and to the evils of the world in which we live. And because today solitude is almost beyond our reach we seek it the more eagerly. Some find it only in dreams; others again on the mountain-tops. The more fortunate, and I count myself among them, satisfy their craving by the side of running streams and lonely lochs. Berdyaev, who will be read when Stalin's name is little more than an unpleasant memory, calls this desire for solitude the nostalgia of the soul; and by this he means, I think, that communication with Nature is the way back for souls that have lost God.
>
> If my own communion with Nature has been made with a rod in my hand, I am no angling maniac, and, although fishing is the thread which runs through this short autobiographical sketch, the tale contains few records of slaughter and no tedious treatise on the mechanics of angling or on the lures and implements which man in his genius has devised for the capture of fish.
>
> . . . I shall not attempt to defend the charge of cruelty. Nature is cruel and man is its child, and although I accept the qualified truth of Fedden's verdict, I think it fair to admit that the angling community is composed of all kinds and conditions of men.

Here, perhaps, we have a point worthy of consideration. Lockhart noted it, and so have the more radical anti-angling lobbies. Firstly, there are such beings as 'angling maniacs'; secondly, and following on from the first, 'the angling community is composed of all kinds of conditions of men'. The radicals observed the soft underbelly of angling and anglers. It was immediately accessible to many of them. They saw the forlorn rows of their cousins and next door neighbours sitting on stools along the local canal bank or river, fishing it seemed without much apparent joy or purpose, and they knew these fishermen for what they were — much like themselves, ordinary folk, not the least bit powerful, not the least bit frightening. Easy targets. Furthermore, they noted as Lockhart did, that anglers come in all sorts and conditions, often with a distinct loathing of some other branch of the sport. In such a manner that, say, a certain type of carp fisherman wouldn't be seen dead talking to a match fisherman; while some trout fly fishermen wouldn't be seen dead talking to either; and a certain type of salmon fisherman would shun and divorce himself from the lot of them.

Make no mistake about it. The reason the antis have picked on angling is because they know and exploit the fact that angling and anglers are divided. And even anglers themselves cannot agree, and differ as to what constitutes cruelty in fishing and whether or not it is reprehensible because of it. The catch and release dry fly fisherman is certain he does no harm and is not cruel, but thinks the coarse match fisherman who stuffs ill-assorted and sundry fish into a keep-net to be ingloriously hoisted and weighed at the end of the day before being emptied back into the water in a slithering mass of half-dead, overstressed creatures, is. Meanwhile the salmon angler sees no cruelty in providing so much valuable food in a single, expensive fish caught fairly and squarely, and despatched quickly and humanely, but perhaps sees the stillwater trout fisherman as behaving reprehensibly in stuffing half dead trout into a small bankside bag while relating the worth of the total weight of his limit catch to the price of the day ticket to fish for them.

Who then, of all of them, is right? Probably none. But we have wandered away from the charge that we anglers are all guilty of cruelty. What are we to do about it? And, if we do nothing, then how are to justify ourselves when accused?

Dr A. A. Luce was a cleric and Professor of Moral Philosophy at Trinity College, Dublin, who possibly wrote best of the ethical angler's dilemma in his 1959 book *Fishing and Thinking*. Reading Dr Luce's book again in the light of writing this chapter one is struck that so few angling writers have concerned themselves with this charge of cruelty. My own belief is that they did not so much systematically turn a blind eye to it, refusing to acknowledge its possible existence, but simply that it never occurred to them — in much the same way that I don't recall my grandfather, or father for that matter, ever talking to me about cruelty to animals — and fish.

True, my father told a tale of how, as a boy, he had once tickled a trout from a Monmouthshire brook and carried it home triumphantly to his parents. Instead of the praise he had expected, he was admonished and instructed to return the long-since-dead fish to the water from which it had been taken — because it was the Sabbath.

Because it still remains the most lucid and informed discussion of the ethics of fishing in published books, Dr Luce's basic tenets were paraphrased in the opening remarks of this chapter. He wrote:

> The ethics of angling is sometimes called in question. Angling is said to be a cruel sport. That is the central charge, affecting us all. Anglers are charged also with wasting time, with neglecting serious things, with fishing to excess, and even with inveracity; but these are subsidiary charges: individual anglers may or may not have to plead guilty to them. The charge of cruelty admits no exceptions. We may fish in moderation;

we may neglect no duty; we may practise fishing as an aid to the performance of duty; we may report the weight of the big fish with mathematical accuracy, without making allowance for atmospheric desiccation or for the incredulity of our friends, and yet, if angling be intrinsically cruel, we anglers, all of us, are doing and encouraging what is intrinsically wrong.

Some readers may feel disposed to brush the charge aside without more ado. They like fishing; it never did them any harm; their fathers and grandfathers before them fished; it is in the blood, and there are many worse ways of spending a day. Fishing keeps the lads out of mischief. Why bother about a handful of dismal croakers who cannot catch fish themselves, and grudge us our amusement?

To Professor Luce the problem was essentially ethical, and not religious; and the main argument should be conducted in terms of right and wrong, not in terms of precept and prohibition. To Luce, therefore, the conclusions reached, if sound, ought to be accepted by all who believe in right and wrong, no matter what their religion, and if they have no religion.

In questioning whether angling is cruel, we have to recognize his belief that 'those people with a conscience who love their fishing rod are placed in a sad dilemma, as long as the question remains unanswered'. We have already seen that, to Luce, what we know to be cruel we know to be wrong. And, if all angling is cruel, then not only is Professor Luce's angling wrong, but yours and mine in no lesser way.

While it is not surprising that a passionate angler like Luce should have philosophized so hard and long and heart-searchingly on the ethics of angling under this charge of cruelty, it is little wonder that, despite some academic interest, the majority of untroubled fishermen will wonder what the fuss is all about, when they do so little harm in pursuance of their occasional sport, and are as unlikely as any men to go home and beat and abuse their wives and children. We must remember what Sir Robert Bruce Lockhart said, 'that angling embraces all kinds of conditions of men', but we must not forget that, to a non-fisherman, as much as to a League of Animal Rights-er, a fishing rod — any fishing rod — is a badge and instrument of evil. A recent article in *The Independent* magazine (5th August 1989) by Germaine Greer — not a person one might expect to be a champion of fishing — would seem to put Animal Right-ers in their proper place and context.

Dr Greer, it seems, is troubled by rats — not so much troubled, but surrounded by them. It makes an interesting point of departure into an essay on some of the social sicknesses of our times. Dr Greer — not an angler, to the best of my knowledge — makes the point that, if you or I made it in some public forum we would be taken to task as cruel philistines. The article in question comes under Home Thoughts, entitled 'Germaine Greer Argues That Rats Are Animals Too':

It must be at least a week since I've seen a rat, which could mean that the plague is over. Perhaps the Pied Piper went past one morning before we were up. The Pied Piper's method of musical entrapment is the only humane one that has ever been suggested for rats. For months we have been involved in orgies of trapping, drowning, poisoning and even shooting of highly developed intelligent animals who have lived as close to man for the last few thousand years as dogs have. Rats are hard to kill; they resist; they fight, bite and scream, but no animal liberationist ever hears them.

After a powerful attack on the often vile and inhumane ways and means of poisoning, trapping, and otherwise killing rats, Germaine Greer continues:

> If animals have rights, then rats have rights, but there is no rat ombudsman. If it is a gross infringement of an animal's rights to kill it, why do we have a duty to kill rats? Because they spread disease? So do most of the other animals that live in close proximity to man; rats don't spread more disease than pigs, and perhaps no more than that most hallowed of all animal parasites, the dog. They certainly make reparation for the disease they spread by the sterling service they offer in our laboratories, which represents the only case in which rats must be humanely killed.
>
> For people who live in towns, killing is an exotic concept; they are the people who feel that the objection that the foetus is 'alive' is an argument against killing it, when in fact it is the necessary condition for killing it. People who live in the country have to observe killing at every turn. The first time I saw 50 rooks clean out my beech trees, chattering lazily in the uppermost branches as they snacked off fledglings grown to a toothsome size, I felt quite sick with horror. Now I am used to it. The first time a racing pigeon came down in my hen run for a drink and a beakful of corn, only to be torn apart by my hens until there was only a pair of silver wings left to show what had become of him, I felt that I hated my hens. But when I heard the rabbit screaming a few weeks ago, when the stoat had it cornered, I watched to see the kill, which was elegant in its utter mercilessness. Yesterday I found the stoat, a parchment stoat under a drift of pinkish fluff. He had been killed but not eaten by a competing carnivore. A mink, perhaps, a descendant of some liberated before I came to this place. (Liberating minks is damn stupid, especially if you are concerned for the endangered species, for minks kill without discrimination or appetite.)
>
> Animal rights must include the right to kill, and to kill messily, for sport or just to get the gastric juices flowing, or to clear the ground for an imperialist takeoever by a single species. Man is an animal, you might argue, and therefore has the right to kill other animals in all the ways that they kill each other. This it seems is not right; man is to be superior to the other animals and stop killing them for sport or fur or any other reason. He is evidently not to breed them or farm them either.
>
> The logic of animal rights seems at least questionable. The propaganda deals only with appealing creatures, whales, tigers, lynxes, seal pups and natterjack toads. When the RSPCA tried to alert people to the suffering caused by overbreeding of dogs, all killed humanely, the picture was considered too harrowing to be seen. Millions of rats were ineptly tortured to death in the same period, but the common perception is that they got no more than they deserved. To rats at least animal liberation must seem pure humbug.

To Dr Greer many thanks for saying something I, as an angler, dared not have said in so many words.

But, as we are discussing angling in particular, we need turn to other anglers to answer those charges of cruelty in terms relating to his sport. In *Letters To A Salmon Fisher's Sons*, A. H. Chaytor had this to say:

> You will often hear fishermen debating the question whether fish feel

pain. It is not that anybody, so far as I know, thinks that fish are wholly proof against the feeling of pain, but many people believe that fish are much less sensible of pain than are warm-blooded animals such as we are. Seeing a long and frantic struggle for life on the part of a beautiful creature which has never given the smallest cause of offence to mankind, a humane fisher is forced to consider whether he is being guilty of wanton cruelty; whether, if he must take fish in order to eat them, he is justified in taking them with the rod, instead of by some means that is either painless — such as stunning them by the use of dynamite or shooting them — or whereby death at least is quickly over, such as spearing them or taking them with a draft net. No doubt the angler puts himself upon his trial with every intention of securing his own acquittal if it be possible. But is he really guilty?

Chaytor goes on to describe the true angler's natural repugnance at the thought of herding fish traps, such as were then common for taking Pacific salmon in British Columbia, and moreso for the use of dynamite and the rifle, such as he had seen on visits to New Zealand where he was born.

Is it merely a selfish desire to capture the fish ourselves, or is it that we feel that a noble fish, even when we need him for food, should have the much greater chance of escape that the rod gives him as compared with the murderous bars of the salmon trap or the toils of the deadly net? It is not merely that the rod gives him a fair chance of escape after he has been hooked; it does not, like the net or the fish trap, sweep the fish off wholesale from the pools or from the narrows through which they are compelled to pass. The rod can take only such fish as are disposed to seize the fly or bait, and we all know that at times such fish are rare indeed, and at no time do they form, I believe, any large proportion of the fish present in the pools.

Anglers are not, as a rule, men given to cruelty in the affairs of life, and yet the fear of possible cruelty in fishing does not impress them as a real one. Some cruelty must be involved in causing the death of any creature, and so long as humane men and women desire to eat slaughtered sheep, cattle, poultry, game, and fish, the angler need not much concern himself beyond proving that his sport involves no greater cruelty than this.

Chaytor goes on to defend against the charge of cruelty by recounting experiences of the trout and salmon's apparent reaction to pain, suggesting that while fish no doubt feel terror and anger at being hooked, they do not feel pain as we and other warm-blooded animals know it, as witnessed that both trout and salmon will take an angler's fly or lure soon after breaking away from a similar previous experience. He further cites how salmon, after being hooked, often simply go down and lie inert and unmoving in the depths of a pool, seemingly suffering little more than discomfort until the angler provokes the fish into movement.

As I, too, feel inclined to do, he also cites the case put forward by that most rollicking and untroubled of all anglers, William Scrope, in his *Days and Nights of Salmon Fishing in the Tweed* (1843). If the anti-angling lobbyists sometimes take a light-hearted and flippant look at fishermen, then why shouldn't fishermen sometimes be permitted to take a similar look at their critics and the fish themselves:

Let us see how the case stands: I take a little wool and feather, and, tying it in a particular manner upon a hook, make an imitation of a fly; then I throw it across the river and let it sweep round the stream with a lively motion. This I have an undoubted right to do, for the river belongs to me or my friend; but mark what follows. Up starts a monster fish with his murderous jaws, and makes a dash at my little Andromeda. Thus he is the aggressor, not I; his intention is evidently to commit murder. He is caught in the act of putting that intention into execution. Having wantonly intruded himself on my hook, which I contend he had no right to do, he darts about in various directions, evidently surprised to find that the fly, which he hoped to make an easy conquest of, is much stronger than himself. I naturally attempt to regain this fly, unjustly withheld from me. The fish gets tired and weak in his lawless endeavours to deprive me of it. I take advantage of his weakness, I own, and drag him, somewhat loth, to the shore, where one rap on his head ends him in an instant.

There can be no doubt that, generally speaking, we nowadays have more care and consideration for all living creatures than previously was the case. It is possible to be considerate to wildlife without being mawkishly sentimental about it. Few commentators on the fly fishing scene are more positive and fair-minded about it than Conrad Voss Bark who recently wrote:

Though still carnivorous, and partial to a trout or two from time to time, it is probably true that we treat trout better than we did, except for those who go in for competitions in killing, which most self-respecting fly fishermen dislike. But our concern does not apply to every creature. Float fishermen are pretty ruthless about maggots and worms.

No scientists, at least none that have come to my notice, have been concerned about the suffering of worms. They must suffer a good deal, one would think, to judge by the wriggle when they are impaled upon a hook and subsequently drowned. In 1870, or thereabouts, an Edinburgh lawyer named Stewart invented a special worm tackle, what one might describe as a crucifix of hooks, which would prolong their lives and extend their wriggling. No one seems to care much for the welfare of worms. There are few exceptions, mostly among fly fishermen. John Gay's

Around the steel no tortured worm shall twine

No blood of living insect stain my line

is a pleasant reminder that there was a worm protectionist movement which started as long ago as 1720. Admittedly, progress is slow. Not that one should be surprised. The habit of worming, like the worm itself, takes time to die.

Conrad Voss Bark, passionate and clear thinking in all matters of fly fishing, uses an engaging and forceful logic against the charge of cruelty. In another piece from the same delightful book, *A Fly on the Water* (1986), he writes:

I met a man once who told me I ought not to go fishing. He said it was cruel and therefore I was wrong to take pleasure from being cruel. He was a nice man, led by various complexities into being a lay preacher and a vegetarian, a combination which together must be regarded as fairly formidable if one comes across them in argument.

I pointed out that Jesus's disciples were fishermen before they became fishers of men. This was no problem to a lay preacher, indeed he leapt upon the point with joy, because he said they did not fish for pleasure or sport or relaxation, or any reason of that kind, but to give people food, for they were an important part of the organisation which provided the loaves and the fishes. In the case of our modern rod and line fishermen they did it for pleasure and not as part of the nation's food supply.

We then went into the question of what professional fishermen actually did when they caught fish, and how the fish were brought in on the trawl, lifted inboard, the purse opened, and several hundredweight of fish dropped into the hold, stunned, suffocated, bruised, drowning in air, left slowly to die or in some cases gutted alive.

One might say, up to a point, that the trawlerman got some pleasure from the catch, for it would pay the mortgage and clothe the bairns, and certainly that would be a point of pleasure or of satisfaction, however pleasure was defined, but might it also not contain a certain modicum of cruelty to the fish. To my surprise my lay preacher friend agreed. I can quote his words for I can still hear him saying them 'As soon as I knew how cod were caught,' he said, 'I gave up eating fish fingers.'

There was nothing further to say, nothing to explore, no possible excuse for continuing. For a man willingly to give up eating the food he liked and face the rest of his life on a diet based mainly on the soya bean is the stuff of sainthood.

A fact perhaps worth mentioning, for it is something my lay preacher was not able to appreciate, is that a good many fly fishermen, quite possibly a large majority of experienced fly fishermen, gain no pleasure from killing and find it distasteful and indeed repugnant. We come up here, of course, against the carnivore and the turning of the blind eye. We do not as a rule see the activity that goes on inside abattoirs or on the boat decks of trawlers so that when we enjoy our roast beef or smoked salmon we do so in a way that seals us off from the past, from any thought of killing or bloodshed or pain that have brought such pleasures to us. The fisherman, landing-net in hand, faces the reality in one way, the vegetarian in another.

It is extraordinarily difficult to be scupulously fair in presenting one's personal views on this matter of cruelty and angling, and of the views of other fly fishermen, in being a passionate angler oneself. In attempting to do so it becomes clear that, while cruelty almost invariably involves the infliction of pain on some poor unfortunate sufferer, the two words, cruelty and pain, are not interchangeable. It is difficult, furthermore, to know when best to stop quoting what other writers may have said on the subject; not because so many of them have, in fact, applied their wits and consciences to the question, because not all that many have, but more directly because it seems like ganging up on those who may have different views. Neither is it much good going to the scientific writers, for they aren't much help when it comes to this matter, however good they might be at explaining the physiology and the private lives of fishes. Even if they are anglers themselves, as well as being ichthyologists, they seem to fudge the issue.

Probably the best book for the layman-angler, of which I am aware, is *The Life Story of the Fish* by Brian Curtis. But in this matter it offers little or no help:

Many people, of whom I am one, shrink from killing a deer, but have no scruples about the often more lingering death which they inflict on a trout. They like to tell themselves that it is because the fish cannot feel pain, while the real reason is that the fish, regardless of what it feels, cannot express pain. If every trout were to scream unceasingly as long as it had a hook in its mouth, trout-fishing would be a nerve-shattering experience which few of its present devotees could undergo more than once.

However, in defence of the fisherman, I find two reasons for believing that the fish's suffering is, comparatively speaking, slight. One is that the actual sensation of pain is apparently not so keen in fish as in some of the higher animals. The other is that the brain of the fish, lacking the cerebral cortex . . . fails to provide a home for the conscious association of ideas, and therefore robs pain of an imagination to work on.

Here Curtis goes on to tell the tale of the trout that was caught with its own eye, showing that the physical sensation of pain felt by the fish was not very keen or else very quickly forgotten.

On second thoughts, however, it is not quite fair to end this enquiry into cruelty in angling by quoting the words of a scientist — albeit a scientist who was an angler. The charge of cruelty in angling, where and by whom it is made, is made directly against anglers and, as it is a serious charge, has to be answered by anglers themselves. It is evident from excerpts already quoted that angling writers have often viewed the charge of cruelty from a wide range of attitudes. Some cynics might say that all angling apologists on the matter are inured to it, and therefore not to be trusted. Many of the fishermen–writers whose beliefs have been recalled were men of great sensitivity, who cannot be so accused. Maurice Wiggin, indeed a man of enormous sensitivity of spirit — and a free-thinking spirit at that, was altogether a most passionate angler, a distinguished journalist and writer, but with the rare integrity of not treating intellectual fools lightly. And one needs to be honest with oneself in order to do that: more honest than most of us could possibly not blush at. While Maurice Wiggin fished with such delight, and was a truly all-round angler (which most of us aren't), he thought and puzzled and worried about it. He didn't necessarily do this because he was worried about the possible charge of cruelty, but because he was puzzled as to why he, and millions of other people, pursued angling with such total all-else excluding passion.

In the aptly named *The Passionate Angler* (1949), Wiggin examines one of his consistently held contentions; that a fish hooked should be landed with as little ado as possible:

I cannot say that I learned more than the very rudiments of angling from the Bloxwich and Essington colliers: but one idea I did absorb — even though it were unconsciously — that I have never lost. And that is, a notion of the decency of landing a fish forthrightly and as soon as may be. The roach pole fisher of the Sneyd had no feeling for the alleged delight of *playing* a fish: his single aim was to get the fish on the bank just as soon as it could be got. And I am sure that this is the best idea. I have no compunction about killing a fish, if need be: which in my case means if I want to eat it, or to give it to someone who wants to eat it. For I have never caught a record fish, and I must say I think stuffed fish in glass cases are among the most mournful of trophies.

Killing cannot be avoided: rats and Colorado beetles (as the vegetarian

Bernard Shaw has pointed out) must be killed. Wasps must be killed, and the King's enemies. There is no need to worry about killing: not wanton killing, but necessary killing. When it is necessary, it is necessary, and there's an end on't. A man has a right to kill a fish. Or so I believe. And indeed, a swift knock on the head is a merciful end: most fish — almost all fish — die 'natural' deaths fouler by far than the angler's 'priest' administers.

But torture is another matter. There is no excuse for cruelty. Anglers who delight in playing a fish right out are cruel. It is sometimes necessary, I know: if the fish is big game, and the tackle fine, he cannot be gaffed or netted until he's played to exhaustion. But why fish with such fine tackle? There is a vogue for extra-fine tackle, and it is pleasant to handle. But I think it is overdone. It is possible to fish *too* fine.

However, it is the deliberate spinning-out of the agony that angers me. Playing cat-and-mouse, prolonging the business, keeping it up so long that the poor fish is utterly spent before it comes to the net. I know that to many anglers, playing the fish is the best of fishing. *Playing*! It shouldn't be. I cannot read of hour-long battles without nausea or anger or both. For while I believe that owing to the structure of its mouth, and the nature of its nervous system so far as can be divined, fish do not feel pain acutely while hooked, I am pretty sure that they feel fear. My objective is (a) to get the fish hooked, and (b) to get him on the bank. And there is little doubt in my mind that in the majority of cases, a fish can be got ashore rapidly and roughly, without finesse. The elaborate tradition of playing a fish to exhaustion is a thoroughly bad one. The man who finds his chief joy in feeling the fish quivering and struggling on the line should look into his soul.

This strongly held doctrine will surprise and even dismay many fishermen. But to be fair to Wiggin, he does follow those paragraphs by a reasoned approach to the technique of achieving that practise without losing too many fish prior to netting. He thought that far too many game fishermen, by and large, spend too much time playing their fish, saying it is amazing what good, fine leader material will stand, if you try it. To Maurice Wiggin, the angler, like the general, must keep the initiative firmly in his hands. Literally, in his hands. He believed that a fish is so surprised to be hooked that in the first few seconds very much can be done, if only you have the nerve and presence of mind to do it.

But the horrid tradition of making the most of it is deep-rooted, especially in angling literature. I am as crafty and cunning as the next man: I will spend hours creeping and crawling up on a fish. I'll go to almost any length to deceive him. But when the fish has taken hold — then it's 'pull devil, pull baker'. If I have misjudged his power, or the strength of my own tackle, good luck to him. But I hate to see a fish turn over on his side.

. . . File the barb of the hook down, and if necessary touch up the point to needle sharpness. Then, when you hook a fish, yank him out without ceremony. I don't suggest that you should *strike* him roughly, of course; that is the way to wreck tackle. A firm flick hooks him, if you are going to hook him at all. But then lose no time. One steady, sure, audacious pull, and it is long odds you will have him on the bank. Fiddle about and rouse him, and then you *will* have a battle on your hands.

In this, however, with due respect to Maurice Wiggin, it is clear that he cannot have fished for and hooked a fresh-run rainbow in the Tongariro River, or a maiden steelhead anywhere along the Pacific Northwest. They would have none of 'pull devil, pull baker', although we take his point.

But this, according to Wiggin, did not apply to salmon fishing, although he comments:

> I read now and then of gruesome battles, lasting hours and hours, and I think, if that's a Christian way to kill one of God's creatures, be damned to it. It's no less wicked than bear-baiting. It's on a level with tying a dog to a stake and letting him break his heart trying to get free. That is all it amounts to, and salmon fishers often admit as much: breaking a fish's heart. I almost prefer the poacher with his dynamite, his sniggle or his net, to these jolly sportsmen.
>
> You see, I am a passionate angler indeed. I love catching fish, the more the merrier: but I don't like slow torture. Out with 'em, that's my motto — up on the bank in one.

Keep-nets have been discussed elsewhere. There is no need to describe Maurice Wiggin's feelings about them because, although a keen coarse fisherman himself, his feelings were entirely of abhorrence. A point he made was that, although the keep-net has come into almost universal use, and is compulsory in most fishing competitions, it is a nonsense to call its use humane:

> The argument runs that if all the thousands of competitors killed the miserable fish they generally catch, there would soon be no fishing left. True. So they slip them into a keep-net until they have been weighed, at the end of the day, and then turn them back into the water. It sounds plausible. But have you ever seen a keep-net full of fish? It's a miserable sight. Fish are easily frightened, as every angler knows, and fish in keep-nets are terrified fish. There is no excuse for keeping wild things in cages, even for a few hours. So what is the answer to the competition anglers? Why it is simple. Have done with competitions! There is something ludicrous in the spectacle of grown men 'weighing-in' a few miserable little fish, for a miserable prize. I say that fishing is one sport which loses its flavour — almost all its flavour — when it is followed communally. I have nothing to say against angling clubs and societies: they are excellent institutions: men get together and are thereby enabled to rent good stretches of water which would be beyond their reach as individuals. Socially, the club is a good thing. But competitions . . . as soon make love all together, in parties. Still, some folk like to do just that.

Lest there be any reader who is aware of Maurice Wiggin's place in British angling literature, but who has not read *The Passionate Angler*, it might be as well to add his own postscript:

> Forgive this didactic interlude. We all have our hobby horses, and this is mine. The endless sporting cant about playing game fish has riled me for years. It is time someone told such sportsmen what is wrong with them.
>
> There will be a lot of hard things said about me on this account, and I shall never be invited to fish the sacred River —. Some will say that I am a contradictory, paradoxical creature, catching fish and at the same time

coddling them: poacher and gamekeeper at once. Well, we are most of us paradoxical and contradictory creatures: show me a single-minded man and I will show you a dangerous fanatic. But I see no inconsistency here so grave that it need worry me. After all, we all subscribe willingly to strict regulations about slaughter-houses. I see nothing ludicrously paradoxical in that odd technical term, 'the humane killer'. That is what I aim to be: a humane killer.

Having digressed perilously into humanities, let us get cheerfully back to our killing.

Until reaching this point of writing I had not intended to give space here quoting chapter and verse of the shrill messages from such bodies as the League of Animal Rights, the Animal Liberation Front, and other kindred organizations. They seem, to me at least, to have none of the informed charm of many of those who defend angling and deny it is, or needs be, a cruel sport.

Yet it would seem wrong, I believe, not to give some mention to at least one such protagonist as portrayed in Maureen Duffy's book *Men & Beasts — An Animal Rights Handbook*. Ms Duffy is, as many will know, a noted novelist, playwright and poet. This Animal Rights book is said to be a blueprint for the way forward and a programme for action by the bewildering multitude of such activists broadly sheltering under the same umbrella. It should be said that the single chapter in the book concerning field and other sports, while vitriolic towards angling and anglers, is moderate when compared with the main onslaught against the eating of meat and all other animal flesh generally, and the farming methods to prepare it for slaughter. For the purposes of this present enquiry we must contain the following comments and quotations to those matters affecting angling — a prime target for Ms Duffy's venom.

I shall do my utmost not to quote out of context, and will not attempt to comment upon such of Ms Duffy's statements that hinge on what seems an unreasonable bitter attack on *all* male (human male, that is) sexuality and the outmoded pseudo-Freudian interpretations she places on her observations of the fisherman and his rod. Similarly, little consequence will be given to the frequent innuendoes that all would somehow be well and 'properly adjusted' in a homosexual, lesbian society!

As for the so-called hunting instinct in man, Ms Duffy seems to admire the hunter-gatherers of ancient times and to subscribe to the outmoded view of the noble savage — until such people were corrupted by modern civilization:

> The hunting anthropoid probably felt the same sort of kinship and near reverence for the creatures he hunted as the Esquimaux. He was after all hunted in his turn and it was easier for him to see himself as part of the natural network of plants and animals covering the earth.

Few fishermen would disagree with much of that. Indeed many of them would still claim that kinship. I do wonder whether Ms Duffy has ever seen a noble 'Esquimaux' clubbing to death a seal pup, or dispatching writhing mounds of netted Pacific salmon? If she has, then does she really believe that this is only because such people have been corrupted by modern civilization?

Up to a point, hunting is separated from other rural sports as being totally reprehensible but — like most contemporary animal rights activists — Ms Duffy singles out anglers and angling for particular virulence because, as has been said, this represents the soft underbelly of the enemy; fishermen being ordinary people, the man next door. Everyone in Britain knows someone, or knows of someone, who goes fishing at times. We see it happening not too far from our own doorsteps. Few people, however, actually know anyone who goes stag hunting, or goes fox hunting. The participants are powerful and distant. They live somewhere else, and they hunt somewhere else. Not so the humble fisherman. But, when it suits, angling is lumped together with the rest of them:

> The point of hunting is to conquer by catching or killing. Whether fishing, fowling, coursing or the chase, is has like masturbation fantasy, two parts, the hunt and the kill even when that is symbolic as in the landing of a fish that is then thrown back.

According to Duffy:

> To deprive an animal of its life or to terrorize it for our pleasure, looked at rationally, is barbarous reversion. Why then, while the more obvious field sports decline, do these two increase? I think it's no accident that birds and fish are both creatures thought to be farthest from human beings, lowest therefore by popular definition, apart from the insects, on the family tree. Human imagination which may with a jump inhabit an intelligent mammal little removed from its domestic pets, finds the bird and the fish, more at home in other elements, beady-eyed, thin-blooded, easiest of all to consider as mechanisms, least understandable, most quickly reduced to the symbols familiar in dreams.
>
> Both sports are relatively solitary and the confrontation is a personal one. The build-up requires patience and endurance, an acquired skill rather than one that's a matter of upbringing. For this reason they are particularly popular with townsmen and their cheapness makes them accessible to all classes. A gun or rod can stand in a cupboard whereas a horse or dog needs the country, food, space and housing at great expense.
>
> Those who are familiar with dream symbolism will know at once that the thing hunted behind these two animals is the same as that behind fox and otter. Indeed the two sports are very much alike. The duck shooter crouching among the reeds in the marshes is another form of the angler on the bank or in the stream; rod and gun are extensions of their owner, letting fly bullet and hook which 'take' the victim.

There can be no doubt by now that fishermen and fishing are the real targets of the activists. Even those Duffy calls 'shooters' become less clearly targeted. Fishers not so:

> But fish are unable to be heard (to express pain) as they gasp in our thin air and their flappings and gill movements are taken as a mechanical attempt of the robot to return to its element. No one stops to ask why a fish has to be so carefully played as it struggles to escape from the usually much larger creature that has captured it. The leaping and twisting of a salmon, the tearing against the hook are not understood as the frantic efforts of a terrified being, still in its element not yet simply reacting mechanically to a rarefied atmosphere, but both experiencing and apprehending fear and pain. It is alleged too that the other animals have

shorter memories. They may indeed be shorter, as on the whole so is their lifespan to which memory may be relative, but memories they have as any old fisherman will bear out with his stories of the wily one that had been deceived by this or that bait before. Even if a fish is put back, which a glance through any angling newspaper will show is the exception rather than the rule, it has nevertheless suffered from the length of time it was 'played', its body may have been injured by the hook or by rough handling. It may be said that the fish deserves it for taking the bait. This is to be grossly anthropomorphic while at the same time applying the kind of reasoning that would blame a housewife who every day shopped in a supermarket for picking the tin of beans that was electrically charged at the whim of an assistant.

One of the chief attractions of fishing is undoubtedly the variety and subtlely of the metaphor. A fish can be found to suit every man's needs. Like all sports it has its ritual, indicating that it is an act of the imagination not of utility. The weighing and photographing are the tell-tales, recalling the comparisons in size and power of small boys, the whole penis folklore. The struggle is to possess magically for oneself that phallic shape. Fathers standing smiling beside curly headed boys with dangling mullet, recalling Tobias and the angel; tough young men display great congers; old men show small but crafty trout.

Now, if I understand Ms Duffy rightly, she is somewhat euphemistically saying in that last paragraph that fishing is so popular because it provides the symbolic masturbator with all kinds of dream and make-believe equivalents of pornographic pictures. Fish — that is women as sex objects — can be found of every size and shape and appearance to satisfy even the most perverted but impotent male. It is an act of the imagination, not utility, as is the case of masturbation. Photographs and dirty jokes are exchanged after 'the orgasm', and they stand around talking about the respective lengths of each other's fish — while they really mean their penises. The fish itself is a coveted phallic symbol. Fathers who take their sons fishing are really indoctrinating them into the dirty and furtive world of fantasy masturbation. Little boys penises are compared to dangling mullet; tough young men liken theirs to conger; while old men think they have penises like 'small but crafty trout'.

The symbolism and the sexual fantasies are mind-boggling, to be sure, and will no doubt seem ludicrous to fishermen. For anyone familiar with Jungian psychology and the symbolism of myths such fantasies would seem disturbed and distorted. But the onslaught hasn't finished yet:

The increasing numbers of fishermen in particular should make us very wary. Obviously there is a strong need which is being fulfilled in this way and that is given no other immediately accessible outlet. While this is so, pleas for the suffering animals are unlikely to succeed; we are too egocentric. It is our equivalent of the circuses for those we are unwilling to educate enough to find an emotional and artistic expression (for fishing, indeed all hunting, is allied to art forms like the happening and the drama or perhaps, in its extreme solitary and meditative Waltonesque manifestation, to novel reading) which will allow them to identify and experience without needing to possess physically. It is also part of the British outdoor, back-to-nature, anti-intellectual character on which we pride ourselves against all the arguings of reason and the advance of technology. The usual paradox of all reform applies, of course. Without legislation against fishing no other outlet will be sought and there will be no legislation until the long process of changing public opinion is far enough advanced. Perhaps knowing what we are really doing will help.

Thus the ninety-five various organizations listed by Maureen Duffy as an appendix to her book are fighting in one way or another to impose their wills on the rest of us. To be fair, not all are animal rights organizations, as such. The list, in fact, shows some strange bedfellows, varying from right-minded and esteemed bodies like the RSPCA, Friends of the Earth, Greenpeace, World Wildlife Fund, RSPB, to the Gay Vegetarians, Animal Activists, Animal Vigilantes, Animal Liberation Front, Council for the Prevention of Cruelty by Angling, League Against Cruel Sports, etc, etc — all of whom, no doubt, think they know better how the rest of us should live and behave. In any case it is an old ploy to list supposedly like-minded organizations, naming highly respected, honourable, long established, and non partisan bodies among the most radical and revolutionary zealots in a clear con aimed at usurping respectability.

Many of them hold well-reasoned and undoubtedly firmly held convictions as to the veracity of their beliefs. As people concerned with our environment and, above all, as fair-minded people it is encumbent upon all anglers to listen to what these people have to say, and to think about the issues they proclaim with such disdain for any other point of view. Only by so doing can fishermen justify their sport, not to the activists who would stop them by any means, but to themselves. Hitherto there may have been little beyond ethics for anglers to consider and work out where they stand regarding the charge of cruelty. It would be folly for anglers to pretend the charge will go away and be forgotten. The chances are that it will become more vehement a charge, and that the ranks of activists will increase as more and more bored and inadequate people look for causes to join to relieve the humdrum tedium of their lives. 'Let's go out and smash something,' seems to be their rallying cry.

Still, knowing that nothing is permanent except change itself, I for one, a passionate angler if there ever was one, hope to go on fishing all the rest of my days, for as long as I can hold a rod and cast, after a fashion, an artificial fly. It does not bother me that Maureen Duffy and her ilk think that I, by so doing, am engaged in pitiful masturbatory fantasy. She is entitled to her views as I am to mine. What does bother me is that she is lobbying to make it illegal for me to go fishing. And that, I believe, neither she nor any of her kind has any right to do. I hope I do go fishing for all the rest of my days, and I hope I will have the right to do so.

But my first hope is of secondary importance to the latter. We have seen how Maurice Wiggin, that erstwhile passionate angler, not all that long ago declared it to be his fondest hope that he would continue fishing until the day he died. But, one day, soon after, he gave it up. Just like that, as he said, I fish no more. What is important is that other men coming after us will have the right to fish, without wanton cruelty, and to know at least some of the bliss and ineffable delights that we, too, have known and shared.

In the final analysis it must remain a matter for the angler's own conscience. For my own part, for what it's worth, mine is clear on this issue, although some part of it still, at times, troubles me. Anglers who are quite untroubled by this accusation of cruelty should fish on with easy minds. Others, who may be sorely troubled by it all, should forswear angling at once.

From my earlier reading of fishing books, I had somehow come to believe that several once passionate and well known anglers had given it up for good for this very reason. Among them I had listed people as diverse as Robert Louis Stevenson, Thomas Masaryk, Lord Byron, Maurice Wiggin — to name a few who spring to mind. But while researching material for this chapter I discovered that, while these men did undoubtedly give up fishing, only in Byron's case had it anything to do with cruelty (or at least that was what he claimed years afterwards, probably when it suited yet another pose). Masaryk gave up fly fishing because his wife felt sorry for the fish. Stevenson had simply had enough of it by the time he was twenty-one, so hardly warrants classing as a complete fisherman. Wiggin, who often wrote that he would carry on fishing with ever new and fresh delight as long as he could crawl to the waterside, gave it up — just like that — at the age of forty-six because he said that, quite suddenly, after a day's trout fishing, it had lost its purpose. None of them, in fact, gave up fishing because of the charge of cruelty.

Chapter 16
Fishing Diaries

There isn't a fly fisherman alive who does not truly believe that he should keep a fishing diary. Yet few do. It is always a matter of starting one at the beginning of next season, yet that rarely happens. Most fishing diaries start off with literary enthusiasm; then dwindle after two or three lessening entries to a few scribbled hieroglyphics regarding the place or the catch: then nothing. A hundred years ago almost everyone kept a diary of sorts. Fishermen, being no exception, undoubtedly kept fishing diaries or, more probably, incorporated their fishing in the general recording of the daily events of their lives. Yet few remain. Even the vast literature of angling holds few fishing diaries as such, and those that exist, I suspect, have been written for publication often long after the events they describe.

Yet many anglers still meticulously note and record the exact details of every catch they make in avoirdupois minuteness and linear measurements to the fraction of an inch or the nearest millimetre. The truth is, of course, that interesting though these details may be, they are of no lasting importance. The day, the event of going fishing, the companionship, the weather and other fishing conditions, the journeys there and back, the day-after recollections, the fish that got away or were never caught: these are the important things and should be the stuff of fishing diaries, not the numbers that went into the deep-freeze.

Arthur Ransome once remarked that fishing diaries are like sundials that tell only the sunlit hours. It is not that they record only successful days; it is that they record only those days on which the diarist fished. The fact that fishermen enjoy reading other men's fishing diaries but, in fact, read so few, does not really matter. It was Ransome, too, who noted that a fishing diary will never find a better reader than the man who wrote it. And this is how it should be.

In a somewhat puckish way Ransome suggested that many fishing diaries are really like totem poles, mere notches on a stick — as, indeed, Dr J. C. Mottram cut notches into his wading stick that forever reminded him of certain notable past captures. In this respect a written diary is useful in checking the proverbial elasticity of fish. It may be scientific fact that a fish will continue to lose weight for some hours after being taken from the water. But it is a fact of human psychology that 'thereafter the fish makes up what he has lost and begins to expand'. Ransome believed that if the most honest fisherman in the world cast his mind back to what he remembered as his most successful day, five, ten or twenty years ago, and asked himself exactly what he caught, then wrote down his answer, and only then turned to his old diary to see what he wrote the moment he came home from the river, he would be astonished:

> Give a fish a chance and he will grow. The only way to keep him within bounds is to write his weight down at once before his post-mortem expansion has begun. No doubt your diary will then be the friend who spoils your best story by reminding you of the facts. You should be grateful. It is only non-fishermen who make jokes about the fisherman's inability to tell the truth. It is nothing to laugh about. Fishermen know that it is hardly worth while to explain to these heathen that in matters of fishing nothing but the truth, the exact truth, is of the slightest interest. Add an ounce to the weight or an inch to the length of a fish and you may as well add a ton or a mile. You have let him escape from real life into space fiction or fourth-dimensional romance. You can no longer reason about him, take him seriously, or compare him with other fish. You might just as well have never caught him.

Notwithstanding such usefulness as a check on the veracity of anglers, it would be unwise for anyone to think there is any merit in a merely statistical diary. Such a document can ruin a man's fishing; turn him into a slab fisherman, fishing for the sake of his diary alone and always seeking to better some past performance. Such an angler finds it increasingly difficult to believe that a blank day may have been a good one. For such a man it seems like defeat.

Despite the fact that few anglers actually keep fishing diaries, most agree that the book chosen for such use should not be a commercially produced, ruled page book, allowing as much space for the barometric pressure and air and water temperatures as it does for the remarks column. Rather, say those who know best, choose a large, strongly bound, plain white paper book that encourages the drawing of pictures, diagrams, and maps of pools and runs and taking places in rivers.

Angling writers are nothing if not divided in their regard for fishing diaries. Some have said that many of the best books about fishing have been based on their writers' diaries. Arthur Ransome went so far as to say he found it hard to believe that a fisherman who has not kept a diary could ever write a good fishing book for other people, although the diary must, in the first place, have been written for himself alone. On the other hand, W. H. Lawrie wondered whether in fact, fewer are kept than has sometimes been supposed:

> There are diaries in the desks and drawers of renowned fishermen still with us which, if they could be obtained, would not only provide interesting reading but also information of much value. As for the departed, what happens to these personal records of sporting careers? Are they destroyed by executors as being worthless or are they preserved privately for reasons of sentiment by relatives? Did George Selwyn Marryat keep a fishing diary? Or Halford? Or W. C. Stewart? How much

the angling community would value such diaries if they did, in fact, exist. We might have learned so much more about the giants of the sport had they had the foresight to leave instructions as to the fate of their records where these were kept. But that never seems to be done, and it is only by chance that one ever stumbles across an interesting diary.

Ransome also commented that what the compiler of a diary does is write a letter to himself when old. He teaches himself as no one else can teach him. He preserves his happiest days in a clearer aspic than memory. There are times when the passing of years sheds greater clarity on past events and fishing occasions. J. W. Hills, author of *A Summer on the Test*, wrote of his old Yorkshire diaries:

I have kept them just as they were written, they were intended for my use only. No one has ever read them and they were certainly never meant to be published. This is their merit. I do not now agree with much that they contain, but I have not altered anything.

Quoting an early entry after a day's fishing he writes:

Out of thirty-two chances I only landed thirteen fish and of these only four were takeable. I attribute this appalling record partly to the fact that I had to fish downstream; partly to my slowness in striking; for the fish were very quick and I am always a slow striker, particularly on the first day's fishing; but partly also to the fact that they came short.

Commenting many years later, he wrote;

There it is, there is the whole story. I fished downstream and I was clumsy. My hand was not in. Writing now, I do not believe that they came short. I believe that the shortcoming was mine. I know it was.

This, indeed, spells out the truth that often comes best in retrospect and gives fresh meaning to the lines Sir Walter Scott copied on the fly-leaf of his Journal:

> As I walked by myself
> I talked to myself
> And thus myself said to me.

Attitudes to fishing diaries are as various as the attitudes of anglers themselves. Dr J. C. Mottram was an essentially practical man and regarded fishing as an essentially experimental business. He did not call the journal he kept, a fishing diary, but a fishing log. He considered it essential not merely to record facts, but to draw conclusions. With scientific precision he recorded each and every fishing experiment, although on one occasion at least he shared odd doubts with his readers:

But, some will say, fishing is a sport, and as such is it worthy of so much seriousness? Fishing is a relaxation; why, therefore, put so much energy into it? Fishing is for the hour only, the present. Neither the past nor the future take a part in it. But this is not so. To the angler fishing is a serious business while he is about it. Other things and thoughts are as nothing when the angler is before his fish. The earth, the universe, life, death, and the unknown disturb him not a whit. He and his fish, these are just the two, and that is all. But, when the fish has gone, they may add, should it not then be forgotten? Is it good to recall it? Will it not distract the mind from the ledger, the brief, the patient, the work at hand? Why not then forget it.

Because it is impossible for those whose minds are built on other lines. Happy is he who can sit in the cocoa-nut grove, beneath the cool graceful boughs, looking across the narrow slip of virgin sand, across the glaring green lagoon, across the roaring breakers and across the unfathomable blue, beyond, to the great infinity. To him, forgetting is an easy matter, but there are some who are not thus happy. They must be doing, progressing, bearing ever forward, struggling with knowledge, dragging it up by the roots, digging deeper and deeper into the hard rock, ever and anon wounding themselves until at last they die with the grit still in their teeth and nails; and not till then will peace come to them. Such as these are also anglers; anglers will and must be such as these, because fishing, far above all other sports, gives hard work both for brain and body. Work is a relaxation provided only it be good and pleasant. Thus the writing of logs is excused and explained.

Not all anglers, however, see themselves in the light of Mottram's views. He then goes on to explain in quite factual terms exactly how a fishing log should be laid out and what should be recorded, although Mottram — being Mottram — goes on to say that the detailed recording of blank days are as important as those when limit bags are taken. To him blank days were often the most interesting and important of all fishing days; hence the need for a detailed log in order to know the reason why.

Not all fishing diaries are kept at the instigation of the diarist: some have been persuaded to keep one throughout a season or seasons for statistical or scientific purposes. Some surprising, and some not so surprising findings came out of such a scheme conducted in New Zealand in the years 1947 to 1952.

In 1946 the work of freshwater fisheries, then under the mantle of the Marine Department, was reorganized following a post-war expansion of research staff. It was necessary to determine which were the most urgent problems calling for study. It was apparent that throughout the country there was a dearth of information as to the state of trout stocks, the quantities of fish being taken by anglers, and the size of the fishing effort. It was also considered necessary to assess the effect of both current and proposed fishing regulations. A much wider coverage of the country was needed than could be achieved by the direct efforts of research staff, and it was obviously necessary to call on the anglers themselves for assistance. The General Diary Scheme came into being. This was under the direction of K. Radway Allen and B. T. Cunningham, research scientists with the Freshwater Fisheries Branch of the Marine Department. Their final report, *New Zealand Angling 1947–1952 — Results of the Diary Scheme*, was published in 1957 and contained some surprising and unexpected findings.

The diaries were supplied to all anglers purchasing a fishing licence. More than 800 detailed diaries covering one or more seasons provided the data on which the study was based. Information requested included the date, water, locality fished, the time of day and number of hours spent fishing; the number, species, and size of any fish killed; and the number of fish returned to the water alive and whether they were above or below the legal size limit. Length was used throughout as a measure of the size of fish, as it was believed that more accurate figures would be provided by anglers for this measure than for weight.

It is not the intention here to examine *per se* the results of this scheme, but only to comment upon how they were completed *as* fishing diaries and what could be read into them, rather than from them.

The average percentage of anglers cooperating ranged from less than 1 per cent in some districts to over 13 per cent in others. It was generally greater in districts containing less than 500 anglers than in the larger districts, and success depended upon the employment of a variety of publicity methods rather than upon the use of any particular and highly effective method.

Between one-third and two-thirds of the anglers keeping diaries dropped out each year, and the proportion tended to go up as the years went by. In these circumstances maintenance of an adequate number of diaries depended upon a sufficient number of new recruits being obtained each year. The number of recruits tended to be greatest in the first year or two, then fall off. The total number of diaries in each district therefore tended to rise for a time and then to fall, slowly at first and then more rapidly.

As an incentive, at the beginning of the diary scheme, prizes were offered in two districts for the best-kept diaries. In offering these prizes stress was laid on the fact that they would be given for completeness and accuracy of the results rather than for quantity of fish recorded. Since no external check on the accuracy of diaries was possible, and since the competition scheme had the definite danger of providing an incentive for sending in good-looking rather than accurate diaries, the response obtained in the districts where competitions were tried was carefully examined to test whether this did actually produce an improvement.

It was generally believed that one of the major difficulties in obtaining a good response was the natural reluctance of anglers to disclose just what they caught and, particularly, where their favourite fishing spots were. Every possible step was made to ensure secrecy, and the diaries were eventually returned to their owners.

One of the first interesting facts to emerge as to individual anglers' efforts showed that while the number of days recorded as fished in one season by one angler varied from 1 to 143, with an adjusted average of between 20 and 30 days in most districts, it was apparent that the average number of days fished in a season increased with the number of seasons for which an angler kept a diary. Either the keeping of the diary stimulated the angler to go fishing more often, or he went fishing more often in order to be able to complete his diary.

The report concluded that, in general, there was no significant difference in catch rates between bait, spinning, and fly fishing. But Dr Donald Scott has subsequently commented that diary returns do not reflect accurately the distribution of effort between methods, nor the catch rate. Further field studies showed the fly fishermen were over-represented in diary schemes both for a simultaneous control and over a 30-year period; this over-representation accounted for diary schemes giving an upward bias in mean catch rates for all methods combined.

Interestingly, by comparing catch rates from diary schemes and creel surveys, it was found that *all* diarists overestimated catch rates, as compared with the more objective creel surveys, and the non-fly anglers appeared to overestimate to a greater extent than fly fishermen. Two basic points emerge:

1.   The more successful anglers tend to return more diaries.
2.   Most anglers tend to omit blank days.

Could there be something, after all, in the claim often made by non-fishermen that all fishermen are congenital liars? Does the keeping of a fishing diary encourage the angler to tell fibs, or at least add a fish or two to his bag, and an inch or two, or a pound or two to their size and weights? Are fishing diarists reluctant to record blank days? It would certainly seem so, as far as solicited diaries are concerned and certainly invalidates their usefulness. Unless a fishing diary remains a private thing there is certainly an incentive to cheat. Fishing competitions also bring out this tendency in some win-at-all-costs people. But the biggest cheat of all is the fishermen who stretches points, as well as numbers and weights of fish, in a private diary no other person may ever see. For then he cheats himself.

Statistical fishing diaries, it would seem, are prone to certain less than desirable pressures. So should diaries limit themselves to recollections of fishing days themselves? The best fishing diary it's ever been my privilege to read is now in its fifth volume, and in describing more fishing expeditions to more wild and scenic high country New Zealand trout rivers than most anglers ever get to see, on more days than most fishermen ever fish, written by the best fly fisherman I know, none of those five volumes contains the death of a single fish. Increasingly, in fact, over the years, these diaries contain fewer and fewer accounts of the capture and release of trout. What they do contain is a wealth of observation about the countryside and the rivers themselves, of brown and rainbow trout stalked and sighted, of studies of stream entomology, of hatches — even of days when there were no hatches and not a single trout sighted, but good days all.

One of the most charming modern diaries published in book form is Oliver Kite's *A Fisherman's Diary*. It has all the hallmarks of a fine diary by a fine and natural diarist, yet was conceived and written as a series of weekly columns in *The Shooting Times*. In one such entry Kite makes a valid point that many would-be amateur fishing diarists are apt to forget in their concern for subject matter:

> A fishing diary is an uneven document, in many ways. There are times of the year when daily entries amount to little more than a comment on the weather, reinforced perhaps with another on tax men or idle tackle manufacturers who take months to execute a repair entailing not more than a couple of minutes' work. At peak fishing times the pen flows more freely, and photographs, sketches, maps, guest cards and the like pack out the pages and enshrine for future years the highlights of glory and of failure, for if a diary is to be of any value at all, it must be frank.

Here, then, may be a key of sorts to the keeping and endurance of fishing diaries. Fly fishermen, as a rule, far from thinking about fishing only when they are about to go fishing, and while they are about the affairs of stream, in fact think about it most of their waking time and, sometimes, even, while they sleep. They have a habit of thinking about fish and fishing even while their wives are demanding their attention towards pressing domestic affairs. They think about fishing in the most unlikely places, meaning anywhere and everywhere. I once found myself deep in thought about a certain delectable stretch of a high country New Zealand trout stream while I was being cross-examined by a noted Admiralty QC in a London court room during a maritime case involving huge sums of money. This particular QC, despite his fairness and charm, was representing what is called 'the other side', and might well have been leading me up some thorny garden path of his own design. Outside the court room the bleak late November rain was beating down on high windows overlooking a Wren church, while my heart and mind had foolishly wandered off to the Te Hoe Stream deep in the remote heart of New Zealand's North Island.

There is no merit in my lapse, although it is the common plight of anglers. For all I know, a few others of that distinguished legal company may likewise, in their hearts at least, have been wandering rod in hand along the more manicured banks of an English chalkstream. The point I am making is that fly fishermen don't only think about fishing when they are fishing. Similarly, a fishing diary need not be necessarily confined to fishing occasions themselves, but should reflect upon the writer's dream fishing.

A few published fishing diaries have been charming as well as decorative, but frothy. Muriel Foster's *Fishing Diary* was such a book. In New Zealand angling literature Alex Gillett's *Taupo Fishing Diary* filled such a place, except that Alex's book was written by a fisherman for fishermen, and like so many other such books was compiled of a composite fishing season, not necessarily one ticked off in the inexorable rolling on of the calendar, which churns on regardless of fish or fishermen.

Every angler should keep a fishing diary. It should not just be a record of numbers and weights, although these, too, have a place. Izaak Walton's *The Complete Angler* is a fishing diary of sorts, and he said of it, 'In writing of it I have made myself a recreation of recreation.'

More recently Sir Robert Saundby wrote of the same matter in terms more reminiscent of Mottram than Walton:

> Some people are natural diarists; they write regularly, easily, and in an interesting way about their daily doings, and the historians are deeply indebted to them. Others find the keeping of a diary irksome; their entries tend to be laboured and sporadic, and it needs an effort of will to prevent them from ceasing altogether. But whichever category he belongs to, the fly fisherman should train himself to keep accurate records. There is no doubt that it is of great value and importance to keep diaries recording daily happenings in shooting, fishing, bird-watching, entomology, and so forth. In no other way can we be certain of our facts and figures, for memory can play strange tricks.
>
> The possession of such a diary enables us to compare one season with another; to verify dates; to make deductions from weather and other conditions; and often to find the answers to present problems. It keeps a tight rein on our imaginations and anchors us firmly to facts. I am aware that those who keep a fishing diary are liable to find that they catch fewer and smaller fish than those who do not, but they will have the satisfaction of knowing that their records are unchallengeable.
>
> . . . For a fishing dairy to have any value the angler must carefully weigh every fish killed, and it is an advantage to measure them also. This adherence to accuracy does not always appeal to those with poetic souls. Halford says, very truly, that anglers are too apt to estimate and not weigh their fish, and that their estimates are invariably too high. He cites an instance of this. After two years' fishing on a water where all trout during that period were carefully weighed and registered, Halford was asked by a 'most respectable professional man' living near the water, who had fished it for many years, about the results of the last two years. Halford replied that over 700 trout, of an average weight of 1lb 9oz, had been killed. The inquirer expressed his disappointment at the number and average weight. Halford then asked him a series of questions, and his

replies, summarized in Halford's own words, amounted to this: 'That the limit of size under the old regime was nine inches; that the fishermen never weighed their fish, but took it as a rule that a nine-inch trout weighed one pound.

And so continues Sir Robert Saundby's exercise in the glorification of angling numeracy. It was a matter of sorrow to him that his earliest fishing records were lost while he was in the Middle East in 1922, and that his fishing diary went back no further than 1 May 1924. According to Saundby, the only saving grace in having lost those 1919–22 fishing diaries lay in the fact that he had undoubtedly caught many smallish trout in earlier days — and they would have lowered the total average weight! As it was, up to the time of writing his book, *A Fly Rod on Many Waters*, in 1961, his diary recorded a total of 1932 brown and rainbow trout, weight just over 2417lb, an average weight of almost exactly 1¼lb, and 2078 undersized trout returned.

There is no gainsaying the occasional usefulness of such detailed records and the near obsession with statistical averages, although for the life of me I cannot see that it matters very much. Fishing diaries should record the events of good days and bad days; should celebrate going fishing as a glorious event, not just add to a running sub-total that might raise the lifetime average by a fraction of an ounce, or raise the total numbers caught to another significant level.

Writing this in New Zealand, I am struck by how spoiled we are by good fishing. I am not a diarist, and in any case the numbers of fish I kill are so small that I am in no danger of forgetting or outrageous exaggeration. Although there is a year-long fishing season I still prefer to fish between an Opening Day on 1 October and the theoretical Closing Day on 30 June. So far this present season, now seven months old, I have killed five trout; all caught on fly in Lake Taupo itself from a rocky promontory drop-off only a few minutes distant from my home. From personal choice, all stream-caught trout — browns and rainbows — have been carefully returned to the water. The five rainbows killed were all caught with the intention of smoking and eating. The most recent was caught yesterday. It was a magnificent maiden rainbow hen weighing exactly 5lb on the kitchen scales, and it measured just over 20 inches, giving it a condition factor of 57and making it an exceptionally good fish, even by the best Taupo standards. But its vital statistics were measured only because my wife asked me to do so, out of passing interest in the superb appearance of the fish before cleaning; not for recording in any fishing diary or for posterity.

Yet, I shall clearly remember the savage take as the fly came up over the lake edge ledge, and the six powerful runs that still didn't run out to the backing, each one punctured by a bright water spilling leap into the westering sun, followed by a hard, deep boring down into forty feet of water outside the ledge; but after each dive being the more ready to be reeled upwards against the arching rod before succumbing to sidestrain and sliding over the rim of the outstretched sunken net. Maybe in New Zealand, anglers are too spoiled by such fishing to regard such a capture as important or as a noteworthy statistic. The only important thing about it was the event of going fishing. Diaries of the sort Sir Robert Saundby advocated would not speak of the celebration of that event; merely of the death of that particular fish.

But New Zealand, too, has always had more than its fair share of angling numerists who equated the excellence of a day's fishing with the size and weight of the bag. George Edward Mannering whose book, *Eighty Years in*

New Zealand, covers the longest recorded span in the country's trout fishing annals, between 1892 and 1942, seems to have weighed, measured and recorded every fish he ever caught.

Some years ago I came across a similar sort of diary among a collection of angling books. It was one of the original New Zealand Diary Scheme issues for the 1948–49 season, and had belonged to a well-known and scholarly angler. Sadly, the top edges and sides of all pages featuring a fishing entry have been eaten away by some insect, making the dates of the entries illegible. The first entry — 1948 records the place to have been the Upper Waihou, fished above Putaruru-Tirau, when between 12.30 and 2.00 p.m. two undersized rainbows were caught on a Brown Nymph, under a hot, bright sun: light NW wind: water discoloured and no fly hatch seen.

The next page records: — 30th 1948, at Arapuni, fishing from Bulls Paddock when, between 7.15 and 7.45 p.m. one 1½lb rainbow was caught on a Dry Red Spinner, when after a light northwesterly, the wind dropped: water very discoloured: and a fair hatch of sedge.

The next entry records a similar evening session at the same place, fishing between 7.00 p.m. and 8.30 p.m. for two undersized rainbows taken on a Dark Sedge. On that occasion it was cooler: water higher: little or no evening rise.

Next comes yet another visit to Arapuni, fishing from Bulls Paddock again, from 7.15 p.m. to 8.30 p.m., taking three undersized browns on a Dark Sedge. The Remarks column records the conditions as being similar, but with a better evening rise. Additionally two eels were taken on the same dry fly, approximately one pound each (2lb 1oz the two).

On the 27th of whatever that month was, he was back at Bulls Paddock at Arapuni, fishing from 2.30 to 7.30 p.m. for a 3lb brown trout taken at 3 p.m. on a Hardy Jock Scott Wiggler, 2 inch, blue and silver. The Remarks have a sad air of finality: 'Strong, rather cold wind: water high: no evening rise by 7.30 p.m. N.B. Four days — 8¾ hours — 2 fish — 7 undersized. No further fishing done — Lack of transport.' The diary ends there, having been sighted and stamped by the Fisheries Laboratory on 22 September 1949. The remaining thirty-four pages are blank, so it would appear the angler ceased keeping the diary because he was without transport. I find this somewhat puzzling as he was a literate, avid, peripatetic angler of some substance, whose book collection revealed loose, slipped-in pages of meticulous and learned notes. I wonder, too, whether this angling diary simply suffered the usual fate of most fishing diaries — that he simply couldn't be bothered to go on keeping it up.

One of the most famous of all known and published fishing diaries must be *The Diary of a Test Fisherman 1809 to 1819* by the Rev Richard Durnford of Chilbolton, Hampshire, which was not published until 1911. Durnford was the sporting English parson exemplified. In those days, even on the Test, although the artificial fly was used at the beginning of the season, the natural fly was used well before the season's end. Blow lines were used a great deal, and the wind became the most important diary entry. Cross-lines were also used, and considered to be fair fishing. Minnows and worm were used as bait whenever it was thought the trout would take them.

Fascinating though Durnford's diary may be, it totally lacks the charm of Dorothea Eastwood's *River Diary* published in 1950, chronicling a fishing season on the River Usk with a lyricism and understanding beyond compare. But, despite its literary charm and compelling reading about a river and its fishing, it is not a fishing diary in the true sense, as Durnford's undoubtedly was.

Dusty attics, garages, damp cellars, long-forgotten cupboards and boxes, in a host of places all over the world must contain hundreds upon hundreds of fishing diaries: good, bad, and indifferent. As they quietly rot away into absolute oblivion, it is somehow sad that other fishermen such as ourselves today, will never read those faded words and learn of triumphs and defeats, joys and frustrations, such as we ourselves suffer and enjoy in our fishing. Perhaps, after all, that is just as it should be. As Arthur Ransome said, a fishing diary is written for the fisherman himself grown old. It will never have a better reader than the man who wrote it.

Chapter 17
Props, Placebos
and Prognostications

The Solunar Theory in Fact and Fiction

One fine sunny English summer's morning many years ago I was picked up by my fishing companion on our way to a day's trout fishing on the River Test. Even before we got on to the New Forest back roads half a mile away I could sense his acute displeasure, and that it was directed towards me. At about that time I made a casual mention of the date: it was the first day of the month; and I recalled that a passenger ship Purser with whom I had once sailed always cloyingly referred to the first of the month, both in talk and in the ship's daily news-sheet, as 'Bunny Rabbit Day'. At the mention of the word rabbit my companion suddenly stopped the car and said, 'Well, that's it. Might as well turn round now and go back. You've ruined our day's fishing.' He was tense with anger.

We did not turn around but continued on our way towards Romsey and the magical trout fishing we shared in those days every Monday throughout the season among the lush water meadows of a Test carrier. But far from being bent on forgiveness my friend further catalogued my transgressions 'First of all you get into my car wearing a green shirt and a green jersey,' he said. 'And if that wasn't enough to ruin a day's fishing you start talking about that unmentionable animal. We might as well not bother. You've spoiled all our chances of a good day's fishing.'

Now this friend of mine was not a superstitious angling beginner but was without doubt the best and most stunningly brilliant angler I have ever known: a born angler to his fingertips and one of Britain's best known all-round anglers and fishing writers. It wasn't simply that he had spent much of his youth among Cornish fishermen that led to these angling 'superstitions' — although this was undoubtedly part of it. Being the demonstrably and consistently brilliant all-round angler he was, this friend of mine, of all men I've ever known, had no need for any angling props, placebos or other fisherman's charms or superstitions such as a lesser, poorer angler like myself might do.

Yet he would never start fishing anywhere without first tossing a coin into the water. This to him was a token, symbolic gesture of 'paying for' the fish he was about to catch. Yet his uncanny skill was such that had there been just one trout and no more in the river that day he would have caught it with superlative ease, skill and certainty.

From time immemorial poor anglers have sought excuses for failure, and encouraged signs and omens to bolster success. One might have thought that better anglers had no need for such props to their self esteem and ability, but this is not always the case. It really depends on whether a man goes fishing for the event of going fishing, or is simply out to catch and kill large numbers of fish. Although in all the years I knew and fished with this friend of mine I never once spoke to him about it, I'm inclined to think that his props and placebos were simply wordless ways of saying something about the magic of the event of going fishing: he was of that rare and fortunate breed of fishermen who goes fishing four or five times a week the year round, and in some of the most delectable places on this earth.

Prognostications concerning the weather and the often subtle interplay of seemingly unrelated conditions have long been of concern to anglers. Air temperature, water temperature, barometric pressure, pressure trends, wind, cloud, rain, thunder, sun, moon and stars, as well as the aches of rheumatic or arthritic joints, the behaviour of cats and dogs, cows and sheep, birds and insects, have all in their time been held as precursory signs of good or bad fishing. Izaak Walton didn't get beyond his Preface before hoping (for the honest angler) that 'the East Wind may never blow when he goes a Fishing'.

Despite all attempts to systematize and explain such phenomena it remains a neglected, murky, self-conscious and only hazily understood area of angling enquiry. It may be that modern man is fast forgetting the instinctive knowledge our ancestors took for granted. Far from getting closer to a real understanding of nature we are, in fact, well embarked on the road to forgetting. Those 'flashes' of understanding one may occasionally experience are not new discoveries as such, but brief and fleeting recollections from a race memory of what being a human being used to be like. Despite all its present day refinements fishing remains one of the few pursuits of man wherein he may on occasion experience briefly an odd flash of part-understanding of the oneness of the natural world. Modern man has all but forgotten that he, too, is part of that same nature he so curiously enquires into while distancing himself from its basic rhythms. The 'discovery' of circadian and lunar rhythms and of their effect on living creatures such as fish should really be no surprise to us for we, too, are subject to and governed by those same rhythms, however strenuously we sometimes deny or ignore them. Our remote ancestors understood such matters well.

Looking briefly at some recurring aspects of these rhythms that have puzzled or concerned the thoughtful angler, James Chetham wrote in 1681:

> In calm, clear and Star-light Nights (especially if the Moon shine) great Fish, Trouts especially, are as wary and fearful, as in dark, cloudy, gloomy and windy days, and stir not, but if the next day prove dark, cloudy, gloomy and windy, and the water in order, you may be sure of Sport, if there be a store of Fish in the River: for having abstained from food all night, they are more hungry and eager, and the darkness and windiness of the day, makes them more bold to bite.

But Chetham was wary enough to disassociate himself from out and out charlatans:

Some may expect me to insert the Elective Times most propitious to Anglers, according to the Rules of Judicial Astrologers, but they must pardon me herein, since I am sufficiently convinced of the Vanity thereof; and it would rather be an Unkindness, than Favour, by puzzling our Angler with their ridiculous Notions, as unserviceable to him, as false in their Foundations. But let our Ingenious Angler elect a cloudy, gloomy or windy Day, and the Wind not Easterly, but either Southerly or Westerly; and use proper and neat Tackle, and suitable Baits for the River, Season, and Fish he designs to catch, and then I doubt not, but he'll conclude with me, that, *Sapiens dorminabitur Astris*.

Most contemporary manuals continue to give warnings of the hopelessness of fishing when the moon is full and well up; suggesting that the fish see far too much by the light of the moon, and that moon shadows will totally inhibit good fishing. Not only are our human assumptions far too simplistic, but we have — by disuse — become dulled to the cues abounding in nature that regulate virtually all other forms of life with far more accurate and predictable precision.

There can be few fishermen who have not frequently experienced that sudden and inexplicable sensation that everything about and around them has spontaneously and suddenly gone dead. With an abruptness that seems heavy with a foreboding of something strange, the birds suddenly stop their song and flying, stream and lakeside animals vanish, fish cease rising; even the river or lake or sea seems quite dead and fishless.

In the same way, and with more good fortune, we may suddenly experience all of nature coming alive again after the stillness. Birds suddenly become active and noisy; insects hatch; fish rise; and all of nature seems on the go again. It is as if something had triggered the opening of a valve. More accurately perhaps it could be compared to one of nature's most important clocks sounding both an alarm and a warning of hunger: eat or be beaten; or perhaps eat and then be eaten in the relentless cycle of many food chains.

The day of the solar cycle is close to being exactly 24 hours long, divided throughout the changing seasons into day and night. The solar rhythm so dominates our lives and our very existence that we tend to neglect the lunar rhythms that strangely regulate everything about us — from the life cycle of human reproduction to the most intricate ways in which we live and die. It is almost as if somewhere along the path of his development man turned his back on the moon. Moonshine, lunacy, lunatic, moonstruck — even the words derived from it have negative connotations. Yet the moon is our closest neighbour in space. It is the earth's own satellite, tethered to earth by gravitational attraction, but itself exerting stranger and subtler forces on our planet than many of us realize.

A tide, as we generally know it, is a vertical movement of oceanic water. All bodies respond to the universal law of gravitation, the intensity of the attraction depending upon the mass of the bodies and the distance separating them. The earth and moon revolve in equilibrium, once a month, around their common centre of gravity inside the earth. This motion is steady because the total gravitational attraction tending to draw the earth and moon together is balanced exactly by the total centrifugal force tending to force them apart. At the earth's centre the centrifugal and gravitational forces are equal and opposite, but elsewhere there is a residual force acting towards or away from the moon. This force is called the lunar tide generating force. The same applies for the sun and earth, but the solar tide generating force is only about three-sevenths of the lunar force because of the greater distance of the sun from the earth.

The tide generating forces act upon every particle of every thing on earth, but only the waters of the earth (and to a somewhat lesser extent the earth's atmosphere that surrounds our planet like an envelope) are free to move. Thus on one side of the earth nearer the sun or moon gravitational attraction overcomes centrifugal force and the water tends to pile up and cause a high tide. On the opposite side of the earth centrifugal force is greater than the gravitational attraction and tends to cause another diametrically opposed high water. Between these two meridionally opposed high waters there is a tendency for two opposed low tides to form.

The earth makes a complete rotation about its own axis in an average of 24 hours, so that any position on the earth is in a direct line with the sun once every 24 hours. The interval between successive high waters caused by the solar tide generating force is thus on average 12 hours. Because of the moon's movement in space any position on the earth is in direct line with the moon once every lunar day, which is on average about 24 hours 50 minutes. The interval between successive high waters caused by the lunar tide generating force is thus on average 12 hours 25 minutes.

The distances of the moon and sun from the earth are not constant because the moon's orbit around the earth, and the earth's orbit around the sun, are elliptical. The tide generating force of either body is greater the nearer the body is to the earth. However, as the declination (which can be defined as the angle at the centre of the earth between the body and the earth's equator extended into space) is constantly changing the tide generating effect of both the sun and the moon will vary.

The combined effect of the lunar and solar tide generating force is complex, but approximately every 29¼ days the moon is between the earth and the sun. This is the new moon and the moon and sun are said to be acting in conjunction. Approximately 15 days later, at the full moon, the earth is between the sun and the moon, and the moon and sun are said to be in opposition. On both these occasions the lunar and solar tide generating forces are acting in the same direction. This is the cause of Spring tides which are those tides that twice in a lunar month rise highest and fall lowest from the mean level.

Between opposition and conjunction the moon will, twice during a lunar month, exert its tide raising force at right angles to the sun. The moon is then said to be in quadrature and the tides experienced will be of less magnitude than at any other time during the lunar month. These are Neap tides and occur at about the times of the first and last quarters of the moon.

As already said the tides vary with the relative positions of the earth, moon and sun. When all conditions tend to increase the height of the high water Spring tides, higher than normal Spring tides will occur. This happens at the Equinoxes in March and September, when the sun and moon have practically no declination. The tides are then known as Equinoctial tides. When all conditions tend to lower the normal Spring tides, at the Solstices in June and December, then lower Spring tides known as Solstitial tides occur.

Man has always been quick to find reasons for the natural phenomena he little understood. It used to be thought that sea fishing was good at the beginning of a flood tide simply because the sea moved in over previously uncovered areas of sand, mud, rocks and estuaries making more food available for shoals of fish moving in on that incoming tide. That, however, is an over-simplification. The fact is that all of nature becomes more active and alive at that time: the tempo of life itself quickens. It is not simply that sea covers more land, but that all creatures then react in one way or another, not simply to the encroachment of water, but to the rising force of the moon coming up. It is the moon that triggers off the feeding activity, not the water itself. And it is felt by all of nature. Hunter and hunted alike are aware of the inexorable rhythms: nature becomes alive again after a period of rest, and with it a myriad organisms throughout the web of the food chain eat and are, in their turn, themselves eaten. Man alone has shackled himself to a different timetable and to different clocks. Only by perusing tide and moon tables, is he now reminded of the cycle.

For centuries, human beings living close to the land and dependent upon the sea have used this knowledge in their fishing, as well as in their folklore and in the myths of their origins and creation. For the American Indians along the sea inlets such as the Straits of Juan de Fuca and the tidal stretches of rivers running into it, up which ran the vast shoals of Pacific salmon on which they depended for subsistence, and for the Torres Strait islanders on the other side of the Pacific, a fishing calendar based on the phases of the moon was the only almanac they knew of or, indeed, needed.

The Maori people of New Zealand, who had no written language, for whom all knowledge and wisdom was oral between one generation and the next, used a fishing calendar based on the age of the moon in successive days. It is used by many fishermen before venturing out. It was nothing but basic:

1st Day	New Moon	Good
2nd Day		Very Good
3rd Day		Fair
4th Day		Good — dawn to noon
5th Day		Fair — noon to sunset
6th Day		Fair
7th Day		Bad
1st Day	First Quarter	Good
2nd Day		Very Good — noon to sunset
3rd Day		Good
4th Day		Good — dawn to noon
5th Day		Fair
6th Day		Bad
7th Day		Bad — if moon rises after sunset
1st Day	Full Moon	Good — if out of sight
2nd Day		Very Good
3rd Day		Very Good
4th Day		Good — noon to sunset
5th Day		Fair
6th Day		Bad
7th Day		Fair — but improving
1st Day	Last Quarter	Good — noon to sunset
2nd Day		Good
3rd Day		Good
4th Day		Fair
5th Day		Bad — dawn to noon
6th Day		Good
7th Day		Very Good

Except to remark that it looks like a calendar devised by someone who didn't particularly like going fishing, and didn't need much of an excuse to stay at home, let us leave the Maori almanac for the moment and pass on to one John Alden Knight, an American angling writer, who during the 1930s first devised and popularized the Solunar Tables, and sought to develop a Moon Up — Moon Down theory to prove them.

To do Knight justice he never claimed to have 'discovered' the Solunar Theory (although that would have at once exposed him to certain ridicule), but he did so over-commercialize his ideas that, with hindsight, it is surprising he did not suffer a far greater loss of credulity among his peers than was the case. Copyrighting information that is published in almost every daily newspaper in the world, while cloaking and slightly amending it with a few mumbo-jumbo words of pseudo-scientific dubiousness was as nonsensical as if someone came along today and claimed to have 'invented' the simple barbed, eyed fish hook, and sought to patent it in order to receive handsome royalties from it. Surprisingly, no one to the best of my knowledge, either at the time or since, has commented on the charlatanic manner in which John Alden Knight introduced his Solunar Tables.

The trouble was that Knight, like so many others, lost his job in the city during the Depression. He was much attracted to fishing and hunting, and would have dearly loved to have been able to making a living out of it. The ingredients were present waiting for an accident to happen: John Alden Knight was looking for an annual income guaranteed for life, and looking around for the ingredients to make it possible. He noted the gullibility of fishermen looking for sure-fire, guaranteed ways to catch more fish more quickly. What he found, though, was that gullibility was only the tip of the iceberg. Far greater numbers of true anglers throughout the world weren't gullible as such, but were still very human. Like anglers since Adam they all in their various ways sought magic potions, irresistible baits, killing flies, super-duper techniques. Most importantly, such knowledge was sought not only to enable the beneficiaries to catch more fish, but to enable them to explain away the reasons for their frequent failure. Most anglers, thank God, go fishing because they want to go fishing: not simply to catch fish. I've yet to hear of a single angler who called off a proposed trip simply because the Solunar Tables told him it would be a waste of time. Instead, he goes fishing, does his best but doesn't catch a single fish, then goes home happy because the tables predicted this would happen. The truth is we need props, placebos and prognostications more to assuage our failures than to compliment our successes.

There can be few anglers who have not sometimes experienced that heady sensation (however briefly) of not being able to do anything wrong. At such a time they cast far and accurately and have almost uncanny control over flyline and fly. They almost tingle with expectancy and excitement — and almost always catch more fish than usual. Now I believe that this is probably due to their brief extra-involvement with what they are about — fishing. For a brief while they are totally involved, right down to their fingertips. Even a placebo or a prop may at times provide the faith to create, however briefly, that intense concentration most of us lack. On the other hand it may well be quite involuntary, the result of the total effect of that time on both angler and fish, a situation in which briefly and occasionally we, too, respond to the solunar rhythms as our forefathers did all the time and took for granted.

But to return to John Alden Knight and his Solunar Tables. These are still published annually by his family and successors and sold throughout the world, as well as being syndicated in hundreds of newspapers and magazines in the USA. Monthly or quarterly Solunar Tables are also syndicated to hundreds of hunting and fishing magazines throughout the world. It is interesting to look at exactly what the tables say, and what they are meant to convey, as well as their claimed exclusive validity.

Recapping briefly on this cosmic scenario, we have seen how it is mostly the mass of the orbiting Moon (with some lesser assistance from the Sun) that tends to pull up the waters of the sea, creating tides that become apparent to greater or lesser degrees everywhere on Earth, but are only visually apparent along the coasts, bays and inlets bordering the world's seas and oceans.

From a ship in mid-Pacific the rise and fall of the ocean tide is not apparent because of the absence of visual or measurable reference points. The shipboard observer in mid-ocean can neither see nor measure, nor in any way feel the tidal forces and the actual physical rising and falling of the sea, so to all intents and purposes, to such an observer, the tide does not exist. When this oceanic scale is reduced to bodies of water such as a lake or a river, there is no immediately measurable or observable tide. This tidal force affects all fluids; the water in lakes and rivers, and even the Earth's atmosphere, in relative ways. Yet in 1971 the Hughes Aircraft Corporation Laboratory in California developed a 'tilt meter' so sensitive it could record lunar tides in a cup of tea.

What the moon does to water on the Earth's surface it also does to our atmosphere, so that twice daily we have the envelope of air that surrounds the Earth pulsating with increasing and decreasing pressures.

Basically what happens is that the Moon will rise at any particular place on Earth from below the eastern horizon, then seem to climb across the sky from east to west along a path governed by both the geographical position of that place on Earth, the declination of the Moon, and the seasonal tilt of the Earth's axis, finally setting below the western horizon.

The tidal force commences with the rising of the Moon; culminating in its greatest attraction when the Moon is at its zenith — which may be relatively low in the sky or even directly overhead — then decreases until the tidal pull zeros again when the Moon sets. In such a manner we have Low Tide at moonrise, High Tide at its zenith, and the following Low Tide when it sets. But as soon as the Moon sets, the same tidal forces begin again because the piling up of the sea on one side of the Earth is offset by an equal piling up of the waters on the opposite side.

Briefly, it is Moon Up — tidal influence begins and increases to a maximum at its zenith, then decreases until Moon Down; immediately following which the tidal rhythm resumes until the maximum influence of the next tide is when the Moon is underfoot.

Naturally there is a delayed effect in all this: the ocean waters lag somewhat behind the passing of the Moon. On some coastlines the topography is such that the delay is even greater as the sea moves in slowly over vast areas of shallows, thus creating a visual awareness of the sea moving in and out laterally; whereas in another area with different landforms the visual awareness is one of a vertical rising and falling of the flooding and ebbing tide.

This time lag or delay between the meridian zenith or the opposite meridian nadir passage of the Moon, and the actual time when the highest tide is expected is known as the Tidal Interval or High Water Interval, and is only ascertained and known by local knowledge. Once known, observed and measured over a long enough period it can then be used to make accurate tidal predictions for that place, based on the astronomical data for all places on Earth on that particular longitude. This means that there is often great variation in the times of tides at places relatively close to each other, and all on much the same longitude. This is all to do with Tidal Intervals. And it is all to do with where John Alden Knight went wrong.

Quite apart from the fact that he knew little about tides and tidal theories, Knight was in a chicken-and-egg situation. He knew, and every thinking outdoorsman knew, as countless generations of 'primitive tribes' close to nature have always known, that fish feed more avidly and are hence more easily caught at certain times, and that this is governed by the phases of the Moon. But he was so over-anxious to meld actual experience with the theory he believed was the cause of it all, that he went from pillar to post, clutching at straws, firmly convinced he was polishing his Solunar Tables into infallible predictions for all time.

It is not unnatural that, in attempting to unravel such secrets about fish, one should become pre-occupied with water itself. Knight dwelt too much on ocean tides, trying to rationalize the Tidal Intervals between places on the Atlantic coast of the USA and the Pacific coast; then — worse, and scientifically invalid — trying to average out these time lags and apply them as corrections to the times of lunar tides in order to make his predictions for inland places throughout the North American continent. This was followed by establishing time corrections for places throughout the entire world. But these corrections are themselves a puzzle because the tables indicate a Nil correction between predictions for the eastern seaboard of the USA and New Zealand. Then there was all this emphasis on 'tides'. Knight's enquiries might have had more validity had he disregarded tides as such and stuck to the times of the rising and zenith and setting of the Moon as being the only pertinent and constant phenomena necessary to consider. His other over-anxiety was to make money out of gullible fishermen.

Basically what Knight claimed was that fishing would be best on any days or succession of days with both AM and PM having Minor and Major times of peak conditions. These would occur at times of Low and High Tides, for approximately one hour each side of the dead low water time, and for approximately thirty minutes either side of the time of high water. He further stated that the Major fish feeding activity took place during the low tide period, and the Minor feeding activity during the following high tide period.

This was old-hat fishing lore — except that no one had previously tried to copyright the notion. Saltwater anglers from time immemorial have believed that fishing was best during the first two hours or so of the flood tide, then peaked again briefly at high water, although there seems no evidence that freshwater fishermen had previously applied such criteria to the likelihood of their success — unless it was to have always been aware that a full bright moon was anathema to good fishing. So what Knight really did was to complicate the issue by bringing Tidal Intervals into the matter. In attempting to refine what is basically the Maori or Indian or Melanesian fishing calendar (although these were, of course, known to indigenous fishermen and hunters throughout the world) Knight actually defiled it by introducing humbug and gobbledegook, then asking fishermen to pay for it.

A direct comparison of the Solunar Tables with the ordinary tide tables for any place on earth shows them to be a pretty meaningless hotchpotch when it comes to solid information about the best times to go fishing. In all they don't make much sense. It hardly requires a relatively expensive annual pocket book of tables produced by Solunar Sales Inc. of Montoursville, Pennsylvania, to haphazardly and often incorrectly tell fishermen and hunters what most of them know already. The chances are that fishing will be best at the time of the rising of the Moon and for the following two hours, and again, briefly but rather less good, for about an hour when the Moon is at its zenith (roughly halfway between Moonrise and Moonset). Fishing may also be good for about two hours immediately after the Moon sets, and again briefly, for perhaps an hour, when the Moon is directly underfoot, approximately halfway between Moonset and Moonrise. All the information necessary for making such predictions is contained in most daily newspapers and pocket diaries.

As for myself I shall continue to go fishing whenever I have the opportunity, the urge to do so, the time, and the beckoning call; whether it is a planned trip to some distant stream or a sudden decision to fish waters closer at hand. I go along with Robert Traver who wrote:

> In the watery and spectral half-world inhabited by trout fishermen there dwell many fanatic sects, each with its own stout band of followers, and each claiming exclusive possession of the one true ladder to trout heaven. At one time or another I have tarried with most of these sects and dallied with their doctrines: the disciples of lunar tables, the pilgrims who yield only to barometric pressures, the worshippers at the shrines of tidal impulses, wind directions, thermal dynamics, water strata, sun spots, spots before the eyes — and all the others. Then one day there came the light, and I became a lamb strayed from the fold, a renegade and a blasphemer. For I now embrace the heresy that the 'best' time to go fishing is when you can get away. I have also concluded that Dr Bile's Almanac (for 1911) is about as good a fishing guide as all the involved scientific claptrap with which so many present-day fishermen clutter their comings and goings.
>
> There is not the slightest doubt, of course, that the fishing is better on some days than it is on others, and that frequently certain parts of the day are better than others. All fishermen know that. My thesis is that I do not believe anyone can predict these times — at least for any appreciable period in advance — and it both amuses and irks me to watch certain self-appointed native witch-doctors blandly arrogate this authority to themselves. Any dolt with a head full of Crisco may suspect that the fishing might be lousy when he sets forth in the teeth of a belting northeast gale, with the barometers crashing all about him, but I am talking about those smug gentry who sit in skyscrapers in January and undertake to tell you what the fishing will be like on Herkimer's Pond at 4.42 PM the following July 17.

Traver rounds off his sage and balanced view with almost self-evident wisdom — leaving us feeling we knew so all the time:

> The more one fishes for trout, then, the more he is forced to the conclusion that no man knows even faintly when or why fishing will be good or bad. Too often have all of us marched forth hopefully on those rare 'perfect' days — when all the licenced fish prophets were for once smiling and nodding in sweet accord — only to return wondering whether all the trout hadn't migrated to Mars. Or again, too often have we braved their collective frowns — and gone out and hit the jackpot. Why? I don't know why, otherwise I would set up shop as a swami myself — and henceforth tramp the trout circuits of the world, fishing away like mad, on the proceeds of my sage revelations.

Most of us tend, generally, to lend to claims made for 'scientifically' backed theories far too ready an acceptance and lack of healthy scepticism. If is often considered ignorant to question 'scientific' revelation, in much the same way as it was once unthought of to question revealed truth in matters religious. There is phony science. To whit one John Alden Knight, unemployed during the Great Depression, took himself off to the US Coast Guard Office in New York one afternoon, before which event he was totally ignorant (by his own admission) of tides and tidal theory. After what was undoubtedly a fairly brief interview with some junior official on front desk duty he emerged transported with what became the Solunar Theory.

Whilst we live in an age of advanced science and technology, far too many men believe that all the problems of living — and fishing — can be solved by applying the pragmatic methods of science to problems that are perhaps essentially insoluble. The same men laugh at the superstitions of our ancestors and at the leaping witch-doctors of present-day primitive tribes, yet themselves gladly swallow enough phony science every day to make even the dizziest witch-doctor look like Albert Einstein.

> I have to add that most trout swamis are a serious, well-intentioned and dedicated crew who genuinely love to fish; they are often highly intelligent men, perhaps lacking only in the saving perspective offered by a sense of humility and humour, whose pretensions after all cause little harm and possibly save quite a few trout. In a sense they are victims of their own hobbies. And sometimes their predictions are dead right, as they are occasionally bound to be, like a man who always plays the same number at roulette. They can't possibly always be wrong. Their occasional home runs are in fact the thing that keeps them in business.

Robert Traver again, and for myself I'd certainly rather have gone fishing with him than with John Alden Knight.

Then there's that other factor. If a disciple of the faith *believes* that the fishing is going to be good he will fish with great care and concentration and is far more likely to catch fish than at other times when the great guru has told him it's a waste of time to go fishing. At such times even *going* fishing is bad: almost as sacrilegious as a born-again Christian saying prayers of thankfulness in a massage parlour.

Many enquiries into the apparent cyclic nature of good and bad fish-taking times have suggested that the rhythmical changes in pressure of the Earth's atmosphere caused by the gravitational pull of the Moon and Sun — in other words 'atmospheric tides' — are the cause of it all.

For what it's worth, my own view tends towards Roderick Haig-Brown's observation:

> I kept a record of barometer readings on fishing days for some fifteen years, but have given up doing so because I could not find the slightest correlation between the vagaries of the barometer and the results of my fishing effort. I seem to catch fish equally well, or equally badly, on a rising, a falling or a steady barometer. I mentioned this to my friend, Tom Brayshaw, who is a mathematician as well as a fine fisherman.
>
> 'Why in hell should a fish worry about the barometer?' Tom asked. 'If it drops an inch while you're out, all he's got to do is go down a foot in the water to find the same pressure. And if it rises an inch he can come up a foot.'

And many is the time in a crystal-clear New Zealand mountain stream pool I've watched big trout swim quietly up through twenty feet of water to take a fly. Haig-Brown observed further:

> But I have a far more serious objection than any of these to rigid systems forecasting the behaviour of fish. It seems to me the fisherman carries an abundance of mental hazards within himself and has no need to add to them. If he is not catching fish he can, and undoubtedly will, wonder if his fly is wrong, his gut too heavy or his choice of pools unsound; he will wonder if the hatch is too late or the day too bright or the river too high or his casting too clumsy. If he must also remember that the mystic tables say the time is too late or too early, he can hardly be expected to fish on with even a remnant of confidence. Worse still, if he is a very faithful believer, he may consult the oracle before he goes out and may decide to stay at home, though the day is lovely and spring is in the woods and fish are rising all over the river.
>
> The time to go fishing is when the chance comes. And the way to go is with a free and hopeful mind, and an eye quick to take note of things. There will be days when the fishing is better than one's most optimistic forecast, others when it is far worse. Either is gain over just staying home.

Notwithstanding all such reveries about the pure joys of going fishing for its own sake, there can be no gainsaying the powerful argument that the fundamental purpose must be in the hope and expectancy of catching fish. So what, then, is wrong with choosing the right time of the right day before setting out with high hopes? The Solunar Tables still sell in thousands of copies around the world. Syndication seems to grow in countless hundreds of magazines and newspapers worldwide. So is there anything in the claims made for them?

Fishermen and hunters who swear by their accuracy are unlikely to know what might have happened had they not consulted the oracle on certain trips. A few years ago, a carefully chosen group of members of the Taupo Fly Fishers' Club in New Zealand, put them to a conducted and controlled test, shortly before I became a member. My colleague and friend John Parsons instigated the test along with Colin Hill. In order to give scientific authority to the proceedings Dr Max Gibbs, a fisheries scientist and club member, took on the task of analysing the results. By early January 1978 the club had gathered a full year's fishing results from six or seven members especially interested in the solunar theory. Max Gibbs painstakingly measured these results against the precise lunar times calculated for the Taupo district for the year, and came up with a set of statistics that proved to John Parsons that John Alden Knight was right. The six or seven who regularly turned in figures for the club's solunar diary caught a total of 2285 trout between 8 January 1977 and 7 January 1978. They fished a total of 3320 rod-hours for those 2285 fish, yielding a catch rate of 0.7 fish per rod-hour.

Max Gibbs established to his entirely scientific satisfaction that the state of the land tide which has greatest significance for the angler is the solunar low-tide condition. He accordingly calculated solunar low-tide times only, disregarding high-tide times. He was also able to calculate which of the two low-tide times in each roughly twenty-four-hour period exerted the major influence and which the minor. Again to his satisfaction he determined that two hours each side of solunar low-tide times (not one hour, as Knight advocated) gave anglers — at least Taupo anglers — the greatest chance of catching fish.

Based on these findings, his figures for the year showed that, of the total of 2285 fish caught, 1152 were hooked in solunar low-tide periods, which aggregated 1105 hours of legal fishing time, or 1.04 fish per rod-hour — *twice the rate at which fish were caught in non-solunar time.*

In his examination of these results in a chapter of his book *A Taupo Season* (1979) John Parsons commented:

> Naturally, some factors affecting the figures are questionable. Is one year enough? Did the anglers record catch-times precisely? Isn't it true that smaller fish and all running rainbows feed all day long? Surely the theory can only be really valid for a resident-fish population? Was the 'other conditions not being unfavourable' factor too often or too infrequently loaded on the side of the fisherman? Did anglers deliberately choose to go fishing at times coinciding with solunar periods?
>
> The answer to the last question is a definite no, but the question itself poses a problem. If the solunar theory works as well as it seems to, won't anglers go fishing only at those times? After all, what's the point of making fish-hooking more certain if you don't take advantage of it?
>
> As Colin Hill put it, if a man knew he could fish either on Saturday or Sunday, but not both, or perhaps was limited to one of the four half-days over the weekend, it would be natural for him to consult the solunar oracle in order to plan grass-cutting, painting, car-cleaning, and other chores, for off-peak solunar hours.

There can be no doubt that the above experiment was conducted with as much scientific exactitude as possible, and that the fly fishermen who took part in the survey were of more than average competence and fishing in waters they knew well. Yet none to my knowledge henceforth became slaves to, or even guided by, the solunar tables. To attempt to explain *why* the increased catch rate was apparent would step beyond the intentions of this chapter. Few fishermen would deny that there is, or maybe there is, something in it. But, equally so, many anglers are prone to function better when propped up by some favourite placebo. If someone really believes that they have their best chance of catching a fish at exactly 2.32 p.m., because it is scientifically forecast that this will happen, or even if stated to them that this happening is in some way pre-ordained, then there is no doubt whatsoever that the fisherman so hyped-up will fish with great care, concentration, stealth, cunning and confidence as the magic hour approaches. Especially confidence. And that may be the key.

As for the tables themselves, if such certainties give the trout or salmon fishermen greater confidence that success will be theirs by going out at the appropriate and happy time, then they are worth every penny of the cost, and should be consulted without fail. Happily there are those of us left who go fishing whenever we can; for whom a blank day is not a wasted day; for whom a fishless day is not a waste of time.

But, there are cases when the use of such information can be made in retrospect, with the added advantage of hindsight. Once thus it happened to me.

Some years ago I wrote a two-part article on the myths and mysteries of the Solunar Theory that appeared in the New Zealand *Flyfisher* magazine. In order to provide authenticity and a means by which readers might measure for themselves the efficacy or otherwise of Knight's theory, but calculated accurately for New Zealand by means of Admiralty Tide Tables and the Nautical Almanac, I set out these times in tabular form with the Solunar Tables' predictions for the same region as syndicated and published in a New Zealand sports magazine, side by side for comparison. This was done for the current month in question. When completed I could not see any real relationship between the times shown in my tables, and those provided by the oracle.

A month or two later I went on a camping-fishing trip with three companions into a remote area of the central North Island at the confluence of two rivers. After fishing hard upstream all day up the more rugged, faster stream, we had returned to camp and after preparing, eating and clearing up our evening meal variously set about quiet evening tasks before turning in. Two of my companions were not only wise and skilful fly fishermen, but avid and knowledgeable entomologists. Bill crouched at the riverside, just a few yards from our tents, ostensibly to bale out a basin of water with which to shave. Suddenly he let out a eureka-like cry of discovery. There, in a plastic mug, he had scooped out a superb and huge larval specimen of *Ichthybotus hudsoni*, the burrowing mayfly, almost 4 centimetres long. It was a splendid and even fierce looking nymph and seemed aggressively huge charging around the bottom of an orange plastic mug. Once common throughout much of New Zealand, *Ichthybotus hudsoni* is now mostly confined to isolated hilly streams flowing through native bush.

While Bill and Nick, my two entomologist-angler friends, discussed the creature so knowledgeably (and prepared to preserve it in my whisky) I looked at it and said, 'That's odd. This afternoon I put a dozen different small nymphs and dry flies in front of, over, and either side of a confidently feeding fish, only to have them all ignored. Looking into my fly-box as if for inspiration I noticed a line of three or four English Richard Walker mayfly nymphs on No.6 longshank hooks. They must have been there for at least five years without even getting wet. But my eyes passed on as I took out and tied on a No.14 Hare and Copper — again without success. I should have used the Richard Walker mayfly nymph!'

With that I set off the few paces to where my fly rod was propped against a streamside bush, and hurriedly cut off the Hare and Copper and tied on the big Walker mayfly nymph.

Bill — an angling purist in the most delightful way — said scathingly, 'You're not going to chuck that monstrous thing at a fish are you?' By which time I was already hotfooting it the twenty yards or so from our camp upstream to the first fast water that tumbled through a narrowing cleft then spread out in the broad shallows close by our tents. Stripping off line as I approached the chosen spot I tossed the nymph upstream, and then with the first half-proper cast dropped it into the downstream tail of the broken water.

With a bang I was into a leaping rainbow that tail-walked around the pool in indignation. Bill, the purist, in mock horror, shook his fist at me, but I looked at him over my shoulder as the fish leapt high and streaked away into the shadows. With tongue-in-cheek I called back, 'Exact imitation, Bill. Even your friend Halford would have to approve!'

The time was 8.25 p.m. The day Tuesday 4th December. I referred readers to Column 6 in the magazine article. There, under the Major Solunar Period, was 2025!

On second thoughts I'm not so sure Halford would have approved, but I'm certain that John Alden Knight would have been delighted.

Chapter 18
Impressionism in Artificial Flies

Another chapter in this book concerns itself with Evolution in Trout and Salmon Flies. In some respects it was not possible to separate a description of the evolution of certain artificial flies from a discussion of undoubted artistic impressionism in their design. Like Jack and Jill, evolution and impressionism are twin beings, yet they are two separate sentient beings each existing in their own right. As a line of enquiry into certain developments in fly fishing it is not always possible to separate the two; yet they are two separate issues. It was not possible to write the chapter on the evolution of artificial flies without mentioning and impinging on the artistic use of impressionism in the design and dressing of the same and other trout and salmon flies. Yet it would have been even more misleading to have developed both theories in the same chapter.

The result is that this quite separate chapter contains some ideas and suggestions that appear in the evolution chapter. They are different sides of the same coin. Evolution is in many ways involuntary, whereas impressionism in artificial flies (while possibly involuntary in that it was sometimes unpremeditated) resulted from a specific way of looking at things, and looking via the experiences and revelations of looking at art. For any too obvious repetition in the two chapters I humbly apologize.

Many early artificial fly patterns happen to have been generally impressionistic, rather than exact imitations, simply because the fly-tyers, by and large, had no clear idea or intention of what they wanted to copy in nature. Such flies were impressionistic by default.

Throughout several pivotal periods of fly fishing for trout in Britain patterns arose that were successful and have lived on, which we recognize (with the wisdom of hindsight) as having been truly impressionistic, because the people who tied and fished these patterns appear to have had little idea, and certainly no pre-conceived knowledge, of what they represented in nature. Soft-hackled flies of the North Country, and Scottish spiders are prime examples of this category of flies. The artificials, and the deadly upstream method of fishing them 'damp', were brought to a fine art long before the fishermen knew what their flies imitated and why they were so successful. It was a matter of a series of truly remarkable flies, and a manner of fishing them, evolving by means of what Arthur Ransome called natural selection.

Admittedly, Ransome's theory was concerned with there having been something akin to natural selection at work in the haphazard development of salmon flies. No one then knew what salmon fed on throughout their life at sea, or even where they went on these oceanic journeys, or that because the salmon ceases to feed on entering fresh water, it could only take an angler's artificial fly out of annoyance or anger, or perhaps because it reminded them of some creature they used to eat at sea. Artificial salmon flies were tied with no other object in mind than attracting the fisherman. They were often bright and gaudy and soon became minor works of art. Some, inevitably, caught salmon. Certain features of the successful flies were almost unknowingly carried over into the design and construction of new patterns. Characteristics that evoked no response from the running salmon were equally unknowingly discarded, until the 'classic' salmon flies all shared certain elements of shape, size, colour, movement, that triggered the salmon to take the fly despite its absolute fast from taking food.

In this manner, and unknowingly to the fly-tyers and the salmon fishermen, and by means of natural selection as absolute as any of Darwin's theories, they often made quite remarkable copies — impressionistic — of one of the main natural foods of the salmon on the high seas. Men who at that time had no knowledge of the existence of the euphausid shrimps of the North Atlantic designed remarkably good copies of this oceanic creature on which the Atlantic salmon grew large and fat.

Even until recent years fishery scientists had little or no idea of the food of salmon in the sea, and it was all too easy to zero in on the euphausiacean crustaceans after the oceanographic round-the-world voyage of the research ship *Discovery II* in 1950-51, important though this breakthrough was in fathoming the secrets of the salmon. To Arthur Ransome and other thinking salmon-fly designers of the time it was sufficient that Atlantic salmon consumed vast quantities of this particular crustacean in their main feeding grounds off Greenland. It was sufficient for Ransome — and an elegant theory, to boot — that, after returning to their natal streams and despite complete cessation of their feeding processes, salmon could be induced to take a fly specifically tied to imitate this shrimp-like creature. It seemed to consolidate and confirm Ransome's theory that natural selection had been at work in the design of salmon flies throughout the previous century, although the fly-tyers concerned had no idea of what they were imitating: simply that some flies with certain characteristics worked, while others didn't.

Subsequent discoveries, of course, have shown that this was over-simplistic: salmon variously feed on a wide range of oceanic life during their long sojourn in the sea. It is no doubt hormonal change that first directs their initial seaward migration, not hunger or the lack of food in their parent rivers. Should they remain in their freshwater habitat, however, there is no doubt there would be insufficient food available for salmon in such huge numbers, or on which they might reach optimum size and weight before returning to the parent stream.

.But once the young smolts drop down to the sea for the first time and adjust their osmotic functions to the salt water, they begin feeding. At first they consume a wide variety of infant pelagic fish still members of the macroplankton, before moving on to elvers, sandeels, then sardines and pilchards, and squid and all manner of prawns, until they come to this great euphausiid soup in the mix of currents off Greenland, on which they and the mighty whales wax huge and fat. Their diet, then, is a fairly catholic one. Like most successful fish they are opportunistic feeders, eating what is best and plentifully available to them along the route of their oceanic wanderings.

This may explain — while still fitting in with Arthur Ransome's theory of natural selection — why the salmon on its return to fresh water will, at times and as readily, take an imitation minnow, or plug, or sandeel, or prawn, or bunch of worms, with as much heartiness as it will a classic traditional fully-dressed salmon fly or one of the newer, sparser, duller, hairwing flies that have now generally succeeded the older style of fly. In all of these artificial baits natural selection has played a similar part.

Now, in all this, it is clear that impressionism was at work, in addition to natural selection — even if the anglers using such flies and devices were unaware of its happening. Impressionism, then, in artificial flies is not new. As in so many human endeavours and activities, nature is copied by means of artistic inspiration rather than straight off the drawing board, as was the case of Leonardo's airplanes and submarines and a host of other discoveries and inventions presaged by an artist's intuitive leap ahead of present-day knowledge.

Ironically, Ransome commented that at least the secret places where the salmon fed so ravenously and well was good news for the fish themselves: 'It must be a place where the salmon are free from all the devices of predatory man. While they are busy, idly and without great effort, absorbing their gargantuan feasts the salmon do not get caught.' Sadly, this was before Danish gill-netters discovered the rich feeding grounds in Davis Strait.

Insofar as natural selection was concerned, it was Ransome's belief that, without certain knowledge of what salmon actually fed on in the sea, no one could tell us better than the salmon what those things were like. It was to the salmon that the fly-dresser continuously appealed. He was the judge who decided on the future of the flies submitted to him. No fly-dresser went on dressing a fly that did not catch fish. A fly may have delighted the human eye, but if it did not interest the salmon little more was ever heard of it. Flies, to Ransome, were like books. Out of many thousands only a very few survived their publication:

> A ruthless form of Natural Selection has been at work for all these years, with the salmon as the Natural Selector. This has applied both to the making of flies that copy known objects and to the making of flies that in some way resemble and in other ways differ from artificial flies that have been approved by fish. This form of natural selection has led to the survival of certain characteristics and the disappearance of others.

By letting himself be caught on certain flies, the salmon has, as it were, expressed his preference, if not for particular feathers, at least for the flies dressed with them:

> Speckled mallard hackles and barred teal feathers hold their place in the fly-dresser's box all but unchallenged. Now why? May it not be that these feathers contribute in some way to the likeness of our salmon flies to creatures we have not been able to copy because we have not seen them, creatures on which we have had as yet no sure proof that salmon feed.

In this matter, I suggest, such feathers provided — albeit unwittingly — that element of pointillism necessary to create an impressionistic creation not only of what the salmon sees in its natural food, but furthermore in *how* the salmon sees, in other words according to the visual processes of fish. In this manner, by accident and by trial and error, fly-dressers had pre-empted the discoveries and experiments of the first impressionist artists, whether the precise pointillism of, say, Seurat, or the shadowy, almost substance-less seas and skies and scenes of Turner's paintings. Until now, this undoubted process of natural selection in the development of salmon and trout flies was not seen for what it was: an anticipation of the artistic and scientific elements of visual suggestiveness. With, perhaps, a new insight into how fish see, and what they see in their watery world.

So, while there is a distant connection between natural selection in artificial flies and impressionism in artificial flies, they are different in application and in their significance to anglers. To begin with, all natural selection is, by definition, unpremeditated and unplanned. It occurs, where and when it does, involuntarily. Impressionism, on the other hand, is designed and planned, as a sort of "fishy" attractiveness or allure built into the fly, but necessarily one quite unalike exact imitation or anything akin to it.

It has long been common to speak of trout flies in much the same language as that of paintings; indeed many people regard fly tying as more of an art than a craft. With regard to fly design Skues once said the imitation might be Impressionist, Cubist, Futurist, Post-Impressionist, Pre-Raphaelite, or caricature — the commonest being caricature. Caricatures are generally black and white line drawings of well known people, often political figures. They are often based on proportions that terribly exaggerate and distort some particular feature of the subject, or may even pick on some habit or gesture that becomes instantly recognizable. Eric Horsfall Turner once wrote:

> The effectiveness of a caricature on our sense is not created so much by distortion of features as by the exaggeration of unusual and individual characteristics. A man with regular features is not easy to caricature; but, a very relevant matter to fly-dressing, a really good caricaturist can often relate a combination of regular features in such a way that they convey the sense of caricature. In passing, the adroit press caricaturist of the politicians will often raise his caricature, even if it is a poor likeness of the victim, to an absolute likeness in the minds of his readers by repetition of the same design.

The absolute recognition characteristic of the caricaturist's art is often some object familiarly associated with the person — Churchill's cigar, or a feature generally associated with them, Mrs Thatcher's hairstyle, President Reagan's hairline. Others still are most extraordinarily difficult for even the most talented and creative caricaturists to create in a few lines. These features, when picked on, are repeated over and over again so that, eventually, the cartoon character seems more like the real life person than would his image in a photograph.

Richard Walker used to liken impressionism in flies to his caricature figure of what he called 'a Chinaman', although he would have been more polite, if less precise, in using the word 'Chinese'. There was the instantly recognizable Chinese coolie figure, accomplished in a very few strokes of the pen:

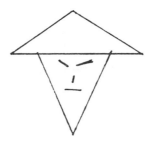

This impressionism, in Walker's view, was of considerable importance to the fly designer and innovative fly-tyer.

Some angling writers have emphasized the benefits of constant repetition even in the case of presenting an obviously phoney artificial fly to a trout. Hewitt, LaBranche, Kite and others have insisted on the success of hammering a trout on the nose with the same fly until it takes.

The principles of art are not easy to convey in words. The best way to study art is to look at it but, however hard and long as one might do, it is not all that simple to come to a way of looking at art and recognizing the 'form' it encompasses and displays without resorting to words suitably explaining what 'form', in this sense, is. Col E. W. Harding was the first angling writer of whom I'm aware to note that form is something much more subtle than a figure bounded by conventional lines:

> It needs a trained eye and understanding to realise the various colours and shades which are combined to give us the sensations of whiteness, cubeishness and position of a white cube on a table. Only portions of the cube are seen at any one instant and a series of momentary impressions of shapes, of light and colour fitting into one another give us that feeling of an 'instantaneous' whole, which we call its form.
>
> Still more complex is the process of seeing movement. We leave out groups of intermediate movements and yet have a sensation of a definite form which is moving. Now that our eyes have been trained, we accept as perfectly normal and correct the instantaneous photograph of horses galloping. We feel a sense of movement about it, yet it is but one phase isolated out of perhaps hundreds that the camera has recorded, and it differs completely from the old conventional drawing of horses in full gallop. When we can realise that the form of objects, especially moving objects, ordinarily visible in the air, are about as substantial as the airy fabric of a dream, we may begin to have some idea of the impressions that the movements of the semi-invisible creatures of the under-water world have upon the trout. Rarely can he see them as simultaneous wholes. He sees them probably as bits of light and colour flowing in a more or less definite sequence of intensity and pattern. And his impressions must vary with the speed of the water in which they are and consequently with the speed with which they are moving.

Study of the vision of trout, and of what the trout sees, reveals that, in the case of the floating fly drifting into the vision of the fish, any attempted precise imitation of the natural is a waste of time. If the artificial is presented by sudden impact inside the area of direct vision through the trout's window, colours and their combinations are quite unimportant compared with outline and size.

In the case of the sunk fly, exact imitation always was aimed for in that era of wet fly fishing preceding the Halford code of exact imitation at all costs. All that happened, in fact, was that the fly-design tenets of the wet fly were transferred to the dogma of the dry fly. It was not unnatural that, when Skues came along with his belief that the sub-surface stages of natural upwinged flies could be imitated, he should have applied his mind towards similar exact imitation of the nymph known to be present.

It was not until the time of Sawyer and Kite that anyone dared to suggest that a simple Pheasant Tail Nymph would take trout as consistently as any other pattern when fished sunk. The Pheasant Tail became a successful caricature of the nymphs of several species as well as that of the freshwater shrimp.

Impressionism in flies had come of age.

Eric Horsfall Turner summed up his view of the matter in this way:

> Why will a splodge of scarlet or bright blue on a poster attract the eye of a passer-by, when a less gaudy creation would have attracted no attention? There are certain colours that have extra impact on the human eye; and undoubtedly there are colours which have similar impact on the eye of the fish. Once the human eye has been attracted to look, the mind becomes active. The fish has no mind in our sense of the word; but it shows considerable reaction to the things it sees. We are back to the speculative in angling, based on the tests of experience; and where imitation fails for lack of colour, the imaginative speculation of caricature may arrest attention. If the creation attracts attention, and looks edible and harmless, the reaction of the fish may be to take it.

Yet it is clear that fly-designers of considerable note were often unaware when their intended exact imitation ended up as caricature. Once again it was the still much unappreciated Col E. W. Harding who first noted that:

> Perhaps the most striking examples of the theory of exact imitation are to be found in the Halford and the Dunne series of dry flies. And they proceed on entirely different principles. Mr Halford used quill or gut bodies which reproduced the colours of the natural flies as seen against a dead white background, whereas Mr Dunne uses artificial silk bodies which when oiled show the colours of the flies when the light shines through their translucent bodies. Mr Halford copied the colours of their legs in his hackles and dressed them with the usual double wings of the dry fly. Mr Dunne, on the other hand, copied the general colour of the wings and legs of the natural fly by hackles only. Mr Halford fished his flies with success for a number of seasons, and Mr Dunne has been successful with his patterns. And over a number of years other fly fishers have fished what may be called the 'Standard' patterns of dry fly also with success. And the standard patterns are supposed to be imitations of the natural fly. Yet, in the air, to the human eye none of these patterns resemble one another, while the Dunne patterns are quite unalike any of them. To the fish they must all, when they are on the water, resemble the natural fly. And that is not the same thing as saying that on the water they resemble one another. The Halford and Standard patterns as imitations may be regarded as belonging to the Pre-Raphaelite school. They are elaborate copies of the colours and shapes of the originals and they miss something of the life of the originals.

The Dunne patterns are Pre-Raphaelite in that they copy, and in my opinion copy successfully, the exact colour of the living insect as it appears when looked at against the light. That is how the fish sees the living insect. But, essentially, these patterns belong to the Impressionist school because they try to reproduce the 'impression' which the trout gets of the fly as he sees it in his window. The trout's window is all important in this theory of imitation, and previously in this book I have given reasons for holding that the trout's window is not so important a factor in the economy of trout life, especially when taking the dry fly, as is commonly supposed.

. . . Mr Dunne, as we have seen, concentrated on the colour of his 'impression'. Dr Mottram goes a stage further in his impressionism. He differentiates between three important qualities of a dry fly — its buoyancy, its transparency and its form, as exemplified by its silhouette. And he defines the silhouette as the outline of the non-transparent parts of the fly. He considers that in varying circumstances of light and water one or other of these qualities must be emphasised; if necessary, at the expense of the other two.

In an illuminating assessment of Mottram's impressionist flies, Col Harding says:

Despite a very commonly held belief, impressionism does not imply careless drawing or absence of exact knowledge of colour and form. On the contrary, it needs both to a very high degree, together with a trained power of selecting the essential characteristics of a subject. As opposed to pre-Raphaelitism, which tries to take in every aspect of a subject and thereby loses itself in detail, impressionism selects the essential details and concentrates on them.

Other fishing writers have taken the artistic comparison to the outer limits. To the American author John Atherton, (*The Fly and the Fish*, 1951), who also happened to be an artist of considerable talent, the colouring of a live dun was impressionistic:

It is built up of many tiny variations of tone such as we find in the paintings of Renoir, Monet and others of the impressionistic school of art. The body usually varies in color from back to belly and from thorax to tail. The thorax contains little accents of color — bright pink, yellow and even bluish tones. The eyes in some naturals are brilliant dark blue or violet. Frequently the legs are spotted, and sometimes of strongly differing colors, the front pair being light and the others darker. All May flies have delicate veined wings and some . . . have very dark and distinct wing spots of brown or black. Add to all this the iridescence of the wings as it reflects the light, and it seems quite remarkable that the trout take our poor imitations at all.

As an artist, realizing how the intelligent use of colour can give life to a picture, I feel that anglers are prone to neglect the possibility of using more living color in their flies. If an artist were to thoroughly mix certain colors to obtain a gray and then apply it to a canvas, the gray would be devoid of any lifelike quality. But, if he should apply the same colors directly to the canvas without mixing them beforehand, the result would have a great deal more vibration, light and life. At close range, the effect would be one of a mixture of colors. But at a slight distance they would appear close to the color and value of his original mixed gray, except that it would be alive and not dead.

Flies used for so discriminating a fish as the trout should, above all, have the appearance of life. For Atherton this lifelike effect could never be obtained by using materials which lacked that quality. John Atherton considered that Impressionism in the materials as well as in the form of flies offered great advantages because it was based on the principles and discoveries of the impressionist painters. As they studied the form which reflected or absorbed light and thus took on certain colour qualities of its surroundings, they were dealing in life, not death. Atherton's advice: anglers should do the same. It was that Skues meant when he spoke of flies tied with 'buzz'.

W. H. Lawrie, writing under the pseudonym Arnold Scott in *The Truth about Trout Fishing* (1951), pondered the earliest known English fly patterns as known from the age of Dame Juliana down via Barker, Cotton, Chetham, Ronalds, etc to the present day. He wondered how much the ideal of accurate representation was there behind the crudity:

> Whether in fact the early flies were of rude and crude appearance or whether the illustrators of fishing books of early times obstinately preferred to depict what *they* considered a trout fly ought to look like, it is fairly certain that these flies must have proved their practical worth, for, even allowing for the cheerful plagiarism so fashionable among early angling authors, certain dressings or patterns are consistently lauded by different writers and would seem to have stood the test of time as only successful patterns could do. Now most of these time-tested trout flies were, as has been indicated, 'imitations' of natural river flies at least in so far as general physical form and coloration could be reproduced with the selected materials; but they must also have incorporated the elusive extra something which appeals to trout, and which Halford and Dunne were not completely successful in securing for their representations. What was it?

The flies under consideration were all wet flies, and the one fact that seemed to stand out was that the majority of successful patterns were flies dressed with *dubbed* bodies, that is with bodies composed of natural wools or furs or a mixture of wools or furs thinly spun over a silk thread of a suitable colour. The dubbed body, one was tempted to suppose, suggested that the early fly fishers knew something about translucency and that the inner colour of an insect was a factor not to be overlooked in dressing an 'imitation'. Is the long-favoured red dubbed-silk body the clue? And, if so, what is the explanation of its success? Lawrie wrote:

> The problem is to discover what quality, or qualities, is, or are, inherent in the dubbed body and lacking in the quill bodies of Halford's representations or in the cellulite bodies of Mr Dunne's flies. For it does seem that where Halford and others of the precise representation ideal went astray was in the choice of materials with which they sought to carry out a sound principle. It is peculiar that a man like Halford, with his undoubted knowledge of the entomology of the sport, should have overlooked or ignored the lesson of history concerning proven fly-

dressing materials, especially so when the clue was there to hand in his early favourite the Gold-ribbed Hare's Ear pattern.

There seemed one possible explanation: the superior light-reflecting qualities of dubbed bodies with consequently a more natural 'light-pattern'. It was obvious that the fly fishers of old were painstaking in the matter of selecting both dubbing and feather material for their flies, and they valued quality above all else. Dubbing wools and furs, and hackle and other feathers, were chosen for their sparkle and for their broken patterns. Every fibre caught and reflected light.

Quite apart from the breaking up of light patterns in the trout's vision of an artificial fly, the sharply barred feathers of the teal, much used in successful patterns, vividly suggests the segmented carapaces of shrimps and many shrimp-like creatures, as well as those of many nymphs.

Perhaps, in such a manner, throughout the centuries of fly fishing, salmon and trout have been steadily helping the fly-tyer by refusing to look at their mistakes. It is fortunate for the salmon and trout that fly-tyers, despite all the innovations and successes, continue to make mistakes. Anglers' flies, by and large, aren't necessarily more effective than they used to be. We really should be thankful for it, otherwise there would be no more fish left to catch, no more to delight, beguile and laugh at us, in refusing everything we care to chuck at them.

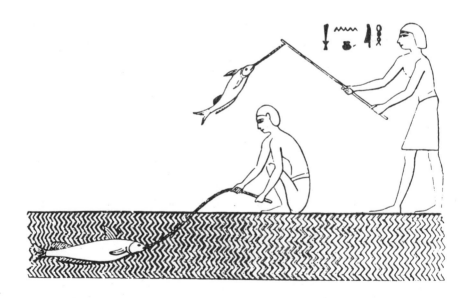

Chapter 19
Competitions and
Competitiveness

With long experience of trout fishing in New Zealand I have been in a unique position to observe a recent phenomenon. The roots of fly fishing for trout in New Zealand are deeply entrenched in British origins and traditions. While it is no longer universally true that fashions, ideas, attitudes currently voguish in Britain travel slowly but inexorably to Antipodean shores, to arrive in New Zealand after a suitable delay of anything from several months to several years, there is no doubt that New Zealand tends to be more influenced by what is happening elsewhere in the world than the rest of the world is influenced by what is happening in New Zealand.

In Britain the sharp division of game and coarse fishing is a by-product of the Industrial Revolution. Before the cataclysmic end to centuries of a rural economy, men went fishing for the species of fish that happened to be locally available. If there was any preference for some species above others, it was probably because on the kitchen table trout taste better than roach; perch have too many bones; tench aren't very good to eat; and that a side of salmon, cold smoked, tastes far better than smoked pike. It should also be noted that in those balmy days before the Industrial Revolution, brown trout and salmon were generally and universally distributed throughout Britain.

One needs but read 15th-century Dame Juliana Berners, 16th-century Samuel and Mascall, 17th-century Walton and Chetham, 18th-century Bowlker and Best, 19th-century Salter and so on, to see that they all fished for pike, perch, dace, roach, tench, eels, barbel, trout and salmon with equal enthusiasm. There were obvious seasonal changes and equally obvious regional differences, but throughout those five hundred or so years the species were spread generally with much the same abundance throughout most regions, excluding perhaps the northern half of Scotland. In those days salmon and trout were as common in the Thames and Trent as any other species and, seasonally, were far more abundant.

While much town fishing was free to the citizens, the outright ownership of rivers, with no free rights of access, and the concept (in England, at least) that the riparian owners also owned the fish — including migratory salmon, sea trout, and resident brown trout — was universal and deeply entrenched in law. While poaching was a universal and ancient art, many of those caught were deported to the colonies for their crimes.

Captain T. Williamson in his *The Complete Angler's Vade Mecum*, published in London in 1808, deemed it necessary to say: 'Once, indeed, I was eased altogether of my cord and lines, but had the satisfaction to learn that the thief, who often gave cautious hints of this trick, was sent to display his dexterity to better purpose at Botany Bay.' And also: 'Laying night-lines, snares, or devices of any kind, for catching fish, without leave from the owner, subjects to heavy fine: if done at night subjects to transportation.'

Poaching existed in the Midlands as it did among the chalkstreams of Hampshire. What was different was that large tracts of Lancashire, Yorkshire, Nottinghamshire, and parts of South Wales rapidly became wastelands and ecological disaster areas as a result of the coal mines, slag heaps, iron foundries, woollen and cotton mills and engineering workshops. Factories in their thousands spewed their filth into the waterways and used the rivers and streams as open sewers. The Revolution created wealth, work and an Empire on which the sun never set, with raw materials from all over the world pouring into Britain in a thousand ships, with another thousand exporting the manufactured products back to a hungry, ever-demanding consumer world.

The enormous wealth and riches these factories heaped upon their owners created a new and wealthy class. The spoliation of their new estates close to the sprawling industrial conurbations was amply compensated for by the new-found riches and power, which provided the wherewithal for the new entrepreneurs to move north, south, east and west to unspoiled parts of the country where they bought or built or married into even bigger and better country estates, where not a drop of effluent polluted the rivers that ran through them.

Moving on to pastures new after despoiling the environment is not exactly new. Not too long ago it was considered to be the natural and obvious thing to do. We are all nomads at heart and our natural tendency, despite all our so-called sophistication, is — metaphorically at least — to defecate on our own doorsteps, then move on.

In England coarse fishing became a cult because of the polluted environment. The salmon and the trout were the first to be driven out or die. Many waters were so polluted that nothing lived on in them, but even in the close environs of many towns and cities the less demanding species of fish only survived in stunted populations in near noxious conditions. It provided the only fishing the mass of working people in such places could afford, or get to.

Because the fishing was so often poor, and the fishing pressure intense, it became the scene of enormous and considerable angling skills and refined techniques. The generally stunted and inedible fish were measured by total catch weight alone. Numbers mattered little; only the total weight was of any consequence. Hence the keep-net. Pollution had made these species of fish inedible anyway, so they were weighed at the end of the day, then returned to the water dead, or alive, or dying. The skills these anglers developed were often quite fantastic. If their catches consisted of tiddlers — and inedible tiddlers at that — it was obvious that some other stimulus and incentive was needed to make the sport worthwhile and satisfy the masses. The lovers of the art would have gone on fishing anyway, but entrepreneurial sorts developed match and competition fishing — where prizes that began as cups and medals, certificates and badges, honour and glory, soon became goods or money or both. The cups and prestige often remained in what otherwise were often bleak and humdrum lives.

It created sponsors, bookmakers, and insatiable appetite for tackle, and even national fame for a few. Contrary to most belief the average trout or salmon angler might only have one fly rod, and spend next to nothing on tackle throughout an entire season, whereas the coarse fisherman constantly aspired to, and even saved and scrimped to add to an ever-growing collection of rods, reels and some of the most fancy tackle ever devised. It fostered, developed and maintained the British fishing tackle industry.

An increasing population and egalitarianism changed all that. The ever-growing demand for water supplies for the towns and cities of England, as well as the parallel demands for electricity, caused a flurry of reservoir building — often huge inland lakes on the outer fringes of industrial belts, but still far enough from the cities to be often situated in some of the most delectable countryside in the land. Furthermore such places were now easily accessible, with increasing affluence, leisure time, and the ubiquitous motor car.

The reservoirs were stocked with brown and rainbow trout — mostly rainbows. Day-ticket charges for the fishing were always acceptably modest. In almost every case they fished phenomenally well for the first few seasons, then mostly dropped off in quality, becoming totally dependent on annual stockings of takeable size fish.

These new fisheries were often large — Grafham, Draycote, Rutland. Others, like Clatworthy, Sutton Bingham, were smaller and more intimate and further afield. Others still, like Damerham, Avington, Leominstead, were smaller still and privately owned and operated, and were not public water supplies. They provided more expensive but better fishing.

The new fly fishers were often converts from coarse fishing, and they soon adapted their coarse fishing skills to those of stillwater fly fishing for trout. Stillwater techniques thus developed with speed, to the delight of the tackle trade, enabling anglers to catch a limit bag of (usually) four fish as quickly as possible. The philosophy of the match coarse fishermen was to catch as many fish as quickly as possible. Going for a happy day out rarely entered into it. With such a background it is hardly surprising they brought with them a highly competitive attitude to fly fishing. As a group they were generally gregarious anglers, used to fishing from ballot-fixed pegs in shoulder to shoulder situations. It didn't take long for organized competitions to start. All the paraphernalia and attractions of the old glamour matches arrived as quickly as the coach and car loads of eager competitors moving to an ever-growing field of 'venues', with prizes, bookmakers, money, and a keepable, edible and saleable catch at the end of it. Such events became a sponsor's delight, and a bonanza for tackle manufacturers and dealers. More fly rods were probably built and sold in England between 1965 and 1975 than in the previous hundred years.

But it was not confined to club level or fishery level. National fly fishing teams appeared everywhere. In the early days it was mostly confined to boat fishing; Scottish loch-style soon to be superseded by the more productive Midland reservoir style. The funny thing was that no one had ever even heard of the people who comprised these national teams, yet they were often billed as such and individuals were proclaimed the fly fishing champion of the world.

In New Zealand, meanwhile, most fly fishermen still owned one generally ancient cane or glass rod and fished in exactly the same waters and in exactly the same way as their fathers had taught them a generation earlier. And so it seemed it would go on that way for ever and ever.

It was mostly a small band of expert coarse fishermen from England who emigrated to New Zealand, who pioneered nymph fishing in that country despite all the many claims to the contrary. It was this expert coterie who in the mid-1970s defiantly faced upstream in the mighty and revered Tongariro River and fished the nymph up fast runs never previously known to hold the fresh-run spawning rainbows, while the old-school downstreamers fished traditional Taupo lures across and down stream through the noted pools, ignoring and never fishing the turbulent, rocky, shallower runs. What is more they caught limit after limit of better rainbows. By the mid-1980s it had become a national craze, but that is another story.

I happened to know most of these innovators who pioneered the Taupo nymph fishing revolution and turned New Zealand trout fishing on its head. While I never heard even one of them hanker for competition fly fishing to be established in New Zealand, or take part in any that already existed, a few had become notable specimen hunters. But they were competing with themselves — not against other anglers — always aiming to catch a bigger trout than their previous 18-pounder.

Strangely, trout fishing competitions in New Zealand are more popular among anglers born in that country, many of whom like the prizes, the brief glory, the perceived glamour and the razzmatazz of the burgeoning list of much-publicized competitions that have spread in recent years from Taupo to Pahiatua and from Waitaki to Turangi. There seems little doubt that the idea will catch on and be encouraged and promoted by some enthusiastic government agencies, while looked at askance, or indeed with grave misgivings, by other agencies of the same government. If anything, trout fishing competitions seem to have an increasing and unfortunately divisive effect on the sport.

It is noticeable that the publicists of these events suggest they are aimed at overseas angler-tourists and, as such, are good for the country's economy. I, for one, have no personal interest whatsoever in competition fly fishing (and even, frankly, distaste for these jamborees), nor have I ever met a single overseas angler who came to New Zealand in order to enter a fishing competition. Most visiting fly fishermen to New Zealand are American or Australian, and both seem generally certain to deplore any suggestion that there is a need for such competitions or that they do any real good.

So far, these fishing competitions are not officially organized international team events — more of which later — but events sponsored, organized and run by tackle manufacturers or, in some cases, by local communities. But it cannot be said with any truth, as is often claimed, that these are fun events intended to foster the pleasures of going trout fishing. There is too much money involved for the competitions to be nothing but fun. To my way of thinking, and to that of really dedicated fly fishermen, they not only encourage even more of the mindless, senseless slaughter of trout than already exists, but go right against the whole principle and good practice of fly fishing. If *winning* is so important people should stick to golf or bowls where the prime objective of the game is to beat the other fellow, and to sort out winners from losers. If competitive fly fishing becomes the reason why we fish, we shall all be the losers.

The heart and soul of any discussion on trout fishing competitions is really concerned with fly fishing, as opposed to all other methods. The New

Zealand competition scene, intended to attract all anglers, usually covers all the permissible techniques in different classes. Thus, the annual Lake Taupo competition, probably the longest established, consists of separate divisions of fly fishing the various streams running into the lake, trolling within recognized limits on the main body of the lake itself, best individual brown trout, best individual rainbow, best total bag weight, best conditioned fish, best ladies' competition, best entered four-man team aggregate, and so on. This offers a wide variety of prizes, and sees the majority of competitors trolling from a boat on the lake. It is billed as being the Kilwell International Trout Fishing Tournament and continues over several days.

The nature of this event is best summed up, I think, by a conversation I overheard at a Taupo supermarket checkout on the first morning of a recent tournament. As previously said I do not care for fishing competitions and believe they do nothing good for the sport. But although I believe that trout fishing should not be a competition between people, and is debased by becoming so, there is ample evidence that hundreds of people think otherwise. They are obviously excited and stimulated by the prospect of a valuable prize and trophy, as well as a moment of glory. It probably does many of those who enter it much good. Anyway, there at the supermarket checkout ahead of me a man decked out in what generally passes for a fisherman's finery was engaging two American tourists in jolly talk, telling them he had towed his boat up from Hawke's Bay for what he told them was the world trout fishing championships. The polite Americans — obviously not trout fishermen themselves — were suitably impressed, and told him he must be very proud to be in such a prestigious event, unaware that it was open to anyone who paid the small entrance fee. The entrant beamed. My own reaction, I confess, was slightly tinged by something close to an amused cringing of the spirit, even superciliousness. But this very personal reaction, I now suggest, however deeply felt, was wrong. That particular fisherman, shopping for the essentials to accompany him out on the lake in his little boat, was going to have himself a ball: not only was he going to catch some trout, but he had as much chance as anyone of catching the biggest and best, and becoming (in his own view, at least) the champion trout fisherman of all the world.

This matter of superiority and lowliness in fishing methods is far from one-sided, as is sometimes supposed, with the fly fisherman considering himself and his kind to be on the top of the heap, and the aspiring world champion in the supermarket to be somewhere near the bottom. The chances are that the man in the supermarket would believe, perhaps with great bigotry, that fly fishing is 'old-fashioned' and an inefficient method of fishing for trout, and that his lead line, Alvey reel, and selection of Cobra lures make him a modern, state-of-the-art practitioner. Bernard Venables once pointed out how deviously fishermen ride their dogmas, how sectarian they are prone to be. But this, all said and done, is simply because *all* human beings are incurably contentious; never ceasing to take irrational stands upon precarious points of principle; loving fierce debates on completely unimportant postulates; and finding in fishing an arena with which theology and politics can hardly contend. Fishermen, then, are prone to take precious attitudes on the propriety of one method over another. But they do believe this, to their own detriment. There is no need to form a vast club incorporating all fishermen, but there is a real need for greater tolerance among them. Despite my earlier description of the development of fly fishing competitions in England, it would be incorrect to think that competitive trout fishing actually began in England in the 1960s in a carry-over from Midlands river and canal banks to the newer stillwater trout fisheries. Over a hundred years ago competition fishing had been a long-established feature of much fly fishing for trout in Scotland, where inter-club matches on many lochs had evolved even their own style of fishing. Indeed, this Scottish influence, so prevalent in the early years of settlement in New Zealand, culminating in the first successful acclimatization of brown trout in 1867, resulted in a competition being organized for the very first day of the very first trout fishing season in that country. The story of that first event is worth repeating here.

It was best recorded by R. Chisholm in the first of *Two Papers on the Introduction and Propagation of Trout into New Zealand*, published in Dunedin in 1897:

> At a meeting of the council of the [Acclimatisation] society, held in the *Otago Daily Times and Witness* Company's office on the 8th October (1874), it was resolved: 'That the Provincial Government be requested to declare the ensuing months of December, January, and February an open season for river trout fishing, and that a fee of £1 be charged to anyone desirous of taking out a fishing license.' A proclamation was accordingly made by his Honor James Macandrew, Superintendent of the Province of Otago, declaring the streams in which trout had been liberated in 1869 and 1870 open for fishing with rod and line. This was the longed-for signal to the disciples of Izaak Walton to awake and buckle on their harness — the dawning of the day when angling was no more a delightful day dream but a reality. Rods, reels, and lines that had long been laid aside and looked upon as relics of the past were now called into requisition. The pulse of anglers beat fast and strong. The last night in November seemed as if it never would pass, and long before a streak of morning light broke across the distant horizon, the enthusiastic angler, fully equipped, could be seen wending his way to the favorite stream. The Water of Leith, from its proximity to Dunedin, was the chief scene of operations. On its bank at early dawn a dark figure is dimly seen, curiosity at whose strange movements, sometimes stooping, sometimes standing erect, bids us draw near; and, as the morning breaks, our joyous surprise finds fit expression in the exclamation of Christopher North: 'By heavens he is fishing with fly! and the Fates, grim and grisly as they are painted to be by full-grown, ungrateful, lying poets, smile like angels upon the paddler in the stream, winnowing the air with their wings into western breezes, while at a careful cast the silvery trout forsakes his fastness beneath the big flat stone, and with a rug and tug, and then a sudden plunge, and then a race like lightning, changes the man into an angler, and shoots through his thrilling and aching heart the ecstasy of a new life expanding in that glorious pastime, even as a rainbow on a sudden brightens up the sky. After careful play he lands a twelve incher on the smooth stones of the only place in the stream where such an exploit was possible, and darting upon him, like an osprey, soars up with him in his tallons to the bank, breaking his line as he hurries off to a place of safety a respectable distance from the stream, and flinging him down on the green grass lets him bounce about till he is tired and lies gasping with unfrequent and feeble motions, bright and beautiful and glorious with all his yellow light and silvery lustre, spotted, speckled, and starred in his scaly splendor before the rising sun that never shone before so dazzlingly.' Such, I doubt not, in some respects at least, was the

experience of our respected townsman and brother angler, Mr A. C. Begg, when between 3 and 4 o'clock in the early summer morning of the first day of December, 1874, he had the distinguished honor and satisfaction of landing from the Water of Leith the first trout caught with rod and line in New Zealand waters. With this difference, however, that I am confident my master and instructor in the gentle art, to whom I owe any success that has attended my feeble efforts for many years, would not, in the happy excitement of the moment, 'break his line'.

The weight of this first caught brown trout was not recorded. In 1881, a Mr Deans landed two trout, each weighing 18lb, from the Fulton Creek on the Taieri, near Dunedin. Records show that this creek was first stocked with young trout in 1870.

Within a few years New Zealand was to become the eldorado of trout fishing. It seems that anglers were far too busy catching large bags of huge trout, returning fish under 10lb, for anyone to think about competition fishing. That first instinct of their Scottish heritage came to be all but forgotten for about eighty years, other than in a very few club matches. Although most anglers undoubtedly fished for sport, the records show that they fished a numbers game. They also went on fishing far beyond their possible maximum food needs.

Quinnat salmon fishing competitions are now an established annual event in some South Island rivers and most certainly cause the slaughter of far fewer salmon than would a local offshore commercial fishing boat or Japanese, Russian, Taiwanese or Korean drift netsmen, probably fishing illegally off the New Zealand coasts.

Both trout and salmon fishing competitions are likely to continue in New Zealand. Inherent in them is the very real danger of human greed. The bigger and better the prizes become, the more likely it is that unscrupulous fishermen will cheat, and this without doubt occurs. Quite apart from fostering wrong ideas about the nature of trout fishing, about why people go fishing in the first place, such competitions will also cover up any deterioration in the quality of the fishing by providing other incentives. Whatever else one might think, one point is clear: competition itself, the drive to compete with other men in a contest of sorts, whether luck alone decides the winner, is a powerful driving force, whether the quality of the fishing itself is good or indifferent or downright poor.

These observations on New Zealand fishing competitions, far from being irrelevant to the contemporary British scene, are worthy of consideration because of recent developments by those who sponsor and foster such events. By this I mean the new so-called 'international' appeal of these events. To me it seems ludicrous that from a very small group of people an event can be staged in some host country or other, after which awards can be made to the World Champion Fly Fisherman on an individual basis, and the World Champions on a team basis. Yet it happens, and it seems likely that the winning contestants somehow really believe they have proved themselves to be just that.

Despite the claim that it is all jolly good fun, I suspect these competitions are entered into in deadly earnest, with no holds barred. It matters little just how these World championships are organized or from whom the teams are chosen. Changes have been made so that the competing teams fish variously on some chosen small stillwater fishery (if one exists in the host country), and even on some hallowed chalkstream (with similar provisos), in addition to the original loch-style drift fly fishing from boats on suitable lakes, lochs or large stillwater fisheries. Doubtless the aficionados among this evolving breed of anglers are a dedicated band of men, amongst whom are many first class fly fishermen. What I suspect about them, however, is their interpretation of what fly fishing for trout is really about, of their potential influence on the sport and on other less well-informed anglers, and of the media-generated image they portray both to non-fishers and to other fishermen. The pages of some sporting journals give unstinting publicity and praise to these events. Fishing, in my belief, and fly fishing for trout in particular, is not about winning or losing, is not a contest between men and fish or men and men, and should not be made to seem so, or it demeans it.

Most thinking, dedicated fly fishermen are convinced that one of the great qualities of the sport is that it is non-competitive. There is enough competition in other aspects of life without including it in one of life's great and magic escapes. The least aspect of competitiveness destroys its most charming qualities, giving it an atmosphere of sly haste, pervading it with petty jealousies, envy and resentment. These sad things are so prevalent in this world that most men go fishing in order to get away from them for a while.

Yes, competitions provide much entertainment and jollity for most of the entrants. Yet anyone who seeks to enter into competition with other men is seeking to win. People who seek to win rarely enjoy losing, and there should be no losing in going fishing.

That is my view. But let us look at what others have said about. It is a claim frequently made by modern protagonists and publicists of competitive trout fishing that their activities have always been central to the main thrust of angling, in England as well as in Scotland, maintaining that trout fishing competitions have a long and honourable history among men of the most altruistic persuasions. It is also claimed that virtually all anglers brought up on coarse fishing — that is people who fished for species other than salmon or trout — not only approve but are best motivated and happiest when fishing competitively. That both these claims are basically untrue and can be seen from the following quotations from well-known-in-their-day and much respected angling writers.

The Reverend J. J. Manley, in *Fish and Fishing* published in 1877, wrote:

> The still progressing popularity of fishing, to which I have already alluded, may be gathered from the wonderful increase in late years of Angling Societies in the metropolis alone . . . there are at the present time about eighty Angling Clubs or Societies in the metropolitan districts, fifty-three of which are associated together under the name of the 'United London Anglers'.
>
> . . . The Metropolitan Angling Clubs are a great feature in the annals of modern fishing. But a few years ago they might have been counted on the fingers of the two hands, but now, as I have said, they have increased and multiplied wonderfully. They hold their meetings, weekly or bi-weekly, in the season, at some congenial hostelry, the landlord of which is generally one of the fraternity. These name are 'fanciful' significative of their craft or indicative of the good fellowship which reigns supreme among anglers. Thus we have the 'Friendly Anglers', the 'Amicable Waltonians', the 'Brothers-well-met', the 'Golden Barbel', the 'Sir Hugh Myddleton', the 'Convivial', the 'Nil Desperandum', the 'Isaak Walton', the 'Silver Trout', the 'Walton and Cotton', the 'Hoxton Brothers', and

the 'Brothers' and 'Anglers' innumerable with an agnomen signifying their particular district. Their club-rooms are decorated with preserved fish, many splendid cases of which they exhibited at the Piscatorial Exhibition at the Westminster Aquarium in 1877, and various piscatorial trophies. At their meetings they 'show' and 'weigh in' their captures, and prizes are given for the 'takes'. It would be more easy almost to enumerate what these prizes are not than what they are, as they range from a set of dining-tables down to a silver thimble, and like Achilles, the least fortunate member values his prize, though it be 'but a little one'. Watches, teapots, lustres, purses, cigar-cases, *et hoc genus omne*, not forgetting fishing-boots, waterproof-coats, and fishing-tackle, serve as testimonials to skill and luck; while coals are also at Christmas time among the rewards of merit, and even a lively young porker and a half-grown donkey have figured among the honoraria.

The establishment of these clubs in London, and in the provinces, where they flourish equally well, has given rise of late years to Angling contests, by which, of course, the 'enterprising landlord' or the --- Arms, who generally gets them up and provides the prizes, contrives to lose nothing by his enterprise. The intense interest these contests excite, and the number of competitors who join in them, must be astonishing to those who are not acquainted with this modern feature of Angling. Not very long ago in the 'North Midlands', a liberal host offered six prizes ranging from 24L to 4L to be fished for, and his friends provided 170 'additional' ones. The competitors, who had to pay 3s.6d entrance each, numbered no less than 500, and they were stationed at twelve yards apart, the line thus occupying a distance along the waterside of three miles and a half. The day being a suitable one for fishing, the aggregate of fish taken was very large, the winner of the first prize scoring 19lb 1½oz. 'The arrangement was most complete', says the historian, 'and everything passed off most satisfactorily' — a fact to be noted, as showing consummate generalship on the part of the managers, and an exceeding amount of good fellowship and 'charity' on the part of the contestant anglers. Still more recently on the Lea, 276 anglers entered for a great roach match, and the day being unfavourable, the winner got the first prize of 40L with 13½oz of fish, which on that particular day were thus worth almost their weight in gold. Matches also between two anglers are now of common occurrence, and these often for very large sums. I remember not long ago seeing a challenge from one first-rate hand to another, to a contest of skill for 100L a side. Whether these contests conduce to the good of 'the craft' is another question; they certainly show the keenness with which angling is now pursued. That betting should take place on these occasions is only what might be expected, as Englishmen will bet on everything 'bettable', such as the settling of flies on lumps of sugar, commonly known as 'Fly Loo'; the trickling of heavy raindrops down a window pane, and the racing power of gentles on a mahogany table.

Almost exactly a hundred years later another literate and passionate angler, Maurice Wiggin, wrote in his acclaimed paean of praise for fishing as a sport, well titled *The Passionate Angler*:

Of course, folk fish for different reasons. There are enough aspects of angling to satisfy the aspirations of people remarkably unalike.

Angling has its pot-hunters, for instance: an affliction it stoically shares with most other pastimes. These are the lamentable folk who see life as a kind of rodeo; the boys who went flat-out for prizes at school and have never grown out of it (as indeed one does not). I find them the least agreeable of all the agreeable folk one meets on the river bank. Desperately keen, ridiculously strung-up; usually highly skilled; offensive in triumph and miserable in failure. I must say I find it slightly ludicrous to make such a fuss about a fish. The vulgar and grubby business of prizes and presentations and glass cases is, in my humble and suspect view as a bungler of excessive mediocrity, the wrong approach to angling. Altogether. There is no keener angler breathing than me, but I do not give tuppence whether I catch a big fish or a small. I understand that there are societies which actually present inscribed cups to their most successful members. This seems to me to be in the exact opposite of the right spirit. But it takes all sorts, as the pike once said to the dace, thoughtfully masticating.

It is worth noting here that Maurice Wiggin was not, as may detractors would suggest, born in a game fishing society which spurned and looked down upon the coarsely labelled coarse fishing. Far from it. Though coming from a family of relative affluence, he was born, bred and brought up in the Black Country and served a most plebian apprenticeship in fishing (of which he was exceedingly proud) with the lads of small towns in south Staffordshire in the 'cuts' and streams and ponds near his home. It was there he cut his angling teeth and learned, both what to do as well as what not to do, from older men whom he has now made famous, although changed in name, in marvellous fishing tales told variously in several of his books.

We have noted the often-made claim by the fishing competition publicists that all anglers who started with coarse fishing are enamoured with, and motivated by, competitive fishing only, whether coarse or trout. Maurice Wiggin again:

There is another form of restraint which I do not care for, and that is the keep-net. The keep-net has come into almost universal use, and is compulsory in most fishing competitions. It is considered humane. The argument runs that if all the thousands of competitors killed the miserable fish they generally catch, there would soon be no fishing left. True. So they slip them into a keep-net until they have been weighed, at the end of the day, and then turn them back into the water. It sounds plausible. But have you ever seen a keep-net full of fish? It's a miserable sight. Fish are easily frightened, as every angler knows, and fish in keep-nets are terrified fish. There is no excuse for keeping wild things in cages, even for a few hours. So what is the answer to the competitive angler? Why, it is simple. Have done with competitions! There is something ludicrous in the spectacle of grown men 'weighing-in' a few miserable little fish, for a miserable prize. I say that fishing is one sport which loses its flavour — almost all its flavour — when it is followed communally. I have nothing to say against angling clubs and societies: they are excellent institutions: men get together and are thereby enabled to rent good stretches of water which would be beyond their reach as individuals. Socially, the club is a good thing. But competitions . . . as soon make love all together, in parties. Still, some folk like to do just that.

Many of the present-day organizers of British and International fly fishing championships for trout would deride such anglers and writers as Maurice Wiggin, calling him — as indeed they would describe me — as (in their own words) an 'only here for the scenery' fisherman, a fake and a fogey. But really he is just someone who does not fish for money, or for freebie trips around the angling world, or for self-aggrandizement or supposed fame and national as well as international honour, or for free fishing in specially stocked waters, or for overlarge and rather vulgar plated silver cups inscribed that so-and-so was in such-and-such a year in such-and-such a place declared to be the Fly Fishing Champion of the World.

Wiggin was of a different mould. He admired excellence in all things and proved himself to have excellence in several fields. Although an avid and addicted collector of fine tackle, he never lost his awareness that such finely crafted tools were simply more pleasurable to use, that they added to his delight in fishing rather than enabled him to catch more and better fish. Yet he had an acerbic eye for those practitioners of the angling art who had, in his view, become mere technicians:

> Then there is the technician. He is the man who would make a business of it, whatever sport he adopted. He is the fellow who can always show you how, and will. If he is a fly fisher, he ties his own flies and is a scholar on shades of hackle. He casts according to the book, and indeed he is a delight to watch. But all else is subordinated to the mere physical act of fishing superbly. Such a man, oblivious of his surroundings, would fish a concrete reservoir if it contained fish. I can best express the attitude of Pezare and me by saying that we would not fish a concrete reservoir if it were so full of fish that you could walk across it on their backs. This sort of expert is often a very decent, cheerful fellow, modest in his demands and the opposite of a pot-hunter. Yet he takes the mechanics of the game too seriously for me. He is really expressing himself through his rod. I cannot bring myself to believe that so simple and unimportant an instrument should be the medium of such devotion. It makes fishing a game like golf.
>
> I am more in sympathy with the naturalist: the man who makes fishing the occasion — I almost said the excuse — for indulging his absorption with wild life. It is true that for most anglers, a good proportion of the charm of angling lies in the fact that it brings one into close contact with the many-voiced life of the waterside: with small, shy creatures not normally met in towns, with trees and flowers and a wonderful world of birds. But it is a certainty that one sees far more of the wild life of the waterside if one leaves one's rod behind.
>
> As I see it, the charm of angling is a subtle compound of a number of separate pleasures. There is the whole delight of being by or on water. There is the natural life around one . . . darting flight of kingfisher, immemorial dignity of heron . . . cosiness of vole, placidity of dabchicks, sheer lovely humdrumness of ducks . . . the talking grasses of the water's edge, and the harmonies of water-loving trees. There is the assuaging pleasure of handling delicate and responsive tackle. And there is the recurring thrill, rooted perhaps too deep in primal instincts to be analysed, of making physical contact with the unseeen, darting, slippery creatures that inhabit another world than ours. Catching fish.

Compare that vision of the quality and true meaning of the event of going fishing with Tony Pawson's statement in his book *Competitive Fly-Fishing*:

> Two Lakes near Romsey is one of the most successful fisheries in
> Hampshire because it caters for the solitary and anti-social instincts of
> most fly-fishermen in pursuit of their prey. That at least is what its
> designer claims was the purpose of turning a round lake into one crinkled
> with little bays and inlets, where each individual can concentrate on
> catching trout undisturbed by other intrusive humans. The Garboesque
> desire to be alone is a part of many fishermen's nature. It is this which
> sends them on happy expeditions to distant hill lochs in pursuit of small,
> dour brownies.
>
> Relaxation from the pressures of the modern world is a main part of
> the sport's charm as they fish on with only the wind and the wild scenery
> for companions. So it is understandable that for many the idea of
> competitive fly-fishing is anathema, a denial of its essential attraction.
> But, however masked, the competitive urge is latent in all of us. One
> magnetic aspect of catching trout or salmon is its trial of skill between fish
> and fishermen, the primaeval hunter's contest. Even the solitary
> fisherman is only too keen to display his large catch as the plethora of
> fishing registers testify, and as those hotels know well that arrange for the
> catches to be publicly displayed each evening. It is evident, too, in the
> tone of the disgruntled salmon fisherman, with a blank behind him, who
> dismisses another's two twenty-pounders with a contemptuous 'Oh,
> caught on a *spinner*', as if he, of course, could have been just as successful
> had he only sunk to using *that* legal lure.

The same writer and avid competition fly fisherman, in his Foreword to
Chris Ogborne's even more recent *Competition Trout Fishing*, writes

> One of the values of competition fishing is that it soon shows whether a
> reputation is deserved or spurious. So many of those 'pundits' who
> pontificate to us about the right way to fish (which usually amounts only
> to an account of their personal preferences and prejudices) are mere
> spinners of phrases and pickers of brains. All the more credit then to
> those like Chris, or Bob Church, or Jeremy Lucas, who are prepared to
> come down from the safe heights of 'authoritative' writing and keep
> proving their genuine ability in competition with the rest of us. There is,
> of course, much more to fishing than catching fish, as the 'only here for
> the scenery' writers continually remind us. But the skills of fishing are
> about trying to outwit and catch the fish: these *skills* are only truly proven
> in competitions.

So much, then, for the 'only here for the scenery' writers who, despite what
is said, almost never claim that theirs is an authoritative overview of fishing or
boast about their skills and the even greater skills of their like-thinking
colleagues. In any case, when has any complete and adequate fly fisherman
ever needed to *prove* anything, whether to the trout themselves that he has
'beaten' them in contest, or to other fishermen that he has, by superior skills,
triumphed in their defeat?

Yet the fact is that some self-proclaimed world championships (and bear in
mind that no one other than the commercial sponsors, the organizers, and the
contestants themselves, declare these events in such grandiose terms) are won
on sometimes paltry catches of equally paltry fish. It is noteworthy, too, that

while such enthusiasts talk so much about proven skills, whenever they coyly mention that element of luck they simultaneously crease with Fourth Form laughter recalling what a jolly good time they all had and saying what good fellowship lies in their jamboree events.

Even the more usually restrained publications are now coming out singing the praises of competitive fly fishing. The 1988-1989 issue of *Where to Fish*, a sound and authoritative but never previously radical sort of publication, had this to say in its editorial:

> This customary review of the angling scene was faced in our 1986/87 edtion with a picture of Tony Pawson displaying the handsome trophy he had won in the 1984 World Flyfishing Championship. This time we show Brian Leadbetter who won the 1987 event, fished this time in England — for the first time — on two reservoirs, Rutland and Grafham, on a small stillwater fishery, Avington, and on the River Test, the hallowed chalk stream which is the nursery of our fly fishing philosophy, and in large measure the whole world's, too.
>
> Not only did an Englishman win the individual trophy in 1987; England won the team event too, with Australia, New Zealand and Wales following in 2nd, 3rd and 4th places. Nor was the margin of victory a narrow one. These events are won on a points system: those scored by the teams just named, in aggregate, amounted to 45% of the total scored by all twenty contending teams.
>
> This triumph chimes nicely with the mood of a year which saw our whole sport climbing towards the crest of a wave; its adversaries in retreat and self-confidence renewed by an expensive programme of motivational research carried out by the fishing tackle trade with results which proclaimed in a most positive way that we anglers are thought of as highly as ever by our fellow-countrymen and women, even if not all of them wish to join us rod in hand at the waterside on the strength of that regard.

Conrad Voss Bark in his *A Fly on the Water* states a different point of view:

> The question raised by a number of fishermen, essentially an ethical one, is whether it is a good thing or a bad thing to have a competition in killing. A typical letter, referring to some teams fishing at Wimbleball reservoir in Somerset, condemned what the writer called 'the wholesale slaughter of yearling rainbows' and continued:
>
> 'I understand that some competitors achieved catches of more than 40 fish, no mean feat, but certainly far from sporting. What on earth would we think if competitions in shooting were to substitute wild pigeons for clays?'
>
> The competitors could no doubt have argued, if they had wished, that as the trout were bred specially for the purpose of being killed it was less of an offence to kill 40 farm rainbows than 40 wild salmon or sea trout. Maybe, but it avoids the main question: whether fly fishermen should become competitive, with considerable prizes for those who kill the most. In this we lapse behind the standards of our ancestors. Dame Juliana Berners:
>
> 'You must not use this arteful sport for covetousness, merely for the increasing or saving of your money.'
>
> Whether there is always scrupulous observance of that advice in the *Treatysse* is doubtful but nevertheless one would have suspected a fairly

general reluctance to win a holiday on the Costa Brava over a pile of dead fish, whether they were born free or born to be killed. An American fisherman put it rather well:

'The statement that a man has killed fifty or one hundred trout makes not the slightest impression on the mind, except possibly a slight feeling of disgust.'

Nothing is conclusive, especially in matters to do with fly fishing, but there seems little doubt that competitions and a growing competitiveness among anglers are here to stay. To this fisherman at least it seems fortunate that not all anglers, probably no more than a very small percentage of the more gregarious, ebullient, ambitious, narcissistic, demonstrative, team-driven, fame-driven types will wholly succumb to its charms. If there aren't any other delights in fishing than the brief moment of glory for the champion, the silver-plate cup on the mantleshelf, the prize, the badges and medallions more outrageous than those of any Latin-American general, the brief acclamation from one's peers, the envy of the losers, and the other attendant if short-lived pleasures, then we all might as well give up trout fishing and find something else to occupy our hearts and minds and leisure.

Lest any reader think that I am being unreasonable or unfair, or that my views are not shared by many others, coarse and trout fishermen alike, let me introduce a witty article by angling correspondent Keith Elliott which appeared in the *Independent* on 25 November 1989.

Under the headline of 'Pegging out in match of the day', the article in question, while specifically relating to coarse fishing competitions, is really about the very nature of competitiveness and competitions in *any* form of fishing. Some may think the words are harsh. Rather that quote just some of it, and be guilty of isolating specific sentences out of context, I quote the text in its entirety:

One of the strangest sights on riverbank or canal is the seemingly endless line of equidistantly-spaced anglers crouching under green umbrellas.

These enthusiasts are called competition or match fishermen, because their catches will generally fit neatly into a box of Swan Vestas. There is a rather cruel joke which runs 'Who has an IQ of 2000?'

'Two-hundred match fishermen.'

This is very unfair, because it would normally not take more than 150. And here is how they get their pleasure.

Competitions are usually on a stretch of water containing very few fish. This hastens the weighing of catches at the end of the day.

The venue appears to make little difference to attendances. The main considerations are that it should be near a Little Chef for an early breakfast, and that cars can be parked close to the water.

This is vital, because competition fishermen lug around more tackle than six normal anglers. It is not unusual for a match man to be still setting up his rods when the whistle blows for the end of the contest.

There are two sorts of competitive angler. One fishes for the glory and a very cheap plastic trophy topped by a gold-painted blob with fins; the other type fishes for glory and money. A successful match man can win more than £10,000 a year, an income which has attracted the prying fingers of the Inland Revenue.

Sometimes, this cash comes from sponsors, who know that such fishermen will wear T-shirts or stick labels on their windscreens bearing the backer's name as long as the colours are bright. Otherwise, the anglers all fork out a tenner and the top four in the event split the money.

But getting to a water before the others will do you no good. Every competitor must draw a number from a hat. This corresponds to a 10-yard numbered space on the bank. On popular stretches, there will be 'pegs'. On others, the cows will have eaten the numbers by the time the anglers arrive.

This patch is yours for five hours. No one else can encroach, but you can't wander off for a more productive spot either.

A whistle indicates the start of the competition. This is also a signal to the fish to bury themselves in the mud for five hours.

To make it harder, each competitor is only allowed to use one rod at a time from the array he has dragged along the bank. You are not allowed to bring fish with you, or to feed up your catches so that they are twice as large at the end of the competition.

With fish at a premium, competitors use all sorts of bait in a bid to trap the unwary. This will mean worms, bread, cheese, sweetcorn, luncheon meat and three different sorts of maggots — big, medium and little — in colours ranging from red to green. White, the maggots' natural colour, is only used by rank beginners.

If anything is caught, it is put in a container in the water called a keepnet. It is so-called because the fish will be freed afterwards. Competitions run in the middle of the day, whereas most fish feed best in the early morning or evening. This means that most catches are of tiddlers, which don't know any better. The mesh on a keepnet is finer than a kitchen sieve and will retain most species of plankton.

At the end of the event, a scales man comes to each peg and solemnly records the weight. The fish are then returned for the following week's competition to catch. Little store is held by the biggest fish or the one with the prettiest fins. All the prizes go to anglers who have the highest total weights.

Afterwards, the competitors invent stories telling why they caught nothing. This is a very important part of the day, because it enables each man later to record a different tale of woe to the one his wife heard the previous week.

The results are read out and there is sparse clapping, generally from the chap who is sharing a car with the winner and who knows he won't get stung this week for his share of the petrol. Everyone else believes that the winner has been pegged in an aquarium.

Then they go home and do the same thing all over again the following week.

The humour of this piece, far from merely poking fun at the eager participants in that forlorn and awful competition, does not disguise the writer's serious distaste for the scene. True, he is writing about a certain type of coarse fishing competition, but to my mind the attitudes, the razzmatazz, as well as the unfunniness of the occasion, are but a mite distant from fly fishing competitions for trout. And therein lies the rub.

Chapter 20
In Praise of Fishing

Anyone but an addicted angler might think that everything remotely possible on this subject had been said in the chapter bravely headed 'Why Men Fish'; but every real angler will at once know that the attempt to answer what at first seems to be a simple question requiring simple answers, has little to do with this present essay 'In Praise of Fishing'. To the best of my knowledge only one book has that title.* It is a slight and simple little book: little in that it fits into the palm of one's hand; simple in that it consists of a mere sixty-four pages. *In Praise of Fishing*, subtitled *An Anthology for Addicts*, was compiled by Colin Willock and published by Frederick Muller in London in 1954. The only copy I've ever seen is in my own collection, although it must be anything but rare because it is one of a series of little books that included such diverse titles as *In Praise of Westminster Abbey, In Praise of Ireland, In Praise of England, In Praise of Scotland, In Praise of Wales, In Praise of Sussex, Yorkshire, Country Life, Kent, Mountains, The British, Good Living, Freedom, Humour, Music, Christmas, The Ballet, Love, Friendship, Churchill, Bernard Shaw, Children, Dogs, Cats, Golf, Cricket, The Theatre, Travel, Trees, Lakes, Horses, The Sea, Birds* and *Flowers*. The list of titles is not meant to advertise a long out-of-print series, but rather to show anglers that the inclusion of *In Praise of Fishing* in no way singles out their personal addiction, but lumps it in with as diverse a selection of book titles as can ever have been included in a single series.

But the truth, of course, as every angler knows, is that every book about fishing ever published is materially a book singing its praise, however poorly or well the author sings the song. The songs of angling praise are few in number, but they come in countless thousands with different words to the same beguiling tunes.

By Walton's time the songs of praise were sung to lutes, the lyrics, romantic, light and frothy:

---

* Since the time of writing, *In Praise of Fishing*, by David Profumo, has been published by Viking Press, London, November 1989.

Doubt not but that Angling is an Art; is it not an Art to deceive a Trout with an artificial Flie? a Trout! that is more sharp sighted than any Hawk you have nam'd, and more watchful and timorous than your high mettled Marlin is bold? and yet, I doubt not to catch a brace or two to morrow, for a friends breakfast: doubt not therefore, Sir, but that Angling is an Art, and an art worth your learning: the Question is rather, whether you may be capable of learning it? for Angling is somewhat like Poetry, men are to be born so: I mean with inclinations to it, though both may be heightened by discourse and practice, but he that hopes to be a good Angler must not only bring an inquiring, searching, observing wit; but he must bring a large measure of hope and patience, and a love and propensity to the Art it self; but having once got and practis'd it, then doubt not but Angling will prove to be so pleasant, that it will prove to be like Vertue, a reward to it self.

Not all angling tunes are best played on the lute or fiddle, or suitable to dance to. By the twentieth century, some were fugues, and the cello and double bass the chief instruments. Take Morley Roberts, whose less sanguine view is resonant with deeper tones:

A fisherman is not properly a social animal. There is no other kind of man who welcomes rain on a holiday. There is no other kind of man who luxuriates in the fact that the whole of the moorland is a bog which holds water for weeks at a time. There is no other human being who can be perfectly happy five miles from home when he is wet through, tired out, hungry and carrying a bag, or creel, which weighs ten pounds. He is the only creature existing whose joy is an increasing burden, a heavier handicap.

Other music is positively rhapsodic in its fulsome praise of fishing; none moreso than that of William Scrope:

Let me wander beside the banks of the tranquil stream of the warm South! in yellow meads of asphodel! when the young spring comes forth, and all nature is glad; or if a wilder mood comes over me, let me clamber among the steeps of the North, beneath the shaggy mountains, where the river comes raging and foaming everlastingly, wedging its way through the secret glen, whilst the eagle, but dimly seen, cleaves the winds and the clouds and the dun deer gaze through the mosses above. There, amongst gigantic rocks and the din of mountain torrents, let me do battle with the lusty salmon, till I drag him into day, rejoicing in his bulk, voluminous and vast.

For Viscount Grey such moments were in a minor key:

It is a great moment when, for the first time of the season, one stands by the side of a salmon river in early spring. The heart is full with the prospect of a whole season's sport. It is the beginning of a new angling year, and the feel of the rod, the sound of the reel, the perpetual sight of moving water are all with one again after months of longing and absence.

Praise often wells up from the near sublime realization of the angler's catch. Negley Farson wrote the words to this particular tune, but there can be few anglers who have not shared a similar heart-throbbing experience when even praise must remain wordless:

> Now began one of the most beautiful battles I have ever experienced. For I had plenty of line in hand now; when he came past I gave him the bend of the rod for all I thought it could stand — determined he should never cross to the other side of that white water again. And every time I checked him. The green water was so glass-clear that when he swung in the swirls sluicing past me the sun caught and reflected the pinkish stripe along his strong sides. I could watch him fighting the hook. And then he spun in the sun, jumping. He was the very essence of fight. Furious, I think — still not frightened.
>
> There is no doubt that in the ingredients of a fisherman's delight there is nothing comparable to being able to watch a fish fight like this. For I could see him, or his shape, nearly all the time.
>
> . . . But by now my gallant rainbow was a slow-moving, sullen thing. His tail working heavily, he lay in the green water about twenty yards out from me. And I looked around for the lee of some rocks and slowly worked him in. I had him in a pool. It was almost still water. He was almost resting against the hook. And then, as the bank was high, and I was an idiot, I signalled the little Chilean boy to wade out and slip the net under him.
>
> . . . The boy did. He was an eager boy . . . so eager that he stabbed the net at the fish . . . pushed him with it! Then he tried to scoop him in from the tail . . . I jumped. As I did, the boy actually got the fish into the net. I seized boy, net, fish, all at the same time, and threw them all up on the bank. There I dived on the fish.
>
> It all goes to prove the hysterical condition into which some fishermen will get themselves. For this rainbow was not much over 6lb. But he was such a beautiful one! That was the point: that small nose, and those deep shoulders, and those firm fighting flanks. This fish had been living in clean water on crayfish galore. I sat on the bank and looked at him for nearly twenty minutes. I had him.

But when the angler cannot say 'I had him', and must admit defeat, there can still be praise for fish and fishing in recollection of the one that gets away, nicely expressed in the anonymous Scottish verse that tells of an angler driven to drink:

> The flask frae my pocket
> I poured into the socket,
> For I was provokit unto the last degree;
> And to my way o'thinking',
> There's naething for't but drinkin',
> When a trout he lies winkin' and lauchin' at me.

Thanksgiving, too, is often an important element in the angler's praise of fishing itself. Thomas Tod Stoddart was another well known Scotsman who became an angler and devoted his life to it. Far from being merely a recreational fisherman, Stoddart — who dropped out of law school before this total conversion — was once approached by a one-time fellow student, now a Judge, in a Scottish riverside inn. When asked by the Judge what he was doing now, Stoddart replied, 'Why man! I'm an angler!'

Angler! that all day hast wandered by sunny stream and, heart and hand, plied the meditative art, who hast filled thy pannier brimful of star-sided trout, and with aching arms and weary back and faint wavering step crossed the threshold of some cottage inn . . . stretch they hand over thy mercies and be thankful!

There can be no doubt that angling holds a powerful sway over the minds and lives of millions of men. Nick Lyons once said that if he wasn't fishing he was thinking fishing. I find such statements reassuring, for being likewise so afflicted I might otherwise have thought myself dangerously obsessed. It may have something to do with the fact that, of most of man's activities, none other has its roots and origins going so far back into only fleetingly remembered racial memories. Detractors of anglers often say there simply is no need for civilized man to fish for food; and that there is no other reason to warrant it. But this is a great over-simplification based on a supermarket, fish-fingers attitude to life. It is rather like saying that because Holy Communion is no longer a shared meal *per se* of breaking and eating bread, drinking water and wine; that because it is no longer a meal in itself, it has become unnecessary.

Hugh Sheringham observed that angling was a branch of human activity with its roots in culture as well as in hunger. Nowadays fishermen have become increasingly specialized and their sport thought of as being entirely dependent upon techniques and equipment; yet the literature of fishing, that yardstick by which its nature is best examined, remains a strange blend of sophistication and tenacious primitivism. An aspect of angling lending credence to these links with man's dimmest past, lies in the recurrence of certain imagery. This imagery often invokes the sense of successive veils being removed from an angler's eyes revealing still further delights and magic still only dimly observed beneath yet more veils. It is as if an angler's chief delights come in instalments and are no sooner revealed than disappear again beneath yet another swirling and diaphanous veil. Why is it, then, that only in a few sporting activities are such journeys to be made? I am told that mountaineers experience something very similar, possibly even more intense. It is easy to sound patronizing when trying to describe an inner glow that sometimes happens in the pursuit of something in which one is personally involved. Why shouldn't there be similar revelations simply by communing with nature on a walk? And why, anyway, do women only rarely experience it? It is certainly not because men make better anglers than women; because women often excel at the sport. But, almost always with women anglers, despite their knowledge and technique and success, they can take it or leave it. However much they love to fish, they can do without it. Far from being a male chauvinist in my personal attitudes to, or relationships with, women, I can't conceive of a single one I've ever known or heard of who *thought* about fish and fishing in the way Nick Lyons meant; in the way that I do, every day of my life, irrespective of where I am, or what I'm doing. Of course, it would be nonsense to suggest that all male anglers are similarly afflicted, or even more than a small proportion of them. In fishing, J. W. Hills wrote: 'I felt receptive to every sight, every colour and every sound, as though I had walked through a world from which a veil had been withdrawn.'

Lest anyone should think that this 'modernity' in angling arose in Walton's England, they should remember that in ancient Chinese civilizations, as far back as 2000 BC, emperors and noblemen and noblewomen fished from specially constructed riverside temples, with light wands of rods and a single human hair.

This preoccupation with water is one of man's most constant memories. Few people — and among anglers none — can cross a bridge over water without stopping and peering down into its depths. Yet not all of us feel the same way about water. W. C. Fields, that ebullient Hollywood comedian who made much of his like of strong drink, was once asked why he never drank water or used it to dilute alcohol. His reply was succinct, if not quite correct. 'Fish fuck in it,' he said.

Others have seen angling's watery dimension in less basic fashion. It was recently observed that there remains one abiding and underlying reason for angling's literary dimension, which really means the way in which angling is best praised:

> The writer repeatedly attempts to transform the world, to see the world anew, to approach it, indeed, as if it were *another* world; the repeated experience of the angler is precisely of a confrontation with another world, or, or what may stand for it, another element. Water, in short, is all. More than anything, it is that glinting, tantalizing horizontal veil, the surface of water, dividing so absolutely one realm from another, which gives angling its mystery, its magic, its endless speculation. 'Water and meditation,' wrote Melville in a splendidly hydrolatrous chapter in *Moby Dick*, 'are wedded for ever', and even the most casual lingerer on bridge or jetty will testify to this truth. The angler becomes curiously affected by and attuned to his watery surroundings; he seems to acquire, as Hills observed, a new perception, to slip beneath the mental surface. It is this sense of blending into the natural ambience and rhythm of his environment which is the subject of *The Fisherman* by W. B. Yeats, himself a keen angler:
>> 'A man who does not exist,
>> A man who is but a dream . . .'
> and it is perfectly evoked by another fishing poet, Ted Hughes, when he describes float fishing:
>> 'You are aware, in a horizonless and slightly mesmerized way, like listening to the double-bass in orchestral music, of the fish below there in the dark.' The encounter with water, furthermore, is dual in nature. If fishing is a meeting with, a peering into another universe, there goes with it a Narcissus-like in-peering, inescapably yearning, entranced, nostalgic. Time and again the strain of paradise lost (sometimes to be regained) finds expression in the literature of angling, frequently focused in the writer's love for a particular hallowed water . . . Yet whatever the specific occasion, the general fact remains true: in water we see the dream, the mystery of ourselves.
> And we also see fish. It is little wonder that these creatures so often embody, as in Kingsley's *Water Babies*, our fantasies of passing into another world; that the literature of fishing is characterized, as Virginia Woolf noted, by a 'confusion between fish and men'; or that Sven Berlin should, in his *Jonah's Dream*, see the Jonah legend as the archetypal myth of the angler. At the very heart of the sport lies a curious imaginative circuitry between fisherman and fish, for the former has to try to think like the latter, the angler has to *be* part fish.

In this Introduction to *The Magic Wheel* the editors, David Profumo and Graham Swift, conjure up a vision of fishing as a contemplative recreation not even anticipated in Walton's bucolic musings on the riverside.

An aspect of the praise fishermen bestow upon fishing lies in the almost shamefaced manner in which they sometimes explain it away. While they *know* that fishing, as well as the recollection of fishing, and the anticipation of fishing, consumes their total interest and a large part of their lives and their thoughts; while they *know* these things, and more, they still feel almost shamefaced in admitting it to non-anglers. No one feels qualms of conscience and guilt about telling anyone who cares to listen why they play golf with such singlemindness; nor should they. Neither should it be any different for anglers. But it often is.

Fishing books often include an almost obligatory part chapter explaining away this unexplainable fact. It is compounded of many things; none of which are very important in themselves, but add up to make the stock figure of the fisherman an odd figure, to say the least. Harold Russell states it baldly, but apologetically:

> Yet compared with the serious things of life, fishing is after all a trivial business. The thoughtful angler must frankly confess this. It adds to the difficulty of the problem when he asks himself why the pleasure of catching a few trout is so great and failure so disheartening. The eagerness and excitement with which one sets about fishing water which holds big fish is almost childish. The value of the prize is in no way comparable to the desire it arouses. When the fish are rising and showing themselves, the longing to hook them which one feels is almost insane. And when we see them feeding regardless of our fly or dashing off terrified at our efforts to delude them, the resentment which the fisherman feels is almost like the anger of a madman.

Not a pretty picture of the contemplative angler, but at least true enough for every honest fisherman to see something there of himself, or once himself. You may well ask what this can possibly have to do with the praise of fishing, but it fits into that somewhat deprecating view the angler sometimes has of himself as a somewhat forlorn, melancholy, wet, solitary and mendacious character, lurking about rivers and lakes in quest of silly fish. It is anglers themselves who don't properly know how to praise the fishing to which they have become addicted; or, if they do, or try to, they stray into the realms of poesy and fancy.

That fish and fishing are indispensable to each other seems obvious, but that relationship may have become stretched the further the purpose of fishing itself has moved away from just providing food. That sage American angler, Sparse Grey Hackle, put it this way:

> Fish are, of course, indispensable to the angler. They give him an excuse for fishing and justify the flyrod without which he would be a mere vagrant. But the average fisherman's average catch doesn't even begin to justify, *as fish*, its cost in work, time, and money. The true worth of fishing, as the experienced, sophisticated angler comes to realize, lies in the memorable contacts with people and other living creatures, scenes and places, and living waters great and small which it provides.

Bill Crawford, the best fly fisherman I know, has reached that stage along the angling path, he has to remember to take along a fly rod when he goes fishing. Nowadays his interests are those of the entomologist, river explorer, and trout-watcher. He sometimes says that he takes along a fly rod on such excursions because he feels such a fool if someone were to see him in such places without one — if he were armed with nothing more lethal than the small hand net in which he collects, and releases, nymphs. As for Bill's fly rod itself being in any way lethal, he hasn't killed a trout for the past seven years. Like Negley Farson, Bill's fly rod is a magic wand that takes him to some of nature's loveliest places.

Fishing, then, in its most perfect form, may after all be much like happiness itself; knowable only in retrospect. The praise of fishing, whether in the pages of angling literature, in shared conversation, or in personal remembrance, is in essence the recollection of days become memorable in that retrospect. There still remains a curious madness about fly fishing. Many anglers discover an assertiveness in themselves very different from their character. A few, less sensitive fishermen mistake this assertiveness for what they wrongly see as the machismo in fishing. But the true and meaningful assertiveness to which I refer is far from being the assertiveness of man against fish. It is the assertiveness of man against inanimate nature, in no way destructive of it or despoiling it.

Vance Bourjaily, the American novelist and fishing writer, was speaking of the fly fisherman's maturity as an angler, rather than about praise for praise sake, when he touched upon the matter:

> I assert that a man does not go fishing or hunting in order to obtain, or kill, as much game as he can. I assert that he does it in order to achieve a certain relationship between himself and wildness, to match himself against the land and against certain of its creatures, possession of which he has taught himself to desire. It is not merely his skill with rod and gun which he wants to exercise . . . there is a more spacious feeling, the feeling of free agency within a large solitude . . . the feeling of being alone and unhampered in one's pursuit, to follow it as one sees fit, by no man's sufferance.

The bond, as it were, between fisherman and fish must be water itself. But not merely the bond; the ineffable separation, too; that which forever keeps both apart. Maybe the sadness that almost always accompanies the angler's killing of a fish is something like this, and never resolved. The angler — the real angler, at least — strives to know the fish he seeks; but the only way he knows how to approach this desired end is to drag them up from their natural element into his own. That this often ends in the death of the fish that gives the angler such delight is, indeed, something of a paradox and a mystery. Catch and release is in part an act of conservation; a deliberate attempt by some anglers not to heedlessly destroy the objects of their hunting by water. It is also an act of the same assertiveness that drives the fisherman to fish in the same place, but without the mindless slaughter.

The magic thread that binds angler to fish is the water itself, not just the fisherman's deceitful line and hook. Someone has said that if there is magic on this planet, it is contained in water. Water reaches everywhere; it touches the past and prepares the future. Aldo Leopold wrote, 'The good life on any river may depend on the perception of its music, and the preservation of some music to perceive.'

It has been said that fish themselves are the attainable goal in fishing — at least sometimes — although it seems, to this fisherman at least, to be a broad generalization. When fly fishing along a stream, particularly a hitherto unknown stream, there can be but few anglers who can hardly bear to stop fishing and come away. There is always the desire to fish on, around the bend, and then around the next bend, ever seeking fresh waters, fresh riffles and runs, fresh pools, fresh wonders and delights. Despite this intense longing to fish on, it is good for an angler's soul not to be able to do so, on at least as many occasions as he can, in order to preserve the unattainable of that particular day in memory and keep the prospect open for some tomorrow. Romilly Fedden, whose book *Golden Days* is redolent of this aspect of fishing, put it this way:

> It is the spirit of fishing, its immeasurable charm and mystery, which ever leads us on beyond the woods where the wild birds sing. Never can we reach our final goal, for always before us lie further fields yet to explore.

Fly fishing is like life, only moreso. Like life itself, much of it is spent in dream. Ian Niall once said:

> If I had a choice of skills and could go back in life to make the choice and use the skill, I should ask simply for the angler's skill and no more. Let everything else be as it is in reality; let fishing be no easier, let me catch nothing a great deal better than the trout I have caught, but let me have time ahead to fish and with that I should have the stuff of dreams, and be content.

There can be little doubt that in the fisherman's most eloquent praise of fishing, the fundamental mystery remains. Only in such essays at praise have most men managed to get near telling *why* they fish. To someone as eloquent as Roderick Haig-Brown it remained a primitive curiosity:

> In the last analysis, though, it must be the fish themselves that make fishing — the strangeness and beauty of fish, their often visible remoteness, their ease in another world, the mystery of their movements and habits and whims. The steelhead lying in the summer pool, the brown trout rising under the cut bank, the Atlantic salmon rolling over his lie, the bass breaking in the lily pads, the grayling glimpsed in the rapid, the enormous unseen trout cruising the lake's drop-off, all these are irresistible temptations to anyone who has held a rod.
>
> It is not that one wants to kill, though kill one may. The appeal is more nearly that of hidden treasure, except that this treasure has life and movement and uncertainty beyond anything inanimate. The thought in the mind is: 'Let me try for him.' The desire is to stir the reaction, respond to it, control it; to see the mystery close by in the water, perhaps to handle it, to admire, to understand a little. Perhaps it adds up to nothing more than a primitive curiosity, but if so it remains powerful and lasting.

Arnold Gingrich was a sophisticate, as well as being a passionate angler, and he often spoke of the *thinking* in fishing. In considering what actually happens with a fish on, he wrote:

> You don't think you're thinking at the time. You actually try to be as nonthinking, as instinctive and intuitive, as the trout or salmon that is your partner of the instant. That's why, both before and after I read Walton, I felt that 'the contemplative man's recreation' was a ludicrous misnomer for this kind of fishing. And yet the fair rewards, the things

that are left with you afterward, are of sweetly silent thought all compact. So the thinking must be retroactive. Maybe angling is not, as old Izaak said, like mathematics. Maybe it's more like sex — and I'm not thinking of that vulgar definition of sex as 'the most fun you can have without laughing'. What I am thinking of is that couple of lines of Houseman:

> The night my father got me
> His mind was not on me.

For fishing seems to me tó be divided, like sex, into three most unequal parts, the two larger of which, by far, are anticipation and recollection, and in between, by far the smallest of the three, actual performance.

The reader will have noticed that in this present examination of views in praise of fishing I have quoted heavily from other men's stumblings around the same arena, the same world fishpond. No apology should be necessary because some of these views are the most eloquent I know of, and are ordinarily spread thinly throughout a great many fishing books. The subject matter of this enquiry is difficult to explain — even to other anglers. The similarities that occur in its various tellings are nothing to do with conscious or unconscious plagiarism, but speak profoundly of the commonality of the fishing experience, however uncommonly difficult it may be to explain.

Thankfully, for the rest of all our fishing days, as well as of those of future generations of anglers, the mystery not only remains, but deepens, as we race on towards wherever we are going, and still further distant from our dimly understood and remembered past — even beyond those veils of the surface of the waters with which we are blessed.

Bibliography

This list contains books from which quotations have been made, as well as those mentioned in passing in the various chapters, or paraphrased with due and proper acknowledgement. The edition mentioned is that which was used.

Allan, P. B. M., *Trout Heresy*. Philip Allan, London, 1936.

Allen, K. Radway & Cunningham, B. T. *New Zealand Angling 1947–1952. Result of the Diary Scheme*. New Zealand Marine Department Fisheries Bulletin No.12, Wellington, 1957.

Atherton, John. *The Fly and the Fish*. The Macmillan Company, New York, 1951.

Bashline, L. James. Night Fishing for Trout. Freshet Press, New York. 1973.

Batten Pooll, A. H. *Some Globe-Trottings with a Rod*. Spottiswoode, Ballantyne & Co Ltd, Eton, 1937.

Bentley, Gerald Eades (Ed). *The Arte of Angling — 1577*. 1st edn with an Introduction by Carl Otto v. Keinbusch, and Explanatory Notes by Henry L. Savage. Princeton University Library Press. NJ, 1956.
  The Same. 2nd edn. 1958. *The Arte of Angling* (1577), plagiarized by Izaak Walton in *The Complete Angler*, 1st edn. 1963, is now attributed to the Rev. William Samuel, Vicar of Godmanchester.

Berlin, Sven. *Jonah's Dream — A Meditation on Fishing*. Phoenix House, London, 1964. Also published by William Kaufmann Inc, Los Altos, California, 1975.

Berners, Dame Juliana. *The Treatyse of Fysshynge wyth an Angle*. Wynkyn de Worde, Westminster, 1496. The old version from Elliot Stock facsimile, London, 1880.
  A modern English version may be found in John McDonald's *The Origins of Angling*. Doubleday, New York, 1963, and *Quill Gordon*, Alfred Knopf, New York, 1972.

Bourjaily, Vance. From an unknown source book. The paragraph used was quoted by V. S. Hidy in the Preface to his book *The Pleasures of Fly Fishing*. Winchester Press, New York, 1972.

Bowlker, Charles. *The Art of Angling*. 5th edn. M. Swinney, Birmingham, 1788. Some earlier editions were published in Ludlow.

Byron, Lord. *Don Juan*, Canto XIII, with Byron's note. 1819.

Chalmers, Patrick. *Green Days and Blue Days*. London, 1925.

Chaytor, A. H. *Letters to a Salmon Fisher's Sons*. John Murray, London, 1910.
  Essays Sporting & Serious. Methuen & Co Ltd, London, 1930.

Chetham, James. *The Angler's Vade Mecum*. 3rd edn. William Battersby, London, 1700.

Chisholm, R. *Two Papers on the Introduction and Propagation of Trout in New Zealand*. Dunedin, 1897.

Curtis, Brian. *The Life Story of the Fish*. Jonathan Cape, London, 1949.

Day, Francis. *British and Irish Salmonidae*. Williams & Norgate, London, 1887.

Deindorfer, Robert G. *Positive Fishing — The Art of Angling Your Outer Limit*. Seaview Books, New York, 1981.

Donne, T. E. *Rod Fishing in New Zealand Waters*. Seeley, Service & Co, London, 1927.

Draper, Keith. *Angling in New Zealand*. A. H. & A. W. Reed, Wellington, 1978.

Duffy, Maureen. *Men and Beasts — An Animal Rights Handbook*. Palladin/Granada Books, London, 1984.

Duncan, David James. *The River.Why*. Hutchinson, London, 1983. First published in the USA by Sierra Club Books Inc.

Dunne, J. W. *Sunshine and the Dry Fly*. A. & C. Black Ltd, London, 1924.
  An Experiment with Time. A. & C. Black Ltd, London, 1927.
  The Serial Universe. Faber & Faber Ltd, London.

Durnford, The Rev. Richard. *The Fishing Diary 1809-1819. The Diary of a Test Fisherman*. Simpkin & Co Ltd, London, 1911.

Eastwood, Dorothea. *River Diary*. Wingate, London, 1950.

Elliott, Keith. *'Pegging out in match of the day'*. The *Independent*, London, 25 November 1989.

Farson, Negley. *Going Fishing*. 1st edn. Country Life Ltd, London, 1942. Several reprints. New edition by Clive Holloway, London, 1981.

Fedden, Romilly. *Golden Days*. 1st edn. A. & C. Black Ltd, London, 1919.

Ferris, George. *Fly Fishing in New Zealand*. 1st edn. William Heinemann Ltd, London, 1954.

Francis, Francis. *A Book of Angling*. 2nd edn. Longmans, Green & Co, London, 1867.

Franck, Richard. *Northern Memoirs*. Written in 1658. New edn. Constable & Co, Edinburgh, 1821.

Gingrich, Arnold. *The Well-Tempered Angler*. Alfred A. Knopf Inc, New York, 1966.
The Fishing in Print. Winchester Press, New York, 1974.

Greer, Germaine. *'Home Thoughts. Germaine Greer Argues That Rats Are Animals, Too,'* The *Independent* magazine, London, 5 August 1989.

Grey, Sir Edward. *Fly Fishing*. 1st edn. J. M. Dent & Co, London, 1899.

Haig-Brown, Roderick. *Fisherman's Spring*. Crown Publishers Inc, New York, 1975 reprint.

Halford, Frederic M. *Dry Fly Fishing in Theory and Practice*. 4th edn. Vinton & Co Ltd, London, 1902.
An Angler's Autobiography. 1st edn. Vinton & Co Ltd, London, 1903.
Modern Development of the Dry Fly. 1st edn. Routledge & Sons Ltd, London, 1910.

Hamilton, Captain G. D. *Trout Fishing & Sport in Maoriland*. Government Printing Office, Wellington, New Zealand, 1904.

Hammond, Bryn. *The New Zealand Encyclopaedia of Fly Fishing*. The Halcyon Press, Auckland, New Zealand, 1988.
and Parsons, John. *New Zealand's Treasury of Trout & Salmon. An Angling Anthology*. The Halcyon Press, Auckland, 1989.

Harding, Col E. W. *The Flyfisher & The Trout's Point of View*. J. B. Lippincott Co, Philadelphia, 1931. Original UK edition published by Seeley Service & Co Ltd, London, 1931.

Hidy, V. S. *The Pleasures of Fly Fishing*. Winchester Press, New York, 1972.

Hill, Raymond. *Wings and Hackle*. E. B. Horwood & Co Ltd, London, 1912.

Hills, John Waller. *A Summer on the Test*. 1st edn. Philip Allan & Co, London, 1924.
My Sporting Life. Philip Allan & Co Ltd, London, 1936.

Hodgson, W. Earl. *Trout Fishing*. 1st edn. Adam & Charles Black, London, 1904.

Jonas, Doris and David. *Other Senses, Other Worlds*. Cassell Ltd, London, 1976.

Kelly, Greg. *The Flies in my Hat. A Book about Trout Fishing in New Zealand*. Hodder & Stoughton, London, 1967.

Kite, Oliver. *Nymph Fishing in Practice*. 1st edn. Herbert Jenkins Ltd, London, 1963.
A Fisherman's Diary. André Deutsch, London, 1969.

Knight, John Alden. *Moon Up, Moon Down. The Story of the Solunar Theory*. Solunar Sales Co, Montoursville, Pennsylvania, 1972.

LaBranche, George. *The Dry Fly and Fast Water*. Scribners, New York, 1926.

Lampman, Ben Hur. *A Leaf from French Eddy*. The Touchstone Press, Portland, Oregon, 1965. Later edition published by Harper & Row, San Francisco, 1979.

Lang, Andrew. *Angling Sketches*. 1st edn. Longmans, Green & Co Ltd, London, 1891.

Lapsley, Peter. 'To fight another day', *Salmon, Trout and Sea-Trout Magazine*, May, 1989.

Leight Hunt, James Henry. *The Indicator and The Companion; A Miscellany for the Fields and the Fireside*, London, 1840.

Leisenring, James E. (with Vernon S. Hidy). *The Art of Tying the Wet Fly & Fishing the Flymph*. Crown Publishers Inc, New York, 1971.

Lockhart, Sir Robert Bruce. *My Rod My Comfort*. Putnam & Co, London, 1957.

Lockhart, Logie Bruce. *The Pleasures of Fishing*. Adam & Charles Black Ltd, London, 1981.

Luce, A. A. *Fishing and Thinking*. Hodder & Stoughton, London, 1959.

Lunn, Alfred. 'What to do with the Evening Rise', in Harmsworth, Lord, *A Little Fishing Book*. 4th edn. Frederick Muller Ltd, London, 1944.

Lyons, Nick. *Bright Rivers*. J. B. Lippincott Co, Philadelphia and New York, 1977.
The Seasonable Angler. Funk & Wagnalls, New York, 1970.

McDonald, John. *The Origins of Angling*. Doubleday, New York, 1963.
Quill Gordon. Alfred Knopf, New York, 1972.

McInnes, John. *Tread Quietly. Stories from a New Zealand Trout Fisherman*. John McIndoe Ltd, Dunedin, New Zealand, 1983.

Maclean, Norman. *A River Runs Through It*. University of Chicago Press, Chicago, 1976.

Manley, The Rev J. J. *Notes on Fish and Fishing*. Sampson Low, Marston, Searle & Rivington, London, 1877.

Mannering, George Edward. *Eighty Years in New Zealand — Embracing Fifty Years of New Zealand Fishing*. Simpson & Williams Ltd, Christchurch 1943.

Miller, Alfred W. (Sparse Grey Hackle). *Fishless Days, Angling Nights*. Crown Publishers, New York, 1971.

Mottram, J. C. *Fly Fishing — Some New Arts and Mysteries*. The Field & Queen, London, c.1914.
Thoughts on Angling. Herbert Jenkins Ltd, London, c.1948.

Mundle, C. W. K. *Game Fishing — Methods and Memories*. Barrie and Jenkins Ltd, London, 1978.

Niall, Ian. *Trout from the Hills — The Confessions of an Addicted Fly-Fisherman*. Heinemann, London, 1961.

Ogborne, Chris. *Competition Trout Fishing*. The Crowood Press, Marlborough, Wiltshire, 1988.

Orton, D. A. (Ed.). *Where to Fish — 1988–1989*. Thomas Harmsworth Publishing Ltd, London, 1988.

Parsons, John. *A Taupo Season*. Collins, Auckland, Sydney and London, 1979.
and Hammond, Bryn (Eds.). *New Zealand's Treasury of Trout & Salmon. An Angling Anthology*. The Halcyon Press, Auckland, New Zealand, 1989.

Pawson, Tony. *Competitive Fly-Fishing*. Pelham Books Ltd, London, 1982.

Pickard, F. W. *Trout Fishing in New Zealand in Wartime*. G. P. Putnam's Sons, New York, 1940.

Profumo, David. *In Praise of Fishing*. Viking Press, London, 1989.
and Swift, Graham (Eds.). *The Magic Wheel. An Anthology of Fishing in Literature*. Heinemann, London, 1986. Softback edition, Pan Books Ltd, London, 1985.

Ransome, Arthur. *Rod and Line*. 1st edn. Jonathan Cape, London, 1929.
Mainly about Fishing. A. & C. Black Ltd, London, 1959.

Raymond, Steve. *The Year of the Trout*. Winchester Press, Piscataway, N.J., 1985.

Roberts, Morley. *A Humble Fisherman*. Grayson & Grayson, London, 1932.

Rubin, Louis D. *The Even-Tempered Angler*. Nick Lyons Books, Winchester Press, New York, Piscataway, 1983.

Russell, Harold. *Chalkstream and Moorland*. Smith, Elder & Co, London, 1911.

Saundby, Sir Robert. *A Fly-Rod on Many Waters*. Stanley Paul & Co Ltd, London, 1961.

Scott, Arnold B. (W. H. Lawrie). *The Truth About Trout Fishing*. Oliver & Boyd, Edinburgh & London, 1951.

Scrope, William. *Days and Nights of Salmon Fishing on the Tweed*. 3rd edn. Hamilton Adams, London & Thos. Morrison, Glasgow, 1885.

Senior, William. *Travel and Trout in the Antipodes*. Chatto & Windus, London, 1880.

Shepard, Odell. *Thy Rod and Thy Creel*. Dodd, Mead & Co, New York, 1930. Softback edition by Nick Lyons Books, New York & Piscataway, 1984.

Skues, G. E. M. *Minor Tactics of the Chalk Stream*. 3rd edn. A. & C. Black Ltd, London, 1924.
The Way of a Trout with a Fly. 3rd edn. A. & C. Black Ltd, London, 1935.
Nymph Fishing for Chalk Stream Trout. 1st edn. A. & C. Black Ltd, London, 1939.

Spackman, W. H. *Trout in New Zealand*. Government Printer, Wellington, 1892.

Stewart, Douglas. *The Seven Rivers*. Angus & Robertson, Sydney, 1966.

Traver, Robert. *Trout Madness*. St Martin's Press, New York, 1960.
Trout Magic. Crown Publishers Inc, New York, 1974.
Anatomy of a Fisherman. Peregrine Smith Inc, Santa Barbara and Salt Lake City, 1978.

Turner, Eric Horsfall. *Angler's Cavalcade*. Adam & Charles Black, London, 1966.

Turner, Brian (Ed.). *The Guide to Trout Fishing in Otago*. Otago Acclimatisaion Society, Dunedin, New Zealand, 1985 with revisions.

Van Dyke, Henry. *Little Rivers*. Charles Scribner's Sons, New York, 1897.

Van de Water, Frederic F. *In Defense of Worms — and other angling heresies*. Duell, Sloan and Pearce, New York, 1949.

Voss Bark, Conrad. *A Fly on the Water*. Allen & Unwin, London, 1986.

Venables, Bernard. *Fishing*. B. T. Batsford Ltd, London, 1953.
The Gentle Art of Angling. Max Reinhardt, London, 1955.

Walden, Howard T. *The Last Pool: Upstream & Down and Big Stony*. Crown Publishers Sportsmen's Classics, New York, 1972. Originally published as two separate books by the Derrydale Press in Limited Editions.

Walker, Richard. *Dick Walker's Trout Fishing*. David & Charles Ltd, Newton Abbot, 1982.

Walton, Izaak. *The Complete Angler*. 1st edn. 1653. A facsimile of the first edition in the Grenville collection is published by Adam & Charles Black, London, 1928.
The Complete Angler. 5th edn. 1676. The first edition to include Cotton's contribution. With few exceptions all the many hundreds of subsequent editions are printed in accordance with this text.

Weeks, Edward. *Fresh Waters*. Atlantic Monthly Press, Little, Brown & Co, Boston, 1968.

Wiggin, Maurice. *The Passionate Angler*. Theodore Brun Ltd, London, 1949 (Limited de luxe edn.). Published simultaneously in a trade edition by Sylvan Press Ltd, London.
Troubled Waters. Hutchinsons, London, 1960.

Wilentz, Joan Steen. *The Senses of Man*. Thomas Crowell Co, New York, 1968.

Williamson, Capt T. *The Complete Angler's Vade-Mecum*. Payne and Mackinlay, London, 1808.

Willock, Colin (Compiler). *In Praise of Fishing. An Anthology for Addicts*. Frederick Muller Ltd, London, 1954.

Wright, Leonard M. *Fishing the Dry Fly as a Living Insect*. E. P. Dutton & Co Inc, New York, 1972.
Fly-Fishing Heresies. Stoeger Publishing Co, South Hackensack, N.J., 1978.

Acknowledgments

Every effort has been made to contact copyright holders, authors, publishers or literary agents in seeking permission to quote or paraphrase material used in this book. In some cases, despite repeated efforts, this proved impossible, or no reply was received. In the very few instances where no reply was received from authors and/or publishers at known addresses and still in business it has been assumed they had no objection to the use of the requested copyright material. This use has been acknowledged in the proper manner. In the event of any inadvertent error or omission in regard to quoted material, the author tenders his sincere regrets, as the policy in writing this book has always been to acknowledge the source material consulted and to obtain direct permission wherever possible.

Thanks are given to the following authors, publishers, literary representatives, for their permission to use copyright material:

Extract and paraphrased material from *A Fly on the Water* reproduced with the kind permission of the author, Conrad Voss Bark, and the publishers Allen & Unwin Ltd. Thanks to Merlin Unwin for his kind assistance. © Conrad Voss Bark 1986.

Extract from *Where to Fish 1988–1989* reproduced with the kind permission of D. A. Orton, editor, and the publishers Thomas Harmsworth Publishing, London.
© Thomas Harmsworth Publishing 1988.

Extract and paraphrased material from *The Independent Magazine*, 5 August 1989, the article by Germaine Greer in 'Home Thoughts' entitled 'Rats are animals too' reproduced with the kind permission of Dr Germaine Greer; and Aitken & Stone, Dr Greer's Agents, with special thanks to Gillon Aitken; and to the Editor of *The Independent Magazine*. © Germaine Greer 1989.

Extract from *My Rod My Comfort* by Sir Robert Bruce Lockhart: grateful acknowledgement is made to the publishers, Putnam, London, 1957, to the Bodley Head, and to Sir Robert Bruce Lockhart's literary executors.

Grateful acknowledgement is made to the literary executors of the late C. W. K. Mundle for paraphrased material from *Game Fishing: Methods & Memories* by C. W. K. Mundle, published by Barrie & Jenkins, 1978. © C. W. K. Mundle 1978.

Thanks are given to Andrew Nurnberg Associates and to Sierra Club Books Inc for their kind permission to quote from *The River Why* by David James Duncan, published in the UK by Hutchinsons, 1983. © David James Duncan 1983.

My thanks are given to John Parsons for permission to use material from *A Taupo Season*, published by William Collins Ltd, Auckland, New Zealand, 1979.
© John Parsons, 1979.

Thanks to John McInnes, and to the publishers, John McIndoe Ltd, for their kind permission to quote from *Tread Quietly*, Dunedin, New Zealand, 1983.
© John McInnes 1983.

Thanks to Julian Shuckburgh of Barrie and Jenkins Ltd for kind permission to quote two passages from *Nymph Fishing in Practice* by Oliver Kite, published by Herbert Jenkins Ltd, 1963.
© Oliver Kite 1963.

Thanks to Hodder & Stoughton Ltd for permission to quote material from *Fishing and Thinking* by A. A. Luce, published by them in 1959. © A. A. Luce 1959.

My thanks are given to Daniel Farson for his personal permission to quote material from his late father's *Going Fishing*, by Negley Farson, published by Country Life Ltd, London, 1941; Harcourt Brace & Co, New York, 1947; Clive Holloway Books, London, 1981. © Daniel Farson 1981.

Grateful acknowledgement is made to the publishers, Thomas Y. Crowell & Co, New York, and to the author, Joan Steen Wilentz, for the use of material from *The Senses of Man* (1968). © Joan Steen Wilentz 1968.

I wish to thank Keith Draper for permission to quote from his book *Angling in New Zealand*, published by A. H. & A. W. Reed Ltd, Wellington, 1978. © Keith Draper 1978.

Grateful acknowledgement is made to the late Maurice Wiggin and to his literary heirs for use of material from his book *The Passionate Angler*, published by Theodore Brun Ltd, London, and the Sylvan Press Ltd, London, 1949.

Thanks are given to Reinhardt Books Ltd for permission to quote excerpts from *The Gentle Art of Angling* by Bernard Venables, published by Max Reinhardt, London, 1955. My thanks are given to Elizabeth Bowes Lyon of Reinhardt Books for her kind assistance in this matter.

My thanks are given to Tony Pawson for his kindness in permitting me to quote excerpts from *Competitive Fly-Fishing* by Tony Pawson published by Pelham Books Ltd, 1982. © Tony Pawson 1982.

My thanks are also given to Tony Pawson for his kindness in permitting me to quote material from his Foreword to *Competition Trout Fishing* by Chris Ogborne, published by The Crowood Press, Marlborough, 1988.
© Chris Ogborne 1988, and for the Foreword © Tony Pawson 1988.

My grateful thanks are given to Jonathan Cape Ltd for permission to quote excerpts from *Rod and Line* by Arthur Ransome, published by Jonathan Cape, London, 1929. Also for their kind permission to quote from *The Life Story of the Fish* by Brian Curtis, published by Jonathan Cape, London, 1949.

Grateful acknowledgement is made to W. H. Lawrie, the author of *The Truth About Trout Fishing* by Arnold B. Scott, published by Oliver & Boyd Ltd, Edinburgh, 1951. Thanks are given to the Longman Publishing Group for their assistance in attempting to locate and contact Mr Lawrie.

Grateful acknowledgement is made to the Century Hutchinson Publishing Group for their informal permission to quote material from *A Fly-Rod on Many Waters* by Sir Robert Saundby, published by Stanley Paul Ltd, London, 1961.
© Air Marshal Sir Robert Saundby 1961.

Acknowledgement is made of the use of material from *Trout Heresy* by P. B. M. Allan, published by Philip Allan, London, 1936. The present Philip Allan publishers bear no relationship to the Philip Allan publishers of the above book.

Thanks are given to Steve Raymond of Seattle, Washington, for his kind permission to quote passages from his book *The Year of the Trout*, published by Winchester Press, an imprint of New Century Publishers Inc, Piscataway, N.J., 1985.
© 1985 by Steve Raymond.

Thanks are given to Brian Turner and the Otago Acclimatisation Society for their kind permission to quote passages from *The Guide to Trout Fishing in Otago*, edited by Brian Turner, published by The Otago Acclimatisation Society, Dunedin, New Zealand, 1983 and 1985. © The Otago Acclimatisation Society.

My thanks are given to Nick Lyons, New York, for his kind permission to quote passages from *Bright Rivers* and *The Seasonable Angler*. *Bright Rivers* published by J. B. Lippincott Co, Philadelphia & New York, 1977. © 1977 Nick Lyons. *The Seasonable Angler* published by Funk and Wagnalls, New York, 1970. © Nick Lyons.

Thanks are given to Nick Lyons of Lyons & Burford Inc, Publishers Nick Lyons Books, New York, for kind permission to quote passages from *Thy Rod and Thy Creel* by Odell Shepard.

Thanks are given to Logie Bruce Lockhart and to the publishers, A. & C. Black Ltd, London, for kind permission to quote material from *The Pleasures of Fishing*.
© 1981 Logie Bruce Lockhart.

My thanks are given to the author and to Grafton Books, a division of the Collins Publishing Group, for kind permission to quote a considerable amount of material from *Men & Beasts — An Animal Rights Handbook* by Maureen Duffy, published by Paladin, Granada Publishing, London, 1984. © Maureen Duffy 1984. My thanks to Doris Zilles of Grafton Books for her kind assistance in this matter.

Thanks are given to André Deutsch Ltd, London, for kind permission to quote material from *A Fisherman's Diary* by the late Oliver Kite, published by André Deutsch Ltd, London, 1st edn 1969. © 1962, 1963, 1964, 1965, 1966, 1967, 1968 Oliver Kite.

Grateful acknowledgement is made to V. S. Hidy and Winchester Press, New York, for the use of quoted material from an unstated source written by Vance Bourjaily and quoted by V. S. Hidy in his Preface to *The Pleasures of Fly Fishing* by V. S. Hidy, published by the Winchester Press, New York, 1972.

Grateful acknowledgement is made to the authors, Doris and David Jonas, and the publishers, Macmillan Co, New York, for the use of material from *Other Senses, Other Worlds*, published in the UK by Cassell & Co, London, 1976. © Doris & David Jonas 1976.

Grateful acknowledgement is made for the use of material from *New Zealand Angling 1947–1952. Result of the Diary Scheme* by K. Radway Allen and B. T. Cunningham. New Zealand Marine Department Fisheries Bulletin No.12, Wellington, 1957. This publication is now in the public domain.

Acknowledgement is made for the use of paraphrased material from *The Fly and the Fish* by John Atherton published by The Macmillan Company, New York, 1951.

Acknowledgement is made for the use of material from *Night Fishing for Trout* by L. James Bashline, published by Freshet Press, New Yorfk, 1973.

My grateful thanks are given to my friend Sven Berlin for his kind permission to use material from *Jonah's Dream — A Meditation on Fishing*, first published by Phoenix House Ltd, London (1964), and in the USA by William Kaufmann Inc, Los Altos, California (1975). © Sven Berlin 1965, © 1975 William Kaufmann Inc.

Acknowledgement is made to Robert G. Deindorfer and the publishers, Seaview Books, New York, for the use of material from *Positive Fishing* (1981). © 1981 Robert G. Deindorfer.

Grateful thanks are given to Phyllis Westburg of Harold Ober Associates, New York, N.Y., and to the Haig-Brown family, Vancouver, British Columbia, for kind permission to use material from *Fisherman's Spring* by Roderick Haig-Brown. © Roderick Haig-Brown 1951, 1975.

Grateful acknowledgement is made and thanks given to Harold Ober Associates, New York, N.Y., for kind permission to use material from *The Fishing in Print* by Arnold Gingrich published by Winchester Press, Piscataway, N.J. (1974). Copyright © 1974 by Arnold Gingrich.

Grateful acknowledgement is made to the publishers, Random House Inc, Alfred A. Knopf Inc, New York, for permission to reproduce material from *The Well-Tempered Angler* by Arnold Gingrich, New York, N.Y., 1965. Copyright © 1959, 1960, 1965 by Arnold Gingrich.

Grateful acknowledgement is made to Mrs Cassie Blair of Taupo, New Zealand, for her kind permission to use some material from *The Flies in My Hat* by Greg Kelly, published by Hodder & Stoughton, London, 1967. © Greg Kelly 1967.

Grateful thanks and acknowledgements are given to the literary heirs of the late Ben Hur Lampman, and to the publishers, Touchstone Press, Portland, Oregon (1965) and Harper & Row, New York & San Francisco (1979) for the use of material from *A Leaf from French Eddy*. This permission is granted by Harper & Row, New York. © 1965 Lena Lampman.

Acknowledgement is made to Lord Harmsworth and the publishers, Frederick Muller Ltd, London, for the use of material by the late Alfred Lunn in *A Little Fishing Book* (1944).

Thanks are given to Norman Maclean and The University of Chicago Press, Chicago, for their kind permission to quote an excerpt from *A River Runs Through It* (1976). © 1976 by The University of Chicago.

Grateful acknowledgement is made to Little, Brown & Co, Boston, Mass., for their kind permission to reprint material from *Fresh Waters* by Edward Weeks, an Atlantic Monthly Press Book published by Little, Brown & Co, Boston, Mass., 1968. © 1968 by Edward Weeks.

Acknowledgement is made to David & Charles Ltd, Newton Abbot, and the late Richard Walker, for the use of a small caricature drawing described in *Dick Walker's Trout Fishing* by Richard Walker (1982).

Acknowledgement is made to Frederic F. van de Water, and the publishers, Duell, Sloan & Pearce, New York, for the use of material from *In Defense of Worms* (1949).

Grateful thanks are given to Nick Lyons of Lyons & Burford, Publishers, Nick Lyons Books, New York, N.Y., for kind permission to use material from *Trout Magic* by Robert Traver, published by Crown Publishers Inc, New York, 1974. © 1974 John D. Voelker.

Grateful thanks are given to Nick Lyons of Lyons & Burford, Publishers, Nick Lyons Books, New York, N.Y., for kind permission to use material from *Fishless Days, Angling Nights* by Sparse Grey Hackle, published by Crown Publishers Inc, New York, 1971. © 1971 by Alfred W. Miller.

My thanks are given to John Bell of Wootton-by-Woodstock, Oxford, for his kind permission to reproduce material from *Mainly About Fishing* by Arthur Ransome, published by A. & C. Black, London, 1959. Grateful acknowledgement is made to John Bell and the Ransome Estate.

Grateful thanks are given to William Heinemann Ltd, London, and to the Editors, David Profumo and Graham Swift, for their kind permission to quote extracts from the Introduction to *The Magic Wheel — An Anthology of Fishing in Literature*, edited by David Profumo and Graham Swift, published by Heinemann, London, 1986, and Pan Books Ltd (Picador Press), London, 1985. © David Profumo and Graham Swift 1985.

A few of the concepts and ideas outlined in this book in some detail were previously discussed in briefer, alternative form in an earlier book of mine, *The New Zealand Encyclopaedia of Fly Fishing*, published by The Halcyon Press, Auckland, New Zealand, 1988. My thanks are given to the publisher Graham Gurr, Halcyon Press Ltd, Auckland, New Zealand, for his kind permission to use this material.
© 1988 Bryn Hammond.

I wish to thank Dr Nick Bradford of Taupo, for his kind permission to quote material from a two-part article on Catch & Release he wrote for the New Zealand *Flyfisher*.

My thanks are given to Colin Laurie McKelvie for editorial advice in the preparation of the final manuscript, and to Alastair Simpson, Managing Director of Airlife Publishing Ltd, for his considerable help in obtaining some of the necessary copyright permissions.

Should any due acknowledgement have been overlooked the author tenders his sincere apologies and regrets. It was not for want of trying.

The chapter head and tail vignettes are from the following books.
Frontispiece: *Halcyon*, George Brennand, London. 1947. Illustrated by C. Walter Hodges. Thanks to A. & C. Black. Introduction:*The British Angler's Manual*, T. C. Hofland, London, 1884. Chapter 1: *Troutfishing*, Norman Marsh, Auckland, New Zealand, 1990. Illustrated by the author. Personal thanks to Norman Marsh and Halcyon Press, Auckland. *The Treatise of Fishing with an Angle*, Dame Juliana Berners, 1496. Chapter 2: *Trout Magic*, Robert Traver. Illustrated by Milton C. Weiler. Crown Publishers, New York, 1974. Thanks to Nick Lyons. *The Angler's Eldorado: New Zealand*, Zane Grey, New York & London, 1926. Chapter 3: Fishing, Vol. 1, edited by Horace G. Hutchinson, Country Life Library of Sport, London, 1907. *Fisherman's Summer*, Roderick L. Haig-Brown. Illustrated by Louis Darling. Crown Publishers, New York, 1975. Thanks to Nick Lyons. Chapter 4: From an old engraving reproduced in *More Recreation for the Contemplative Man*, compiled by Laurenda Daniells & Stanley Read, The Library of the University of British Columbia, Vancouver, Canada, 1971. Chapter 5: *Beneath the Rising Mist*, Dana S. Lamb. Illustrated by Tom Hennessey. Stone Wall Press Inc., Boston, Mass., 1979. Thanks to the publishers. Chapter 6: *An Angler's Anthology*, edited by Eugene Burns. Illustrated by Louis Macouillard. The Stackpole Company, Harrisburg, Pennsylvania, 1952. Acknowledgements to the publishers. Chapter 7: Taken from the Wellington Acclimatisation Society's *Centennial Year Annual Report*, Wellington, New Zealand, 1971. *British Fresh-Water Fishes*, The Rev. W. Houghton, London, 1879. Chapter 8: *The Trout Waters of England*, Walter M. Gallichan, London, 1908. Chapter 9: Reproduced in *The Ultimate Fishing Book*, edited by Lee Eisenberg and DeCourcy Taylor, Houghton Mifflin Co., Boston, Mass., 1981, acknowledged to the Kienbusch Collection, Princeton University Library, Princeton, NJ. *Mr Briggs and His Doings* by John Leech (mid-nineteenth century). Fishing, Vol. 2, edited by Horace G. Hutchinson, Country Life Library of Sport, London, 1907. Chapter 10: *My Life as an Angler*, William Henderson, London, 1879. *The Complete Angler*, Izaak Walton, 5th Nicholas Edition, London, 1875. Engraving by Thomas Inskipp. Chapter 11: *Troutfishing*, Norman Marsh, Auckland, New Zealand, 1990. Illustrated by the author. Personal thanks to Norman Marsh and Halcyon Press, Auckland. Chapter 12: *The Way of An Angler*, David Scholes, The Jacaranda Press, Brisbane, Queensland, Australia, 1963. Thanks to the publishers. Chapter 13: *Troutfishing*, Norman Marsh, Auckland, New Zealand, 1990. Illustrated by the author. Personal thanks to Norman Marsh and Halcyon Press, Auckland. *Fisherman's Spring*, Roderick L. Haig-Brown, 1975. Illustrated by Louis Darling. Acknowledgement and thanks to Crown Publishers Inc., New York. Chapter 14: *Halcyon*, George Brennand, London, 1947. Illustrated by C. Walter Hodges. Thanks to A & C Black, London. Chapter 15: Reproduced in *The Ultimate Fishing Book*, Boston, Mass., 1981. Attributed to Sandy Scott, El Paso, Texas; detail of an etching done for *Gray's Sporting Journal* (1981). *The Angler's Eldorado: New Zealand*, Zane Grey, New York & London, 1926. Chapter 16: *The Trout Waters of England*, Walter M. Gallichan, London, 1908. Chapter 17: *The Contemplative Man's Recreation*, compiled by Susan B. Starkman & Stanley E. Read, The Library of the University of British Columbia, Vancouver, Canada. Taken from an unnamed English nineteenth century fishing book. Chapter 18: *The Book of the Fly Rod*, edited by High Sheringham. Illustrated by George Sheringham. London, 1931. This illustration taken from a much older engraving of an ancient Egyptian fishing scene. *Peches des Jadis de Naguere et d'Ailleurs*, Jerome Favard, Editions Bornemann, Paris, 1976. The illustration captioned *Pech a la ligne ne Egypte ancienne (avec et sans canne)*. *Sepulture de Beni Hassan, 12 dynastie*. Chapter 19: *The Angler's Eldorado: New Zealand*, Zane Grey, New York & London, 1926. Chapter 20: *Trout from the Hills*, Ian Niall, London, 1961. Illustrated by Toni Goffe. Thanks to Heinemann Ltd., Publishers. From a nineteenth century fishing book. Possibly after Thomas Bewick. Endpiece: *My Life as an Angler*, William Henderson, London, 1879.

Index